T0309584

Interface Support for Creativity, Productivity, and Expression in Computer Graphics

Anna Ursyn
University of Northern Colorado, USA

A volume in the Advances in Multimedia and
Interactive Technologies (AMIT) Book Series

Published in the United States of America by
    IGI Global
    Information Science Reference (an imprint of IGI Global)
    701 E. Chocolate Avenue
    Hershey PA, USA 17033
    Tel: 717-533-8845
    Fax: 717-533-8661
    E-mail: cust@igi-global.com
    Web site: http://www.igi-global.com

Artwork within the cover image "Timetable" © 2018, by Anna Ursyn. Used with permission.

Library of Congress Cataloging-in-Publication Data

Names: Ursyn, Anna, 1955- editor.
Title: Interface support for creativity, productivity, and expression in
  computer graphics / Anna Ursyn, editor.
Description: Hershey, PA : Information Science Reference, [2018]
Identifiers: LCCN 2018024580| ISBN 9781522573715 (h/c) | ISBN 9781522573722
  (eISBN)
Subjects: LCSH: User interfaces (Computer systems)
Classification: LCC QA76.9.U83 I555 2018 | DDC 005.4/37--dc23 LC record available at https://lccn.loc.gov/2018024580

This book is published in the IGI Global book series Advances in Multimedia and Interactive Technologies (AMIT) (ISSN: 2327-929X; eISSN: 2327-9303)

British Cataloguing in Publication Data
A Cataloguing in Publication record for this book is available from the British Library.

The views expressed in this book are those of the authors, but not necessarily of the publisher.

For electronic access to this publication, please contact: eresources@igi-global.com.

Advances in Multimedia and Interactive Technologies (AMIT) Book Series

Joel J.P.C. Rodrigues

National Institute of Telecommunications (Inatel), Brazil &
Instituto de Telecomunicações, University of Beira Interior,
Portugal

ISSN:2327-929X
EISSN:2327-9303

Mission

Traditional forms of media communications are continuously being challenged. The emergence of user-friendly web-based applications such as social media and Web 2.0 has expanded into everyday society, providing an interactive structure to media content such as images, audio, video, and text.

The **Advances in Multimedia and Interactive Technologies (AMIT) Book Series** investigates the relationship between multimedia technology and the usability of web applications. This series aims to highlight evolving research on interactive communication systems, tools, applications, and techniques to provide researchers, practitioners, and students of information technology, communication science, media studies, and many more with a comprehensive examination of these multimedia technology trends.

Coverage

- Mobile Learning
- Multimedia Technology
- Audio Signals
- Web Technologies
- Multimedia Streaming
- Internet Technologies
- Gaming Media
- Multimedia Services
- Digital Games
- Digital Technology

IGI Global is currently accepting manuscripts for publication within this series. To submit a proposal for a volume in this series, please contact our Acquisition Editors at Acquisitions@igi-global.com or visit: http://www.igi-global.com/publish/.

Titles in this Series

For a list of additional titles in this series, please visit: www.igi-global.com/book-series

Intelligent Multidimensional Data and Image Processing
Sourav De (Cooch Behar Government Engineering College, India) Siddhartha Bhattacharyya (RCC Institute of Information Technology, India) and Paramartha Dutta (Visva Bharati University, India)
Information Science Reference • copyright 2018 • 429pp • H/C (ISBN: 9781522552468) • US $235.00 (our price)

Real-Time Face Detection, Recognition, and Tracking System in LabVIEW™ Emerging Research and Opportunities
Manimehala Nadarajan (Universiti Malaysia Sabah, Malaysia) Muralindran Mariappan (Universiti Malaysia Sabah, Malaysia) and Rosalyn R. Porle (Universiti Malaysia Sabah, Malaysia)
Information Science Reference • copyright 2018 • 140pp • H/C (ISBN: 9781522535034) • US $155.00 (our price)

Empirical Research on Semiotics and Visual Rhetoric
Marcel Danesi (University of Toronto, Canada)
Information Science Reference • copyright 2018 • 312pp • H/C (ISBN: 9781522556220) • US $195.00 (our price)

Exploring Transmedia Journalism in the Digital Age -
Renira Rampazzo Gambarato (National Research University Higher School of Economics, Russia) and Geane C. Alzamora (Federal University of Minas Gerais, Brazil)
Information Science Reference • copyright 2018 • 348pp • H/C (ISBN: 9781522537816) • US $195.00 (our price)

Image Retrieval and Analysis Using Text and Fuzzy Shape Features Emerging Research and Opportunities
P. Sumathy (Bharathidasan University, India) P. Shanmugavadivu (Gandhigram Rural Institute, India) and A. Vadivel (SRM University, India)
Information Science Reference • copyright 2018 • 183pp • H/C (ISBN: 9781522537960) • US $145.00 (our price)

Multimedia Retrieval Systems in Distributed Environments Emerging Research and Opportunities
S.G. Shaila (National Institute of Technology, India) and A. Vadivel (National Institute of Technology, India)
Information Science Reference • copyright 2018 • 140pp • H/C (ISBN: 9781522537281) • US $165.00 (our price)

Handbook of Research on Advanced Concepts in Real-Time Image and Video Processing
Md. Imtiyaz Anwar (National Institute of Technology, Jalandhar, India) Arun Khosla (National Institute of Technology, Jalandhar, India) and Rajiv Kapoor (Delhi Technological University, India)
Information Science Reference • copyright 2018 • 504pp • H/C (ISBN: 9781522528487) • US $265.00 (our price)

701 East Chocolate Avenue, Hershey, PA 17033, USA
Tel: 717-533-8845 x100 • Fax: 717-533-8661
E-Mail: cust@igi-global.com • www.igi-global.com

Table of Contents

Preface xiv

Section 1
Interfaces That Support Communication

Chapter 1
An Intuitive Interface for Interactively Pairing Multiple Mobile Devices: Dynamic
Reconfiguration of Multiple Screens and a Variety of Content Designs 1
Takashi Ohta, Tokyo University of Technology, Japan

Chapter 2
Expressive Avatars in Psychological Intervention and Therapy 27
Ana Paula Cláudio, Universidade de Lisboa, Portugal
Maria Beatriz Carmo, Universidade de Lisboa, Portugal
Augusta Gaspar, Universidade Católica Portuguesa, Portugal & Universitário de Lisboa,
*   Portugal*
Renato Teixeira, Universidade de Lisboa, Portugal

Chapter 3
Creating Characters for Various Interfaces 49
Anna Ursyn, University of Northern Colorado, USA

Chapter 4
Visual Storytelling for Various Interfaces 82
Anna Ursyn, University of Northern Colorado, USA

Chapter 5
How We Hear and Experience Classical, Computer, and Virtual Music 110
Robert C. Ehle, University of Northern Colorado, USA

Chapter 6
Dialogue With Interfaces: Beyond the Visual Towards Socio-Spatial Engagement 129
 Ana Paula Baltazar dos Santos, Universidade Federal de Minas Gerais, Brazil
 Guilherme Ferreira de Arruda, Universidade Federal de Ouro Preto, Brazil
 José dos Santos Cabral Filho, Universidade Federal de Minas Gerais, Brazil
 Lorena Melgaço Silva Marques, University of Birmingham, UK
 Marcela Alves de Almeida, Universidade Federal de São João del-Rei, Brazil

Section 2
Interfaces That Support Art

Chapter 7
The Forking Paths Revisited: Experimenting on Interactive Film 150
 Bruno Mendes da Silva, Centro de Investigação em Artes e Comunicação, Portugal
 Mirian Nogueira Tavares, University of Algarve, Portugal
 Vítor Reia-Batista, Centro de Investigação em Artes e Comunicação, Portugal
 Rui António, Centro de Investigação em Artes e Comunicação, Portugal

Chapter 8
CulturalNature Arga#2 167
 Tiago Cruz, Instituto Universitário da Maia, Portugal
 Fernando Faria Paulino, Instituto Universitário da Maia, Portugal
 Mirian Tavares, University of Algarve, Portugal

Chapter 9
Aesthetic Composition Indicator Based on Image Complexity 185
 Adrian Carballal, University of A Coruña, Spain
 Luz Castro, University of A Coruña, Spain
 Carlos Fernandez-Lozano, University of A Coruña, Spain
 Nereida Rodríguez-Fernández, University of A Coruña, Spain
 Juan Romero, University of A Coruña, Spain
 Penousal Machado, University of Coimbra, Portugal

Chapter 10
Approach to Minimize Bias on Aesthetic Image Datasets 203
 Adrian Carballal, University of A Coruña, Spain
 Luz Castro, University of A Coruña, Spain
 Nereida Rodríguez-Fernández, University of A Coruña, Spain
 Iria Santos, University of A Coruña, Spain
 Antonino Santos, University of A Coruña, Spain
 Juan Romero, University of A Coruña, Spain

Chapter 11
The Origins of Music and of Tonal Languages 220
 Robert C. Ehle, University of Northern Colorado, USA

Section 3
Interfaces That Support Learning

Chapter 12
Leveraging Computer Interface to Support Creative Thinking 246
Robert Z. Zheng, University of Utah, USA
Kevin Greenberg, University of Utah, USA

Chapter 13
Cognitive Learning Through Knowledge Visualization, Art, and the Geometry of Nature 266
Jean Constant, Independent Researcher, USA

Chapter 14
Augmented Reality in Informal Learning Environments: A Music History Exhibition 281
José Duarte Cardoso Gomes, Universidade do Algarve, Portugal
Mauro Jorge Guerreiro Figueiredo, Universidade do Algarve, Portugal
Lúcia da Graça Cruz Domingues Amante, Universidade Aberta, Portugal
Cristina Maria Cardoso Gomes, Universidade do Algarve, Portugal

Chapter 15
Building Virtual Driving Environments From Computer-Made Projects 306
Carlos José Campos, Polytechnic of Porto, Portugal
Hugo Filipe Pinto, Polytechnic of Porto, Portugal
João Miguel Leitão, Polytechnic of Porto, Portugal
João Paulo Pereira, Polytechnic of Porto, Portugal
António Fernando Coelho, University of Porto, Portugal
Carlos Manuel Rodrigues, University of Porto, Portugal

Compilation of References 321

About the Contributors 344

Index 353

Detailed Table of Contents

Preface... xiv

Section 1
Interfaces That Support Communication

Chapter 1
An Intuitive Interface for Interactively Pairing Multiple Mobile Devices: Dynamic
Reconfiguration of Multiple Screens and a Variety of Content Designs 1
    Takashi Ohta, Tokyo University of Technology, Japan

We designed an intuitive user interface to connect multiple mobile devices over a network and relate the applications running on them. We proposed a pinching gesture for making a connection between two devices, which is realized by swiping the touch screens of the two annexed mobile devices as if to stitch them together. We believe that this user interface can create new user experiences for multiple-screen usage, especially by designing the application content to react instantly to the connection and disconnection triggered by the gesture. We expect this interface to fulfill a great potential in inspiring application designers to conceive various ideas, particularly suited for visually fascinating content that takes advantage of the dynamic reconfigurable multi-display feature. To demonstrate the potential, we produced some prototype applications. In this article, we explain the idea and details of the interface mechanism, and introduce the design of the sample applications.

Chapter 2
Expressive Avatars in Psychological Intervention and Therapy 27
    Ana Paula Cláudio, Universidade de Lisboa, Portugal
    Maria Beatriz Carmo, Universidade de Lisboa, Portugal
    Augusta Gaspar, Universidade Católica Portuguesa, Portugal & Universitário de Lisboa,
       Portugal
    Renato Teixeira, Universidade de Lisboa, Portugal

A wide range of applications for virtual humans can be envisaged for the needs of both research and intervention in Psychology. This chapter describes the development and preliminary testing of an interactive virtual reality application "Virtual Spectators" – whereby virtual humans with expressive behaviour modelled on the basis of field research in human facial expression in real emotion contexts can be configured to interact with people in an interview or jury. We discuss the possibilities of this application in cognitive behavioural therapy using virtual reality and in nonverbal behaviour.

Chapter 3

Creating Characters for Various Interfaces 49
Anna Ursyn, University of Northern Colorado, USA

This chapter is focused on the theme of creating characters for visual storytelling discussed in practical, theoretical, and historical terms. The description includes a discussion of artistic forms acting as characters for telling stories, various meanings conveyed by characters in semiotic terms, the creating of characters by drawing, and then a set of learning projects follows, on creating characters for various interfaces.

Chapter 4

Visual Storytelling for Various Interfaces 82
Anna Ursyn, University of Northern Colorado, USA

This chapter is focused on text visualization and storytelling delivered in various literary styles adopted for various delivery systems. Discussion pertains first storytelling by drawing, both with traditional techniques and digital storytelling for various media and technologies. Transition from a sketch to sculpted forms converted to 3D printing, animation, and video is then discussed. Projects offer practical examples of the visual storytelling production and examine the possible usage of visual storytelling for different kinds of interfaces conducive to human communication through mass media, digital interactive, social, and printed media, with the use of mobile apps, web app, or application software.

Chapter 5

How We Hear and Experience Classical, Computer, and Virtual Music 110
Robert C. Ehle, University of Northern Colorado, USA

This chapter examines occurrences and events associated with the experience of composing, playing, or listening to music. Discussion of popular music and computer music begins the chapter, including issues pertaining the tuning systems, digital interfaces, and software for music. It then recounts an experiment on the nature of pitch and psychoacoustics of resultant tones.

Chapter 6

Dialogue With Interfaces: Beyond the Visual Towards Socio-Spatial Engagement 129
Ana Paula Baltazar dos Santos, Universidade Federal de Minas Gerais, Brazil
Guilherme Ferreira de Arruda, Universidade Federal de Ouro Preto, Brazil
José dos Santos Cabral Filho, Universidade Federal de Minas Gerais, Brazil
Lorena Melgaço Silva Marques, University of Birmingham, UK
Marcela Alves de Almeida, Universidade Federal de São João del-Rei, Brazil

This chapter grapples with the hegemony of the visual and its pervasiveness in current urban installations. It discusses how technology and the visual are fetishized instead of used in their dialogical potential to engage people in socio-spatial transformation. This chapter presents the trajectory of the Graphics Laboratory for Architectural Experience at Universidade Federal de Minas Gerais, Brazil (LAGEAR) in its theoretical and practical development. This chapter then discusses LAGEAR's main drives, which are the playful interaction, the distinction between interface, and interaction and dialogue, in order to create interactive interfaces that actually engage people in socio-spatial transformation. It presents examples of the authors' works, drawing from visually based to bodily engaging and socio-political installations.

Discussion concerns the problematization that leads to the need of engagement rather than the bodily engagement. Emphasis was put on working with the socio-spatial context and proposing interfaces that take into account the process in its openness and indeterminacy instead of prescribing a product (even if an interface-product).

Section 2
Interfaces That Support Art

Chapter 7
The Forking Paths Revisited: Experimenting on Interactive Film... 150
Bruno Mendes da Silva, Centro de Investigação em Artes e Comunicação, Portugal
Mirian Nogueira Tavares, University of Algarve, Portugal
Vítor Reia-Batista, Centro de Investigação em Artes e Comunicação, Portugal
Rui António, Centro de Investigação em Artes e Comunicação, Portugal

Based on the triad, film-interactivity-experimentation, the applied research project, The Forking Paths, developed at the Centre for Research in Arts and Communication (CIAC) endeavors to find alternative narrative forms in the field of cinema and, more specifically, in the subfield of interactive cinema. The films in the project invest in the interconnectivity between the film narrative and the viewer, who is given the possibility to be more active and engaged. At same time, the films undertake a research on the development of audio-visual language. The project is available at an online platform, which aims to foster the creation and web hosting of other interactive cinema projects in its different variables. This chapter focuses on the three films completed up to the moment: Haze, The Book of the Dead, and Waltz.

Chapter 8
CulturalNature Arga#2.. 167
Tiago Cruz, Instituto Universitário da Maia, Portugal
Fernando Faria Paulino, Instituto Universitário da Maia, Portugal
Mirian Tavares, University of Algarve, Portugal

CulturalNature Arga#2 is an interactive audio-visual installation intended to explore the concept of landscape as a verb (to landscape) questioning and reflecting about the semiotic discourses associated with this concept. The landscape as something natural, static, peaceful, silent, etc. is a semiotic discourse with roots in a past related with the representation of a point of view, not only perceptual but also conceptual, ideological. These representations informed the visual culture leading to a particular discourse. The installation proposes a reflexion about the way different elements associated with a particular territory shape this territory's landscape, giving it a dynamic existence, a product of cultural activity.

Chapter 9
Aesthetic Composition Indicator Based on Image Complexity 185
Adrian Carballal, University of A Coruña, Spain
Luz Castro, University of A Coruña, Spain
Carlos Fernandez-Lozano, University of A Coruña, Spain
Nereida Rodríguez-Fernández, University of A Coruña, Spain
Juan Romero, University of A Coruña, Spain
Penousal Machado, University of Coimbra, Portugal

Several systems and indicators for multimedia devices have appeared in recent years, with the goal of helping the final user to achieve better results. Said indicators aim at facilitating beginner and intermediate photographers in the creation of images or videos with more professional aesthetics. The chapter describes a series of metrics related to complexity which seem to be useful for the purpose of assessing the aesthetic composition of an image. All the presented metrics are fundamental parts of the prototype "ACIC" introduced here, which allows an assessment of the aesthetics in the composition of the various frames integrating a video.

Chapter 10

Approach to Minimize Bias on Aesthetic Image Datasets.. 203
    Adrian Carballal, University of A Coruña, Spain
    Luz Castro, University of A Coruña, Spain
    Nereida Rodríguez-Fernández, University of A Coruña, Spain
    Iria Santos, University of A Coruña, Spain
    Antonino Santos, University of A Coruña, Spain
    Juan Romero, University of A Coruña, Spain

Over the last few years, numerous studies have been conducted that have sought to address automatic image classification. These approaches have used a variety of experimental sets of images from several photography sites. In this chapter, the authors look at some of the most widely used in the field of computational aesthetics as well as the capacity for generalization that each of them offers. Furthermore, a set of images built up by psychologists is described in order to predict perceptual complexity as assessed by a closed group of persons in a controlled experimental setup. Lastly, a new hybrid method is proposed for the construction of a set of images or a dataset for the assessment and classification of aesthetic criteria. This method brings together the advantages of datasets based on photography websites and those of a dataset where assessment is made under controlled experimental conditions.

Chapter 11

The Origins of Music and of Tonal Languages 220
    Robert C. Ehle, University of Northern Colorado, USA

This chapter offers the author's theory of the origins of music in ancient primates a million years ago, and what music would have sounded like. Origins of nasal and tone languages and the anatomy of larynx is discussed, and then a hypothesis is presented that these creatures would fashioned a tone language. They had absolute pitch that allowed them to recognize other voices, to read each other's emotions from the sounds they made with their voices, and to convey over long distances specific information about strategies, meeting places, etc. Having an acute sense of pitch, they would have sung, essentially using tonal language for aesthetic and subjective purposes. Thus, they would have invented music. Then the physicality of the human (or hominid) voice is discussed and the way an absolute pitch can be acquired, as the musicality still lies in the vocalisms it expresses. The reason for this is that music is actually contained in the way the brain works, and the ear and the voice are parts of this system. The final part discusses the origins of musical emotion as the case for imprinting in the perinatal period.

Section 3
Interfaces That Support Learning

Chapter 12

Leveraging Computer Interface to Support Creative Thinking 246

Robert Z. Zheng, University of Utah, USA
Kevin Greenberg, University of Utah, USA

How to design computer interface that facilitates learners' creative thinking can be challenging. This chapter discusses the cognitive processes, the types of divergent thinking, visualization, and brain-functions in relation to human learning. Informed by the research in previous areas, the authors examine the features of computer interface that aligns with brain-functions to support various types of creative thinking. An example is included to demonstrate, at the conceptual level, how computer interface can be leveraged to support learners' creativity, imagination, originality, and expressiveness in learning. Discussions are made with respect to the implication and limitation of the chapter. The chapter concludes with suggestions for future research and studies.

Chapter 13

Cognitive Learning Through Knowledge Visualization, Art, and the Geometry of Nature 266

Jean Constant, Independent Researcher, USA

Scientific modeling applied to the study of a mineral structure at the unit level provides a fertile ground from which to extract significant representations. 3D graphics visualization is equal part mathematics, geometry, and design. The geometric structure of 52 minerals was investigated in a specific modeling program to find if meaningful visualization pertaining to the field of art can be extracted from a mathematical and scientific resource. Working with the lines, spheres, and polygons that define crystal at the nanoscale provided the author with an exceptional environment from which to extract coherent visualizations sustainable in the art environment. The results were tested in various interactive platforms and opened a larger debate on cross-pollination between science, humanities, and the arts. Additionally, the experiment provided new ground of investigation for unexpected connections between mathematics, earth sciences, and local cultures.

Chapter 14

Augmented Reality in Informal Learning Environments: A Music History Exhibition 281

José Duarte Cardoso Gomes, Universidade do Algarve, Portugal
Mauro Jorge Guerreiro Figueiredo, Universidade do Algarve, Portugal
Lúcia da Graça Cruz Domingues Amante, Universidade Aberta, Portugal
Cristina Maria Cardoso Gomes, Universidade do Algarve, Portugal

Augmented reality (AR) allows computer-generated imagery information overlays onto a live real-world environment in real time. Technological advances in mobile computing devices (MCD) such as smartphones and tablets (internet access, built-in cameras and GPS) made a greater number of AR applications available. This chapter presents the Augmented Reality Musical Gallery (ARMG) exhibition, enhanced by AR. ARMG, focused on twentieth century music history, and aimed at the students from the 2nd Cycle of basic education in Portuguese public schools. In this chapter, the authors introduce AR technology and address topics like constructivism, art education, student motivation, and informal learning environments. They conclude by presenting the first two parts of the ongoing research conducted among a sample group of students contemplating the experiment in an educational context.

Chapter 15

Building Virtual Driving Environments From Computer-Made Projects.. 306

    Carlos José Campos, Polytechnic of Porto, Portugal
    Hugo Filipe Pinto, Polytechnic of Porto, Portugal
    João Miguel Leitão, Polytechnic of Porto, Portugal
    João Paulo Pereira, Polytechnic of Porto, Portugal
    António Fernando Coelho, University of Porto, Portugal
    Carlos Manuel Rodrigues, University of Porto, Portugal

The virtual environments used in scientific driving simulation experiments require extensive 3D models of road landscapes, correctly modeled and similar to those found in the real world. The modeling task of these environments, addressing the terrain definition and the specific characteristics required by the target applications, may result in a complex and time-consuming process. This chapter presents a procedural method to model large terrain definitions and adjust the roadside landscape to produce well-constructed road environments. The proposed procedural method allows merging an externally modeled road into a terrain definition, providing an integrated generation of driving environments. The road and terrain models are optimized to interactive visualization in real time, by applying most state-of-art techniques like the level of detail selection and spatial hierarchization. The proposed method allows modeling large road environments, with the realism and quality required to perform experimental studies in driving simulators.

Compilation of References 321

About the Contributors 344

Index 353

Preface

This book is a collection of essays where professionals in selected fields from science to art discuss the user interface designs that support our communication, art, and learning environments. The goal for collecting authors' contributions is in the emphasizing the role of creating and designing points of interaction between computer systems or components and diverse areas of human artistic, social, and productive activities. Essays written by authors contributing to the previous issues of the *International Journal of Creative Interfaces and Computer Graphics* constitute a considerable part of this book, while digital artists inspiring themselves with science and technology contributed with their input. The topic of interfaces is relevant to the use of computers and computing. We can see programming and computing as significant revolutions in science. Advances in interactions between a computer and humans, their aesthetic appeal, ease of use, and learnability that are made possible due to the creation of user interfaces result in further progress in science, aesthetics, and practical applications. The role of user interfaces grows in importance because of the pervasive presence and common use of cell phones, apps, tablets, boards, bots, and games. They are in most cases networked, interactive, and often supported by augmented reality techniques relying on many senses. Like in a Newton's cradle, each application unites its digital content with the physicality of the device, thus addressing our sensory perception.

The title *Interface Support for Creativity, Productivity, and Expression in Computer Graphics* contains a notion of computer graphics. This domain means a study, creation, and use of art and image data for creating and displaying on the computer the static or motion pictures. This means, images created with the use of graphical hardware and software may be presented and manipulated as two or three dimensional, and they may be animated or brought into other platforms as well. Interfaces for electronic devices intensify user experience. In this book, the reader will find a variety of examples of the user interface design.

The title of this book includes also a notion of creativity. As a faculty indispensable in thinking, creating art, or generating new data, information, and knowledge, creativity is one of the significant skills that are essential to work, learn, and cooperate. While deliberations on creativity carry on from the times of Plato and Aristotle, a generally accepted framework for the creative thinking process has been described by E. Paul Torrance (1979) in his book *The Search for Satori and Creativity* as fluency, flexibility, originality, and elaboration. Then, the standard definition of creativity has been offered by Runco and Jaeger (2012), with the notion of creativity involving the generation of useful novelty in many fields. All the time, the notions of creativity, talent, problem solving, aesthetics, and beauty retain their value. While some people cannot appreciate computer art because they know little or nothing about coding (Boden, 2016, 2018), computational creativity gains growing interest of researchers from various domains, including computer science, psychology, cognitive science, robotics and arts (al-Rifaie, Cropley, Cropley, & Bishop, 2016).

al-Rifaie et al. (2016) introduced a concept of the weak vs. strong computational creativity that fits in with the current state-of-the-art development in the field of computational creativity. Creativity gains a new meaning when it is related to production of devices like tablets, VR systems, and apps for phones or the web. Visual storytelling, video storytelling, poetry, and visual poetry created by a computer and the conceivable computer creativity may serve as other examples of such visual styles.

Support that can be attained by designing creative interfaces is described in many ways depending on a discipline in which they are applied. This book examines cognitive tools and solutions for enhancing computing-based endeavors in the domains of communication, art, and learning. Authors' contributions examine the ways the film, augmented and virtual reality, visualization, and other electronic media may augment our multisensory experiences concerning thinking, aesthetic assessment, learning, communication, and other areas of interest and expertise. Discussions about such concepts may serve for computing solutions in ever-changing technology that targets more of our senses.

Visual learning projects, exhibitions, and presentations are seeking for the progressive, proactive, and inclusive ways of thinking about achieving knowledge, creating meaning-based art, or providing amusement and enjoyment. They combine computing (a tool) and knowledge (a goal) with visual arts (the means). Topics support cognitive learning by interlocking, due to specified interfaces, selected concepts with particular fields of science, mathematics, art, and technology. Computer graphics and visuals display practical applications to technology-based creativity, computing, and programming. Projects bridge a gap between science and everyday problems by imaging data and concepts with the user interface design techniques.

ORGANIZATION OF THE BOOK

This book is comprised of three sections.

Section 1, "Interfaces That Support Communication," deals with the topic of strategies and solutions regarding the user interface applications in service of communication between humans, the apps they use, and their sensory environment.

In the Chapter 1, "An Intuitive Interface for Interactively Pairing Multiple Mobile Devices: Dynamic Reconfiguration of Multiple Screens and a Variety of Content Designs," Takashi Ohta presents an intuitive user interface connecting multiple mobile devices over a network, which improves human-machine interaction, and allows the devices instantly react to user gestures. In Chapter 2 entitled "Expressive Avatars in Psychological Intervention and Therapy," Ana Paula Cláudio, Maria Beatriz Carmo, and Augusta Gaspar describe an interactive Virtual Reality application Virtual Spectators where virtual humans with expressive behavior interact with people. In Chapter 3 entitled "Creating Characters for Various Media," Anna Ursyn is focused on the theme of creating characters for visual storytelling discussed in practical, theoretical, and historical terms. Description includes artistic forms acting as characters, the meanings conveyed by characters in semiotic terms, and the creating of characters by drawing. A set of learning projects follows, on creating characters for various interfaces. The next Anna Ursyn's chapter, "Visual Storytelling for Various Interfaces," is focused on storytelling delivered in various literary styles adopted for various delivery systems. Drawing is discussed, both done with traditional techniques and digital storytelling for various media and technologies. Projects offer practical examples of the visual storytelling production. Chapter 5, "How We Hear and Experience Classical, Computer, and Virtual Music," written by Robert C. Ehle, discusses the experience of composing, playing, or listening to music: popular music, the computer music, and then the tuning systems, digital interfaces, and software for music. An experiment on the nature of pitch and psychoacoustics of resultant tones completes the chapter. Ana Paula Baltazar dos Santos, Guilherme Ferreira de Arruda, José dos Santos Cabral Filho, Lorena Melgaço Silva Marques, and Marcela Alves de Almeida discusses in Chapter 6, titled "Dialogue With Interfaces: Beyond the Visual Towards Socio-Spatial Engagement," the interactive urban installations strongly based on digital technology.

Section 2, "Interfaces That Support Art," examines computational solutions related to interfaces supporting artistic digital media, interactive film, video, and the related aesthetic assessment.

In Chapter 7, entitled "The Forking Paths Revisited: Experimenting on Interactive Film," Bruno Mendes da Silva, Mirian Nogueira Tavares, Vítor Reia-Batista, and Rui António present a research project available at an online platform which is based on three films: Haze, The Book of the Dead, and Waltz, and is aimed at finding alternative narrative forms in the field of Interactive Cinema and examining the development of audio-visual language. The interconnectivity between the film narrative and the viewer provides the possibility to activate and engage the viewers. Tiago Cruz, Fernando Faria Paulino, and Mirian Tavares present Chapter 8, "Culturalnature Arga#2," which is an interactive audio-visual installation intended to explore the concept of landscape as a verb (to landscape) and questioning the semiotic discourses associated with this concept. The installation and a semiotic discourse are related with the representation of a point of view not only perceptual, but also conceptual, ideological. The installation proposes a reflexion about the way different elements associated with a particular territory shape the dynamic existence of the landscape. In Chapter 9, "Aesthetic Composition Indicator based on Image Complexity," Adrian Carballal, Luz Castro, Carlos Fernández-Lozano, Nereida Rodríguez-Fernández, Juan Romero, and Penousal Machado describe a series of metrics for assessing the Aesthetic Composition of an image, facilitating beginner and intermediate photographers the creation of images or videos with a more professional aesthetics. The prototype "ACIC" is introduced, which allows an assessment of the aesthetics in the composition of the various frames integrating a video. Chapter 10 entitled "Approach to Minimize Bias on Aesthetic Image Datasets" and authored by Adrian Carballal, Luz Castro, Nereida Rodríguez-Fernández, Iria Santos, Antonino Santos, and Juan Romero, addresses the issue of automatic image classification; they review the studies in the field of computational aesthetics, and describe a set of images built up by psychologists in order to predict perceptual complexity as assessed by a closed group of persons in a controlled experimental setup. A new hybrid method is proposed for the construction of a set of images or a dataset for the assessment and classification of aesthetic criteria. Chapter 11, written by Robert C. Ehle and entitled "Origins of Music and of Tone Languages," offers the author's theory of the origins of music and of nasal and tone languages. The anatomy of larynx is discussed, and a hypothesis how having the absolute, acute sense of pitch, the ancient primates would have sung using tonal language for aesthetic and subjective purposes, and how they thus would have invented music. The final part discusses the origins of musical emotion as the case for imprinting in the perinatal period.

Section 3, "Interfaces That Support Learning," focuses on solutions aimed at supporting brain functions, creative thinking, cognitive learning, interactive visualization, and the augmented and virtual reality environment.

In Chapter 12 titled "Leveraging Computer Interface to Support Creative Thinking," Robert Z. Zheng and Kevin Greenberg examine, at the conceptual level, the features of computer interface that facilitates learners' creative thinking and supports learners' creativity, imagination, originality, and expressiveness in learning. This chapter discusses the cognitive processes, types of divergent thinking, visualization, and brain-functions, in relation to human learning, that support various types of creative thinking. Chapter 13 entitled "Cognitive Learning Through Knowledge Visualization, Art, and the Geometry of Nature" by Jean Constant presents the geometric structure of 52 minerals investigated in a specific modeling program designed to find if visualization pertaining to the field of art can be extracted from a mathematical and scientific resource. Working with the lines, spheres and polygons that define crystal at the nanoscale provided the author with an environment enabling visualizations for the art environment. Chapter 14, "Augmented Reality in Informal Learning Environments: A Music History Exhibition" by José Duarte Cardoso Gomes, Mauro Jorge Guerreiro Figueiredo, Lúcia da Graça Cruz Domingues Amante, and Cristina Maria Cardoso Gomes presents the Augmented Reality Musical Gallery (ARMG) exhibition, enhanced by augmented reality (AR), which allows that computer-generated imagery information overlays onto a live real-world environment in real-time. ARMG, aimed at the students in Portuguese public schools, focuses on the twentieth century music history, introduces AR technology, and addresses topics such as constructivism, art education, student motivation, and informal learning environments.

Chapter 15, "Building Virtual Driving Environments From Computer-Made Projects," authored by Carlos José Campos, Hugo Filipe Pinto, João Miguel Leitão, João Paulo Pereira, António Fernando Coelho, and Carlos Manuel Rodrigues, discusses the virtual environments used in scientific driving simulation experiments, which require extensive 3D models of road landscapes, correctly modeled and similar to those found in real world. The authors present a procedural method to model large terrain definitions and adjust the roadside landscape to produce well-constructed road environments. The road and terrain models are optimized to interactive visualization in real time, by applying the level of detail selection and spatial hierarchization.

REFERENCES

al-Rifaie, M. M., Cropley, A., Cropley, D., & Bishop, M. (2016). On evil and computational creativity. *ResearchGate*. Retrieved from https://www.researchgate.net/publication/297751482_On_evil_and_computational_creativity

Boden, M. A. (2016). Skills and the Appreciation of Computer Art. In *Computational Creativity, Measurement and Evaluation, Connection Science*. Taylor & Francis. doi:10.1080/09540091.2015.1130023

Boden, M. A. (2018). Artificial Intelligence: A Very Short Introduction. Oxford University Press.

Runco, M. A., & Jaeger, G. J. (2012). The standard definition of creativity. *Creativity Research Journal*, 24(1), 92–96. doi:10.1080/10400419.2012.650092

Torrance, E. P. (1979). *The Search for Satori and Creativity* (1st ed.). Creative Education Foundation.

Section 1
Interfaces That Support Communication

Chapter 1
An Intuitive Interface for Interactively Pairing Multiple Mobile Devices:
Dynamic Reconfiguration of Multiple Screens and a Variety of Content Designs

Takashi Ohta
Tokyo University of Technology, Japan

ABSTRACT

We designed an intuitive user interface to connect multiple mobile devices over a network and relate the applications running on them. We proposed a pinching gesture for making a connection between two devices, which is realized by swiping the touch screens of the two annexed mobile devices as if to stitch them together. We believe that this user interface can create new user experiences for multiple-screen usage, especially by designing the application content to react instantly to the connection and disconnection triggered by the gesture. We expect this interface to fulfill a great potential in inspiring application designers to conceive various ideas, particularly suited for visually fascinating content that takes advantage of the dynamic reconfigurable multi-display feature. To demonstrate the potential, we produced some prototype applications. In this article, we explain the idea and details of the interface mechanism, and introduce the design of the sample applications.

INTRODUCTION

Through our attempts of using a multi-display environment for interactive content, we have particularly focused to realization of a system that allows to change its screen layout flexibly and easily. Our objective was to pursue multi-display usage that can enrich representation of digital content. Herein, we designed and implemented a reconfigurable multi-display system with commodity mobile devices, and used a pinching gesture as the intuitive interface for establishing network connection between the different devices.

DOI: 10.4018/978-1-5225-7371-5.ch001

A multi-display environment is generally used for offering extremely large and high-resolution virtual screens (Ni et al., 2006; Li et al., 2000). The display composition for such a system is generally static and permanent. The main application domains that use such environments are scientific visualization and virtual reality. If interactive applications (such as media artwork) are run on a multi-display system, the larger composite screen would create a greater impact on an audience than a normal single display would do. However, if multi-display is constructed only to form a single large virtual screen, no different user experience would be provided other than the impact given by the screen size.

In pursuing the potential of multi-displays as a platform for interactive content, we decided to seek a way in which the display layout can be reconfigured interactively. Our concept of a "reconfigurable" system is not restricted to the aspect of changing the screen layouts. We also want to add and remove devices freely to and from the multi-display configuration at any time. We believe that more interesting representations are possible by making a change in screen layout itself trigger an application response.

We do not like to use specifically designed devices because we want our technology to be commonly available. Therefore, we chose mobile devices such as smartphones and tablet PCs as the hardware platform. These are ideal for our approach, because of their mobility and high-resolution displays. It is also helpful that many people now own such devices. We also wanted to avoid mechanisms that would only work at previously prepared places, or require extra sensing devices or manual network configuration. The latter points would be a significant obstacle to the ideal of dynamic interaction. Many different approaches and interfaces can be designed for realizing dynamically reconfigurable multi-screen systems, but we believe that a great difference exists between one that merely achieves the function and one that provides a new user experience. The latter cannot be realized merely by designing an interface that is simple and intuitive. Such an interface must be organically integrated into usage scenarios and applications. We chose to employ a pinching gesture to establish a network connection between two devices because the gesture would imply the intention of connecting two things. The gesture is performed by holding a forefinger and thumb on each of two annexed screens, and moving the fingers together in a pinching motion, as though stitching the screens together. To break the connection, we chose a shaking or tilting action to accomplish the task. With these gestures for forming a multi-display environment, we designed "Pinch"-able applications, which react instantly without further prompting other than connecting or disconnecting of devices. This arrangement enables a user to have the illusion that his or her hand has come to possess a magical power that can connect digital content.

We introduce in this article the applications we created to demonstrate the technology's potential for producing a variety of content design and new user experiences. We designed them with special emphasis on dynamic interactions.

DYNAMICALLY RECONFIGURABLE SCREENS

Displaying visual content on a multi-display can strengthen the impression it makes, by offering an extremely large screen. However, in terms of the audience's experiences, it would not be much different from the case in which the content is played on a single display, as long as the application of multi-display is restricted to providing a single large screen. Having a different display formation such as the CAVE system may offer a different user experience, but each different display arrangement provides only one alternative. What we desire here is to add more flexible and interactive features to the usage of multiple displays.

To make it easy for reforming the layout of multi-display, we designed a tool that automatically configures an application to adjust it to various arbitrary screen layouts in a tiled arrangement (Ohta & Tanaka, 2010). We did this work to allow visual applications to try different screen layout more easily. The tool not only accommodates the flexibility of the display arrangement but also supports the changes in the number of displays to form a multi-display environment. We believe the tool can help application designers examine their visual applications more casually with various different screen layouts and find the best representation. Another of our experiments introduced interactivity to the usage of multiple displays, by putting sensors to note-PCs for detecting the other PC when it is placed at the neighbor (Ohta, 2008). We created a sample application that reacts instantly to the screen layout change, so that the graphics are displayed properly on the new screen layout (Figure 1). The application is sufficiently simple, in that it shows only a ball moving through the display's boundary at an annexed edge to the next screen.

Despite the application's simplicity, we found playing with it to be an engaging experience, and became convinced that such an interaction could add fascination to interactive content. From these experiences, we also became convinced that reconfigurable multi-display is a content platform of great potential in producing unique interaction and user experience. We chose mobile devices such as smartphones and tablet-PCs as our hardware platform because we can find no use cases that involve the more bulky and difficult-to-maneuver note-PCs and PC displays.

INTERFACE DESIGN FOR INTERACTIVE PAIRING OF MULTIPLE DEVICES

To accomplish our intentions, the system needs to be aware of the relative placement of the displays, whenever it changes. We can conceive of various approaches to accomplish that. We can grasp their overall location using an image processing technique, or deduce the overall relation by letting each display detect its neighbor using a sensor, and relay that information. However, we neither want to attach extra sensors to devices, nor need to open up a configuration panel for every layout change; we would not be

Figure 1. Experiment of dynamically reconfigurable multi-display with note PCs (© 2018, T. Ohta. Used with permission)

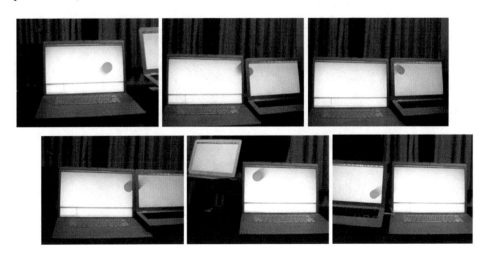

content even if it was a simple interface that provided easy manipulation. What we want to achieve is not an efficient and practical interface to achieve the task – we wish to create an entire new user experience. Therefore, it does not suit our purpose to relegate responsibility to the devices to notice each other; that would not be amazing to the users, because when something occurs automatically, people tend to assume the existence of some advanced technical mechanism behind the trick.

With these requirements in mind, we decided to adopt a pinching gesture for the interface (Ohta & Tanaka, 2012). Swiping two juxtaposed screens simultaneously using forefinger and thumb executes a pinching gesture, which enables detection of adjacent devices. Knowing which devices had their screens swiped simultaneously leads to them getting paired. By applying this action sequentially, connecting an additional device to the already connected devices, one can increase the number of displays forming that screen. The pinching gesture not only provides a simple and intuitive interface but also gives a feeling that one is actually stitching digital content together as if it was made from real objects (Figure 2). That feeling – something that would not be established merely by having an appropriate interface – is what we would like the interaction to convey. To create the illusion that one has stitched two devices into one, the application content needs to react instantly to the gesture. To create a novel experience, our comprehensive design does two things in response to a pinching gesture – it connects two devices over a network, and makes the content respond appropriately.

In addition to the interface design, we wish to enable interaction such that the screen layout can be changed repeatedly, and at any moment, even when applications are running on the devices. We also would like to have the system so that it allows devices to be connected in any relative orientation and alignment (Figure 3). Such flexibility would strengthen furtherly in rendering stickable character to the digital contents.

Figure 2. Pinching gesture provides a metaphor for stitching things together (© 2018, T. Ohta. Used with permission)

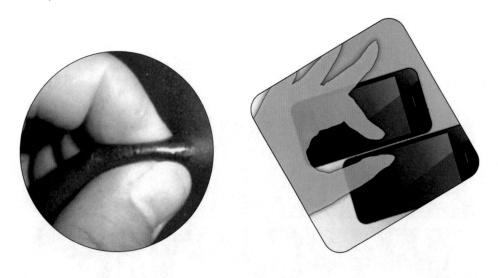

Figure 3. Flexibility of screen's orientation and alignment for connection (© 2018, T. Ohta. Used with permission)

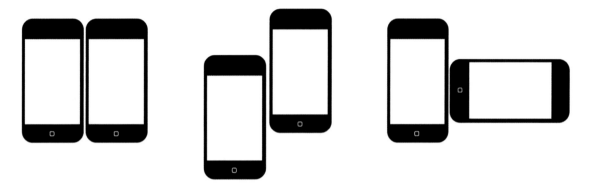

RELATED STUDIES AND WORKS

Research has been done on the concept of dynamically reconfigurable multiple screens. "Data Tiles" consists of a flat display and tiny transparent tiles (Rekimoto, Ullmer, & Oba, 2001). Each tile has an RFID tag, with reading sensors mounted on the panel, so that the system can recognize when a tile is placed on the panel. When a tile is placed, content associated with each tile's category is displayed automatically on the panel. This research demonstrates a kind of interface in which multiple display units are used, and physical interaction such as placing a unit onto a panel triggers the content to react.

While Rekimoto's work uses a panel to create an independent displaying area within a single larger panel, there are other studies that examine the use of physically independent display devices. "ConnecTables" (Tandoor, Prante, Müller-Tomfelde, Streitz, & Steinmetz, 2001) is about a system that dynamically connects two displays, thereby producing a single virtual screen to produce a collaborative workplace. A display unit, called a ConnecTable, is a graphic tablet equipped with a built-in-sensor. These units detect each other when they are placed so that their boundaries are attached to one another; this prompts their screens to get connected into a single screen. On the connected screen, users can share information by moving displayed items between devices. Hinckley (2003) proposed bumping displays together to trigger a connection (Hinckley, Ramos, Guimbretiere, Baudisch, & Smith, 2004). An acceleration sensor can detect a vibration from the bump. Then, display regions are connected to form a single workplace. "Stitching" (Hinckley et al., 2004) similarly builds a collaborative workplace using multiple displays. This work uses a stylus pen for connecting displays. The system recognizes the pen's continuous movement spanning over multiple displays, and forms a temporary single screen by deducing the relative positions of displays by rendering the pen's trail as a continuous line. These studies present variants of the approach. Some use sensors to detect physical contact between displays, some use a gesture to signal the same intention, while others use a pen's trail to sense positions more precisely.

The following papers describe the works that assemble multiple mobile devices for building a larger virtual screen (Johnston, 2012; Intelity, 2011). These works are done mainly for displaying demo contents, and the display arrangement is fixed. The "Junkyard Jumbotron" (Borovoy, 2011) is an application that combines devices including smartphones or/and PC displays, and binds them into a single large virtual screen. It configures the relative position of each device by detecting specific graphical markers displayed on each display using a camera. This work provides a method to configure randomly-arranged multiple displays, but does not have any interactivity.

A lot of research has been done to examine dynamically changing the placements of multiple screens by adopting a variety of different approaches in detecting the relative position of devices. "Shiftables" (Merrill, Kalanithi, & Maes, 2007) introduces a specific tiny block device, which equips a display and built-in-sensors on its four sides to detect the other devices. The approach to use a sensor for detecting a connection with the other device can be characterized as resembling ConnecTables and Hinckley's work. There are researches using common mobile devices for achieving a multiple-display environment with interactivity. HuddleLamp (Rädle, Jetter, Marquardt, Reiterer, & Rogers, 2014) uses a lamp equipped with RGB and a depth-tracking camera to detect the positions of multiple devices to enable multi-device interaction. Li and Kobbelt (2012) let mobile devices observe a graphic marker through built-in cameras so that the devices could calculate their own positions and orientation in the marker's coordinate system (Li & Kobbelt, 2012). A variety of approaches for realizing multi-device interaction have been intensively surveyed and discussed by Rädle et al. 2015.

Differences in research objectives explain the differences between the aforementioned projects and ours. Our approach resembles "Stitching," in which a display's relative position is surmised through the trail drawn on screens, but we emphasize a dynamic changing of display layout. We use the pinching gesture for not only prompting connection of the displays but also turning it into an interface for producing a reaction from applications. Other studies have been aimed mostly at proposing a method for establishing a working environment for cooperation with multiple devices. Another difference is that we chose the gesture of "pinching" as a physical analogy of gluing two things together, so that a user can have the sensation of actually connecting devices manually. Junkyard Jumbotron was designed to create a single large screen with temporarily assembled devices, whereas ours work is intended to produce an application platform that uses a change of display layout as a means of interaction. Therefore, Junkyard Jumbotron detects and configures the display positioning as a whole at one time, whereas ours uses no such configuration approach. Shiftables specifically demands tailored devices, whereas our approach uses commodity devices. Using temporarily assembled devices is the salient feature of our approach. Shiftables assumes that a single person possesses all the necessary devices for playing applications, whereas we assume that a person will call friends to bring their devices before playing together. We expect that applications with our approach will encourage social interaction.

This field of research is not limited to pursuing the realization of a particular mechanism. One project assessed the social impact of using multiple devices collaboratively (Falchuk, Zernicki, & Koziuk, 2012). They specifically examine the necessary system architecture and clarify problems to be solved for realizing such a service, especially considering video streaming applications as a candidate example. Some studies have adopted the interactivity that comes from the reconfiguration of digital blocks for use in specific applications. Dertien, Dijkstra, Mader, & Reidsma (2012) proposed the use of a set of cubic blocks as an education tool for children. Each block installs RGB LEDs and an LCD display on its surface, and changes color when connecting to the other blocks. "t-words" (Sylla, Gonçalves, Branco, & Coutinho, 2012) uses blocks with a recording function for cultivating children's pre-literate skills. By changing the order of the blocks in connections, different sentences are uttered from devices. The same function can be realized as a PC application with which a user can manipulate virtual CG blocks appearing in a PC display. However, making such functional blocks into real objects not only provides an easy interface for children but also renders the play to be more fun, which works as positive feedback for learners. These examples of research suggest that approaches such as the one used in our research are promising for wider use in many application areas.

MECHANISM AND IMPLEMENTATION OF PINCH INTERFACE

In this section, we explain the mechanism of using a pinching gesture to make a connection between devices. To realize a dynamically reconfigurable multi-display, a network connection should be established among devices to enable mutual communication. Next, they need to sense their own relative locations. Finally, the visual appearance of the content should react instantly, and accordingly. The interaction proceeds through four major steps other than the installation of applications, as portrayed in Figure 4, to implement the requirements explained above. These steps will be performed repeatedly when the layout undergoes a change.

For implementing the mechanism of these steps, we imposed upon ourselves the following requirements. First, because we chose commodity devices for our platform, we did not want to attach extra sensors to devices for automatically detecting the existence of other devices. We also did not want to introduce a manual pre-configuration process for registering the devices. Moreover, we wanted to avoid explicit preparation of a device solely dedicated to management and control. We wanted the applications to be usable on any occasion, and not just in a specifically tailored situation. Therefore, we wanted the system to be completed solely by the use of the mobile devices themselves and network.

RECOGNITION OF DEVICES

When an application starts, it instantly begins to seek other devices on the same network. Once it has found other devices on which a compatible application is running, the application registers the network addresses of the devices and establishes a mutual connection. Finding others on a network is accomplished automatically using Apple's Bonjour protocol. This protocol is useful for publicizing a network service to other devices. The bonjour protocol deals with the identifier, designating a kind of service,

Figure 4. Procedure of relating devices (© 2018, T. Ohta. Used with permission)

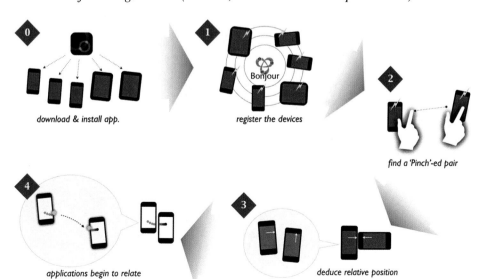

and a transport protocol of the type in a format such as "pinch. tcp." In this way, the application can find other fellow "Pinch"-able applications on the network. We prepared the function for network connection so that it can use either of Wi-Fi or Bluetooth. No direct connection among the devices is established at this stage. Each device only notices candidates for establishing a connection.

As may be apparent from the explanation above, no central architecture exists for managing the information as a whole. Network communication is performed peer-to-peer among the devices. The applications are running independently on the respective devices, only exchanging the necessary information on demand with corresponding devices. Additionally, the platform needs no extra device, such as sensors attached to the display devices. Detecting a gesture applied to the touch screen provides sufficient information to configure the connection. These features — having no centric server, and no extra attachment — provide great advantages for implementing multiple displays using only temporarily assembled commodity devices.

IDENTIFYING A PINCHED PAIR AND ESTABLISHING A NETWORK CONNECTION

Once devices are mutually registered as a group, as described in the previous step, they are ready to send and receive information of a pinching event. The system needs to know which two devices from all the candidates should be paired, when the pinching gesture is applied. On each device, the application detects whether a swiping motion has been applied to its screen. When the application notices a swipe applied on the screen, it broadcasts that information to all the other devices (Figure 5).

The pinched pair can be determined by finding two devices that are swiped simultaneously because we can assume that swiping motions on two devices caused by a pinching gesture happen at the same instant. A broadcasted information of a swipe consists of the data shown in Table 1. Each device receiving that information examines if a swipe is applied to itself at the same moment. If there is such a device, it continues to check the following conditions to examine if it really is one of a pinched pair.

1. If the motions occur simultaneously (happen within a very short period)
2. If a screen's surface is directed to the same orientation
3. If the swipes move in opposite directions

These conditions can also be satisfied by a false action, one other than a valid pinching gesture. One such example is the simultaneous application of two independent swipes to two separately placed devices. Our system does nothing to prevent such ambiguous actions. Connecting the devices by such a false action will not give a useful outcome to a user, especially when an application is designed so that it requires the displays to be annexed to show a meaningful response. Therefore, we believe that users would eventually comply with the intended usage without being forced to do so, to appreciate the benefits that this interface and the application can offer.

Figure 5. Broadcasting information on a swiping action (© 2018, Ohta. Used with permission)

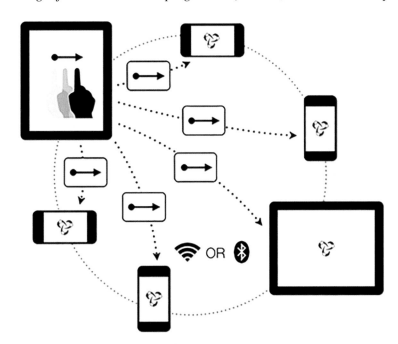

Table 1. Information on a swipe

Attributes	Explanation	Value
Timestamp	time when swipe is applied	h:m:s
Screen Size	screen size (in pixel)	{width, height}
Location	swipe's terminal position	{x, y}
Direction	swipe's direction in screen	right, left, up, down
Orientation	screen's orientation	portrait, landscape
Roll	roll of device's position	roty (degree)
Pitch	pitch of device's position	rotx (degree)
Yaw	yaw of device's position	rotz (degree)

DEDUCING RELATIVE PLACEMENT OF THE DEVICES

After a pinched pair is discovered, it is necessary to determine the relative screen coordinates of the paired devices. The idea is based on the assumption that swipes applied by the forefinger and thumb in a pinching gesture would be on the same straight line. Therefore, we can deduce the orientation and alignment of two connected screens by obtaining the swipe locations. For example, if the swipes on displays of pinched devices are located as illustrated in the left hand Figure 6, then the device positioning is deduced by finding the relative position at which these swipes are on the same line in an opposite direction (right hand figure of Figure 6).

Figure 6. Relative placement of devices is deduced by the swipe's location and direction (© 2018, T. Ohta. Used with permission)

Each device of the pair has information about the swipe, which was applied on the other device. This information includes the swipe's terminal position, which is the coordinate value of the cross point of the swipe motion and the screen's edge, as depicted by the red circle in Figure 7. It is possible to infer the relative position from combining this data.

The procedure to determine relative screen coordinates is the following. In Figure 8, these steps are illustrated by using the values of Figure 7.

1. Position screen B so that its center matches A's center.
2. Move screen B by the distance between swipe A's location and screen A's center position.
3. Rotate screen B by the difference of the two devices' directions.
4. Move screen B further by the distance between swipe B's location and screen B's center position.

By these procedures, an application on each device can obtain the connected screen's relative location. Using this knowledge, the application can convert a certain position on the screen of the other

Figure 7. Swipe data in screen coordinates (© 2018, T. Ohta. Used with permission)

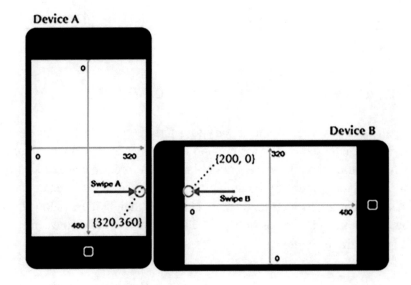

Figure 8. Steps for determining relative screen coordinates (© 2018, T. Ohta. Used with permission)

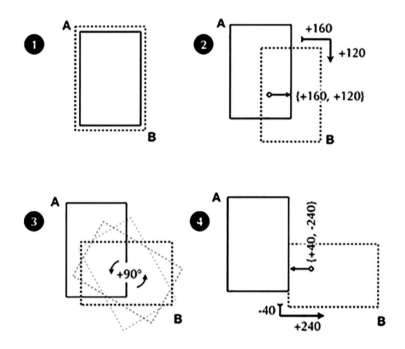

connected device to its own coordinates, making it possible to display a graphic object moving from one screen onto another. Because the data of a swipe's terminal position reflects the screen's size, this process is also applicable to a pair of different screen sizes. Therefore, the procedure works well with combinations as smartphones and tablet PCs.

INTERFACE FOR BREAKING A NETWORK CONNECTION

For implementing a flexibly reconfigurable multi-display, we created two different interface designs for disconnecting the devices, making them intuitive and instant. Shaking a device (left hand of Figure 9) is one approach to do so. Shaking an object is a good physical metaphor for breaking a connection. We also adopt tilting of a device as another way to disconnect. Although shaking would be more appropriate when a user has the devices in hand, it is bothersome to do so when the devices are placed on a table. Both interfaces differ only in the sensitivity criteria for detecting the device's acceleration. Therefore, it is easy to judiciously choose one over the other for a certain application and occasion.

DESIGN OF THE APPLICATION'S REACTION

To make it look as if the pinching gesture connects the devices, it is necessary to design an appropriate application reaction. Recognizing a pinching gesture alone will not realize the interaction of our intention. The gesture can produce a magical feeling only when it smoothly integrated with the instant reaction of an application. When applications are running in relation, a reaction is made not by nominating a central

Figure 9. Two different interfaces for breaking a connection (© 2018, T. Ohta. Used with permission)

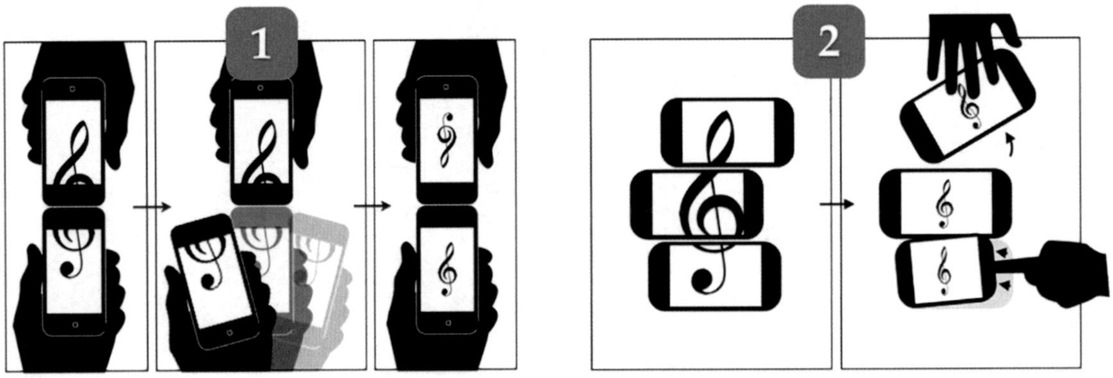

controller device and letting other devices to follow the order from it. Reaction is formed as an ensemble of each device's independent reaction to user input, or to a change in state of a neighboring device.

We designed a programming framework to develop applications that employ the interface. The framework provides functions such as handling the networking, detection of pinching action, conversion of screen coordinates, relaying messages among multiple devices, and disconnection by the shaking gesture. It covers most of the system work and saves a developer from coding these parts. Figure 10 portrays the framework's functional layers. Using the framework, developers can concentrate on the coding of logic that is specific to the application, graphics, and reactions. Figure 11 depicts the class structure of the programming framework. It is readily apparent that the "Pinch" functionality implemented in several classes is ultimately congregated in the class named "PinchController." By preparing its own Controller class inheriting PinchController, an application can call the necessary "Pinch" functions through the methods and classes provided by the framework.

Figure 10. Programming framework layers (© 2018, T. Ohta. Used with permission)

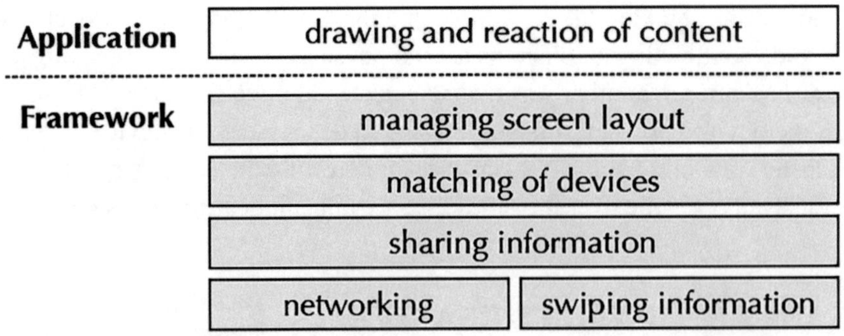

Figure 11. Class structure (© 2018, T. Ohta. Used with permission)

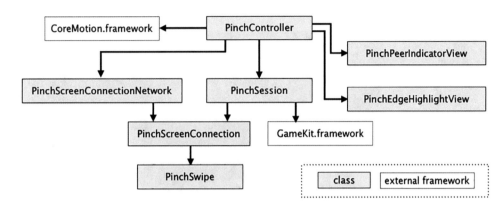

VARIATION OF CONTENT DESIGN

We developed applications that employ the "Pinch" interface to ascertain whether the system works as expected. Additionally, we designed various applications to demonstrate the potential of this user interface for producing a variety of content. Although we believe that the user interface can be used by a variety kind of applications, we focused on creating visually-oriented applications because such content would be better at demonstrating the interface's features. We think that an application is most effective with this interface when it is playable even on a single device and can add extra fun when it is played by using multiple devices. The sample applications introduced here are simple ones, but they can demonstrate the interface's potential to produce fascinating interactions.

TRANSFERRING OF GRAPHIC OBJECTS

The first example is very simple: a graphic object can move among multiple displays that are interconnected. When the application is started on one device, a ball appears to be moving on the screen. It bounces back when it hits the boundaries. When it is connected with other devices, the ball can go through the boundaries of one device to the other device's screen (Figure 12). Connecting additional devices further enlarges the area within which the ball can move around. The devices can be connected with any orientation or alignment (Figure 13). The ball bounces back again when the connection is broken. The screen layout can be reconfigured repeatedly. When the screen is tapped, a new ball is generated, and starts moving around.

The mechanism for making a graphic object look like it is going through physical screen boundaries is described in the following steps. The assumption is that the object is originally located on device A.

1. Get the object's location and destination in terms of device A's screen coordinates.
2. Deduce these positions in terms of device B's screen coordinates.
3. Generate a copy of the graphic object on device B by converting the original object's position from device A's coordinates to device B's coordinates (Figure 14).
4. Move graphic objects on both screens simultaneously.

Figure 12. A ball goes through the boundaries when devices are connected (© 2018, T. Ohta. Used with permission)

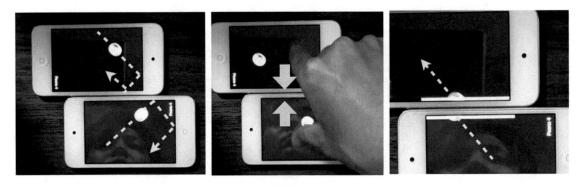

Figure 13. Flexible arrangement of devices (© 2018, T. Ohta. Used with permission)

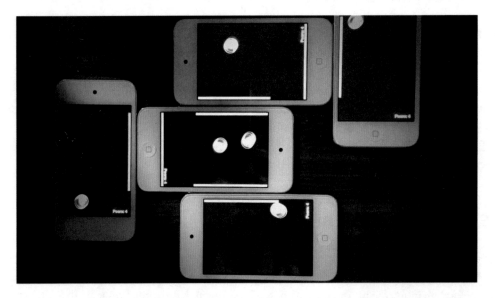

5.   Remove the original object from device A after the object moves beyond the screen's boundary.

As explained above, the object's motion is executed by copying the object instance to a new device when the object moves to a different screen. Information regarding the object's properties, including its coordinates, is shared over a network. This approach differs from the way in which a central device does all the calculation and management about the graphical object's movements for all displays, and broadcasts them to the devices. This approach benefits the choice of smartphone as our platform because no device is indispensable, and any device can be removed from the connection at any time. This means that any owner who are offering his/her device to play an application can leave anytime by retracting it.

Using this feature can lead to new ideas for creating game applications. In the game shown in Figure 15, a user is required to keep a character moving along the displayed course by repeatedly reconnecting the devices to keep the course from being broken. In order to prevent the character from being blocked

Figure 14. Conversion to coordinates of a different screen (© 2018, T. Ohta. Used with permission)

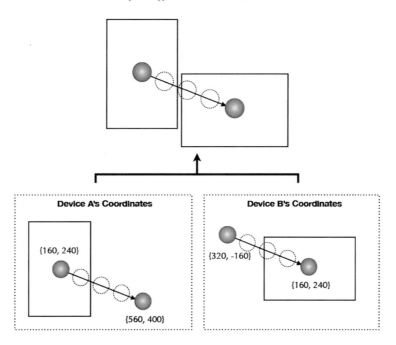

at a boundary, the user needs to react quickly to bring devices around. The challenge is to keep moving devices into appropriate alignments to make the course continuous in time. The other game (Figure 16) also aims at moving a character continuously by reconnecting devices repeatedly. A step appears on each screen, and the player is required to enable a character to reach it by adjusting the device's alignment.

In these games, rearranging devices is not merely for forming a screen to display content but is the interface for playing the game, and that interaction gives a main fun part of the playing.

DYNAMIC RECONFIGURABLE, ARBITRARILY-ARRANGED MULTI-DISPLAY

The application introduced here creates a single virtual screen by connecting multiple devices, the same way it is done with an ordinary multi-display approach. A larger screen is constructed by repeatedly attaching a device to any one of the many devices forming a screen, by applying a pinching gesture

Figure 15. A game to keep a character moving on a course (© 2018, J. Tanaka. Used with permission)

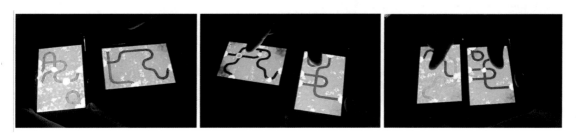

Figure 16. A game to keep a character moving through a generated field (© 2018, A. Yeh, S. Nilsson, M. Tyrén, and A.Weiss. Used with permission)

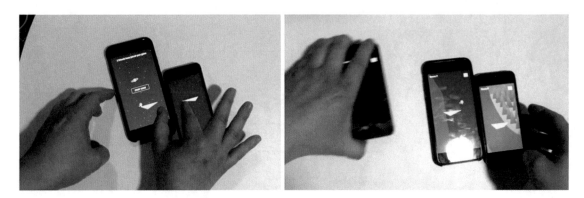

to connect them. Because there is no central controlling unit in the system, a multi-display screen is made as a sum of the connections of two devices. The difference between our application and ordinary multi-display systems is that a virtual screen can be formed and re-formed dynamically by attaching and retracting devices freely, and such manipulation can be done even while a movie is playing on the screen.

For this application, the same movie file is delivered to every device in advance, because the file is incorporated into the application. A static image is displayed when the application starts on a device, and tapping the screen plays a movie. When another device is attached to form a multi-display, the movie is enlarged to fit inside a newly constructed virtual screen. Each device is responsible for a part of the movie's full area, which is calculated from the total screen size and each device's relative placement within that screen. The size and orientation of the movie extending through the connected screens is also adjusted dynamically to appear as large as possible within the virtual screen (Figure 17). The size of the full virtual screen is adjusted at the instant that a display is added or removed from the formation. The region that each device is responsible for is also determined at this event. This process is done without stopping the movie. Movies played on different devices are synchronized to make a single screen output if the movies were played at different time positions before the devices were connected. The signal for the synchronization is issued from the device located at the center of the virtual screen.

When an additional device is connected to an existing multi-device construction, the device causing the change obtains the virtual screen's information from the annexed device, and updates it by accumulating its own screen size. When a device is extracted from the construction, the counterpart of the connected pair updates the screen's information. Because no specific unit is responsible for managing the information on all the system, there needs to be a mechanism for relaying the update to the applications running on all the connected devices. A device responsible for updating the data sends out the information to its direct neighbors, and makes them update their own information. Subsequently, each device re-sends the information to its own neighbor(s). The updated information of the virtual screen's size is therefore relayed to all devices through iteration. To prevent the information from circulating endlessly, a unique identifier is added to the information. A device stops forwarding the information when it receives a message with an old identifier. An example of message routing is depicted in Figure 18. The devices relay the virtual screen's size and their own screen ranges in global coordinates. Therefore, every device updates its responsible display area at the same instant.

Figure 17. Displaying a visual over multiple screens (© 2018, T. Ohta. Used with permission)

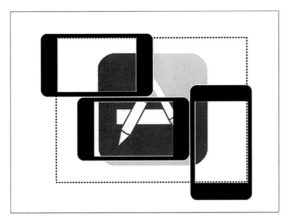 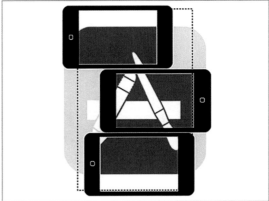

Figure 18. Relaying a message to all devices (© 2018, T. Ohta. Used with permission)

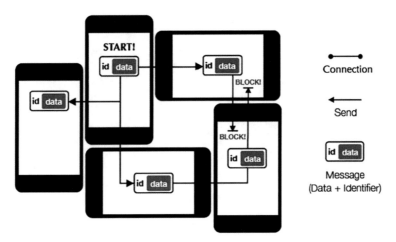

Fitting a movie to a virtual screen is made possible by each device knowing to display the part of the movie's area it is responsible for. This is possible because each device knows its own position in the virtual screen's global coordinate system, and the screen size of its own display. A virtual screen is therefore established as the coordinated sum of individual devices. Images in Figure 19 and Figure 20 portray how the application works.

This multi-display construction can be extended to handle a greater number of devices for providing a platform for digital signage by introducing a server architecture (Ohta & Tanaka, 2015). Further, the arrangement of devices is not limited to two dimensions, but can be extended to 3D compositions shown in Figure 21. Such compositions can render a realistic presence to the content.

Figure 19. Pinching two annexed displays to make them form a single screen (© 2018, T. Ohta. Used with permission)

Figure 20. Playing a movie on a virtual screen formed by multiple devices (© 2018, T. Ohta. Used with permission)

PROPAGATION OF EVENTS

What we introduce here are applications that propagate an event to a connected device. They use the same graphical expression mechanism explained in the preceding sub-sections, but the main interaction is based on event propagation.

The first application is a music sequencer for composing and playing music. Initially, only a rectangular space appears on the screen. The leftmost image of Figure 22 shows that the player can place a tiny silver circle over the dots in the rectangular space, by tapping the screen where the player wants to position it. A sound is played when a scan line traverses the screen and hits these tiny circles. The sound pitch is determined according to each circle's position. Although a single device's screen affords only a very short melody, adding extra devices can elongate it. When the scan line reaches the end of one device, it sends a message to the next device to begin its turn. When the scan line reaches the end of the last device, scanning begins again from the first device. Relaying of a message is necessary to

Figure 21. 3D screen composition (© 2018, T. Ohta. Used with permission)

Figure 22. Tuneblock: a music sequencer application (© 2018, T. Ohta. Used with permission)

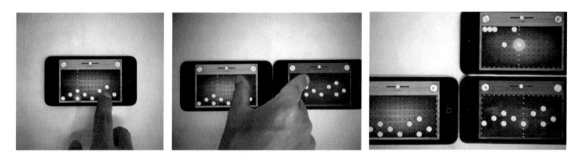

realize this looping of playing sound. Connecting of the devices works not only for elongating a musical note: tunes set in different devices are played in chorus when devices are connected in parallel to the scanning line's direction of movement (rightmost image, Figure 22). Although the same setting of circles remains on each device, altering the display layout can play a different piece of music. With this application, friends can have fun by appending their own musical segments to produce a new piece of music. This usage suggests that our interface and approach can provide a new way of cooperation and sharing an experience, not in a virtual space but in real life.

One other application with a similar approach is for playing visual images and sounds. As shown in Figure 23, tapping on the surface creates an expanding circle of random color and produces a fancy sound. When devices are connected, the circle propagates beyond multiple screens as it expands. The event is propagated to a neighboring device when the circle graphic reaches a boundary. Data transmitted includes the circle's center position in global coordinates, as well as the radius and the graphic color.

Figure 23. Ripple-like graphics caused by a touch propagate through multiple screens (© 2018, T. Ohta. Used with permission)

EVALUATION

This section describes assessments of the system's functionality, and presents feedback regarding usability received from audiences at several conferences where the applications were exhibited.

FUNCTIONALITY

First, we examine whether a connection is established promptly, and whether the system can deduce the correct direction for the connection. Many combinations exist in the orientation of devices for a connection, more so when one considers that there are four sides on which to put other devices. We examine this by observing whether a virtual screen's coordinates are built consistently with the displays' physical placement. We use the moving ball application to verify that combinations of two to five devices are handled properly. Thereby, we confirmed that all of these are processed correctly.

We observed a slight discrepancy in the alignment of devices arising out of matching screen coordinates. This cannot be avoided when obtaining a position to align by using a finger's touch on the screen. Approximately 2.5 mm of slip is observed on average, with a maximum value of 5 mm, although this quantity is expected to differ among people, and individual styles of moving fingers. Touch by thumb was found to have greater slippage. However, we do not need high accuracy for our purposes. A small slip between the juxtaposed screens does not deter us from regarding the two displays as connected. A larger slip is observed when a pinch action is applied in not perpendicular to a display's boundary but along in a diagonal line.

Because a pinching action is used for not only connecting devices but also prompting applications to react, the response time to the action is critical for the realization of interaction. We measured the elapsed time for connection and disconnection of different protocols. The response is almost instantaneous both with Bluetooth and Wi-Fi.

Finally, we examined how many devices can join the connection simultaneously. With the Wi-Fi protocol, we observe that the connection is successful up to 28 devices. We were not able to test for a larger number because we did not have access to more devices. We believe that more devices can be accommodated, but it would become difficult because network communication increases drastically with an increase in the number of devices. We experienced that the connections become unstable for several large conferences. We suppose that the existence of many Wi-Fi network channels in one place negatively affects the mechanism's working. With Bluetooth, we can use only up to four devices because of a restriction in the current software specification of Bluetooth.

PUBLIC RESPONSE

We have presented applications at several conferences and exhibitions. Responses from the audience were favorable, and showed great enjoyment. The applications even received an award at a conference as the most impressive demonstration, decided by the attendees' votes. Our research was also acknowledged to be an "Innovative Technology" by the Japanese Ministry of Economy, Trade and Industry (DIGITAL CONTENT EXPO, 2012).

On one such occasion, at an academic conference titled "Interaction 2012" held in Tokyo, where we presented our applications in a demonstrative session, we administered questionnaire surveys and interviewed some audience members about their evaluation of the content and interface. The attendees responding to the questionnaires were mostly university faculty members, company researchers, graduate students in the research field, and a few non-researchers who came to see the demonstrations. Their ages varied from 20 to 60.

We asked respondents if they felt that the interface was natural for connecting displays (Q1), and if it inspired new ideas of applications (Q2). When a respondent was an independent developer, we asked this additional question; did he/she want to develop applications using the interface (Q3)? The reason for the fewer answers to Q3 is that not all the respondents were application developers. We obtained extremely positive answers to all of these questions. We were especially gratified to learn that a majority of people answered that the interface inspires new ideas, and that they wanted to develop their own applications using it. Table 2 presents the results of the questionnaire survey.

Table 2. Questionnaire about the Pinch interface

	Question	Yes	No
Q1	Do you feel the interface intuitive and natural?	30	2
Q2	Can you come up with any application ideas with the interface?	27	5
Q3	Do you want to develop an application by yourself? (for developers only)	20	1

There were also many positive comments posted on Twitter to a demonstration movie broadcast on a web news site (DIGINFO TV, 2012), such as "A great UI & UX," "looks very interesting," "anticipate a great potential," or "expect it can produce various applications." In addition, we received inquiries about the feasibility of various application ideas. Ideas for advertisements, games, and education are majority of them, but some wanted to know the plausibility of using the interface for sharing files, or even for transferring service authentication. Having shared discussions with several interested parties, we noticed that they were intrigued mainly by the dynamic construction of the multi-display at first. Therefore, many ideas focus solely on using that feature, and consider neither the reconfiguration of the layout, nor utilization of the flexible alignment of the displays' relative positions. For example, one gaming idea uses the interface only to expand the field by connecting additional displays. Furthermore, most of the ideas remain in suggesting of application only. We expect our approach can create applications of a social kind. We believe that an application should be positioned within an external global campaign to realize that potential. After we hinted at plausible application design that could be achieved by introducing the dynamic reconfiguration feature, or the potential of a social campaign with a 'Pinch-able application as its core, the interested parties seemed to find these scenarios more promising.

For example, a certain party created an application with our advice for advertisement purposes (welovead, 2013). The content is similar to our example application for displaying a movie in a flexible layout. Instead of adjusting a movie to a newly established layout, adding a new device will reveal a part of a movie that is hidden until the extra display is added. If a movie is fascinating enough to make people want to watch it at full size, we can expect a user to call friends to join him/her to gather enough devices to form a virtual screen that can display the movie's entire area. Once the number of devices reaches a pre-defined criterion, there appears a secret movie on the screen, which can be shared to attendees through a screenshot. Although such an application could be created as fascinating enough by the content itself,, we believe having a use of an application of this kind would be a good scenario for promoting an advertisement campaign.

CONCLUSION

We devised a new interface that dynamically connects multiple mobile devices. We also created applications that react automatically to a change in the display arrangement. The objective of our approach is the creation of a dynamically reconfigurable multi-display environment as a new platform for interactive media content. Using the "Pinching" action to prompt a connection of the displays provides an intuitive interface, because the gesture is a physical metaphor of stitching things together. Additionally, we created applications to react directly to the change in display arrangement, which means that the pinching action is useful not only as an interface for connecting displays but also as a trigger that causes an application's response. We believe that the fun and engagement of our approach derives mostly from this instant reaction to a layout change.

In terms of functionality for connecting multiple devices over a network, we may conceive various approaches and interfaces to achieve the purpose. Some interfaces would be easy and simple to set up. However, we believe there would be a huge difference between those that merely implement the function, and those that can provide a new fun experience. What we desire is an interface that provides a new user experience and an application platform that invites various new ideas.

We created several prototype applications, hoping to demonstrate the interface's potential for delivering new user experiences. We also want to appeal that the interface could become a platform that can produce a variety of applications. All of these applications are designed not only playable on a multi-display; the applications are designed so that they are playable on a single screen, but they have an extra fun that emerges when devices get connected with each other. This design principle can enable people to play the application either alone or with friends. In addition, different types of interaction can be anticipated with the interface. For example, currently only co-planar connections are possible but with a slight alteration, construction of 3D displays becomes possible. This feature would greatly expand the potential of the interface in producing a variety of applications. We have received favorable feedback and comments from the audience at some conferences and exhibitions, and also from the Internet. Although the applications are simple in terms of their content, the idea of the interface was appreciated, as we had anticipated.

The other merit of our approach is the selection of the hardware platform. Mobile devices such as smartphones and tablet-PCs are now sold and owned as commodity gadgets. Today, many people own more than one such device. Therefore, we can expect that there would be plenty of occasions on which several devices can be gathered at the same spot. A group of friends or colleagues could gather to play, because one person might not be able to afford so many mobile devices. In such a situation, we would be able to develop social applications of a new type. The applications require face-to-face communication. Therefore, it is useful in viral advertising. Pursuing this aspect of the interface, and the applications it can support for encouraging people to have communication with physical contact, is a future objective of our research endeavors.

ACKNOWLEDGMENT

This research was supported by MEXT KAKENHI Grant Number 24500154, funded by MEXT (The Ministry of Education, Culture, Sports, Science and Technology, Japan).

REFERENCES

Borovoy, R. (2011). Junkyard Jumbotron, *MIT Center for Civic Media.* Retrieved December 27, 2017 from http://civic.mit.edu/blog/csik/junkyard-jumbotron

Dertien, E., Dijkstra, J., Mader, A., & Reidsma, D. (2012). Making a toy educative using electronics. In A. Nijholt, T. Romao, & D. Reidsma (Eds.), Advances in Computer Entertainment, LNCS (Vol. 7624, pp. 477–480), Springer. doi:10.1007/978-3-642-34292-9_39

DIGINFO TV. (2012). Pinch interface connects the displays of multiple devices simultaneously. Retrieved December 27, 2017 from https://www.youtube.com/watch?v=jRGLkj-PsCc

Falchuk, B., Zernicki, T., & Koziuk, M. (2012). Towards Streamed Services for Co-located Collaborative Groups. In *Proceedings of the 8th IEEE International Conference on Collaborative Computing: Networking, Applications and Worksharing*, IEEE Computer Society. 10.4108/icst.collaboratecom.2012.250426

Hinckley, K. (2003). Synchronous gestures for multiple persons and computers. In *Proceedings of the 16th Annual ACM Symposium on User Interface Software and Technology (UIST 2003)* (pp. 149–158). ACM, New York. 10.1145/964696.964713

Hinckley, K., Ramos, G., Guimbretiere, F., Baudisch, P., & Smith, M. (2004). Stitching: pen gestures that span multiple displays. In *Proceedings of the Working Conference on Advanced Visual Interfaces (AVI 2004)* (pp. 23–31). New York: ACM. 10.1145/989863.989866

Intelity. (2011). The Intelity 64 iPad Wall. Retrieved December 27, 2017 from https://vimeo.com/

Johnston, J. (2012). Universal Mind, The iPad Table. Retrieved December 27, 2017 from https://medium.com/universal-mind/the-ipad-table-66129e030b8c

Li, K., Chen, H., Chen, Y., Clark, D. W., Cook, P., Damianakis, S., ... Zheng, J. (2000). Building and Using a Scalable Display Wall System. *IEEE Computer Graphics and Applications*, *20*(4), 29–37. doi:10.1109/38.851747

Li, M., & Kobbelt, L. (2012). Dynamic tiling display: Building an interactive display surface using multiple mobile devices. In *Proceedings of the 11th International Conference on Mobile and Ubiquitous Multimedia* (pp. 24:1–24:4). New York, NY: ACM. 10.1145/2406367.2406397

Merrill, D., Kalanithi, J., & Maes, P. (2007). Siftables: towards sensor network user interfaces. In *Proceedings of the First International Conference on Tangible and Embedded Interaction (TEI 2007)* (pp. 75–78). New York: ACM. 10.1145/1226969.1226984

Ni, T., Schmidt, G. S., Staadt, O. G., Livingston, M. A., Ball, R., & May, R. (2006). A Survey of Large High-Resolution Display Technologies, Techniques, and Applications. In *Proceedings of the IEEE Conference on Virtual Reality (VR 2006)* (pp. 223–236). Washington, DC: IEEE Computer Society.

Ohta, T. (2008). Dynamically reconfigurable multi-display environment for CG contents. In *Proceedings of the 2008 International Conference on Advances in Computer Entertainment Technology (ACE 2008)* (p. 416). New York: ACM. 10.1145/1501750.1501866

Ohta, T., & Tanaka, J. (2010). Automatic configuration of display ordering for multi-display environments. In *Proceedings of the 2010 International Conference on Advances in Computer Entertainment Technology (ACE 2010)* (pp. 24–27). New York: ACM. 10.1145/1971630.1971638

Ohta, T., & Tanaka, J. (2012). Pinch: An Interface that Relates Applications on Multiple Touch-Screen by 'Pinching' Gesture. In *Proceedings of the 2012 International Conference on Advances in Computer Entertainment Technology (ACE 2012)* (pp. 320–335). New York: ACM. 10.1007/978-3-642-34292-9_23

Ohta, T., & Tanaka, J. (2015). *MovieTile: Interactively Adjustable Free Shape Multi-Display of Mobile Devices. In SIGGRAPH ASIA 2015 Mobile Graphics and Interactive Applications.* New York: ACM. doi:10.1145/2818427.2818436

Rädle, R., Jetter, H. C., Marquardt, N., Reiterer, H., & Rogers, Y. (2014). Huddlelamp: Spatially-aware mobile displays for ad-hoc around-the-table collaboration. In *Proceedings of the Ninth ACM International Conference on Interactive Tabletops and Surfaces (ITS '14)* (pp. 45-54). New York, NY: ACM. 10.1145/2669485.2669500

Rädle, R., Jetter, H.-C., Schreiner, M., Lu, Z., Reiterer, H., & Rogers, Y. (2015). Spatially-aware or spatially-agnostic? Elicitation and Evaluation of User-Defined Cross-Device Interactions. In *Proceedings of the 33rd Annual ACM Conference on Human Factors in Computing Systems (CHI '15)* (pp. 3913–3922). New York, NY: ACM.

Rekimoto, J., Ullmer, B., & Oba, H. (2001). DataTiles: a modular platform for mixed physical and graphical interactions. In *Proceedings of the SIGCHI Conference on Human Factors in Computing Systems (CHI 2001)* (pp. 269–276). New York: ACM. 10.1145/365024.365115

Sylla, C., Gonçalves, S., Branco, P., & Coutinho, C. (2012). t-words: Playing with sounds and creating narratives. In A. Nijholt, T. Romao, & D. Reidsma (Eds.), Advances in Computer Entertainment: LNCS (Vol. 7624, pp. 565–568). Springer.

Tandoor, P., Prante, T., Müller-Tomfelde, C., Streitz, N., & Steinmetz, R. (2001). Connectables: dynamic coupling of displays for the flexible creation of shared workspaces. In *Proceedings of the 14th Annual ACM Symposium on User Interface Software and Technology (UIST 2001)* (pp. 11-20). New York: ACM.

Tokyo University of Technology, School of Media Science. (2012). Pinch: an interface for connecting multiple smartphone screens. In *Digital Content Expo 2012*. Retrieved December 31, 2017, from http://www.dcexpo.jp/archives/2012/en/program/exhibition/detail.html#IT201210

welovead, (2013). Pinch Pinup. Retrieved December 31, 2017 from http://www.welovead.com/en/works/details/aaeElowx

KEY TERMS AND DEFINITIONS

Arbitrary Arranged Multi-Display: The devices are placed arbitrary to form a free shaped screen. You can place a device to any four edges at any positioning of another device to form a multi-display, and also in any orientation. However, it is not completely free. A device cannot be placed apart nor in a slanted position.

Event Propagation: In general, a content is divided and delivered to each display in order to form one screen by multiple displays. We employ a different approach for designing some applications; an event is transmitted to a directly attached device in order to make a consistent visual effect at each local application. The summation of all the application's local response will present a consistent visual as one screen. This application design is more suitable for our dynamically reconfigurable multi-display.

Interactive Multi-Display: In general, "Interactive Multi-display" would mean a multi-display environment that has an interactivity with users. In this document, we use the word to represent a system that can be configured or reconfigured interactively.

Interactive Pairing: In this article, paring two devices means to connect two devices via network. We attach "Interactive" to express that the paring is done in interactively. That includes not only paring of devices, but also releasing of established network connection and reconnecting with a different device.

Network Connection: With our system, all the running application know other applications' existence when they start to run and are ready to broadcast an information when it is. When two devices are decided to be a pair, they directly exchanging information between them but not broadcasting it to all.

Pinch Gesture: In ordinary mean, Pinch gesture is a swiping action applied onto one touch screen by forefinger and thumb for zooming the screen. In this article, we use the gesture to make a connection of two devices over a network, by putting forefinger and thumb to each of annexed devices.

Reconfigurable: We call it reconfigurable especially when the arrangement of displaying devices consisting a multi-display can be altered during applications are running on them, and the applications will react so that the content will fit into the newly arranged environment.

Relative Placement: In order to make one virtual screen by assembling arbitrary placed multiple display devices, it is necessary to know each devices' placement in the entire screen. Because it is assumed that all the devices are connected, the placement of all the devices can be deduced by knowing relative positioning of every two devices.

Chapter 2
Expressive Avatars in Psychological Intervention and Therapy

Ana Paula Cláudio
Universidade de Lisboa, Portugal

Maria Beatriz Carmo
Universidade de Lisboa, Portugal

Augusta Gaspar
Universidade Católica Portuguesa, Portugal & Universitário de Lisboa, Portugal

Renato Teixeira
Universidade de Lisboa, Portugal

ABSTRACT

A wide range of applications for virtual humans can be envisaged for the needs of both research and intervention in Psychology. This chapter describes the development and preliminary testing of an interactive virtual reality application "Virtual Spectators" – whereby virtual humans with expressive behaviour modelled on the basis of field research in human facial expression in real emotion contexts can be configured to interact with people in an interview or jury. We discuss the possibilities of this application in cognitive behavioural therapy using virtual reality and in nonverbal behaviour.

VIRTUAL REALITY IN PSYCHOLOGY

Information Technologies (ITs) designed for human social interaction are currently living their heyday: daily all over the world, social robots make the news, and when not social robots, then artificial intelligence solutions, or the ever more realistic virtual reality games. These ITs hold so much promise for every field of human life, indeed, but entertainment, sales and industry seem to be those that are currently taking the most advantage of their potential.

DOI: 10.4018/978-1-5225-7371-5.ch002

A great deal of emphasis for ITs' applications has been put in Health, including Mental Health (e.g. Jarrett, 2013; Maheu, Pulier, McMenamin, & Posen, 2012) for purposes that range from aid in diagnostic to "tele-counselling" to the design of psychoeducational environments for therapy and/or specific skill learning (e.g. Lane, Hays, Core, & Auerbach, 2013).

Two decades ago virtual reality (VR) opened new possibilities for psychological intervention with the generation of virtual scenarios for the desensitization treatment of people suffering from a variety of phobias, such as flying, open spaces or spiders (Glantz, Durlach, Barnett, & Aviles, 1996; North, North, & Coble, 1997; Rothbaum, Hodges, Watson, et al., 1995, 1996), a trend that continues to this day with the implementation of increasingly realistic VR scenarious (e.g. Shiban et al., 2017). But the scope of interventions with VR has widened somewhat with their incorporation into mobile devices, gaming and distance communication technology. The creation of online virtual worlds where people act and interact assuming the role of a customized avatar, such as *Second Life* (url-SecondLife), also provided a venue for research in Psychology, especially behavioural research (Jarrett, 2009). Virtual humans are being increasingly incorporated into interventions in Psychology, including: the assessment of emotion and eating disorders (Gaggioli, Mantovani, Castelnuovo, Wiederhold, & Riva, 2003), the therapy of eating disorders (Gutiérrez-Maldonado, Ferrer-García, Dakanalis, & Riva, 2017), schizophrenic hallucinations (Jarrett, 2013) and exposure-based treatment of phobias (e.g. Baus & Bouchard, 2014; Haworth, Baljko, & Faloutsos, 2012).

The therapy of social phobia has caught our interest and we have been developing over the last five years VR solutions to enable both therapist-conducted and programmed sessions and self-help simulations (Cláudio, Carmo, Pinheiro, & Esteves, 2013; Cláudio, Gaspar, Lopes, & Carmo, 2014; Cláudio, Carmo, Gaspar, & Teixeira, 2015a; Cláudio, Carmo, Pinto, Cavaco, Guerreiro, 2015b).

In this chapter we describe the rational and the developmental stages of an application that was originally designed to interact with people suffering from Social Anxiety Disorder or Social Phobia – a human condition characterized by intense anxiety when the individual faces or anticipates public performance (APA, 2013). The application has a much wider scope of uses – a topic we will discuss towards the end of the chapter.

Virtual Reality and the Treatment of Social Phobia

Social Anxiety Disorder (SAD) is a condition that can be very crippling in the personal, social and professional domains, as those bearing it withdraw from social contact; it also has a high comorbidity with depression (Stein, 2000). People with SAD fear negative social judgments and are hypervigilant for signals in other's behavior, thereby identifying faster and more efficiently than other people facial clues to threatening or negative content (Douilliez, 2012).

Therapy approaches to SAD include medication, relaxation methods, and psychotherapy, mainly Cognitive-Behavioural Therapy (CBT). CBT produces the most efficient and persistent improvements, especially when it is applied as Exposure Therapy (ET) (Beidel & Turner, 2007), which consists in exposing the patient to the feared situation. VR has been used in ET since the early 90's, being called Virtual Reality applied to Exposure Therapy (VRET).

Several studies have concluded that VRET has a positive effect in anxiety disorders (Wortein, 2015) and produces results that are similar to traditional exposure therapy (Klinger, 2004; Herbelin, 2005, Wortein, 2015). VRET allows a precise control over the habituation (and extinction) to the fear of the phobic object and offers thus, several additional advantages over classic ET (which is based on images and later contact with *in vivo* situations).

Compared with traditional ET, VRET presents some important advantages: (i) it allows scenario configuration and interactions in order to fulfill each patient's needs and progress levels along the therapy; (ii) it provides better preparation of the patient before facing a real life scenario, avoiding the risk of a premature exposure to a real situation; (iii) it reduces the risk of taking steps backwards because of overreactions, allowing a more stable and progressive environment towards predictable and solid results; (iv) it assures patient privacy.

The design of the first VR application aimed at treating public fear before an audience goes back to the work of North and colleagues (1998). This application included a scenario with up to 100 characters. During a therapy session, the therapist was able to vary the number of characters and their attitudes, using pre-recorded video sequences. The patient/client wore a Head Mounted Display (HMD), listening to the echo of his/her own voice. Slater, Pertaub, & Steed (1999) created a virtual room with 8 characters with random autonomous behaviors, such as swinging the head and eye blinking. The initial study gathered 10 students, with different difficulty levels in public speaking, and was later expanded so as to include phobic and non-phobic participants (Pertaub, 2001; Pertaub et al., 2002; Slater et al., 2006).

James et al. (2003) proposed a double scenario: one subway wagon populated by characters that expressed neutral behaviors, which is considered a non-demanding situation from a social interaction point of view; and a more demanding situation that took place in a bar with characters that look uninterested. The characters' behavior included eye gazing and pre-recorded sentences.

Klinger et al. (2004) conducted a 12-session study with 36 participants to evaluate changes in fear before public speaking. Virtual characters were created from photos of real in typical situations. Participants were allocated to one of two groups, submitted either to CBT or to VRET. A higher reduction in social anxiety was reported in the VRET group.

Herbelin (2005) with a 200-patient validation test, demonstrated that his platform fulfilled the requirements of therapeutic exposure in social phobia and proposed that clinical evaluation may be improved with integrated monitoring tools, such as eye-tracking. The inclusion of physiological measures such as electrocardiogram or skin conductance is a common feature of more recent studies (e.g. Esteves, Isberg, Cláudio, Carmo, & Gaspar, 2016; Shiban et al., 2017).

All the referred approaches resorted to HMD equipment. In a study described by Pertaub and colleagues, half of patients tried one of the virtual environments through a HMD, while the rest of the group used a desktop (Pertaub, 2002). Herbelin and Grillon, in addition to an HMD and a computer screen also used a big projection surface (Herbelin, 2005; Grillon, 2009).

Haworth, Baljko, & Faloutsos (2012) implemented virtual scenarios to be visualised simultaneously by patient and therapist in computer screens, possibly in different physical locations and over the internet. Scenarios are oriented to patients suffering from acrophobia (fear of heights) or arachnophobia (fear of spiders). A Kinect is used to control patent body movements (url-Kinect). The results of this study suggest that this type of low-cost solution is effective in these phobias.

In another experiment, Wortwein, Morency, & Scherer (2015) studied the effect of a virtual audience on anxious public speakers, without immersive VRET, using two projections to render a life size audience. These projections were positioned in such a way that the presenter had to move the head to look at the whole audience. Results pointed to the conclusion that anxious participants reduced public speaking anxiety and improved their performance after four training sessions.

VRET has therefore gained recognition for being a useful tool the therapy of social phobia and particularly public speaking anxiety. Its drawbacks are the high cost of the immersive virtual equipment (e.g., HMD, CAVE) and possible, though uncommon, secondary effects (cybersickness) (LaViola, 2000).

THE VIRTUAL SPECTATORS PROJECT

Virtual Spectators is our VRET approach to the fear of public speaking. The work described in this chapter follows from the team's previous work. A first version of the application recreates an auditorium populated by virtual characters with controllable behaviors but with few facial expressions (Cláudio et al., 2013); a second version considers a simulation of a jury composed by a group of virtual characters with body and facial expressions controllable by the therapist in real time (Cláudio et al., 2014). In the current version (Cláudio et al., 2015a) the virtual humans (henceforth VH) are endowed with voice and use simple sentences.

The development of each version has been a multidisciplinary work where the developers of the application teamed up with psychologists and a non-verbal behavior expert psychologist, so as to identify major features to be incorporated, particularly facial and body expressions that potentially convey to the observer a positive, a neutral or a negative feedback.

In addition to describing the development of this VR application, we also report results from a validation study concerning the VH's facial expressions, along with the theoretical assumptions and previous empirical research underpinning the creation of the facial actions' menu. We also provide the output of usability tests performed with psychotherapists in order to study the suitability of the application and its potential effectiveness to VRET.

In this project we envisaged an environment where the patient stands before a jury in an evaluation context, in a job interview or in a similar situation. In a therapy session, while the patient/client faces a jury of one-to-three virtual characters (displaying facial and body expressive behavior), the therapist controls these characters according to the level of stress he/she wants to induce in the patient. This control is accomplished through an interface (conceived to be available to the therapist) which, among other options, triggers and modulates specific facial and body movements that, combined, may convey neutral, positive or negative affective content or various degrees of attention or lack of interest.

Before each therapy session, the therapist defines the setup of the scenario by choosing the characters and some aspects of their appearance (hairstyle, clothes and glasses), their relative position at the table (center or one of the sides) and also the room's decoration style (classical or modern furniture, different wall colors). The simulation scenario is projected on a canvas or a wall, in such way that characters are displayed in real size, to enhance the sense of presence (that is, the feeling of being there, inside the room, facing a jury).

Our application is also a useful tool to non-verbal behavior research: the communication effect related to facial or body actions is not entirely known, and it is currently object of intense academic debate (Gaspar, Esteves, & Arriaga, 2014; Russell & Fernandez-Dols, 1997; Russel, 2017). The application allows the individual visualization of a virtual human's face and supports many combinations of body and facial behavioural units. It also supports a fine-tuning control over a single individual facial action, whilst others are kept constant. Evaluating the impact of these combinations in observers may clarify the communicative role of single and composed actions, giving clues about the treatment of social anxiety. It may also assist various other research lines in the field of interpersonal perception and the affective and cognitive processing of non-verbal behavior signals. Other authors have similarly used VH to customize appearance variables in order to conduct fundamental research on interpersonal perception (e.g. Hirsh, Callander, & Robinson, 2011; Wohlrab, Fink, Kappeler, & Brewer, 2009), manipulating VH's variable features such as gender, ethnicity, and age and detailed facial expressions, as Hirsh and colleagues did, or tattoos, as in Wolrab's study.

Our application has two types of users: the therapist who is an active user, and the patient/client, a passive user. The patient, while speaking in front of the virtual jury, receives visual and sound stimuli from the characters; the therapist, while observing the patient's behavior and reaction to these stimuli, interacts with the application to modify the simulation accordingly, whether by varying the characters' behavior, or by triggering multiple events in the simulation scenario. The initial setup of the scenario is a task also performed by the therapist, as previously mentioned.

The equipment required to run the application is rather common: a computer, two sound columns, a projector and a canvas or wall used as a projection surface. The application opens two separate windows: (i) the simulation window which displays the virtual jury and must be projected and (ii) the interface window which should be displayed in the screen of the computer, to be used by the therapist. The sound columns must be close to the projection to increase the degree of realism of the simulation.

The equipment is inexpensive and easy to install; the projected image should contain the models of the VH in real size with the aim of providing the patient a good sense of presence. With this solution it is possible to have several people observing simultaneously the simulation, a valuable asset for research or in the training of students or therapists. Additionally, all the unpleasant secondary effects reported by some users when using VR equipment are not a concern here.

The Current Version of Visual Spectators

One of the main goals in the development of Virtual Spectators was to provide virtual characters with a good level of realism, but not compromising the application's performance, which had to respond in real time to the therapist's control. Finding a balance between the characters' final appearance and the most critical aspects of the application (number of polygons of the meshes, the textures' resolution and the complexity of the illumination algorithms) was crucial to achieve real time response.

In the current version we combined different models (or parts of them) from the software Poser (url-Poser) and from online repositories. In such a way, we were able to create two males and one female characters of seemingly different ages, who were named John, Carl, and Jessi. These characters can be observed in Figure 1, which displays several screenshots of simulations with different jury compositions, distinct facial and body behaviours.

Figure 2, Figure 3, and Figure 4 show several variations in the look of the virtual characters. The animation of these characters was accomplished using Blender (url-Blender) and a free version of Unity3D (url-Unity). The application was also developed in Unity3D.

Figure 1. Different jury: John, Carl, and Jessi (© 2018, A. P. Cláudio. Used with permission)

Interface Functionalities

The interface displayed when the application starts contains the functionalities to configure the simulation scene and the virtual characters (Figure 5). At the top there is a menu to choose amongst different scenarios (the application is ready to include new scenarios that might be relevant to consider in the future).

To configure the jury, the user uses a drag-and-drop mechanism that allows the choice of the characters: the user selects the picture that represents the character and drags it to the corresponding position in the table contained in the virtual scenario; the photo of the character turns grey signalling that it is no longer available to be chosen. It is possible to choose a formal or informal clothing style, and a formal or informal hairstyle (except for Carl that is bald). These choices are independent, so it is possible to combine several options.

There is also a preview option to visualize the selected and modified character and it is possible to observe a face close-up.

Figure 2. Jessi model exhibiting two different hairstyles and facial expressions (© 2018, A. P. Cláudio. Used with permission)

Figure 3. Carl model with different expressions (© 2018, A. P. Cláudio. Used with permission)

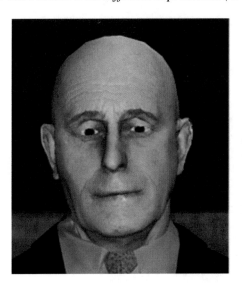

Along the configuration phase, all choices made using this interface are immediately exhibited in the simulation window, which is also visible.

When pressing the button "Start Simulation", the simulation interface is displayed. To avoid excessively complex interaction tasks for the therapist, the application supports user control of only one character at a time; so while one VH is being controlled in real-time, the other characters are exhibiting behaviour that was previously configured. These control modes are called interactive and automatic

Figure 4. Variations in the look of the virtual characters (© 2018, A. P. Cláudio. Used with permission)

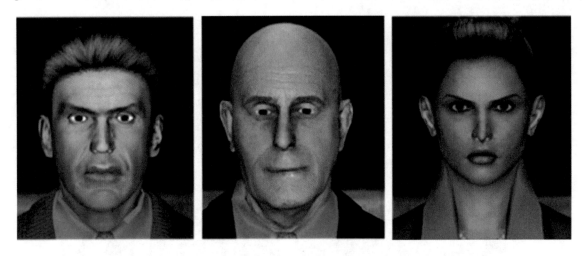

Figure 5. Two screenshots of the configuration interface (© 2018, A. P. Cláudio. Used with permission)

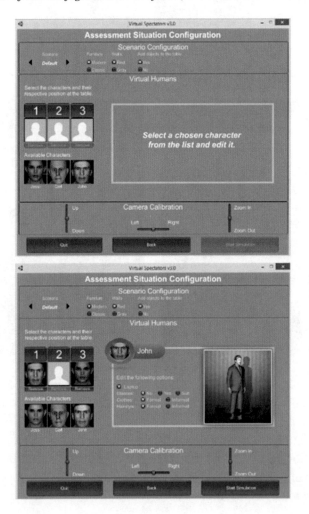

mode, respectively. Throughout the simulation, the therapist is free to switch the characters to control interactively (for details see Cláudio et al., 2014).

Figure 6 shows the simulation interface for a pre-configured jury of 2 elements, one on the middle (position number 2) and one on the right (position number 3). The character in position 2 is in interactive mode of control while character in position 3 is in automatic mode. The difference in the number of available options in each mode is quite clear; the interactive mode is significantly more complex, offering much more options.

There are six automatic modes that can be chosen in alternative: Attentive (neutral), Attentive (agreeing), Attentive (disagreeing), Distracted (agreeing), Distracted (disagreeing) and Leaning backward, inner brow down, arms crossed. They correspond to predefined animations executed by the VHs. At the bottom of the interface there are three types of functionality (Figure 6, from left to right): (i) a slider to control light intensity; (ii) keys to trigger sound events in the environment (plane flying over, phone ringing, traffic in the outside, rain, a conversation in the hallway); (iii) keys to control the position and zooming of the camera. This last set of controls offers the following three possibilities: to visualize all characters (option by default), only the body and the face of the VH in interactive mode or only its face. This feature is particularly suitable to focus the observer's attention on a particular character.

The interface area to control the VH in interactive mode (see position number 2 in Figure 6) has three sets of keys: i) to define two possible states of attention (Attentive, Distracted); ii) those that define what we called by Actions (Disagree, Agree, SMS –answers to a text message that has just arrived– Use laptop, Sleep, Look to the right, Whisper –starts a conversation with the character sitting next, as illustrated in Figure 1) and, finally, a key to open the facial expressions menu, explained ahead. At the bottom of the interface, there are keys to control body postures: Leaning neutral, Leaning forward, Leaning backward, Cross arms, Leaning backward arms crossed. Some, like nodding yes (Agree button) have a predetermined execution time, while others, like Use laptop, are executed as long as the therapist desires. It is possible to combine some of the animations like, for instance, Cross Arms and Agree.

Figure 6. The simulation interface (© 2018, A. P. Cláudio. Used with permission)

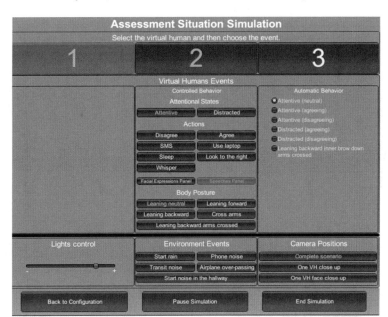

The interface that allows the user to control facial expressions is illustrated in Figure 7. It contains keys that switch on Action Units (AU) from Facial Action Coding System (FACS) (Ekman, Friesen, & Hager, 2002); for two AUs (AU4, AU12) there are options to increase intensity. Our choice of facial elements to include, and the scope of expressions that can be composed with them is based on current validated knowledge on the content of human facial behavior (for an updated review see Gaspar et al., 2014). Although there are applications, games and films today with a wide range of expressive behavior, the way expressive behavior is decoded by people and what exactly do real people convey with their facial and body behavior is still largely debated in emotion Psychology (Russell, & Fernandez-Dols, 1997; Russell, 2017) so we opted for a range of AUs and possible combinations, that has been most consensually derived from behavioural studies of spontaneous facial behavior (e.g. Gaspar & Esteves, 2012; Gaspar et al., 2014).

Furthermore, these facial compositions can also be associated with several body postures. Our selection of postures is based on cross-cultural studies of human non-verbal communication (Eibl- Eibesfeldt, 1989).

Figure 8 shows the same model with different AU combinations. The neutral face (upper left corner), with no AU activated and a positive-emotion expression, a combination of AU1+2+5, full brow and eyelid lift, with AU12, lips up (upper right corner). In the lower right, we see a combination of AU4 and AU15, both related to negative affect. In the lower left corner we see a combination of AU4 and AU6+12 ("smile" button). The AU6+12 combination is known as "Duchenne smile", and has been consensually associated to positive affect more than any other smile form (Gaspar et al., 2014).

Speaking Characters

Verbal communication plays an important role in human interactions, and as our main goal is to attain realistic human-like characters, we planned to include speech as a key feature of the characters. However, to provide a VH with the ability to speak is a complex and highly time-consuming task. To accelerate the process we conceived a simple but effective and satisfactory solution.

Figure 7. Keys that switch on Action Units (© 2018, A. P. Claudio. Used with permission)

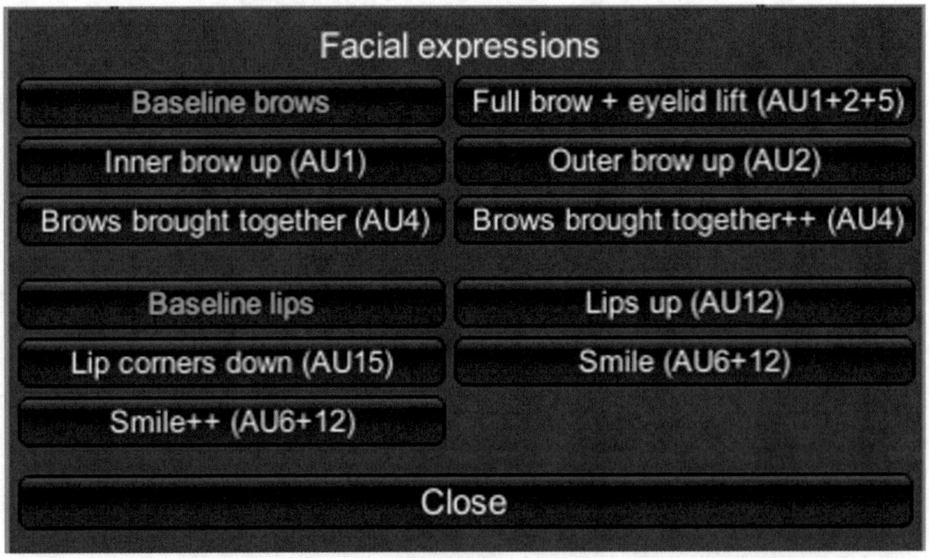

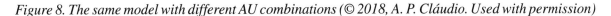

Figure 8. The same model with different AU combinations (© 2018, A. P. Cláudio. Used with permission)

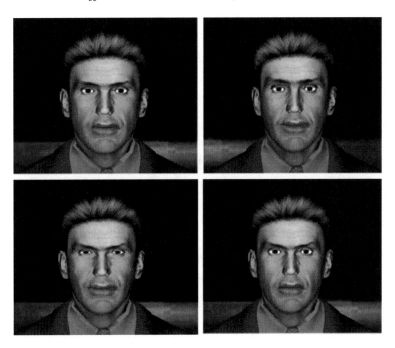

Our main idea was to predefine a set of verbal expressions that each character could reproduce (with sound synchronized with lip movements) and that were controllable and triggered by the therapist during the simulation. On a first trial, we implemented this solution for a single character, John.

The main stages involved in this process are the following:

1. Record the intended set of speeches to include in the application. It can easily be accomplished using the microphone of a laptop, recording a real person speaking.
2. Define and shape all mouth positions involved in the process of animation of the characters considering the sounds that need to be reproduced. On a first instance we defined just 5 shapes/states only for the Portuguese language: Base (baseline), A, E, O and U.
3. Each shape corresponds to an animation. Therefore, this includes a process of animating the characters to be able to visually reproduce these different states. The only bones affected belong to the mouth area, namely, the jaw and the lips.
4. Deconstruct the sentence that the character should be able to reproduce, in such a way that it corresponds to a sequence of animations that the character can process and verbalize. For example, the sentence "Hello world" should be translated to a language recognizable to the character and it would correspond to the sequence of animations (E,O,U,O, Base). This process involves the following steps:
    a. Decomposing the sentence into smaller segments. The division of the sentence is somewhat similar to division by syllabus. However, each segment must contain a single vowel. Given the example, it would be "He-llo-w-o-rld" (in this approach, letter w is considered as a vowel);
    b. Evaluate each segment according to the sounds it needs;

c.   Add the corresponding animation to the buffer of all animations that need to be played. For example, a segment "He" will correspond to state *E*, "llo" to *O*, and so on.

5.   Reproduce sequentially all the animations. It is defined a time interval between each animation so that all animations can be synchronized with the sound that starts playing as the therapist triggers the event.

This approach provides a simple but nonetheless realistic and satisfactory solution. It is a good starting point towards a more robust and complete approach. New states can be considered to include a wider range of sounds.

Assessing and Validating the Application

We carried out two assessment procedures: (1) a validation study in order to verify the assumptions supporting the current facial actions' menu and (2) a usability tests with 6 expert volunteers (therapists) aimed at assessing the suitability of the application and its potential effectiveness in VRET.

1.   Content Validation Study

One distinguishing feature of our approach is the concern with testing assumptions underlying the behavior of the VHs. Therefore, adding to the theoretical framework supporting the selection of expressive elements included in the VHs, based on human expressive behavior, we designed a study to test whether the content attributed by observers in the expressive behavior displayed by the VHs was indeed the content we had expected. This was also an important stage in the development of the application, preceding the writing of a handbook with guidelines for therapists willing to plan comprehensive intervention programs with the different levels of positive/negative affect/intimidation that the VH´s may convey, to be customized in a fine grained, increasing intensity along the many weeks that a CBT program generally takes to produce effects (12-16 weeks typically).

Participants (31F; 7M) (age 18- 25 yrs old) were recruited in two universities campuses through advertising in related courses. After providing informed consent, student volunteers were assigned to groups of 8-10 individuals that were tested simultaneously. They were instructed on their tasks, which consisted on watching and rating each and every one of 28 animated clips (3" duration; with a close-up view of a VH) showing either a baseline or one of 13 expressive faces composed of single AUs or AU combinations, that were replicated with precision in each VH face. In the first task participants rated the clip with two onscreen pictorial scales assessing (1) emotional arousal (the felt physiological activation), (2) valence (a dimension that has the very negative experience at one end and very positive at the other end) and (3) dominance/sense of control, that comprise the Self-Assessment Manikin (SAM), developed by Bradley and Lang (1994) to ascertain how one perceives his/her own emotional experience at a given moment in response to a stimulus ("how it makes me feel"). In the second task they appraised the clip using an onscreen close-ended questionnaire with 8 content options (Fear, Happy, Surprise, Angry, other positive emotion, other negative emotion, neutral, don't know).

Procedures comprised providing detailed instructions on the two appraisal tasks that followed the presentation of each stimuli and the stimuli projection in a random order (to control for possible order effects). Participants rehearsed the tasks a minimum of 3 times, and until they had mastered it with a different set of stimuli from that in the test. Images were projected on canvas 2-3 meters away and in front of participants creating real life size projected VHs (see Figure 9 with screenshots from the experiment). Test sessions were conducted in a dim light room.

Stimuli VR video clips displayed faces with the following AUs/AU combinations:

- Baseline eyebrows + Baseline lips
- Eyebrows brought together AU4
- Eyebrows brought together (more intense)++ (AU4)
- Full brow up and eyelid lift (AU1+2+5)
- Inner brow up (AU1)
- Outer brow up (AU2)
- Lips up (AU12)
- Smile (AU6+12)
- Intense smile ++ (AU6+12)
- Lip corners down (AU15)
- Eyebrows brought together++ (AU4) + Lips up (AU12)
- Eyebrows brought together++ (AU4) + Lip corners down (AU15)

Figure 9. Screenshots from the experiment (© 2018, A. P. Cláudio. Used with permission)

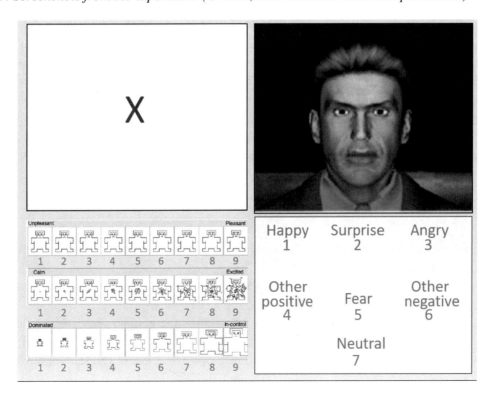

- Inner brow up (AU1) + Lips up (AU12)
- Inner brow up (AU1) + Lip corners down (AU15)

Results showed great convergence in both content attribution and emotional impact to many facial expression patterns, thereby validating our content assumptions while choosing the expressive units to include.

As regards emotional content attribution, we observed high convergence in the interpretation of clips, with 12 out of 28 clips presenting convergence above 75% (6 on the label angry, 4 on happy, 1 on surprised and 1 on neutral) with a highly significant association between images and label (X^2=2088.07; p <= .001; N = 978), as shown by the independence X^2 test performed on the cross tabulation of composition and content. Importantly, convergence was congruent with the expected content in all convergent pictures. Table 1 shows the aforementioned 12 clips.

As to emotional impact (see Table 2), images generally did not elicit high Arousal (only 3 clips scored higher than the Median). Pleasure was highly convergent, fitting a narrow bell curve, with 100% of data below SD=1.9 and Mean=4.53, approaching the Median=5. Regarding Dominance/control, 19 clips scored higher than the Median, in an also centered distribution where Mean=5.16 approaching the Median=5 and 100% of data fell below SD=1.9; the highest scores on feeling dominant occurred in response to target faces that had been convergent on positive content in the labelling task and resulted from exposure to the female avatar, for the equivalent patterns in male avatar faces. The virtual human's expressions in the stimuli clips were never customized to extremely high intensities, which is likely to explain why elicited arousal was almost never high. In addition, this validation tests were carried out with volunteers from a normative population, not with sufferers from fear of public speaking or SAD.

With this study we were able to achieve two important goals: on the one hand that of tabulating values for relevant affective impact parameters - a crucial step towards guidelines in a therapist's handbook - with validated content and intensities, so as to enable the customization of CBT with these virtual humans; on the other hand we have been able to create a platform database of stimuli for studies of impression formation and perception of emotion, by having precise manipulation of action units combined with different facial features and gender. Further manipulation is possible, controlling for the effect of a formal vs. informal outfit and hairstyle. Another test yet to be conducted with these virtual humans is to create patterns that elicit higher levels of arousal and Dominance/control. And, of course extending the tests to the clinical populations with full blown SAD, just with fear of public speaking, or even with Generalized anxiety disorder (GAD)- an exaggerated worry about everyday events and an unrealistic fright of the worst outcomes - which may hold different results for some of the stimuli.

2.   Usability Tests

We carried out yet another study with the goal of evaluating the application on two main features: usability and VH realism.

For these purposes, we recruited 6 therapists (5F; 1M) ages 34- 59 years old. In this group, only 2 participants had not tried the previous version of the application. Tests were conducted individually with each therapist, in a dim light room (to improve visualization of images and sense of presence). The apparatus for tests was identical to that of the typical application use: a portable computer connected to an LCD projector displaying the image onto a projection canvas. Both client and server were executed in

Table 1. The 12 clips that presented convergence above 75% (© 2018, A. P. Cláudio. Used with permission)

		No answer (I do not know)	Fear	Happy	Neutral	Other negative	Other positive	Surprise	Angry
	Image 10- Jessi intense smile (AU6+12)++	5.7%	0.0%	**91.4%**	0.0%	0.0%	2.9%	0.0%	0.0%
	Image 12- Jessi brows brought together ++ (AU4) ++	11.4%	0.0%	0.0%	0.0%	5.7%	0.0%	2.9%	**80.0%**
	Image 16- Jessi full brow and eyelid lift (AU1+ AU2+AU5)	5.7%	11.4%	0.0%	0.0%	2.9%	2.9%	**77.1%**	0.0%
	Image 19- Jessi brows brought together (AU4)	8.6%	0.0%	0.0%	0.0%	0.0%	0.0%	2.9%	**88.6%**
	Image 18- Jessi Smile (AU6+12)	5.7%	0.0%	**80.0%**	0.0%	5.7%	5.7%	0.0%	2.9%
	Image 24- Carl brows brought together ++ and lip corners down (AU4++ and AU15)	5.7%	0.0%	0.0%	2.9%	5.7%	0.0%	5.7%	**80.0%**
	Image 28- Jessi lips up (AU12)	5.7%	0.0%	**80.0%**	0.0%	0.0%	14.3%	0.0%	0.0%
	Image 4, Jessi brows brought together (AU4)	11.4%	0.0%	0.0%	2.9%	0.0%	0.0%	2.9%	**82.9%**
	Image 6- Jessi baseline (neutral expression)	5.7%	2.9%	0.0%	**85.7%**	0.0%	2.9%	2.9%	0.0%
	Image 7- Carl smile (AU6+12)	8.8%	0.0%	**76.5%**	5.9%	0.0%	8.8%	0.0%	0.0%
	Image 8- Jessi brows brought together ++ and lip corners down, (AU4++ and AU15)	8.6%	2.9%	0.0%	0.0%	0.0%	0.0%	0.0%	**88.6%**
	Image 9- Carl brows brought together (AU4)	5.7%	0.0%	0.0%	11.4%	5.7%	0.0%	0.0%	**77.1%**

Table 2. Emotional impact (SAM scale) (© 2018, A. P. Cláudio. Used with permission)

Image id	Arousal		Pleasure		Dominance	
1	4,44	(1,71)	3,66	(1,59)	4,82	(1,14)
2	3,41	(1,76)	4,48	(1,48)	5,09	(1,74)
3	3,08	(1,78)	4,06	(1,53)	4,94	(1,85)
4	4,69	(2,12)	3,66	(1,51)	5,43	(1,57)
5	4,37	(1,75)	3,89	(1,49)	4,80	(1,41)
6	2,97	(2,00)	5,06	(1,32)	5,29	(1,38)
7	4,50	(2,35)	6,00	(1,73)	5,54	(1,50)
8	4,83	(2,12)	3,31	(1,38)	4,80	(1,25)
9	4,17	(1,83)	3,66	(1,41)	4,63	(1,21)
10	4,58	(2,58)	7,26	(1,26)	5,91	(1,54)
11	3,22	(1,91)	4,71	(1,10)	5,09	(1,56)
12	4,69	(1,95)	3,59	(1,43)	5,29	(1,50)
13	4,89	(1,85)	4,43	(1,77)	4,71	(1,70)
14	4,03	(2,28)	5,49	(1,65)	5,26	(1,66)
15	2,75	(1,76)	4,77	(0,80)	5,29	(1,48)
16	4,56	(1,81)	4,59	(1,04)	5,38	(1,65)
17	5,58	(8,33)	3,94	(1,30)	5,20	(1,99)
18	4,00	(1,93)	4,03	(1,24)	5,37	(1,81)
19	4,67	(2,23)	3,51	(1,22)	5,11	(1,49)
20	4,03	(2,05)	3,77	(1,43)	5,11	(1,69)
21	5,06	(1,95)	4,43	(1,48)	5,11	(1,32)
22	4,61	(2,25)	6,60	(1,48)	5,86	(1,53)
23	4,61	(1,79)	3,57	(1,21)	4,77	(1,28)
24	4,92	(1,96)	3,31	(1,32)	4,54	(1,38)
25	5,17	(1,87)	3,97	(1,80)	4,57	(1,54)
26	4,47	(2,19)	3,54	(1,26)	5,00	(1,83)
27	3,89	(2,23)	6,31	(1,15)	5,63	(1,37)
28	3,94	(2,31)	7,12	(1,12)	5,97	(1,38)

localhost. Whilst the therapist interface is shown in the laptop screen, the client interface is projected onto the canvas approaching real-life size. Two sound columns were connected close to the projection canvas.

The evaluation was divided into 4 distinct phases: character evaluation regarding realism (compared to the previous version), usability of the implemented functions, realism of the application as a whole, and an open answer questionnaire section. Each part was evaluated as the user performed each respective task.

As a result, in every section therapists considered the new characters to be more realistic than those of the previous version. The modifications made to the configuration interface were welcomed as improvements. Suggestions made to this interface were:

- Increase the number of available scenarios and characters for higher versatility and the options to edit each character;
- Add new body animations (such as, looking at the watch or touching the hair).

Each therapist was further asked to trigger a specific speech in the "John" character and none had difficulty performing this task. The favorite feature of therapists in the new version is the VH's ability to speak.

Finally, every therapist mentioned that if available, they would likely use the application in their therapy sessions.

CONCLUSION AND FUTURE WORK

One of the main questions related to the use of VRET by the therapists is the cost of the immersive equipment and some degree of discomfort associated with its use. Having this in mind, we sought to implement an affordable solution that is both effective at assisting in the CBT approach to SAD resorting to VRET, especially in the specific and more common problem of fear of public speaking, and at assisting researchers and teachers in the domain of non-verbal behavior.

The approach we propose involves conventional everyday equipment: computer, sound system (two sound columns are enough), projector and canvas (or a wall) to project the simulations. The software for this project (with no budget whatsoever) was developed using freeware and free or very low cost 3D models. The main disadvantage of this approach is the difficulty in obtaining highly photo-realistic models.

Notwithstanding, results from our content validation study, demonstrated that facial expressions in our present models are consistently interpreted by normative observers and are decoded according to expectations derived from emotion and expression science, which can be construed as indirect evidence of realism. These gives us the confidence to use the application to generate animation clips to be used in the research domain of non-verbal communication.

Tests performed with therapists further confirm that the current models are more realistic than those of the previous version. Speech articulation was seen as a major improvement, and in general the idea of using this tool in a clinical environment was welcomed with enthusiasm.

The main follow up steps for Virtual Spectators will be: i) to further test these virtual humans in more AU compositions, with the alternative informal look, and extend tests to more virtual humans, in order to ascertain the contingent impact of facial features and outfit with facial action units; ii) to develop and integrate in the application an artificial intelligence module toward the simulation of emotions; iii) and, to subsequently validate the usefulness of the application with a clinical population in a therapeutic context.

ACKNOWLEDGMENT

We are thankful to all the therapists and volunteers that participated in our study with no other reward than contribute to the research. We thank the Research Unit BioISI, UID/MULTI/ 04046/2013 funded by FCT/MCTES/ PIDDAC, Portugal for providing the main resources that enabled this study.

REFERENCES

American Psychiatric Association (APA). (2013). *DSM-V*. Washington, DC: American Psychiatric Publishing, Inc.

Baus, O., & Bouchard, S. (2014). Moving from Virtual Reality Exposure-Based Therapy to Augmented Reality Exposure-Based Therapy: A Review. *Frontiers in Human Neuroscience*, *8*, 1–15. doi:10.3389/fnhum.2014.00112 PMID:24624073

Beidel, D. C., & Turner, S. M. (2007). *Shy Children, Phobic Adults: Nature and Treatment of Social Anxiety Disorder* (2nd ed.). Washington, DC: APA.

Bradley, M. M., & Lang, P. J. (1994). Measuring Emotion: The Self-Assessment Manikin and the Semantic Differential. Journal of Behavior Therapy and Experimental Psychiatry, *25*(1), 49–59. doi:10.1016/0005-7916(94)90063-9 PMID:7962581

Cláudio, A. P., Carmo, M. B., Gaspar, A., & Teixeira, R. (2015a). Using Expressive and Talkative Virtual Characters in Social Anxiety Disorder Treatment. In *Proc. GRAPP 2015, 10th International Conference on Computer Graphics Theory and Applications* (pp 348-355). SciTePress.

Cláudio, A. P., Carmo, M. B., Pinheiro, T., & Esteves, F. (2013). A Virtual Reality Solution to Handle Social Anxiety. *International Journal of Creative Interfaces and Computer Graphics*, *4*(2), 57–72. doi:10.4018/ijcicg.2013070104

Cláudio, A. P., Carmo, M. B., Pinto, V., Cavaco, A., & Guerreiro, M. P. (2015b). Virtual Humans for Training and Assessment of Self-medication Consultation Skills in Pharmacy Students. In *Proc. IEEE ICCSE 2015- 10th International Conference on Computer Science & Education*, Cambridge, UK (pp 175-180). 10.1109/ICCSE.2015.7250238

Cláudio, A. P., Gaspar, A., Lopes, E., & Carmo, M. B. (2014). Virtual Characters with Affective Facial Behavior. In *Proc. GRAPP 2014, 9th International Conference on Computer Graphics Theory and Applications* (pp 348-355). SciTePress.

Douilliez, C., Yzerbyt, V., Gilboa-Schechtman, E., & Philippot, P. (2012). Social anxiety biases the evaluation of facial displays: Evidence from single face and multi-facial stimuli. *Cognition and Emotion*, *26*(6), 1107–1115. doi:10.1080/02699931.2011.632494 PMID:22122070

Eibl-Eibesfeldt, I. (1989). *Human Ethology*. NY: Aldine de Gruyter.

Ekman, P., Friesen, W. V., & Hager, J. C. (2002). *Facial action coding system*. Salt Lake City, UT: Research Nexus.

Esteves, F., Isberg, N., Cláudio, A. P., Carmo, B., & Gaspar, A. (2016). Psychophysiological responses to a virtual reality scenario for the treatment of social anxiety. *International Journal of Psychophysiology*, *108*, 138. doi:10.1016/j.ijpsycho.2016.07.403

Gaggioli, A., Mantovani, F., Castelnuovo, G., Wiederhold, B., & Riva, G. (2003). Avatars in clinical psychology: a framework for the clinical use of virtual humans. *Cyberpsychology & Behavior: The Impact of the Internet, Multimedia and Virtual Reality on Behavior and Society*, *6*(2), 117–125. doi:10.1089/109493103321640301

Gaspar, A., & Esteves, F. (2012). Preschoolers faces in spontaneous emotional contexts – how well do they match adult facial expression prototypes? *International Journal of Behavioral Development*, *36*(5), 348–357. doi:10.1177/0165025412441762

Gaspar, A., Esteves, F., & Arriaga, P. (2014). On prototypical facial expressions vs variation in facial behavior: lessons learned on the "visibility" of emotions from measuring facial actions in humans and apes. In M. Pina & N. Gontier (Eds.), *The Evolution of Social Communication in Primates: A Multidisciplinary Approach, Interdisciplinary Evolution Research* (pp. 101–145). New York: Springer. doi:10.1007/978-3-319-02669-5_6

Glantz, K., Durlach, N. I., Barnett, R. C., & Aviles, W. A. (1996). Virtual Reality (VR) For Psychotherapy: From the Physical to the social Environment 1. *Psychotherapy*, *33*(3), 464–473. doi:10.1037/0033-3204.33.3.464

Grillon, H. (2009). Simulating interactions with virtual characters for the treatment of social phobia. Doctoral dissertation, EPFL.

Gutiérrez-Maldonado, J., Ferrer-García, M., Dakanalis, A., & Riva, G. (2017). Virtual Reality: Applications to Eating Disorders. In W. Stewart & A. H. Robinson (Eds.), *The Oxford HandBook of Eating Disorders* (2nd ed.). Online Publication. doi:10.1093/oxfordhb/9780190620998.013.26

Haworth, M. B., Baljko, M., & Faloutsos, P. (2012). PhoVR: a virtual reality system to treat phobias. In *Proceedings of the 11th ACM SIGGRAPH International Conference on Virtual-Reality Continuum and its Applications in Industry* (pp. 171-174). 10.1145/2407516.2407560

Herbelin, B. (2005). Virtual reality exposure therapy for social phobia [Doctoral dissertation]. EPFL.

Hirsh, A. T., Callander, S. B., & Robinson, M. E. (2011). Patient demographic characteristics and facial expressions influence nurses' assessment of mood in the context of pain: A virtual human and lens model investigation. *International Journal of Nursing Studies*, *48*(11), 1330–1338. doi:10.1016/j.ijnurstu.2011.05.002 PMID:21596378

James, L. K., Lin, C.-Y., Steed, A., Swapp, D., & Slater, M. (2003). Social anxiety in virtual environments: Results of a pilot study. *Cyberpsychology & Behavior*, *6*(3), 237–243. doi:10.1089/109493103322011515 PMID:12855078

Jarrett, C. (2009). Get a second life. *The Psychologist*, *22*(6), 490–493.

Jarrett, C. (2013). Avatar therapy. *The Psychologist*, *26*(7), 478.

Klinger, E., Légeron, P., Roy, S., Chemin, I., Lauer, F., & Nugues, P. (2004). Virtual reality exposure in the treatment of social phobia. [PubMed]. *Studies in Health Technology and Informatics*, *99*, 91.

Lane, H. C., Hays, M. J., Core, M. G., & Auerbach, D. (2013). Learning intercultural communication skills with virtual humans: Feedback and fidelity. *Journal of Educational Psychology, 105*(4), 1026–1035. doi:10.1037/a0031506

LaViola, J. J. Jr. (2000). A discussion of cybersickness in virtual environments. *ACM SIGCHI Bulletin, 32*(1), 47–56. doi:10.1145/333329.333344

Maheu, M. M., Pulier, M. L., McMenamin, J. P., & Posen, L. (2012). Future of telepsychology, telehealth, and various technologies in psychological research and practice. *Professional Psychology, Research and Practice, 43*(6), 613–621. doi:10.1037/a0029458

North, M., North, S., & Coble, J. (1997). Virtual reality therapy for fear of flying. *The American Journal of Psychiatry, 154*(1), 130–142. doi:10.1176/ajp.154.1.130b PMID:8988975

Pertaub, D. P., Slater, M. & Barker, C. (2001). An experiment on fear of public speaking in virtual reality. In *Studies in health tech. and informatics* (pp. 372-378).

Pertaub, D. P., Slater, M., & Barker, C. (2002). An experiment on public speaking anxiety in response to three different types of virtual audience. *Presence, 11*(1), 68–78. doi:10.1162/105474602317343668

Rothbaum, B., Hodges, L., & Kooper, R., & Opdyke, D. (1995). Effectiveness of computer-generated (virtual reality) graded exposure in the treatment of acrophobia. *The American Journal of Psychiatry, 152*(4), 626–628. doi:10.1176/ajp.152.4.626 PMID:7694917

Rothbaum, B., Hodges, L., Watson, B., Kessler, G. D., & Opdyke, D. (1996). Virtual reality exposure therapy in the treatment of fear of flying: A case report. *Behaviour Research and Therapy, 34*(5-6), 477–481. doi:10.1016/0005-7967(96)00007-1 PMID:8687369

Russell, J. (2017). Toward a Broader perspective on Facial Expression.Moving on from basic Emotion Theory. In J. M. Fernández-Dols & J. A. Russell (Eds.), *The Science of facial Expression* (pp. 93–105). Oxford University Press. doi:10.1093/acprof:oso/9780190613501.001.0001

Russell, J. A., & Fernandez-Dols, J. M. (1997). What does a facial expression mean? In J. Russell & J. M. Fernández-Dols (Eds.), *The psychology of facial expression* (pp. 3–30). New York, NY: Cambridge University Press. doi:10.1017/CBO9780511659911.003

Shiban, Y., Diemer, J., Müller, J., Brütting-Schick, J., Pauli, P., & Mühlberger, A. (2017). Diaphragmatic breathing during virtual reality exposure therapy for aviophobia: Functional coping strategy or avoidance behavior? A pilot study. *BMC Psychiatry, 17*(1), 1–10. doi:10.118612888-016-1181-2 PMID:28100203

Slater, M., Antley, A., Davison, A., Swapp, D., Guger, C., Barker, C., ... Sanchez-Vives, M. V. (2006). A virtual reprise of the Stanley Milgram obedience experiments. *PLoS One, 1*(1), e39. doi:10.1371/journal.pone.0000039 PMID:17183667

Slater, M., Pertaub, D. P., & Steed, A. (1999). Public speaking in virtual reality: Facing an audience of avatars. IEEE Computer Graphics and Applications, *19*(2), 6–9.

Stein, M. B., & Kean, Y. M. (2000). Disability and Quality of Life in Social Phobia: Epidemiologic Findings. *The American Journal of Psychiatry*, *157*(10), 1606–1613. doi:10.1176/appi.ajp.157.10.1606 PMID:11007714

North, M. M., North, S. M., & Coble, J. R. (1998). Virtual reality therapy: An effective treatment for the fear of public speaking. *The International Journal of Virtual Reality*, *3*, 1–6.

Wohlrab, S., Fink, B., Kappeler, P. M., & Brewer, G. (2009). Differences in Personality Attributions Toward Tattooed and Nontattooed Virtual Human Characters. *Journal of Individual Differences*, *30*(1), 1–5. doi:10.1027/1614-0001.30.1.1

Wortwein, T., Morency, L.-P., & Scherer, S. (2015). Automatic Assessment and Analysis of Public Speaking Anxiety: A Virtual Audience Case Study. In *Proc of IEEE Affective Computing and Intelligent Interaction* (pp. 187-193). 10.1109/ACII.2015.7344570

ADDITIONAL READING

Blender. (n.d.). Retrieved from http://www.blender.org/

Microsoft. (n.d.). Kinect. Retrieved from https://www.microsoft.com/en-us/download/details.aspx?id=44561

SecondLife. (n.d.). Retrieved from http://secondlife.com/

Smithmicro. (n.d.). Poser 3D animation software. Retrieved from http://my.smithmicro.com/poser-3d-animation-software.html

Unity. (n.d.). Retrieved from http://Unity.com/

KEY TERMS AND DEFINITIONS

Cognitive-Behavioural Therapy (CBT): This is a type of psychotherapy that is focused on modifying cognitive biases and restructuring behavior patterns (for example learning to face one's fears), which has been demonstrated to be effective in a wide range of problems such as anxiety disorders, depression, substance abuse, eating disorders, among other problems.

Fear of Public Speaking: This is a form of social anxiety disorder people have whereby fear is focused mostly on performance in the context of public speaking. It may co-occur with other problems as well, such as in people who stutter.

Nonverbal Behaviour Research: A cross-disciplinary field of Psychology and Anthropology that is focused on nonverbal behaviour expression, comprising facial and vocal expression, posture, gait and gestures.

Social Anxiety Disorder (SAD): A trait characterized by intense fear of finding oneself in situations where one is observed and possibly scrutinized by others. The individuals with this form of anxiety dread negative evaluations and are biased towards perceiving such evaluations.

Virtual Reality: Virtual reality is a technology that enables the creation of lifelike scenarios and characters in a computer and the simulation of presence for a user that feels as if he/she is interacting with real people in a real place.

Virtual Reality in Exposure Therapy (VRET): Because of its extraordinary potential to simulate reality, Virtual reality became a useful tool to replace *in vivo* (real life) exposure in the therapy of phobias and other disorder.

Chapter 3
Creating Characters for Various Interfaces

Anna Ursyn
University of Northern Colorado, USA

ABSTRACT

This chapter is focused on the theme of creating characters for visual storytelling discussed in practical, theoretical, and historical terms. The description includes a discussion of artistic forms acting as characters for telling stories, various meanings conveyed by characters in semiotic terms, the creating of characters by drawing, and then a set of learning projects follows, on creating characters for various interfaces.

INTRODUCTION

Both traditionally drawn and computer drawn characters are a great part of our everyday experience including communication, learning, productive work, and artistic activities. Many types of traditionally created characters have found their continuation in computing-based media, especially when accomplished in a digital, interactive, and shared environment. Interaction techniques for digital transfer from the old resources to a currently demanded destination start from the old cut, copy, and paste operations, often without any concern about the copyright issues.

Drawings can have strong storytelling properties. By adding characters as visual storytelling to traditional drawing, character makers become immersed in a fourth dimension, wandering across time and space. Storytelling by drawing characters is about delivering emotions: visceral, emphatic, or voyeuristic. When we paint colors on a computer screen we evoke emotional responses from the audience. Animation in storytelling allows us to slice through the time dimension to enhance dramatic actions, show suspenseful obstacles, and build tension before resolving a conflict. Figures and characters offer flexibility in communication path through transformations or by inducing interactivity.

DOI: 10.4018/978-1-5225-7371-5.ch003

Storytelling by drawing characters can act as a crucial interface between the visual and the verbal. We might see this capacity in sketches that serve as a starting point to create manga, blogs, and even products and architectural schemes. Characters may evoke personal experience in the mind of the viewer through received and perceived information. Thus, the viewer becomes the co-creator of the art. Digital storytelling can coexist with other techniques such as video, performance with physical and virtual interaction, visual surveillance, motion tracking, and artificial intelligence.

ARTISTIC FORMS ACTING AS CHARACTERS FOR TELLING A STORY

Creating characters may serve as a way to communicate within many literary and not only literary forms, including:

- Illustration
- Portrait
- Comics, Comic book
- Graphic novel
- Doodling
- Cartoon
- Manga
- Data visualization
- Timeline
- Infographics
- Sequential art
- Joke, Cartoon
- Web tree, Web cloud
- Storyboard
- Architectural drawing
- Abstract graphics
- Mathematical equations
- Chemical molecules
- Physical laws – visual description
- Electrical circuit
- Road signs
- Signage
- Marketing
- Advertisement
- Clipart
- Music notation
- Calligraphy
- Realistic drawing versus the essence of the object – among many other options.

Also, smartphone images and emoji digital images, especially when animated. (Emoji exist in various genres, including facial expressions, common objects, places, types of weather, and animals. They are much like emoticons, but emoji are actual pictures instead of typographics).

Puppets

Puppets can be considered the storytelling characters acting as an extension of our body: you can take a dead object and give it a new life and expression. Puppet performances have been part of the theater from early times. The word 'puppet' comes from Latin 'pupa' (a doll). Puppets are representations of human or animal figures that can be manipulated to give an illusion of life.

There are many kinds of puppets:

- The hand puppet, where puppet's head and arms can be moved by the fingers of the operator's hand. This may include the sock puppet, and finger puppet.
- The shadow puppet, with a flat cutout held against a screen and illuminated by a lamp from behind, or hands casting shadow. Paper puppets create moving shadows. In Indonesia, tinted translucent materials are used to produce colored shadows.
- The rod puppet, controlled from below by long, thin rods.
- The marionette, which is controlled from above by strings connected to a control bar; its name, which means in French 'little Mary', is traditionally derived from the use of such figures in medieval sacred dramas. Puppets can be made from metal, ceramics, plastic, and wood, which is most popular for glove-puppet heads and marionettes.

The earliest puppets were used in religious ceremonies. In classical Greece puppets were used for entertainment. In the Far East, puppetry was considered a high dramatic art. Japan evolved the form of Bunraku. In Europe, puppets are being used for satirical performances or serve the simpler tastes. In Sicily and southern Italy, marionettes dramatized medieval tales of heroic chivalry. English and Italian puppeteers toured with plays, even Shakespeare's works. The Yiddish theatrical-literary culture came about in 1925 with music as an integral part. Wladyslaw Starewicz (1892-1965) (1999) created first puppet-animated films and 3D stop-motion animations using dead insects and other animals as protagonists (Bendazzi, 1999). The Salzburg Marionette Theater in Austria performs Mozart operas. The Bread and Puppet Theater, which combines masks, puppets, and human actors, has been a politically radical and educational puppet theater founded by Peter Schumann in New York City's Lower East Side in the years 1962-1963. It is one of the oldest, nonprofit, self-supporting theatrical companies in the United States (Bread & Puppet, 2017). Masks from Africa and Asia are also used in festivities as a potent tool for storytelling, as well as Venice carnival masks, theatrical characters such as in Japanese masked drama theater Noh, along with many other cultural traditions.

The storytelling with the use of puppets has been serving also for children's entertainment. The Muppets are widely known through their exposure on television and in films. Jim Henson (1936-1990) who was the creator of The Muppet Show had also developed characters for the Sesame Street television series. In Czechoslovakia there have been over 2,000 puppet theaters. Two types of puppets delivered stories: the loutkove divadlo used the string-operated puppets, and Bramborove Divadlo operated like hand puppets (Shershow, 1995). One of the most celebrated animators Jan Švankmajer created his characters in surrealistic animations and films (Hames, 2007). In 1960s and 1970s Jiří Trnka made his animated short films with puppets, often adaptations of literary works.

Shadow Play

Shadow play was one of the earliest media presentation systems. Shadows transform shapes of objects and thus serve as a link between the real and imaginary or virtual world. Since many centuries artists of puppetry create transformation of shadows by moving both the puppets and the light source. In India the shadow puppetry began with Hombaiyah who considered the shadow puppets a gift from the god Rama, and then with Togalufombeatta where the puppet was made of colored biological skins and fibers; and early moving images were often believed as infused with a living force. The first screens were silk, and then celluloid was made from plants and animals.

The Greek philosopher Plato (428-348 BCE) used the unreal appearance of changeable shadows to discuss the relation between our experiences and real world. In his work 'Republic' Plato (2014) created the Allegory of the Cave in the form of a dialogue about people chained to the wall of a cave all of their lives, facing a blank wall. Watching the shadows projected on the wall by things passing in front of a fire behind them, people ascribed forms to these shadows and experienced them as if they were reality. Plato poses that the philosopher is like a prisoner freed from the cave that understands that the shadows are not reality. According to Plato, forms (ideas) but not the material, observable world make the fundamental kind of reality. Plato also thought artists could imitate but not create (Plato, 2014, The Republic, 597D).

Artists from various cultures such as China, Taiwan, India, Greece, Nepal, Cambodia, Thailand, and Turkey have been creating magical effects of shadows casted by cutout figures held between a source of light and a translucent screen. Performances called Chinese shadows were also popular on Montmartre in Paris in 18th century. In Malaysia and Indonesia, especially Java and Bali, shadow puppet theater with figures made from buffalo skin is called Wayang Kulit Kelantan. This artistic form is threatened with imminent extinction. In 2003 UNESCO has designated Wayang Kulit Kelantan in Malaysia as a Masterpiece of Oral and Intangible Heritage of Humanity. The use of visualization and computer graphics techniques for the Wayang Kulit Kelantan preservation has been examined in its four major aspects: puppets, shadows, screen for shadow projection (Kelir), and the light source (Ghani, 2011).

Multimedia artists in Malyasia are now examining possibilities of using computer graphics to capture visual style of Wayang Kulit Kelantan performances. In India, shadow puppets are cut out of leather, which has been treated to make it translucent. Shadow puppets are pressed against the screen with a strong source of light behind it. The manipulation between the light and the screen make silhouettes or colorful shadows visible for the viewers who sit in front of the screen (Puppet Forms in India, 2012). The theatrical shadow puppet tradition, in the folklore, popular, court, and contemporary Western versions, is still continued in Turkey (Senyer, 2017). In the United States animation was for some time dominated by the Disney style, which in turn drew inspiration from European children books. In Germany from before the Nazis, Otto Fischinger and Lotte Reininger were considered modern animation pioneers, with animations showing references to both expressionist movement and the Oriental art (Rall, 2009). The renaissance of German animation came in the eighties with production of independent animation films. Current trends in contemporary South Asian animations based on old myths and traditions: Indonesian ones based on wayang kulit, Chinese hybrid production with the presence of traditional cultural heritage, Thailand animations based on shadow play nang yi, the ancient Indian epic tale of the Ramayana, and many others from Philippines, Vietnam, and Singapore has been described by Hannes Rall (2009) in a book "Tradigital Mythmaking."

MEANINGS CONVEYED BY CHARACTERS IN SEMIOTIC TERMS

Signs, Symbols, and Iconic Images as Characters in Storytelling

While working on the creating a character we must remember that a character rarely exists without an action. However, in some cases a character acts as a symbol, such as a Statue of Liberty. Characters that appear in a story, avatars, each one representing a particular person, emoticons and emoji images used in electronic messages, favicons associated with the website URLs, logos adopted to identify organizations' products, and other visual signals, all occur simultaneously with the extensive use of signs, symbols, iconic objects, and metaphors. Nature, art, social interactions, fashion, food, sex, interaction with technology, machines, and practically everything else can be interpreted as signs. One may say face cards for playing can be considered characters that define each suit. Figure 1 presents playing cards designed by my student Doiana Caro.

My student Morgan Hurtado offered another solution for playing cards and also books about card games design (Figure 2).

A character in a story should convey its personality, integrity, and important features in a simplest, most concise way. It is important to avoid unnecessary details or embellishments in the characters' image. This process of eliminating unnecessary details and deciding what is crucial to the basic message is called abstracting.

Abstract concept, not just a real thing is often communicated in a linear way as they form signs, symbols, and descriptors. Symbols have a power to replace words. They are used in various areas of life and different disciplines, beginning from transportation (as road signs e.g., 'slippery when wet'), architecture and industrial design (as blueprints), through mathematics, sciences such as physics or chemistry (as chemical formulae), to biology (as systematic classification or a DNA visualization). Furthermore,

Figure 1. Doiana Caro playing cards (© 2018, D. Caro. Used with permission)

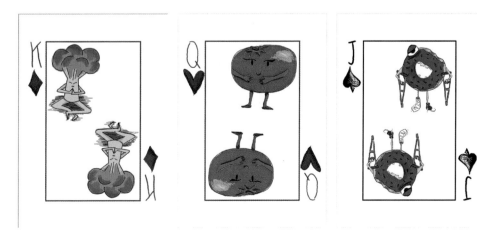

Figure 2. Morgan Hurtado playing cards and books (© 2018, M. Hurtado. Used with permission)

as documented in numerous dissertations in the fields of instructional technology and nursing, drawing characters is used as a tool in the processes of memorizing, relaxation, stress management, and spending a pleasant time.

We can find examples of symbols in everyday life, and many of them take form of a well-known character. A symbol of the ying-yang interplay of contrasting and complementary forces that originate and sustain the universe: an electric diagram that uses abstract symbols for a light bulb, wire, connector, resistor, and switch; an apple for a teacher, a bitten apple for a Macintosh computer. A map is a typical abstract graphic device. Colors are often used as symbols, for example, they signal the cold-warm water on faucets. We apply many abstract symbols in graphics, when we draw charts (bar chart, pie chart, organizational chart, flow chart), graphs (with the x and y axes), diagrams (e.g., link-node diagram) or a pattern language that groups symbols into relationships using its own grammar.

An icon represents a thing or refers to something by resemblance to it (thus a picture, a photograph, or a mathematical expression can be seen as iconic). An old-style telephone may be regarded as an iconic object. Icons and symbols help compress information in a visual way. The meaningful use of icons and symbols is a main topic of semiotics – the study of signs and symbols, codes, and conventions that allow communication of all kinds, mainly in art and literature. Semiotics analyzes culture as a series of sign systems in various cultures. The name 'semiotics' is derived from the Greek word 'semeion' which means "sign."

On Figure 3 my student Jake Collins presented his day/night schedule of activities in a visual way using simple symbols that are ubiquitous online. Each of the 12 segments contains a symbolic depiction of tools he uses, time of day or night, and a figure representing what he is doing.

A metaphor indicates one thing as a representation of another, difficult one. Thus metaphors enable us to make mental models and comparisons. For the metaphors, we usually choose concepts and objects that we hold to be easily understandable and familiar to our audience. Abstract images that resemble something through the metaphors may make learning easier. Telling stories verbally and visually involves structuring the data toward different metaphorical representations of a person as a character. Creating

Figure 3. Jake Collins, The day/night schedule (© 2018, J. Collins. Used with permission)

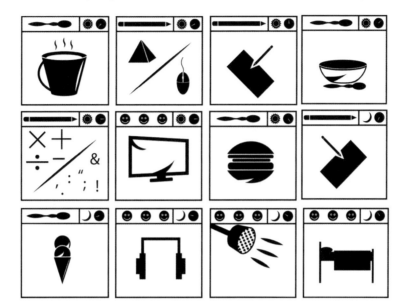

metaphors for a set of factors that make up a profile or a portrait will allow showing individual features of a character. In order to portray an imaginary character, one may want to depict a person in a literary way, the artistic way, or in the both ways. One may write a profile (verbal portrait) or convey graphically a mental image (visual portrait) of the chosen person. Imaging mental and emotional processes is truly important in creating visual communication. Depending on the kind of a character one is working on, whether it would be a personal, cultural, social, political, or psychological portrait, one has to cope with a different set of variables that must be taken into account.

Many times characters depicted visually may carry iconic significance. For example, an image of a snake as a character may evoke several different connotations. It may mean the Aesculapian snake that was important in ancient Greek and Roman mythology. The Apo's son Aesculapius (Asclepius in Greek), who was a god of medicine, healing, and physicians, was pictured in ancient mythology carrying a serpent-entwined staff. The chemist Friedrich August Kekulé (1829-1896) described his dream about the snake, which led to the invention of the ring structure of benzene and aromatic organic chemicals (Read, 1957/2011). Also, the snake is an important character in *The Little Prince* by Antoine de Saint Exupéry (1900-1944). Ouroboros (or uroboros) is a circular symbol depicting a snake that eats its own tail. In ancient Egypt, India, Greece, Norse legends, and other places this magic symbol symbolized introspection, the eternal return, nature's cyclic creation and destruction, life, death, and despair (Soto-Andrade, Jaramillo, Gutierrez, & Letelier, 2015; Hodapp, 2010).

A sword may be considered another iconic object. According to an ancient story, a sword of Damocles was hanging on a single hair of a horsetail, above the throne; the legendary sword Excalibur from the medieval Welsh poetry was associated with the King Arthur, the Knights of the Round Table, the Holy Grail, and the wizard Merlin. In more recent times, sword plays important role in American action films, for example, the 2010 R. Rodriguez and E. Maniquis' movie "Machete Kills," and its 2013 sequel "Machete Kills Again."

The evil eye talismans have been created as magic objects to protect against a malevolent curse and defy evil forces. They may have originated at the Upper Paleolithic Age (Late Stone) Age; the evil eye forms were found in cuneiforms on Mesopotamian clay tablets from 5,000 years ago, and they are present in Jewish, Christian and Muslim, as well as Buddhist and Hindu cultures.

In the cinematic and theatrical arts, sports, shows, and more, an iconic character may comprise a group of people that may make a collective character.

Figure 4 presents a chess set created and then 3D printed by my student Oksanna Worthington. These informational chess pieces are designed to inform the novice player about the rules how each piece moves, so these chess pieces act as characters with their motion built into each design. This is done with a typographic approach to express the movement of each piece. For example, the King is a plus sign to move one square at a time; the Queen is an asterisk as she moves vertically, horizontally, or diagonally; the Bishop is shaped as an X as it moves diagonally; and the Knight is L-shaped.

The Semiotic Approach: A Long Way From Generic to Meaningful

Recognition (just by looking) not always means comprehension that is bound to thinking: we may remember we have seen something before, but we may not know what does it mean. In the process of comprehension, we perceive the relationships of the object to other categories, which have irreducible properties (for example, knife and fork belong to 'silverware' – it does not matter if it is silver, green, or wooden). Images, symbols, and words lie along a continuum from the concrete to the highly abstract. Abstracting is considered a thought process occurring on non-verbal level. Due to abstracting, on a long way from generic to meaningful, we take in those features that are good for creating categories, and suppress those features that are not generic but are basic to comprehending it. This way we show the scissorness of the scissors. In order to give structure and meaning to our experience, we get rid of similarities and unimportant features (visible or semantic) that are not crucial, and thus we suppress non-basic features. Alfred Korzybski (1879-1950), a Polish/American linguist who initiated the movement called General Semantics drew attention to a difference between a thing and a word. According to

Figure 4. Oksanna Worthington, A wireframe for chess figures (© 2018, O. Worthington. Used with permission)

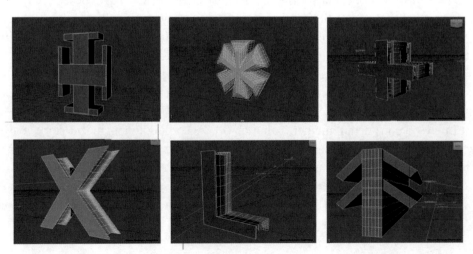

Korzybski (1933/1995), language comes between someone and the objective world, sometimes causing a confusion between the signifier and the signified. Because of that, we allow language to take us up the 'ladder of abstraction'.

A Canadian/Japanese linguist and semanticist Samuel Ichiye Hayakawa (Hayakawa & Hayakawa, 1991) followed the ideas of Alfred Korzybski and built the abstraction ladder of categories (S. I. Hayakawa's term), with four up to eight levels, which could be applied to various areas of our experience.

The abstraction ladder of categories, with a word "cow" as an example, comprises:

- A general physical reality, everything we see: all cow's characteristics are infinite and ever changing;
- Reality perceived (a particular cow – the object of experience selected from the totality by one's nervous system); many of the characteristics are left out;
- The word "Bessie" is the name of the cow, an object that we have seen in (2), which is not an object but stands for the object as a name. Now, Bessie does not mean those characteristics that were omitted;
- The word 'cow' stands for the characteristics abstracted for a common cow but not exactly for Bessie;
- When Bessie is referred to as 'livestock', only those characteristics she has in common with pigs, chicken, goats, etc., are referred to;
- When Bessie is included among 'farm assets', reference is made only to what she has in common with other salable items on the farm (corn, wheat, grain)
- When Bessie is referred to as an 'asset', still more characteristics are left out;
- The word 'wealth' is an extremely high level of abstraction, omitting almost all reference to the characteristics of Bessie.
  - A general physical reality, cows we see: all cow's characteristics are indistinct and ever changing.
  - Reality perceived, the particular cow - the object selected by our senses: many of the characteristics are left out.
  - The word "Bessie" is the name of the cow, a name that stands for the object. Bessie does not mean the features that were omitted.
  - The word 'cow' stands for the characteristics abstracted for a common cow, but not exactly for Bessie.
  - When Bessie is referred to as 'livestock', only those characteristics she has in common with pigs, chicken, goats, etc., are referred to.
  - When Bessie is included among 'farm assets', reference is made only to what she has in common with other salable farm items (corn, wheat, and grain).
  - When Bessie is referred to as 'asset', still more characteristics are left out.
  - The word 'wealth' is an extremely high level of abstraction, omitting almost all reference to the characteristics of Bessie.

The following example (Chung, 2012) shows abstraction ladders having four levels, based on the Hayakawa's ladder of abstraction.

- Level 1 tells about specific, identifiable nouns, such as: my blue Levi 501 jeans, Tina's newborn sister, a three-bedroom house on Hollis Street, African violets, Mina;
- Level 2 identifies noun categories as more definite groups; for example: teenagers, middle class, clothing industry, parents, a college campus, a newborn child, house plants;
- Level 3 defines noun classes as broad group names with little specification, e.g.: people, men, women, young people, everybody, nobody, industry, we, goals, things, television;
- Level 4 describes abstractions, for instance: life, beauty, love, time, success, power, happiness, faith, hope, charity, evil, good.

Below are some of my students' reactions to the abstraction ladder theme.

- There is a blade of grass, upon which I stepped to make my way to class today
- On another, separate occasion, this blade of grass witnessed a murder in the middle of June last year, one of the many thousands of witnesses that evening.
- This blade of grass is a member of a university, a silent member of a student body too many to count at the entrance of the Kepner Hall
- Each of these blades of grass maintain a similar shape, a triangle exponentially repeated to create a meadow
- Each triangle is green, making the field a reflection of cosmic particles
- This blade of grass is thus only a green triangle.

Nick Carlson

- I have these skills that are relevant and specific.
- I have some of the skills that are needed to do the job.
- I want that specific job.
- I want a job.

Taylor Duryea

1. Christmas Tree
2. Spruce trees
3. Trees in general
4. Plants
5. Vegetation
6. Life on Earth
7. Life in the Universe
8. Life

Ethan Funkbreay

Going From Generic to Meaningful Characters in Storytelling

Going from concrete to abstract can be also seen in the realm of art. Abstract, non-representational art often uses symbols and symbolic drawings. Many works of abstract art convey messages about universal forces. Below are examples of art works that progressively abstract the essence of the picture theme.

- Photography shows everything we see. Rudolph Arnheim (1988, 1990) wrote that photographs might affect our observation by singling out accidentals as readily as essentials, making everything equally important. This is not true anymore, since the Canon company introduced multifocus touch screen.
- A portrait painted by an artist enhances characteristics that are specific for a sitter.
- A caricature deliberately exaggerates the subject's distinctive features or peculiarities. It often produces a comic or grotesque effect.
- Another approach to abstracting important issues has been taken by artists who developed such styles in art as the conceptual art, abstract expressionism, or minimalist art.

A question arises, why so many people do not like abstract art. It seems that liking or not liking abstract images depends on the easiness of communication with the intentions of the artist. The message coming from abstract art does not end at the aesthetic level. Harry Broudy (1991) introduced the notion of the allusionary base – a stock of meanings with which we think and feel, which everybody is building during lifetime and while appreciating art. The allusionary base is based on images. Concrete images, perceptions of shapes, colors, and motions convey meaning (the rustle of leaves means danger). Abstract imagery influences the learning of languages, skills, concepts and attitudes.

Components used for drawing materials for different surfaces are transferred to computers to mimic them and then add the computer's incomparable precision by using lines with their repetition and code-based transformations. At the same time, computer natives who always have access to devices and applications, make the visual unwritten notes before they even begin to work on a computer. Such visual mental notes work efficiently as characters, especially when animated. The environmental trends result in discoveries of the self-cleaning (microwaveable) sketchbooks. This continuous correspondence between the visual and verbal contexts erases the division between a notebook and a sketchbook. As a result, there is a constant need to visually document ideas and inspirations, which leads to the new ways of thinking and creating characters to visualize the results.

The coding and preserving visual messages was analyzed and discussed in cognitive terms. The cognitive approach to design helps to bridge the sophisticated language of abstract art with messages coming from pictograms, cartoons, advertisements, TV animations, and even signs used on the streets. A Russian painter Wassily Kandinsky (1866-1944) derived his language of abstract forms from physiological characteristics of human perception. In a similar way, an American painter Arthur Pinkham Ryder (1847-1917) considered his landscape paintings as being kind of abstract, as he conveyed his messages beyond the representational appearance. Decoding the message of the artist is possible when a message is decoded on a basis of a code shared by both the artist and the viewer. However, the codes of the addressee are often different from those of the sender. For example, it would be such a case, were American painter Arthur Pinkham Ryder evaluated as a seascapist only, and the German painter Arnold Böcklin as an illustrator of mythology. There are also deliberately open messages using symbols or signs that could be freely interpreted and also generated cooperatively by the viewer. Umberto Eco (1989) studied such open messages and asked: "How to produce texts by reading them." Abstract artists choose their own means of expression, so their paintings gained a feature of an ambiguous, open work with loose relation between signs and meanings. Thus, the paintings of Rothko, in spite of their recognition in the world of art, may be annoying for someone who can see there only the colorful rectangles.

A Canadian psychologist Allan Paivio (1971, 1986, 1991) put forward a dual-coding theory of cognition. Paivio proposed that the human mind can transform information into two cognitive codes, to be transferred to long-term memory, and then compared to something previously learned, stored, and organized as a cognitive structure. The two cognitive codes include (1) A visual or iconic code, a visuo-spatial scratchpad for images and (2) An auditory or semantic code with verbal language rules: semantic, syntactic, and orthographic. The performance in memory and other cognitive tasks is mediated not only by linguistic processes but also by a distinct nonverbal imagery model of thought. We receive both verbal and imaginal stimuli, and form representational associative structures. Verbal associations and visual imagery can both expand on learned material. Visual and verbal information, processed in different ways, create separate representations of information. Thus, researchers hold that mental imagery supports recollection of verbal material, when words evoke corresponding images.

One may discern at least two approaches to creating art, either leading to the precision and accuracy of ready solutions or the artist's individual style. Each of them often evokes a dislike toward another style, as undeserving to be named art. Several artists who work in the fields both art and mathematics (e.g., such electronic artists as Manfred Mohr or Helaman Ferguson) found a way to develop their individual artistic style through applying mathematical rules that are seemingly reverse to artistic expression. Some computing savvy individuals look for artistic solutions using applications, to respond to the market demands; they search the Internet and use plenty of tools, applications, and solutions found on websites. On the other hand, many times artistically talented people are determined to create art with whatever is at hand: a computer or a broom. Their powerful visual reasoning evokes an outburst of strong emotions. Moreover, while looking at the artwork consisting from a few simple strokes everybody feels they could do the same easily.

Completely different outcomes may result from these two approaches. We may compare perfect works of electronic design, completed with first-rate tools, with intentional deformations characteristic of traditional mainstream art, for example, those created by Francisco Goya, Alberto Giacometti, or Amedeo Modigliani. Geometry has been often neglected in works by Paul Cézanne, Pablo Picasso, or Vincent Van Gogh, proportion was often changed by Henri Matisse, Jonathan Borofski, or Fernando Botero, and so on. For the technology-oriented people, teamworking with an artist may bring a conflict. On the other hand, we may find purposeful deformations in electronic art resulting from translating, scaling, slanting, and otherwise distorting the initial image, aimed to depart from what the eye can see. One can imagine many reasons for such transformations and distortions. For example, some advertising messages are successful due to impressive imaging that gives a shorthand summary of patterns of ideas. With purposeful deformations, we may address some cognitive processes or make mental shortcuts, reacting to synthetic signs, and implying connotations to symbols or icons.

CREATING CHARACTERS BY DRAWING

Drawings can act as an interface between the visual and the verbal, so they are the strong tools for visual storytelling. Communication goes both on visual and verbal levels, and even numbers are translated into lines, for instance to show a bell curve. As well as statistics, drawing is a form of a world's description: a drawing uses a line, while statistics uses means and averages. In art, a line is used in an every medium, from drawing, printmaking, or painting, to 3D structures, serving to define dimensions so it goes from shapes to forms. Such lines can be organic such as during Secession, Art Nouveau and Jugend style, or geometric such as in Art Deco or Cubism. A line serves also to create a character. A line, and even a dot may become a meaningful character, as in a book illustrated and written by Norton Juster (2000) entitled "The Dot and the Line: A Romance in Lower Mathematics."

On a computer, a line is a collection of pixels in a digital system of zeros and ones. A transition of a pixel from a rectangle into a square can be compared to the invention of a wheel because it eliminated the heavy jagging and a need for anti-aliasing. On a computer, jagged edges on curved lines can be smoothed out with an anti-aliasing technique. Within an analog recording system, a line is defined by a mathematical equation controlled by points and functions. The user can change a curvature, thickness, color, pattern, and a character of a line. As analog line is resolution independent, even a big billboard would be perfect, without any distortions. When sketching, the searching of a line often defines a volume. It is a paradox that we say that a text and time-based media and music are linear, while a line can be perceived during any amount of time that a user chooses to spend. You cannot comment on a music composition before you spend as much time as a composer decided the music would last.

Drawing characters conveys to a computer screen the visceral, emphatic, or voyeuristic emotions and evokes emotional response from the audience. The same may be told about the effectiveness of animation in storytelling, as adding the time dimension enhances dramatic actions, shows suspenseful obstacles, and builds tension before solving a conflict. Line drawing serves as a preferred tool in many disciplines. Sound waves are depicted on the parallel lines and spaces between them that host notes denoting their pitch. Other disciplines may apply line to depict a heartbeat, a molecular structure, geological folds, or a multitude of shapes, forms, and abstract denotations.

Read about the elements and principles of design in arts, as well as in other disciplines such as coding. Elements of design refer to what is available for the artist/designer or any person willing to communicate visually, while principles of design describe how the elements could be used. For example, one may ask whether the line, which falls into the elements category, is repeated, is applied with the use of symmetry, is it spiral or radial, black or of any other color. Color and value, shape and form, space, line, and texture are called the elements of design. These elements are known as the fundamentals for all works of art because without them art could not be created. All of these elements exist in the world around us in nature and in the environment we create for ourselves. Various disciplines: music, science, mathematics, as well as different forms of art use a lot of the same elements and principles of design. Talent, creativity, thought, or abstract concepts are common to all those areas. Write your own statement on this theme. Figure 5 presents a work by Anna Ursyn entitled "Dot." by Anna Ursyn. While taking a test or an exam on a rainy day your attention may be distracted by sunrays conquering the grayness. We use dots to mark our answers, and suddenly we may realize how dots may serve other purposes: to organize, summarize, categorize, inform, order, and position, to say nothing about small dots of rain gathering on window panes. The pattern they create travel as we carry through our progress.

To create a male or feminine character using shapes only (triangles, circles, rectangles) you may use geometric shapes first, and then save a file under different name, and add organic shapes, in order to depict and emphasize their unique features. Then you may transform the image into 3D. Figure 6 shows three characters built of simple shapes, all in a work "Threeall" by Anna Ursyn.

Figure 5. Anna Ursyn, Dot (© 2017, A. Ursyn. Used with permission)

Figure 6. Anna Ursyn, Threeall (© 2017, A. Ursyn. Used with permission)

Principles of design may guide the composition, for example a scale, proportion, or hierarchy to make one person larger, or emphasis/dominance through the use of color in order to show importance. Then, using the principles of design you may combine codes for people, objects, and a background, so the content would overlap into a composition: people with trees in the background, still life in front, and wind above. The way of using lines in the context of the elements and principles of design is determined by the artist's temperament.

One needs also to remember that every color coexists with others. Below is a verse by Anna Ursyn "Still Life." Asterisks indicate links when it is in written in an interactive format.

Still Life

Favorite color?
No color exists alone, like a note in a music composition,
Or a frame in a movie. *
I may say, a blue pen. You will say, it's cobalt one,
placed on a green book, actually a sap green,
with one corner covered by a red apple, a symbol. **
Well, maroon with salmon speckles,
supported by a piece of yellow cheese, the kind with holes.
Swiss cheese, we would say to simplify, ***
to communicate better, or faster.
Precise description of a color may confuse,
make conversation longer, less interesting,
or even destruct it; change the meaning of what we are saying,
like shouting or whispering.
Leave it to a painter.

* A Frame in a movie

An artist works a lot to be able to see progress made
or not made
or made after three weeks would pass.
Hard to see, judge, or value it
right after the task is completed.
Like in a key frame in animation: two frames are looking almost same.
Much work is needed to make or see the progress.

*** **Are you an artist because you make art,***

or you make art because you are an artist?
Symbols for a meaning shield a musician, a poet, or a mathematician.
A drawing is open for comments, suggestions, and friendly remarks.

No reason is left for rephrasing its visual sentence.
No timeframe is set for viewing it, to finish its perception,
organize what's left of thoughts, connotations, and memory of order.

*** Stereotypes

A small change makes a big difference.
We all know about the origins, uses, abilities, or problems.
It's faster and more efficient to classify, and find order and importance
knowing what to expect from a person
or from an object for each situation.
We have a saying, a sentence, a word or, much simpler, a gesture.
A vocabulary of symbols makes us well rounded.

Sketches

Drawing is used to organize and communicate in the form of sketches and even interactive sketches. We used to sketch in order to communicate better and quicker. We can guess the meaning of a shape that was just started. We can make visual memories and at the same time we can use a line in a particular, highly specialized way, for instance in the time-based media, storyboards, web 3D applications, blueprints, diagrams, web trees, wireframes, etc., often accompanied with a text.

Sketches may serve as a starting point to create characters for manga, blogs, even product and architectural schemes, and other forms. Sketching has a cognitive power, enhances the eye–hand–brain coordination, as well as the mind–brain–eye–hand coordination. Application of sketching is often used in storyboarding, brainstorming, for designing cognitive maps, making web trees, planning events and competitions, or arranging conflict reduction. A Dan Roam's (2013) book "The Back of the Napkin" discusses such cases. Figure 7 presents sketches made by my student Emrey Winter showing various face expressions.

Introductory Project: Drawing a Shoe and a Human Figure

Start with taking your shoe off and placing it in front of you. Sketch your shoe for 3 min. Now, turn the shoe, and use 1 minute for the same task. You'll have time for less lines to describe it, thus you'll need to make some decisions what is really important about this she. The third sketch should take only 30 seconds. Now, you'll need to eliminate what is not relevant. Examine your three sketches. Which one is the best? Many will say the last one. Anyway, we have a camera for detailed drawing.

Make sketches for your story. Familiarize yourself with sketches made by artists such as Ken Bernstein, and Danny Coyeman who used to sketch patrons on the receipts in the stores he visits. Also, make some drawings: draw a manikin that serves for learning drawing or a mannequin usually used for displaying garments on it. Draw also some geometric sketches and explore by sketching the positive–negative space relations. Consider links of drawings, architecture, and design with mathematics, physics, and the functioning of the brain and body (Halpers, 2014).

Figure 7. Emrey Winter, Sketches for face expressions (© 2018, E. Winter. Used with permission)

CREATING CHARACTERS FOR VISUAL STORYTELLING

Characters exist in their environment. That means a research is needed, about various characters and their traits, before you would decide whether your character is big, fast, strong, and wise. To tell the story, we need a set of characters, which may be humans, animals, plants, objects, or creatures resembling humans. In *The Little Prince* (*Le Petit Prince* by Antoine de Saint-Exupéry, 1900-1944) we may encounter all of these kinds of characters.

The whole storytelling may change depending on factors such as the mood, inspirations, emotions (altered states included), the costume style, a narrator's style, and the tools and media used for production. In case of visual storytelling, the same characters and objects would be different when created with different tools. While creating your own characters you may want to give them the appearance typical of new materials and technologies (such as 3D printing), or provide them with techno-textile designs of their garments that are made of new materials with wearable technology (Ryan, 2014). Figure 8 entitled *Kardelup Family* results from creating and then 3D printing a family of imaginary characters.

Adding Meaningful Components to the Character

It may be useful to add meaningful components to the characters. The introduction of iconic props while designing one's own character may induce many viewers to form their own notions and opinions about this character. For example, one character may be equipped with the evil eye jewelry, which in many cultures can protect the wearer from a curse that might be cast by a malevolent glare and cause misfortune or injury. Another character may wear a rosary – a string of beads for keeping a count of prayers in the Roman Catholic Church or other religions. Yet another character may wear a dream catcher made of yarn, feathers, and beads by American Indians to catch the nightmares and give its owner good dreams.

Figure 8. Anna Ursyn, Kardelup Family (© 2014, A. Ursyn. Used with permission)

Sometimes props may act as characters. For example, Walt Disney used saucers, a wardrobe, and more objects to act as characters. Theatrical and film production directors provide their actors with props and then with the stage design in theaters or the first-rate background. In the United States storytelling for animation was for some time dominated by the Disney style, which drew inspiration from European children books. The film industry such as Warner Brothers, film companies such as Lucasfilm (which produced Star Wars in 1980s); The Walt Disney Company, Pixar, DreamWorks, Blue Sky Production and more, and visual effects companies such as Industrial Light and Magic (from 1975 by George Lucas) are striving to maintain their own identity. Digital effects FX (sound and visual effects used in film, TV, and music) may include Simulation FX, Matte painting, and Compositing. My students present their own versions of iconic creatures: Adel Alanmi on Figure 9, and Matthew Rodriguez on Figure 10.

You may want to create some imaginary, un-existing characters. In literature, we often see transformations, sometimes coming from translations from old languages (Beowulf). In Greek religions, there are Gods, and Half-Gods. Each of them had powers and weaknesses mirroring the earthly, human, and unnatural forces. In his book titled "Bestiary" Nicholas Christopher (2008) discusses the fate of those animals that missed the Noah's Arc. They became werewolves and other harmful and quite unfriendly creatures. Figure 11 presents a set of impossible creatures, with descriptions, drawn by Katie John as characters for visual storytelling.

Creating Characters Presenting Biology Based Strategies for Designing New Products and Materials

While creating imaginary characters for visual storytelling you may want to inspire yourself with the use of bio-inspired ways for designing new materials, devices, and applications. Translation of form to function is often discussed in terms of the old 'form follows function' approach by Lamarck, where the form is altered by required function, for example, while examining a symmetrical makeup of the butterfly's wings. Contrary to that, according to Darwin, form (variation) precedes function determined by selection, so some organisms in a population are more successful in functioning and reproduction.

Scientists are now imitating the living systems in order to create materials that can function and respond to external stimuli in a similar way as living beings; this is another way of translation of biological

Figure 9. Adel Alanmi, Creatures (© 2018, A. Alanmi. Used with permission)

ADEL'S CREATURE CREATIONS

MINOTAUR   GARGOYLE   RED DRAGON

HIPPOCAMPUS   PEGAUSUS   PHOENIX

@ 2018 Adel Alanmi

Figure 10. Matthew Rodriguez, Creatures. (© 2017, M. Rodriguez. Used with permission)

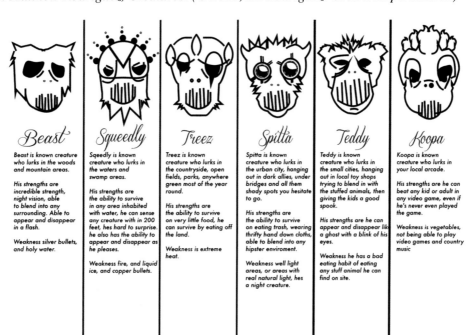

Beast

Beast is known creature who lurks in the woods and mountain areas.

His strengths are incredible strength, night vision, able to blend into any surrounding. Able to appear and disappear in a flash.

Weakness silver bullets, and holy water.

Squeedly

Sqeedly is known creature who lurks in the waters and swamp areas.

His strengths are the ability to survive in any area inhabited with water, he can sense any creature with in 200 feet, hes hard to surprise. he also has the ability to appear and disappear as he pleases.

Weakness fire, and liquid ice, and copper bullets.

Treez

Treez is known creature who lurks in the countryside, open fields, parks, anywhere green most of the year round.

His strengths are the ability to survive on very little food, he can survive by eating off the land.

Weakness is extreme heat.

Spitta

Spitta is known creature who lurks in the urban city, hanging out in dark allies, under bridges and all them shady spots you hesitate to go.

His strengths are the ability to survive on eating trash, wearing thrifty hand down cloths, able to blend into any hipster enviroment.

Weakness well light areas, or areas with real natural light, hes a night creature.

Teddy

Teddy is known creature who lurks in the small cities, hanging out in local toy shops trying to blend in with the stuffed animals, then giving the kids a good spook.

His strengths are he can appear and disappear like a ghost with a blink of his eyes.

Weakness he has a bad eating habit of eating any stuff animal he can find on site.

Koopa

Koopa is known creature who lurks in your local arcade.

His strengths are he can beat any kid or adult in any video game, even if he's never even played the game.

Weakness is vegetables, not being able to play video games and country music

Figure 11. Katie John, Index (© 2015, K. John. Used with permission)

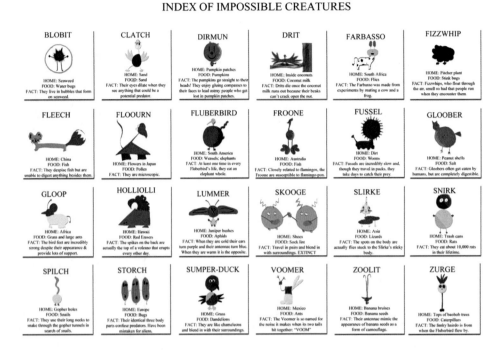

Connections between biology, engineering, and material sciences result in growing partnership among academia, laboratories, and industry. Scientists focus on biology-inspired research to understand how biological systems work, and then create systems and materials that would have efficiency and precision of living structures. According to the National Research Council of the National Academies (2008), strategies for creation of new materials and systems may be characterized as bio-mimicry, bio-inspiration, and bio-derivation. By applying bio-mimicry people design structures that function in just the same way as living systems and create synthetic materials that respond to external stimuli. With bio-inspiration people strive to create structures acting in different scheme than the living systems to perform the same functions. Bio-derivation means incorporation of biomaterials into human-made structures. The National Research Council provided examples of these three strategies:

Bio-mimicry – learning the principles used by a living system to achieve similar function in synthetic material and also create materials that mimic cells in their response to external stimuli. For example, certain cells such as T-lymphocytes can sense particular external stimuli, and then deal with pathogens. The challenge is to design bio-inspired systems and devices for detecting hazardous biological and chemical agents and strengthen national security systems.

Bio-inspiration – developing a system that performs the same function, even with different scheme. For example, the adhesive gecko foot, the self-cleaning lotus leaf, and the fracture-resistant mollusk shell are examples of inspiring structures. The cutting-edge optical technology solutions can be found in animals as well: multilayer reflectors, diffraction gratings, optical fibers, liquid crystals, and structures that scatter light. For instance, Morpho butterfly has iridescence sparkle and blue color visible from hundreds of meters due to periodic photonic structure in scales on wings, without any dye involved.

Bio-derivation – using existing biomaterial to create a hybrid with artificial material, such as incorporation of biologically derived protein into polymeric assemblies for targeted drug delivery. The eyes of higher organisms and the photosynthesis mechanism in plants are examples of biological structures and processes that can support harvesting light and also fuels (by converting cellulose polymer to ethanol). Deciphering force and motions in proteins driven by sub-cellular, molecular motors can advance clinical diagnostics, prosthetics, and drug delivery. Molecular motors convert chemical energy (usually in form of ATP – adenosine triphosphate) into mechanical energy. Contrary to Brownian movements, solely thermal effects do not drive them. Scientists strive to create self-evolving, self-healing, self-cleaning, and self-replicating super-materials that could mimic the ability to evolve and adapt. The challenge is not easy to meet: for example, the gecko's adhesive works in vacuum and under water, leaves no residue, and is self-cleaning; adhesion is reversible, so geckoes alternatively stick and unstuck themselves 15 times per second as they run up walls. As for now, "all attempts to mimic their design or to synthesize artificial polymers that are analogous to the bio adhesives in structure or function have been largely unsuccessful … and the magic of a gecko's "dry" glue with its reversible attachments remains unsolved, unmatched, and more challenging than ever" (National Research, 2008, pp. 63-64).

Choosing the Traits of Characters

Some characters are fascinating, erudite, or romantic, while other are boring. They are present in our life and also exist in literature starting from children books, short stories and novels, books of many other kinds, live performances, dramatic arts, films, television programs, and role-playing games. They are visually depicted, in two, three, or more dimensions in digital storytelling, illustrations, comics, manga, infographics, interactive video games, animations, and stereoscopic installations, among many other options. Depending on the genre, characters may be imaginary or real, historical or technology-based, magical, or supernatural. In a great measure the quality of the story depends on the distinctive attributes of characters as well as on their visual quality.

Characters that appear in a story, avatars, each one representing a particular person, emoticons and emoji images used in electronic messages, favicons associated with the website URLs, logos adopted to identify organizations' products, and other visual signals, all may occur as characters in storytelling, with the extensive use of signs, symbols, iconic objects, and metaphors.

Characters may be inspired with their literary descriptions. Artists that create visual storytelling or illustrate a literary text may imply their characteristics. A character may help integrate a text with images and sounds into a powerful message. Many times, we create the traits and features of our characters in a personally motivated way. Since the time we encountered impressive characters in our childhood they keep our company for years. They have an effect on our judgments and affect our sets of values. For this reason, illustrations play such important role in education. Many kinds of book awards for illustrators have been established, such as the Caldecott Medal, the Caldecott Honor Books award, and the Newberry Medal.

Developing one's own characters and creating one's own style is often a self-fulfilling and fun activity. Apart from their literary description, characters exist in our minds as visually imagined beings; sometimes they may convey a significant meaning that is important to us. Figure 12 presents Groober, a character for visual storytelling drawn by Galt Tomasino.

In case you prefer to choose some existing sources in spite of creating your own visual story, countless characters existing in our collective memory may support you in finding inspiration. Examples may include Greek drama, ancient tragedies and comedies (e.g., Antigone from a tragedy by Sophocles, characters from the Aristophanes' comedies); old epic stories such as Iliad or Odyssey. Monsters and ghosts populate folk stories from different nations. Aladdin of the Middle East origin and the stories of the "One Thousand and One Nights where Scheherazade narrates "The Arabian Nights," along with a parrot acting as a storyteller; in the Romantic tradition, the "Hunchback of Notre Dame," "Phantom of the Opera" (A Night at the Opera was a 1935 film with the Marx Brothers: Groucho Marx, Chico Marx, and Harpo Marx); characters acting in the 20th century literature, cartoons, and movies, such as Atticus Finch from the 1960 Harper Lee novel *To Kill a Mockingbird*; Garfield from a comic strip created by Jim Davis; a duo of characters Wile E. Coyote and the Road Runner from the Looney Tunes; the Leon Schlesinger's *Merrie Melodies* a 1931-1969 series of cartoons; Looney Tunes, and Bugs Bunny by Chuck Jones. Maybe you would prefer to choose the supernatural characters or transparent characters dressed in a coat of invisibility.

However, taking characters from famous books, movies, theatrical performances (such as from the Bread and Puppet theater), games, or animations may generate the copyright infringement. There are many groups of animators who are following the style of companies such as that of Disney, Dr. Seuss,

Figure 12. Galt Tomasino, Groober (© 2015, G. Tomasino. Used with permission)

Jim Henson, Hayao Miyazaki, or the manga, League of Legends, etc. Moreover, there is not much instruction on how to develop a new character. Figure 13 presents a character with a description, designed by Brian Phelps.

LEARNING PROJECTS: CREATING CHARACTERS FOR VARIOUS INTERFACES

A Project: Creating Characters With Abilities

Design an creature and then, on the scale of one to ten as a maximum, assign numbers for each of three abilities: intelligence, speed and weaponry (Figure 10). How much would you distribute for intelligence, and how much for speed (maybe power?). The rest goes to weaponry, but the total may not exceed 10. Would the one with higher intelligence win over the one with higher speed, or the one with better weaponry would take down the one with lower intelligence?

Figure 14 presents a character drawn by Galt Tomasino for further designing of a visual storytelling, along with a characterization of the character's abilities and developed skills. Tomasino based the design of his characters on the Howard Gardner's theories of multiple intelligences (Gardner, 1983, 1993) to create a game as an interactive, interdisciplinary storytelling.

Figure 15 presents a set of such characters with the description of their traits and abilities.

Figure 13. Brian Phelps, a creature (© 2001, B. Phelps. Used with permission)

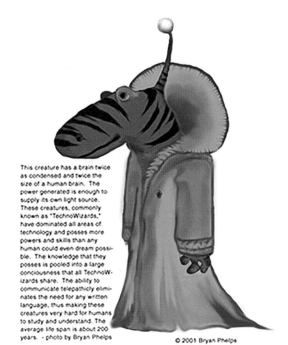

Figure 14. Galt Tomasino, Conri Seach (© 2015, G. Tomasino. Used with permission)

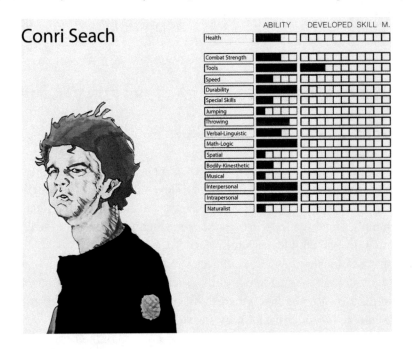

Figure 15. Galt Tomasino, characters (© 2015, G. Tomasino. Used with permission)

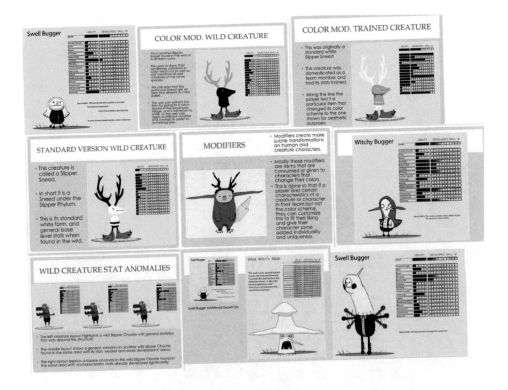

A Project: Creating Characters With Expressive Faces (or Talking/ Singing Mouths)

We are emotional creatures. Emotions are written on someone's face, body language, gestures, and the way one moves. While thinking about our characters we may refer to ancient psychological theories about fundamental personality times: sanguine (cheerful, active, and social), choleric (short-tempered, fast, or irritable), melancholic (analytical, wise, and quiet), and phlegmatic (relaxed and peaceful) (Boeree, 2002; Wikipedia). Presently, neurochemical models of individual temperaments are examined along with their social and environmental influences.

In order to picture varied facial expressions, begin with taking photographs of your own face showing many different moods (Figure 5). First, compose and print out a list of moods, and then place a set of sheets of paper in front of you. Read a name of the mood from your list, and imagine how a selected mood would be affecting your face. How would you look like? Make that face and take a picture of it. Most computers have picture-taking abilities, as software able to record faces sitting in front of the machine. Smart phone and many devices can do the same. For example, a Photo Booth application not only can record one's face but also change it into a foggy looking face, an alien, a two-headed monster, etc.

Now, you may put on your list of moods a checkmark by that mood. Name your file with your name and the name of this mood. For example: Your_name_happy.jpg. Take lots of photographs mimicking each mood, and take pictures of your various face expressions. Now, apply on a computer some effects to your faces, and then name again each file with your name, mood, and the effect used. For example, Your_name_frivolious_butterflies.jpg.

Open files with your photographs and begin sketching your faces. Before you will begin sketching a set of your own characters start by thinking of how many lines are needed to show a face. A circle or an ellipse is not enough. A vertical line inside a circle drawn to suggest a nose is not enough either. But when you add one horizontal line (straight or curved) for an eye, a face will emerge. Then, you may add another line for the second eye, vertical this time, and you have a face showing emotion. Then, you may add a line for the lips: vertical, horizontal, a circle, or yet another one, and this way you will show many faces with different emotions. Make your sketches fast, but carefully follow characteristics of your own face. Now, scan or photograph your sketches.

Take your photographs and sketches into Adobe Photoshop, a free editor Gimp, or a free painting program Krita, and by going to the Edit-Transform- tool try to change one of the photographs by distorting the image of your face, scaling it, applying perspective, slanting, or even warping it. Do the same on one more photograph, but use the Edit-Puppet Warp tool instead. Now, open a photograph, apply Select all, Copy, then Paste into Adobe Illustrator. The "Trace Image" button will appear. It will provide you with many options. Try them all, and when you will see anything interesting, export your file as a jpg and name it appropriately. You may want to use a puppet-warp function in the Adobe Photoshop to alter your face.

Now is the time to apply various filters to your photographs and your scanned sketches. Every time you would like the result, save it under a different name. This way you will end up with a large collection of faces showing various expressions in one way or another.

Choose your best faces, open them and resize your canvas. Apply Image: Canvas size, and add a set of larger numbers). Look at each face. What kind of an animal, object, plant, atmospheric event, or creature does it remind you of? Then grab an image of that animal, object, etc., and add the body to your altered face following the information on the image. Stay away from copyrighted material. Use images as a reference only. For example, an angry hammer might be a productive or dangerous one, while a happy hammer could compose some music. Keep in mind that the same photograph of a face might serve for developing various characters.

Try to avoid stereotyping; do not intellectualize by associating a specific mood with a particular animal, such as an angry lion or a happy panda. Sometimes it is difficult to guess the iconic source of a product's particular name. For example, Baby Ruth – an American candy bar owned by the Swiss company Nestlé was named after the President Grover Cleveland's daughter Ruth Cleveland (but not after a baseball player Babe Ruth).

Examine each drawing or an altered photograph, and imagine the animal you would like to associate with each mood presented. This way you'll have your own very unique growing set of characters, still avoiding the mimicking, inspiring with others' work, and refraining from the copyright infringement. Now you can choose characters for your next story you will work on. Below are drawings of my student Joel Raynor based on the making of his own face expressions (Figure 16).

A Project: Interactive Programs About Senses and Feelings

When going from the programming to art exercises, we may design an assignment about senses (such as sight, hearing, touch and haptic experience, smell, taste, and many more) and feelings. This exercise will facilitate the concept of conditions in programming by writing programs that tell how particular senses respond to specific changes in environment, and what emotions they may evoke. Changes in environment may, for example include visual, acoustic, chemical, tactile, electrical, and seismic signals.

Design an imaginary character set in a changing environment, which has many senses. Senses connect our perception with changes in our surroundings. The program may determine responses of particular sense to a change in environment. For example, a change of color will evoke a response from the character's sight; a noise or music will stimulate its hearing; a presence of a rose or cheese will stimulate the

Figure 16. Joel Raynor, Drawings of characters based on making face expressions: as annoyed chimney and then as a chameleon (© 2015, J. Raynor. Used with permission)

©Joel Raynor

© Joel Raynor

smell receptors in its nose; an apricot, when grabbed, will trigger a response from the sense of touch; drinking a lemon juice or licking honey will cause a response from its taste buds. An earth tremor may stimulate its internal mechanoreceptors or geospatial sense of the direction.

Changes of our surroundings can be good or bad for us. We may also perceive them as good or bad (we may approve hot air when we are feeling cold or we may avoid it when we feel overheated such as in a condition of hyperthermia). They may thus act at physical level (for example, a hot surface can burn our skin), physiological level (e.g., climbing at a high elevation can cause change in our blood level), and psychological level (for example, by evoking emotions such as 'I like it' 'I don't like it' 'I'm afraid of it'). Emotional reactions can act as learned, cliché responses (e.g., color blue means sadness), or may result from complex reactions coming from various brain structures.

We can also devise a program about conflicting emotional reactions to perceptions coming from senses, where one's wish, inclination, or desire is conflicting with fear, a dislike, or an avoidance re-action. For example, one can know that sunbathing can cause a skin cancer but one can love tanning; one can realize that drinking a lot of coffee (that was not decaffeinated) may advance osteoporosis by lowering the bone calcium level but one may like the taste and smell of coffee and good feeling coming from rise of the blood pressure.

This may become more complicated when we would try to devise a program about how these good, negative, or conflicting emotions can evoke a feeling of self-indulgence in our mind, controlled by brain structures and mediators. Even more complex would be description how memories emerge, based on sensual perceptions and the resulting emotions. We may start from activity: take pictures of your face showing different emotions, and then draw these emotions on your phone.

A Project: Creating a Story About a Bio-Inspired, Bio-Mimicry, or Hybrid Creature

1. Imagine yourself as an ornithologist, a beekeeper, a researcher of the ocean life and processes, or any other specialist involved in animal life. Think about special features or abilities displayed by animals under your attention that you would like to possess. Try to understand the nature of these capacities and ponder about their micro- and nano-structures in order to understand them better. Consider which bioimaging (or other) technologies would you apply to examine structures enabling these animals to surpass human abilities in particular areas. Then, think about selecting technologies that could be helpful in devising bio-inspired applications based on these special features, creating biomimicry-based materials, or create a hybrid of the animal structures with artificial materials.
2. Draw an avatar on a computer, with a pencil, or any other artist's tool. It doesn't have to look like you; it may be quite fantastic. Make it a bioinspired, biomimicking, or hybrid creature that would be able to exceed your own capabilities in an area you choose.
3. Create animation, a cartoon, or an illustrated story where your avatar would be presented as super clever and proficient because of having abilities characteristic of the animals you are working on or with. In a background of your image, present the animals that inspired you in developing applications or materials that make you (and your avatar) exceptional. Design an action where your abilities become crucial to solve harmful problems to be dealt with, win, or survive.
4. Record your facial expression using software such as PhotoBooth, or some smart phone apps. You may apply your faces to your creatures.

When working in a group, a shared folder may become useful to create a scene with an action involving all tailed characters. It would serve for the good of one's own composition and allow learning about a collaborative environment. Utilizing classmates' characters, and sharing own creations of all participants can be used to build a collaborative environment, so important in the working environments of the most media based companies. The following step is to create a 3D tailed creature to be executed as a 3Dprinted sculpture moved from Adobe Illustrator to Rhino.

A Project: The Tail – A Tailed Avatar

1. Imagine and then design a character with a tail, which can serve you for many purposes. Write a storyboard for a game, which involve the characters' tails. Your storytelling supporting the game events may be based on mythological tales and involve fantastic or legendary creatures; however, don't make a yet another dragon game that would look similar to many existing ones. How would you design a costume?

2. Invent a game where a tail would be your asset: a tool, a weapon, and means of communication. First, define an objective of you game and a goal you want to attain. Determine ways of communication with the use of your tail, both friendly and threatening.

3. Design an avatar for a game. Draw and describe a character with a tail, which would serve as your avatar in the game. Draw possible opponents, competitors, and also obstacles to achieving the goal of the game. Devise the ways your avatar could succeed in dealing with the opponents and how would this avatar overcome the obstructions and stumbling blocks using its marvelous tail. Think about the ways of using the tail to attain a faster movement when running on a surface, vaulting over barriers, and jumping into the air. You may also make your avatar suspending, thus resembling the way primates and sloths hang from tree branches. It may be applied to use locomotion in trees, swing on rock piles, feed by hanging on a tail while using both hands, or apply hanging or suspension of the body to rest and regenerate while feeling safe.

Remember to apply the laws of physics while you work on the game characters' movements. For example, when designing a swinging movement, you will examine the periodic motion of your character, which repeats back and forth movements around the central position in equal intervals of time (HyperPhysics, 2014). This pertains to a concept of the simple harmonic motion that means periodic motion where the force (F) is proportional to the displacement from the equilibrium position. Simple harmonic motion can be described by period (T) of the swinging that means the time the swinging character makes a full move back and forth, and amplitude (A) which means the maximum distance your avatar will move from the equilibrium position (in equilibrium position, there is no movement and only gravity counts).

Your character will swing on its tail resembling a pendulum and obeying the rules of the simple harmonic motion. If you want to determine the period (T), you have first to determine the length (L) of the tail your character is swinging on. Then you may apply the equation $T=2\pi(L/g)^{1/2}$ where g is the acceleration of gravity, 9.8 m/s^2. The force of gravity is proportional to the distance from the equilibrium position, and 2π refers to the description of sinusoidal oscillation. Thus, the period (T) depends on the length of the character's tail and the acceleration due to gravity, which results from applying work by you or your avatar (work would mean force multiplied by distance). Applying work is needed to start swinging by building gravitational potential energy mgh (your character's weight m, times gravity g, times distance from the ground h). Now gravitational potential energy, which pushes one towards the earth, converts to kinetic energy $1/2 \, mv^2$ (where m is mass and v is velocity – distance per time measured as m/s), so your character moves upward. Now you can design your character's movements based on a reliable source of information.

4.   Design an educational material that conveys information using a 'tail' metaphor. It may be a handout, a graph, a newsletter, a pamphlet, a brochure, a video clip, or a poster. You may choose to describe the laws of physics that shape the use of a tail along with the speed and agility of its owner, recount changes in time due to evolutionary processes, or tell about the environmentally determined features of selected running, flying, or swimming animals with tails living on land or in water.

A Project: Creating a Story About Light and Radiative Energy

Apply information driven from astrophysics related knowledge to device a story about creatures that possess different levels of strength projected as light. This means each creature can signal its power by sending off the light. Also, each type of light could give the animal a special power represented by special wavelengths. Create a system where a specific power depends on the emission or the absorption of the radiative energy. Special powers are represented by specific wavelengths. Present the power of each animal in a graphical way, for example, through the colors or textures of bodies of your animals.

Create a group of impossible creatures, and then write a story about them, as they coexist, react to changes in illumination, cooperate or compete for light, communicate and survive. Find the electromagnetic system that would apply to trees, plants, flowers, or mushrooms. You may also show the relation between the animal's brightness and its speed and agility; for example, showing a gazelle in a yellow and a turtle in a brown color. How could you learn about creatures' powers and speed by measuring wavelengths they emit? Since this environment is set as a color-coded, one can develop own expectations just by looking at the color of each creature. Construct different levels of departure from the earthly laws.

CONCLUSION

The process of creating characters for visual storytelling may cause us to think of the practical, theoretical, and historical approaches. Characters may serve as an extension of our personalities or may convey prevailing attitudes and behaviors. Several artistic forms may act as characters, some resembling humans, other real or impossible creatures, or the dead objects endowed with a life and expression. In semiotic terms, stories they tell often communicate meaningful notions, both general and abstract. The creating of characters usually involves electronic or hand drawing and then a set of learning projects is offered, on creating characters for various interfaces.

Media offer now many possibilities. As a result, the majority of new ideas expand into the multivariable, multidimensional communications going beyond the xyz coordinate system. They become interactive with a dynamic environment, science-inspired, and multicultural projects. For these reasons collaborative efforts are in high demand, to create time-based, animated presentations supporting the new ideas that result from participants' creativity, abstract thinking, and inventiveness. Drawing and sketching characters based on research, observation, and note taking is probably the shortest way to get there. So, sketch and draw daily as a way of thinking, and use the camera when some level of accuracy is needed.

REFERENCES

Arnheim, R. (1988). *The power of the center - A study of composition in the visual arts*. Berkeley: University of California Press.

Arnheim, R. (1990). Language and the Early Cinema. *Leonardo, Digital Image-Digital Cinema Supplemental Issue, 3-4.*

Bendazzi, G. (1999). *Cartoons: One hundred Years of Cinema Animation (Reprint Edition)*. Indiana University Press.

BoereeC. G. (2002). *Early Medicine and Physiology*. Retrieved from http://webspace.ship.edu/cgboer/neurophysio.html

Bread and Puppet Theater. (2017). Retrieved from http://breadandpuppet.org/

Broudy, H. S. (1991). *The Role of Imagery in Learning (Occasional Paper 1)*. Getty Center for Education in the Arts.

Christopher, N. (2008). The Bestiary. Dial Press Trade (Reprint ed.).

Chung, D. N. (2012). *Language Arts*. Western Washington University. Retrieved from http://faculty.wwu.edu/auer/Resources/Hayakawa-Abstraction-Ladder.pdf

Eco, U. (1989). *The Open Work* (A. Cancogni, Trans.). Cambridge, MA: Harvard University Press.

Ghani, D. A. (2011, January-June). Visualization Elements of Shadow Play Technique Movement and Study of Computer Graphic Imagery (CGI) in Wayang Kulit Kelantan. *International Journal of Art, Culture and Design Technologies, 1*(1), 50–57. doi:10.4018/ijacdt.2011010105

Halpers, O. (2014). *Beautiful Data: A History of Vision and Reason since 1945 (Experimental Futures)*. Duke University Press Books.

Hames, P. (Ed.). (2007). *The Cinema of Jan Švankmajer: Dark Alchemy (Directors' Cuts)* (2nd ed.). Wallflower Press.

Hayakawa, S. I., & Hayakawa, A. R. (1991). Language in Thought and Action (5th ed.). Harvest Original. (originally printed in 1941)

Hodapp, C. L. (2010). *Deciphering the Lost Symbol*. Ulysses Press. (originally printed in 1873)

Juster, N. (2000). The Dot and the Line: A Romance in Lower Mathematics (1st ed.). Chronicle Books. (originally printed in 1963)

Korzybski, A. (1995). *Science and Sanity: An Introduction to Non-Aristotelian Systems and General Semantics* (5th ed.). Brooklyn, NY: Institute of General Semantics. (Original work published 1933)

National Research Council of the National Academies. (2008). *Inspired by Biology: From molecules to materials to machines*. Washington, D.C.: The National Academies Press.

Paivio, A. (1970). On the functional significance of imagery. *Psychological Bulletin, 73*(6), 385–392. doi:10.1037/h0029180

Paivio, A. (1971). *Imagery and verbal processes.* New York: Holt, Rinehart, and Winston.

Paivio, A. (1990). Mental Representations: A Dual Coding Approach. Oxford University Press. (originally printed in 1986)

Paivio, A. (1991). Dual Coding Theory: Retrospect and current status. *Canadian Journal of Psychology, 45*(3), 255–287. doi:10.1037/h0084295

Plato. (2014). The Republic (B. Jowett, Trans.). Simon & Brown.

Puppet Forms in India. (2012). Centre for Cultural Resources and Training. Retrieved from http://ccrtindia.gov.in/puppetforms.htm

Rall, H. (2009). Tradigital Mythmaking: Singapore Animation for the 21st Century. Singapore: Dominie Press.

Read, J. (2011). *From Alchemy to Chemistry.* Dover Publications. (Original work published 1957)

Roam, D. (2013). *The Back of the Napkin: Solving Problems and Selling Ideas with Pictures (Expanded ed.).* Portfolio Penguin.

Ryan, S. E. (2014). *Garments of Paradise: Wearable Discourse in the Digital Age.* The MIT Press.

Şenyer, E. (2017). *Traditional Turkish Puppet Shadow Play Karagößz Hacivat.* Retrieved from http://www.karagoz.net/english/shadowplay.htm

Shershow, S. C. (1995). Puppets and Popular Culture by Scott Cutler Shershow. Cornell University Press. ASIN: B01FJ0UM1W. (originally printed in 1894)

Soto-Andrade, J., Jaramillo, S., Gutierrez, C., & Letelier, J.-C. (2015). *Ouroboros avatars: A mathematical exploration of Self-reference and Metabolic Closure.* MIT Press.

StarewiczW. (1999). Retrieved from https://www.awn.com/heaven_and_hell/STARE/stare1.htm

ADDITONAL READING

Boden, M. A. (2010). *Creativity and Art: Three Roads to Surprise.* Oxford, UK: Oxford University Press.

Boden, M. A. (2016). *AI: Its nature and future.* Oxford, UK: Oxford University Press.

Borges, J. L. (2006). The Book of Imaginary Beings (A. Hurley, Tran.). Westminster, UK: Penguin Books.

Christian, B., & Griffiths, T. (2016). *Algorithms to Live By: The Computer Science of Human Decisions.* New York: Henry Holt and Company.

Damasio, A. (2010). Self Comes to Mind. New York, New York: Pantheon.

Editors of Phaidon. (2012). *The Art Book.* London, UK: Phaidon Press.

Hanson, R. (2016). *The Age of EM: Work, Love, and Life when Robots Rule the Earth.* Oxford, UK: Oxford University Press.

Lima, M. (2011). Visual Complexity: Mapping Patterns of Information. New York: Princeton Architectural Press.

Lima, M. (2014). *The Book of Trees: Visualizing the Branches of Knowledge*. New York: Princeton Architectural Press.

Tufte, E. R. (2001). *The Visual Display of Quantitative Information* (2nd ed.). Cheshire, CT: Graphics Press. (Original work published 1983)

Tufte, E. R. (2005). *Envisioning Information*. Cheshire, CT: Graphics Press. Third printing with revision. (Original work published 1992)

Yau, N. (2011). *Visualize this: The flowing data guide to design visualization and statistics*. Hoboken, NJ: Wiley.

Yau, N. (2013). *Data Points: Visualization That Means Something*. Hoboken, NJ: Wiley.

KEY TERMS AND DEFINITIONS

Animatic: A simplified mock-up, a series of still images as an initial version of animation, video, or film containing successive sections of a storyboard and a soundtrack with rough dialogues. Storyboards and animatics allow pre-visualizing a project to get an insight about how the motion, soundtrack, and timing will work together before beginning the production.

Avatar: A representation of a person (a user) or a character created by this person in a form of a figure or an icon, used in video games, motion pictures, online forums, virtual reality, etc.

Fiberoptics: Optical fibers transmit information in a form of light pulses going through the core of a transparent fiber made of glass (silica) or plastic. The transparent coating material has a low index of refraction, and light signals travel along the core with very little loss of strength.

Icon: icon represents a thing or refers to something by resembling or imitating it; thus a picture, a photograph, a mathematical expression, or an old-style telephone may be regarded as iconic objects. Thus, an iconic object has some qualities common with things it represents, by looking, sounding, feeling, tasting, or smelling alike.

Liquid Crystal: Matter in an intermediate state between the solid crystalline state and the liquid state (for example, a gel), which may flow like a liquid but has molecules oriented in a way resembling a crystal. Liquid crystals exist in the natural world such as minerals, living organisms with their proteins and cell membranes; they have many technological applications, e.g., in electronics.

Motion Graphics: A sequence of abstract or thematic electronic images – parts of a film, animation, a multimedia project, or a trademark, supported by fragments of soundtrack; motion graphics provide illusion of motion or rotation but usually do not tell a story.

Pictograph: A symbolic image representing a word or a sentence wide used in ancient cultures such as in Egipt, Mesopotamia, or Indian pictographs and petroglyphs. Also, a pictorial representation (an icon, a symbol, or a picture) presented on a computer screen, or a chart, showing the value of the data or comparing the sets of the data; pictographs are used to replace or enhance graphs that present the data as lines, curves, or bars.

Semiotics: the study about the meaningful use of signs, symbols, codes, and conventions that allow communication. The name 'semiotics' is derived from the Greek word 'semeion' which means "sign". "Meaning" is always the result of social conventions, even when we think that something is natural or characteristic, and we use signs for those meanings. Therefore, culture and art is a series of sign systems. Semioticians analyze such sign systems in various cultures; linguists study language as a system of signs, and some even examine film as a system of signs. The semiotic content of visual design is important for non-verbal communication applied to practice, especially for visualizing knowledge.

Sign: a conventional shape or form telling about facts, ideas, or information. It is a distinct thing that signifies another thing. Natural signs signify events caused by nature, while conventional signs may signal art, social interactions, fashion, food, interactions with technology, machines, and practically everything else.

Storyboard: A graphic organizer containing sequenced images (usually drawings), simple directions, and dialogues designed to pre-visualize animation, film, motion graphics, or a sequence of interactive media.

Symbol: symbols no resemble things they represent but refer to something by convention. We must learn the relationship between symbols and what they represent, such as letters, numbers, words, codes, traffic lights, and national flags. A symbol represents an abstract concept, not just a thing, and is comparable to an abstract word. Highly abstracted drawings that show no realistic graphic representation become symbols. Symbols are omnipresent in our life. Examples may include: an electric diagram, which uses abstract symbols for a light bulb, wire, connector, resistor, and switch; an apple for a teacher or a bitten apple for a Macintosh computer; a map – typical abstract graphic device; a 'slippery when wet' sign. Signs, icons, and symbols are collectively called signage. Icons and symbols help compress information in a visual way. Designers choose signs, symbols, and icons that are powerful and effective; for example, a designer may look for an icon showing the essence of the meaning related to scissors and common features characteristic for this product. Effective design of a complicated product may help memorize and learn how to use the product.

Tree Structure: A data structure usually used for abstract data built up from nodes (vertices) and edges; tree structures often have many hierarchical levels but they do not form a cycle.

Visualization: the communication of information with the use of graphical representations. Interactive visual representations of abstract data use easy-to-recognize objects connected through well-defined relations.

Chapter 4
Visual Storytelling for Various Interfaces

Anna Ursyn
University of Northern Colorado, USA

ABSTRACT

This chapter is focused on text visualization and storytelling delivered in various literary styles adopted for various delivery systems. Discussion pertains first storytelling by drawing, both with traditional techniques and digital storytelling for various media and technologies. Transition from a sketch to sculpted forms converted to 3D printing, animation, and video is then discussed. Projects offer practical examples of the visual storytelling production and examine the possible usage of visual storytelling for different kinds of interfaces conducive to human communication through mass media, digital interactive, social, and printed media, with the use of mobile apps, web app, or application software.

INTRODUCTION

Storytelling

Generally, storytelling refers both to the archived oral tradition in storytelling in different cultures, times, and places, and to digital storytelling using a variety of media formats, and involves words or written texts, images, gestures, sounds, and animated graphics to let the recipient know about incidents, occurrences, or events, and thus convey education, games, entertainment, (along with edutainment as a form of entertainment aimed at educating as well as entertaining) or cultural and moral traditions. The raw data such as observations, equations, structural formulas, or spectra are useless without the narrative theoretical framework that makes a story out of them. For many multi-media communication complex institutions, communicating by using fiction storytelling techniques can be a more compelling and effective route than using only dry facts. Stories also help us make sense of the world (Hensel, 2010).

DOI: 10.4018/978-1-5225-7371-5.ch004

Storytelling in the past often carried spiritual content, such as when Australian Aboriginal storytellers painted symbolic visual stories on sand or rocks, following the path of the spirits controlling their hands. Storytelling before the emergence of writing served for preserving memory of important events, such as in the case of a Greek epic poem Iliad ascribed to Homer, retold by centuries with many improvised embellishments. Some stories were not recorded at all but repeated by storytellers often enough to preserve its presence in a society, played with the use of shadow puppets or masks, as theatrical performances, games, or serial events. Stories often evolved by being told by people with different personalities and perspectives.

With the advent of writing, the writings recorded on rocks, wood, bamboo, clay, pottery, silk, papyrus, or paper complemented visual storytelling. Folklorists discern legends and fairy tales as the main groups of oral tales. Folkloric storytelling includes fairy tales about not necessarily true, often supernatural events, along with legends about true events happening in particular places and times, as well as extraterrestrial and ghost stories. Writers tell stories in their poems, novels, biographies, articles, museum displays, theatrical plays, and films. Many times, the same story about what happened is retold several times by the characters in a play or a movie, with similar props but changed events in each story. Actors, singers, and comedians use legends or folkloric materials along with historical data to engage their audience interest. The audience visualizes the events by creating personal mental images, reacting to the words and gestures of the storyteller, and thus becoming co-creators of the spectacle and motivating the teller to improvise. Children books with traditional stories often contain educational content, sometimes at the expense of a time-honored tale. For example, in some American editions a bottle of wine has been removed from a basket carried by a girl from the Charles Perrault's (2012) 'Little Red Riding Hood' (rewritten later by Brothers Grimm).

One might say that whatever we do is a potential story. Visual storytelling, especially digital storytelling combines visual and verbal communication. There are a growing number of interfaces to introduce our story. With the use of a computer we can do it by creating an image and then transform it into other dimensions: from a two dimensional to a three-dimensional rotational object, a time based visual story, or a virtual reality based scenario. Tools for enhancing visual literacy and thus supporting learning about science may comprise visual storytelling, animations, video clips, simulations, and augmented reality environments, among other solutions. Visual storytelling adds the fourth dimension as it allows wandering across time and space to follow the events that happen to the characters we draw. It makes possible the retrieving, visualizing, representing, and sharing our knowledge through visual and verbal metaphors, and also involving our senses in the process. Music and sound effects also serve as the ways to transfer information. We may send out our stories on the web, and this would allow the user/visitor's interactivity through the web. We may make a transition from a sketch to a 3D printed form, to animate it, and to interact with; while watching an interactive movie the gaze of a viewer can be tracked via an eye-tracking device.

Visual Storytelling as Sequential Art

Storytelling is an art form that can be annotated as sequential art that uses a string of images to produce a graphic storytelling or deliver knowledge. It is an old form of art, as the cave paintings, Egyptian hieroglyphs, pre-Columbian pictorial artifacts wall paintings from different times and places, old friezes, vases, tapestries, embroideries, scrolls, and later, printed series of graphics and numerous paintings – all depict informative stories to document their times. Contemporary examples of sequential works are comics printed in newspapers and magazines, for example comics created by Scott McCloud (2006). They are often presented later as films and animations, web comics, storyboards used for preparing motion pictures of different kinds such as a motion graphic, film, animation, or interactive presentation for the social media or interactive websites.

Drawings are the strong tools for storytelling as they can act as an interface between the visual and the verbal. Visual storytelling adds the fourth dimension as it allows wandering across time and space to follow the events that happen to the characters we draw. Storytelling achieved by drawing pictures conveys to a computer screen the visceral, emphatic, or voyeuristic emotions and evokes emotional response from the audience. The same may be told about the effectiveness of animation in storytelling, as adding the time dimension enhances dramatic actions, shows suspenseful obstacles, and builds tension before solving a conflict. Sketches may serve as a starting point to create manga, blogs, even product and architectural schemes, and other forms.

Digital Storytelling

We grow up with stories. Depending on who delivers it, we create our own visual representations, connotations, and memories. When a book is adapted into a movie, almost everyone has something to say about how the actors do not necessarily fit their own imaginative description of them. Some believe that the real magic comes with interactive storytelling, as each word in each story is cross-linked, clustered, cited, extracted, remixed, reassembled and woven into the story texture. Interactive novel and interactive adventure games were created with many other kinds of software; e.g., early versions created with a Hypertext. For example, a poet and a speechwriter for Ronald Reagan Robert Pinsky is an author of the interactive fiction game *Mindwheel* developed in 1984 by Synapse Software and released by Broderbund. It was an interactive storytelling on a black-and-white screen of an early Macintosh computer, where the story would unfold differently depending on choices and decisions made by a reader. *Killer: the Game of Assassination* has been the first live a role-playing game about 'killing' other players without hurting them (Jackson, 1981;2018).

Teaching drawing and computing techniques including computer graphics becomes a part of the collaborative interdisciplinary curricula designed for art and computer science undergraduates. Storytelling Studies became an interdisciplinary field, or as a discipline unto itself. One may find on the Internet long lists of storytelling courses delivered all over the world, workshops, and textbooks. One can also learn about digital storytelling and new media narrative (Caputo, Ellison, & Steranko, 2011). On Vimeo, one can find short videos on the future of storytelling. Storycenter (2018) is a network of storytelling specialists from science, research, management, design, media and art. Transmedia storytelling is the technique of telling stories across multiple platforms and formats using current digital technologies, involved in branding, performance, ritual, play, activism, spectacle, as other logics (Jenkins, 2011).

Crafting a story is a challenging task because a story should be engaging both intellectually and visually. Readers and listeners convey the words into a virtual environment in their own mind (Zeng & al., 2003). A story has to evoke the audiences' response and meet their cognitive and emotional needs for gaining new information, binding with a story heroes, participating in a conflict, feeling suspense resulting from threat and uncertainty, enjoying the completion, and being entertained, many times in voyeuristic, visceral, and vicarious way. Digital storytellers work on multiple levels: combine words and ideas into a story structure, select the level of interaction, and include audio, photo, and video. They often apply a comic strips metaphor, or animate the events.

Anyone can tell their story in their own way. People using computers and personal photographs make videos with a digital camera, edit them (or not), and upload the films onto the video-sharing site YouTube. Digital stories (short films) make a new medium that is present on popular web sites. A story may comprise separate stories set against the common ground in past, present or future. Audiences follow the troubles, hopes, and efforts of the characters, and thus they explore the issues presented by the storyteller. For example, an interactive web-based video series lonelygirl15 achieved massive popularity in the years 2006-2008, and then was put to end as fictional.

Brian Alexander (2011) describes platforms for tales and telling, as the Web 2.0 storytelling, social media storytelling, and gaming storytelling on a small and a large scale. He also comments on the combinatorial storytelling involving networked books, stories designed for mobile devices, alternate reality games, and for augmented reality where digital content is linked to the physical world. Telling stories may involve Web 2.0 tools, technologies, and strategies to be posted at social media. As Alexander & Levine (2008) put it, "Stories now are open-ended, branching, hyperlinked, cross-media, participatory, exploratory, and unpredictable. And they are told in new ways: Web 2.0 storytelling picks up these new types of stories and runs with them, accelerating the pace of creation and participation while revealing new directions for narratives to flow."

Combined use of natural language processing and 3-D computer graphic techniques can enhance human-to-human interaction. Within a storytelling medium readers and listeners convey the meaning of the words into virtual environment (Zeng, Mehdi, & Gough, 2003). The non-professionals can generate an interactive 3D virtual story environment based on a story-based natural language input, where a sentence in human language acts on a language engine and a graphic engine. This approach bridges the gap between scripting/storyboarding by a nontechnical creative writer and rendering characters and scenes by a graphics specialist.

We may notice many functions of storytelling. Digital storytelling, used in television to show the news and ubiquitous in multimedia in the form of text and animated graphics, coexists often with other techniques and is an important factor in managing communication in the news, business, education, and training. Online journalists and TV reporters combine text, image, sound and movement into a dynamic environment, and thus they are able to tell, show, explain, demonstrate, and discuss the issues, which is appealing for Internet newsreaders. In many cases digital storytelling combines performance with physical/virtual interaction, visual surveillance technology, motion tracking, and artificial intelligence. Visual storytelling may assume multidimensional, interactive features. Ricou & Pollock (2012) created an about 8 ft diameter soft sculpture, the *Spiral of Life*, a symbol for the evolution of life based on a Tree of Life web project http://tolweb.org/tree/ and an interactive Tree of Life website http://itol.embl.de/. Their "soft sculpture doubled as a storytelling stage and a tactile playground … when Ricou performs the Story of Evolution, reading the sculpture like a book with children, exploring horizontal and vertical processes as physical structures" (Ricou & Pollock, 2012, p. 24).

Several industries use serious games for various purposes, such as education, scientific exploration, health care, emergency management, city planning, engineering, and politics. Interactive visualization projects are also made with a medical, especially therapeutic perspective or for supporting defense military resources. Interactive computer video games serve both educational and medical purposes. For example, Corwin Bell produced interactive games with biofeedback sensors measuring heart rate and skin conductance; players not only learn to control their breathing, build mental serenity, and reduce stress; they also can access their innate power of visualization and see how their thoughts and emotions may impact their ability to play the game or deal with the real-life actions. A game *Journey to the*

Wild Divine, my former student's Master of Arts in Computer Graphics project, was the first computer biofeedback game (Figure 1). Other programs, especially those designed for children involved clickable objects that could be triggered by a touch of a mouse to be animated, speak their names in various languages, or change their position. For example, students from the University of Northern Colorado Cameron Grimes, Emrey Winter, and Olivia Koval created a game about the journey to the Earth center using a virtual reality learning tool zSpace.

Other programs, especially those designed for children involved clickable objects that could be triggered by a touch of a mouse to be animated, speak their names in various languages, or change their position, (with one of the early prototypes *Just Grandma and Me* or *The Manhole*).

Visual story might be done in many ways and for various purposes, for example:

- An e-book, a visual novel, an interactive fiction story
- Electronic novel, graphic novel, or visual narrative
- A mixed-media novel comprising of images made out of 3D sets made of paper, paper cutouts, clay, glass and mirrors, with added light effects, sculpted, or 3D printed elements and characters
- A Mixbook, an Internet-based photo design and photo production service that allows designing books and other printed matter through its online interface
- Recorded steps for painted images
- Drama: a script for a theatrical play
- A script for time-based visual media, film, video, and moving images
- A libretto for an opera and operetta, for a ballet or a musical, often in a confined space

Figure 1. Corwin Bell, Interactive games with biofeedback sensors (© 2009, C. Bell. Used with permission)

- Poetry: a poem, a limerick, haiku, e-poetry, visual poetry
- Sequential art
- A web art combining technologies, focusing on collages of poetry, image, sound, movement and interaction
- Manga
- Comics
- Portrait, visual and verbal (for a cultural study, interpretation), often practiced by journalists
- Interpretative or explanatory drawing
- Data-, information-, and knowledge visualization
- A story complementing a scientific illustration or drawing
- Technical writing explained visually
- Description for a design of a product
- A story for VR environment, or a Second Life with the use of avatars
- A story with visual approach to social networking: YouTube, MySpace, FaceBook, Flaxo for interactive Fiction games, Linkedin, blogs, user groups, groups such as Delicious.com, Plaxo – an online address book, etc.
- A story for wireless technology: Nintendo, e.g. Nintendo E3 2018, animation, inter-global participation (Super Mario Cart where each player selects a character as alias standing on a particular place of the globe, so other players are not informed if they are playing with an elementary school student, or with someone's grandma who happens to be at their place up at 3 o'clock in the morning and in a playful mode); cell phone communication, where a group of strangers would play poker and would grin at the one leaving the electronic table); or a game that would mimic the local weather by sharing rain, snow, or the sunshine); PDAs; Zoom; Coliseum; videoconferencing; Skype; etc.
- A story for a game with graphics or anime-style art, gaming of various kinds, such as serious games serving education, entertainment, self-improvement, health, fitness, or biofeedback
- An ad in TV or a magazine.

Teaching drawing and computing techniques including computer graphics becomes a part of the collaborative interdisciplinary curricula designed for art and computer science undergraduates. Storytelling Studies became an interdisciplinary field, or as a discipline unto itself. One may find on the Internet long lists of storytelling courses delivered all over the world, workshops, and textbooks. One can also learn about digital storytelling and new media narrative (Caputo, Ellison, & Steranko, 2011). On Vimeo, one can find short videos on the future of storytelling. The Center for Storytelling is a network of storytelling specialists from science, research, management, design, media and art. Transmedia storytelling, also known as multi-platform storytelling is the technique of telling stories across multiple platforms and formats using current digital technologies.

Computer graphics and art may be created in several ways:

- Through writing algorithms (instructions about sequential steps for carrying out operations)
- Using graphic software packages and applications
- Changing a pre-written code (for example, Processing (2018), HTML, Blender with Python + HTML, and

- Combining the 3D immersive world of augmented or virtual reality with actions performed by users.

One may manipulate images scanned or drawn on a screen, using graphic or painting software, applying multimedia packages, video, animation, visualization systems, or real time interactive communication through art. Structures can be shared or translated between media to visualize images, forms, music, poetics, and interactive fiction.

To create a digital storytelling we may use computer graphics and art, using techniques applied in digital illustration, which encompass the 2D, 3D, interactive, and many other types of illustrations. We may consider smart graphics, intelligent, and adaptive graphics, which are often used for the production of mailing postcards, flyers, brochures, door hangers posters, business cards, magnetic plastic cards, presentation folders, stickers, labels, and also sketch-based interfaces and rendering techniques for the 3D models (Knödel, Hachet, & Guitton, 2009).

There are many possible options to choose from when commencing a visual/verbal project. It may take form of activities performed for creating images, music, and text:

- Writing a statement to a picture
- Drawing a picture for a story
- Improvisation to a musical theme, just combining music, a picture, and a verbal content; it may be text for a song, with illustration
- Reacting to a set of icons, such as road signs
- Writing a story about a scientific material, for example, a planetary system
- Creating an encyclopedia of symbols and gestures as visual metaphors
- Making use of preformatted themes coming from everyday activities. However, one has to keep in mind the copyright issues. One may use a clipart (accordingly to the company's agreement), a supply from stock photography, free music, digital libraries, websites such as CGTextures.com, resources for open source, or use items or designs from libraries for a specific software, inclusive websites (give and take), or for an easy, friendly automatic website design.

CREATING ANIMATIONS AND MOVIES FOR VISUAL/VERBAL INTERACTIONS

The task described below is to develop, with the use of software, coding, or both, dynamic presentation of various kinds of data in the form of a visual story. The reader is requested to participate actively in the following exercise by creating a visual story. The purpose for which the storytelling is to be created as animation or a movie is to develop, sometimes with the use of coding, a visual presentation of various kinds of data. To create animation, start with a figure and then change the communication path through transformations. You may start with visually programming a set of 3D images, and then creating an own story and then a storyline for animation. This requires thinking about the tentative audience, creating and sketching characters and their environment, choosing a media container, and then developing a storyboard on a template.

The task of creating animation or a movie consists of several steps. The story has to be envisaged and then put into words and visuals in order to create a storyline. You may want to plan your actions and mentally visualize your ideas, purpose, and message, so you will be ready to write a short script that may later serve as the audio for your story. Later on, the products will be added to the database for comparing codes, discussing them, and for making critiques of the projects. Another venue pertains to interactive animation.

Writing a Storyline

Create visually your own story. Every story needs a storyline to communicate the process of storytelling. The narrative of a fictional or true research-based story is usually a collaborative experience. You may want to begin with writing a short story. It may be helpful to write the storyline the way you would tell it to your friend on your cell phone; it should be short, interesting, without visual cues, that means not requiring putting on view any objects.

First, choose a theme, a subject that is being dealt with, and objects to which actions will be directed. Decide whether your story would be a fairy tale or a realistic description of issues and events. A conventional fable often begins with a "once upon a time, behind 7 rivers, behind 7 mountains" opening. Yeki Bud Yeki Nabud, which means in Persian, "There was one and there wasn't one" is referring to an indefinite time and place. Then, make a timeline that would define when and where your story takes place, and then establish the chronological order of the events you are telling about. Decide the sequence how the main events will appear on the screen. Perhaps you may decide your story would not be linear – it may shift or travel in time, flash forward or backward, change the point of view or even the narrating person, or it may have more then one outcomes.

Describe the key events and thus the key scenes you will show – how your story will begin, what kind of action would happen with possible conflicts and their solution, and how the story would end. Think how the plot would develop and indicate changes of the setting when action switches to another place (Video, 2013). At first your description of the story will be general, and then it will serve for creating a more detailed material for designing a storyboard. Animated storyboard is often called an animatic. Storyboards and animatics serve for pre-visualizing your project before beginning its production (Bloop Animation Studios, 2017). You will be thinking about particular scenes and their illustrations on the storyboard, which later will be brought into an editing program and integrated with sound effects.

Consider the underlying processes, products and effects of actions, external and internal forces defining the concept development. You may want to decide about who would be the hero, what would be an objective of the story, when and where the action would happen, why the conflict would ensue, and how would you design the fabric of the story. A theme for your story will determine a mood, a sequence of story actions that structure the tale and will support an introduction of characters that will act there; also it will dictate the way of describing their garment such as shirts and trousers, headgear, and weapons or tools. It's a good time to include some surprises, a thought-provoking statement from your point of view, or an insight, so the story becomes interesting and not predictable.

In many cases, a storyteller wants to tell about the sense of right and wrong, thus conveying a moral of the story. For example, an angel and a devil metaphorically sitting on the character's arms can speak out your voice of conscience. Also, you may want to convey your thoughts about the future – what do you want to happen in the world.

When you write it on a computer or a tablet computer such as iPad, it is time to name and save your story (However, a title such as "How Jonny Killed the Dragon" does not seem a good solution as it shows the ending up-front). The story may now serve as a source for creating its various containers. You may want to choose from many persuasive forms of rhetoric and change your story into a short poem, a limerick, a pun, or a script for a TV play. A limerick, a comic, or a nonsensical verse is a concise form of telling a story.

Addressing the Audience of a Story

Composition of the project starts with choosing a character and its environment, followed by thinking about the recipients of the project, and considering possible ways of redesigning this storyline for a particular audience. Every audience may have their own needs and likings, so it is vital to meet them both in the visual and written parts of the project. Images may be sized up differently depending on how old are the viewers, how familiar are they with computer technologies, or how much time they spend online. For instance, viewers belonging to various age groups would best understand and share the feelings of characters when they are drawn in a style that is familiar to them, be it an accurate depiction, or a manga-style drawing.

As for the verbal part, typography, which means setting types and the appearance of printed material, is important: when they are well set for given recipients, the written part of the project is legible, readable, and appealing for them. For example, small type is not good for small children and also for the elderly people, while a big font size may be seen offensive for high school students.

Think about possible ways of redesigning your story for various audiences. A good many of viewers prefer humans as characters of a story because they can identify themselves with the heroes and feel empathy toward them. For that reason many universities put pictures of students on their websites in spite of placing informative depictions of their departments. In the same way we may find happy faces on the snack wrappings.

Many traditional stories share similar themes with minor variations. The story will surely evoke an interest of the audience when they anticipate that you'd introduce a problem, fear about a conflict between the characters, probably some ambiguity and misunderstandings, a worry about the ensuing actions and obstacles causing tension, they are anxious about events resulting from actions, and finally hope to release their tension seeing the means of solving a conflict and dealing with a difficult situation. The audience may want to satisfy their need for information about your characters' passions or dilemmas about important decisions, and even may want to share these feelings and tensions; they may also expect some entertainment coming from your project when they find your story suspenseful, surprising, and exciting. The ending of the story may represent universal truths and even provide a moral of this story.

Characters

Composition of the project starts with choosing a character existing in its environment. After making search about various characters and their traits you would be able to select a set of characters and decide which your characters is big, fast, strong, and wise. They may be humans, animals, plants, objects, or creatures resembling humans. A character in your story should convey its personality, integrity, and important features in a simplest, most concise way. The process of eliminating unnecessary details and deciding what is crucial to the basic message is called abstracting. Figure 2 presents Chupo, a characre drawn by my student Joel Raynor.

Avatars – characters that appear in a story represent a particular person; emoticons and emoji images are used in electronic messages, favicons associate with the website URLs; companies and organizations adopt logos to identify their actions and products, for example Mickey Mouse acts as a character of this

Figure 2. Joel Raynor, Chupo (© 2016, J. Raynor. Used with permission)

type. All such visual signals may occur as characters in storytelling, with the extensive use of signs, symbols, iconic objects, and metaphors. Figure 3 presents a character Tento who performs electronic fortune telling.

Creating the Background Environment for a Story

After the choosing of characters is completed it is time to provide them with suitable, individually created environments, and also reactions of your invented characters (avatars) to changes in these environments. That means a research is needed, about the characters' habitat, and also various factors such as symbiosis, dangers, characters' equipment and implements. As a response to environmental changes, invented characters (avatars) would react in different characteristic ways. The background may change in time. For instance, the moon may travel across the sky; a background may reveal detailed objects (leaves, small birds, owls, frogs, bats, or car headlights).

Mystery can be conveyed by a character, task, or landscape. Also, the impressive lighting, a set of textures, auditory and visual cues, and a design signifying depths can convey a mood. First, the understanding is needed of underlying processes, products, and forces that define the setting for a story. Therefore, start your project with a research about characters and their habitat, and also factors such as symbiosis, dangers, characters' characteristics, and equipment. Is your main character big, fast, strong, and wise? How about other characters? Figures 4 and 5 present drawings by my student Galt Tomasino aimed at creating landscapes and characters for visual storytelling.

Figure 3. Anna Ursyn, Fortune Teller Tento (© 2010, A. Ursyn. Used with permission)

Choosing a Container of a Story

Advances in the time-based and interactive technologies may convince us that our stories require a container, as every story needs to be told differently for each medium, be it a graph, animation, web, manga, film, theater, radio, podcast, or comic. Choosing a container of a story will define how the story is being delivered in a specific setting, told and retold differently for each medium. Digital storytelling is becoming an important factor in managing communication in business, education, and training. Teaching drawing and computer graphics is now part of the collaborative interdisciplinary curricula for many art and computer science undergraduates.

Telling the same story in another medium may require another setting. Digital storytelling may combine several modes of presenting visual material such as a graphic, a comic strip or a comic book, an animated cartoon, manga, an animated film, a theater performance, VR, web, a game, a movie, a radio show, podcasting, or other means by which it is communicated. The writer needs to retell the story to match the framework, timing, and technical requirements of each medium. Old, popular tales are often treated that way in various media. A blogspot entitled A Look into Later: "27 ways to tell a story in

Figure 4. Galt Tomasino, Landscapes for storytelling (© 2015, G. Tomasino. Used with permission)

Figure 5. Galt Tomasino, Landscapes for storytelling (© 2015, G. Tomasino. Used with permission)

VR" (May 13, 2018) discerns several options for designing a virtual reality project: passive that is like watching a movie, active that is like playing a traditional video game, open which is like having a stage you're free to roam around on, and a combo or combinations of these methods. virtual reality.

Animation is a popular way to deliver a story; it often supplements a video footage. To create the animated visual storytelling you may choose to animate text and vectors (which designate a type of graphical representation using straight lines to construct the outlines of objects) using key-framing and adding effects. Animated visuals that tell stories can be then put on the web and social media networks.

It might be entertaining to write a short story and then rework it in several ways, thus creating various kinds of containers for the same story according to a specific literary style, with specific settings and styles. You may want to re-create your story in other literary styles, every time changing its design according to the goal and purpose. Visualize your writing and assign visual containers to your story by creating illustrations or animations. Avatars may convey their stories through music, dance, and text. A coded program or a computer graphics may serve for defining a container for a story. After that, explain the features of particular types of writing and write a critique of your visual and verbal creations.

The way we unfold and deliver the story depends on our purpose for storytelling and the environment. For example, a web page developer should not only design a project but also make it fit for the changes in an environment actually perceived by the user. Therefore we have to analyze cultural implications of our products from the perspective of the viewer, not only in the artist's frame of reference. It may cause a need for interdisciplinary training, to become equipped to not only to produce pretty pictures but also be able to bring about a cross-cultural impact, since the product delivery is usually tested under specific technical or cultural conditions. Moreover, it may create a need for exploration of the tastes and needs of recipients. For instance, there may be a tension existing between the precise way of drawing and scientific thinking that is typical of engineers and analysts and the expressive drawings as an instrument of thinking through art. Even so, scientists, business managers, and production specialists produce artwork for analyzing and disseminating information in a visual form, for example, when creating a real-time portfolio textures to visualize financial data.

Now it would be a good time to visualize your writing and assign your story some visual containers. Having the written part of your story ready, visualize your story by creating illustrations for it. Assign your story some visual containers by creating illustrations or animations for this story. This way you will be creating various kinds of containers for the same story. A coded program or a kind of computer graphics may serve for defining a container for a story.

With another approach, you may choose to design a shape poem – a concrete poetry made of a typographical arrangement of the words contained in your story, or a poster with pictures showing the course of events. You may also draw a cartoon showing satirical interpretation of your story, comics – a comic strip with simple drawings and short texts about what the characters have to say, or manga – a cartoon in Japanese style showing your fantasy about the story events. It may also become an animation (black-and-white, color, or 3-D animation), a short film, or vimeo (a video-sharing website). It could be amusing to actually do it according to the rules set up for of each medium (posted online) or breaking some of them. The use the hypertext links would allow the viewers to access parts of your project.

It would be useful to take into account the elements and principles of design for each depiction, and think about a 2-D space versus lighting and the camera work, in case you would like to take shots with your digital camera or a smart phone. It may be a challenging task to apply many media – audio (music and voice), text, and visuals altogether to show, explain, and discuss the ideas that would be appealing for the viewers, evoke their response and meet their emotional needs.

Whatever is the container for your digital (or traditionally crafted) story, it will be told in your distinctive, individual way, especially when you would use your personal photographs and videos made with a digital camera, edit (or not) and download them to enrich your work. If you decide to use pictures taken by others, be sure to add such information as the copyright, author, and date at the bottom of a page. It may then be interesting to upload this homemade work onto YouTube.

A Template

Free printable storyboard templates are available on the Internet. Digital storytelling storyboard templates (Ohler, 2012a, b) maybe found helpful in this task. Pick one template that meets your aesthetic and intellectual needs. It may look like the one pictured on Figure 6.

A Storyboard

A storyboard helps to organize a story and focus on the main features of a story against time (Storyboard, 2017). For an online presentation, a storyboard may also help to figure out what medium to use for each part of the story: video and music video, still photos, audio, graphics, and text (Storyboarding, 2016). The 2D or 3D storyboard software is available on the Internet. As defined by Essley, Rief, & Rocci (2017), "A storyboard is a writing format, generally a set of boxes (or rectangles, circles, or other shapes) placed in a logically sequenced order. Each box or frame is a place for the writer to put information, pictures, symbols, or text." The authors think of Chinese pictographs and ancient Egyptian hieroglyphs (etched in stone or written on papyrus) as storyboards, as they organize a society.

Figure 6. A template for designing a storyboard; an example of a template from the web (© 2013, LetterHead Template Sample, letterheadtemplate.org. Free documents download storyboard template)

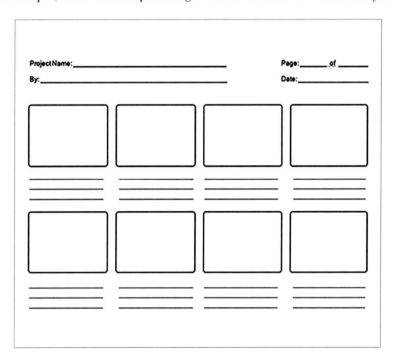

The next step will involve storyboarding, drawing a comic strip, with pictures working in sync with words and sentences in your script. Pictures may contain symbols or metaphors but not necessary decorations that are not connected with the story. Storyboards are used for pre-visualization of your video, animation, motion picture, motion graphic, or any interactive medium. This graphic organizer would be a set of drawings or sketches going together with dialogue and directions. It shows the shots you will make for your production. Write captions under every change that will explain each dynamic action.

After your storyline is ready, make a storyboard that will organize graphically your storyline with the use of illustrations or simple drawings combined with spare text. Images and text support and reinforce each other (Essley, Rief, & Rocci, 2017). You may use your computer in many ways in order to create your storyboard (Educational Uses of Digital Storytelling, 2017). You may download a storyboard template as PDF (Download, 2018); create your storyboard in Microsoft Word (Create, 2018); create a PowerPoint storyboard template.ppt; or make a digital storytelling storyboard template by coding.

For your visual storytelling, your drawings or sketches combined with text will serve as frames on a strip of your animation or your movie. In video technology a frame is a coded image. First make the general template consisting of the starting and ending points of the story, changes of setting or the timing of the movement. A keyframe is a drawing defining the starting or ending points of a transition between the drawings – the timing of the movement. To create animation or a movie, select your keyframes defining the starting point and the ending point for smooth transitions between images. A set of keyframes will define the movements seen by a viewer. Select your sketches of major key frames, and then insert them into the template. In order to secure a smooth transition, insert the remaining frames as inbetweens between the keyframes. One may also consider making mental key frames in the programming process.

Your drawings or sketches will serve your projects better than premade images or clip art because you will use drawing as a thinking tool. Images will provide you with synthetic information along with entertainment. While looking like thumbnails, they illustrate the key scenes. Each scene should contain some action and convey some emotions. If your story is long or complicated, for example takes place in several places or times, make more than one storyboard. Figure 7 shows a storyboard drawn by Christian Eggers for a story about insomnia, while Figure 8 presents a storyboard by Galt Tomasino for his animation.

Below each picture describe each cell of your storyboard, so everybody would know what you want to present and what action would be pictured on each scene. Especially, write captions under every change that will explain each dynamic action. Indicate the setting of the main action and of the background. Write the dialogues for each scene where they are needed.

After completion of the first stage of working on your storyboard, start reviewing it as a whole, checking if you have identified key points well. Then examine each sketch. Sketches should be as simple as possible, make sure they make sense to somebody else apart from you. Inspect the design of each frame whether it shows what you wanted to show. Think about composition of your sketches, whether they show light or darkness, right colors, correct relation between foreground versus background, and perspective. Maybe it's better to place your actors in perspective, not just standing in the same distance from the front line. To create an illusion of perspective, place some actors nearer by making them bigger and lower in the foreground; partially cover farther actors by the nearer ones; and apply lighter shades in front of and darker in the back of the space of your scene.

Show the difference between actors that do the action, whether they are people, animals or animated objects, and objects/props that are only acted upon. Also, you may add some objects/props to the scene that would better explain the action. Think about adding some actions indicating tension, emotion, and

Figure 7. Christian Eggers, Investigation of an insomniac (© 2017, C. Eggers. Used with permission)

© Chrisitan Eggers 2017

a reason for further action. For example, your character may take some steps, look in the direction of the next event, or say something before this event or action happens on the following scene. Finally, edit your storyboard to improve its integrity, but be careful to maintain your personal style.

EDUCATIONAL IMPLICATIONS

Digital storytelling serves as an educational tool providing knowledge of oral tradition in storytelling in different cultures. The medium of storytelling uses a variety of media formats: text, image, sound, animated graphics, time-based and interactive projects (such as websites). Computer graphics are essential for developing a container: how the story is being delivered. Every discipline or medium – archeology, history, geology, online environment, a game, to name just a few – can be seen, or even should be seen as a set of stories, moreover, visual stories. The way we unfold and deliver the story depends on the

Figure 8. Galt Tomasino, Storyboard (© 2015, G. Tomasino. Used with permission)

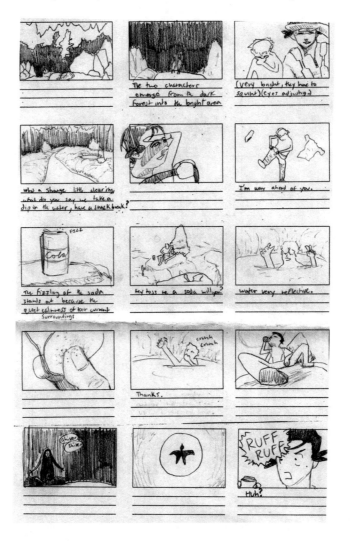

learner's needs and the environment. Thus, we should analyze cultural implications of our products from the perspective of the user, not only in the artist's frame of reference.

Interpreting and constructing visual representations such as diagrams can lead to better understanding of science concepts (Tippett, 2016). Presenting learning material through mental imagery supports both immediate and long-term recall as compared to studying material in a traditional, lecture-based method. In the ArtScience Program individuals of diverse cultures, educational backgrounds, interests, and professions communicate, transform, and share knowledge by learning to make and explore symbolic models through Metamorphing (Siler, 2012).

As it was declared in the Adobe Education White Paper (2011), digital storytelling has become an essential method of enhancing education by making abstract or conceptual content more understandable, in a way that is more engaging than plain text. Digital communication skills associated with digital storytelling have an impact on liberal arts, humanities, and cross-curricular humanities/technology collaborations. It may involve the illustration of story elements using photographs, graphics tools, and free and open source tools. Digital storytelling brings together any combination of visual art, motion (video and film), sound, graphics, and text, frequently written and read in nonlinear fashion, often with a specific point of view. "Increasingly, however, digital storytelling has evolved to include more complex forms of digital expression requiring video skills, such as micro-documentary production. In some cases, digital storytelling is dependent upon computer programming skills for application development and augmented reality" (Adobe Education White Paper, 2011, p.2). Digital storytelling as a cross-curricular technique provides structure for both sharing and understanding new information. Used in fields such as medicine, it helps to humanize the patient-physician experience.

Artistic quality of a website is often affected by unintended presence of a banner or a video with an advertisement, therefore a webpage developer should not only design a product but also make it fit for the environment as perceived by the user. The developer should be therefore trained interdisciplinary, ready for not only producing ready pictures but also making a cross-cultural impact, since the product delivery is often tested under particular technical or cultural conditions.

Digital Storytelling in Online Learning Environment

Traditional myths, legends, fairytales, folktales, parables, and fables found their place in the current multimedia storytelling techniques. Present-day story visualization technologies combine storytelling with multimedia formats such as text, images, sound, and movement with narratives, commentaries, and depictions in a dynamic, often interactive environment. Traditional and online classroom can be enhanced by digital storytelling. Using visual media for digital stories teachers may enliven and then capture their instruction, while students may present their work. Students become the co-creators of the art, and thus digital storytelling becomes a constructivist-learning tool of choice. Students may use for this purpose a variety of tools and apps such as Microsoft PowerPoint, Flickr, Movie Maker, digital photos and videos. Through digital stories they may address issues and challenges, enrich information, evoke responses, and emotionally involve other learners. Thus digital storytelling may serve for making news, as well as for creating the business-related, marketing, educational, and training applications.

Digital storytelling can be brought to the K-12 classroom with the use of the iPad devices, smart phones, and other mobile devices with audio and image capture capabilities. However, according to research (Ostashewski, & Reid, 2012) these activities require a simple workflow for successful implementation. Digital stories used for learning can be shared online using the Web 2.0 tools that enable presenting online the dynamic user-generated content. In a quasi-experimental study (Wu, & Yang, 2009), instruction with the use of digital storytelling resulted in the improvement of students' critical thinking, problem solving, and academic achievement.

Visualization is helping to analyze huge resources of information such as libraries, email archives, applications running the World Wide Web, or things such as a blog, a wiki, a tweeter feed. Text representation goes on three levels: lexical (transformation of strings of characters into a sequence of tokens), syntactic (identifying and annotating each token's function), and semantic level, which extracts the meaning and relationships between pieces of knowledge derived from the structures identified at the syntactical level (Ward, Grinstein, & Keim, 2015). Users select the level of interaction and decide how they would like to access the content.

Digital storytelling can be considered an interactive active learning tool, along with a mind mapping or a figure analysis method. According to Johnstone and Selepeng (2001) chunking information facilitated by mind mapping helps in main idea selection and relation of ideas, reduces the amount of information for processing, and increases the capacity of the working memory, which creates more space for critical thinking. Consistently with the mental model approach, Leopold & Leutner (2012) demonstrated positive effects of the drawing strategy instruction in contrast with the text-focused strategy instruction. According to Wiles (2016), the fact that visual literacy is often overlooked in undergraduate science education may create a challenge while incorporating active learning techniques into advanced courses such as molecular biology. An active learning technique called figure analysis helps interpret visual information through analysis, criticism, and discussion (Wiles, 2016). In the spirit of active learning Wilson, Copeland-Solas, & Guthrie-Dixon (2016), applied a mind mapping technique (Buzan, 1976; Davies, 2011) to organize information visually.

Visual projects interpret parts crafted in other media. Picture books, theatre, television, and movies extract abstract information of the story (that may refer to fiction or nonfiction) into concrete visual scenes to enhance experience and evoke emotions. There is a National Storytelling network with a web page www.storynet.org dedicated to advancing the art of storytelling. There are also many websites and online projects presenting digital storytelling environment. The Center for Digital Storytelling is an international organization for training and research assists youth and adults in using digital media tools to craft, record, and share stories in ways that enable learning, build community, and inspire justice. For example, Colorado universities are working with this Center to deliver a graduate-level Digital Storytelling Certificate Program.

Photography as a Teaching and Learning Tool

Visual tools such as photographs have a strong impact on our mental activity, memory, and our emotional reactions to the learning content. The art and science of photography support observation of the objects' features and details. Research that relates to memory function and brain development showed that people's memories of images are far stronger than their verbal memories (Wirth, 2008; Wirth & Perkins, 2008). A visual approach to learning contains cognitive and emotional scopes with respect to the reception and the mien of visual connection (Pantaleo, 2015). With the visual approach to educational technology, a teacher delivers and explains knowledge to students using instructional photography. As visual teaching tool photography allows the analyzing, creating, and estimating, which leads to an increase in critical thinking. Photography serves as means of communication, thus improving the educational setting and the instructors' teaching style. Photography enables teachers to increase student understanding and clarify the difference between the reality and the imagination. Photographs support visual literacy and present events from the previous days throughout history (Buhamad, 2016). Visuals recommended by educators include large-scale maps, pictures, and models (Park, 2004; Park & Hannafin, 1993). The use of photographs in education serves to exemplify and clarify difficult procedures and study field data in detail (McKenzie, Mims, & Ozkan, 2010). Visuals and drawings made by the students help them build the essential knowledge and disregard non-essentials (Park, 2004).

The use of images has been an important component in instructional technology. Instructional photography allows students to interact by responding to the learning environment; it is measured as a student learning style. It includes the capability to read and understand media, to be able to produce data and images through digital manipulation, and to assess and apply new information expanded from digital environments. During the first 20 years of the 20th century teachers set out a list of skills and qualities considered necessary for success in teaching. The appendix in the report of the *Reorganization of Science in Secondary Schools (*National Education Association, 1920) stressed a need to focus on visual education such as drawings, sketches, and charts as well as the use of bench and machine tools "computers." The production of photographs and light slides is another qualification of great value for all teachers (National Education Association, 1920). Today, photos play an important role in journalism. Starting in the late 19th century, newspaper and magazine stories depended on photographs as a fast way to transport information. Journalists worked with sense of sight to meet their needs and grab the audiences' attention. The use of photos expanded in the mid-20th century, especially in television, online journalism, and in the news (Sterling, 2009). According to Baker (2013), the Pew survey showed that about 83% of individuals snap photos on their cell phones and upload huge numbers of photos onto their several websites.

Instructional photography should fulfill several essential requirements. It must be able to change the students' beliefs, not just narrate the lesson (Buhamad, 2016). Teachers need to present the education material in a way that ensures that it is stored in long-term memory (Moreno & Mayer, 1999).). Photos made for an educational setting should appear as works of art with the right colors and balance. Strong colors for the main elements may represent the importance of those elements thus engaging the learners. Instructional photo should be a good representation of the learner's environment, tie contents of the lesson with things that exist in their lives such as their school, home, and daily life, in order to motivate the learner and speed up the transition of knowledge. Instructional photo should speak to learner's mind and imagination, be connected to the lesson, and be relatable to the learners` culture and background. Photos must have a specific purpose, address viewers' backgrounds and their own prior experiences in order to provide the required knowledge (Holm, 2008). A strong instructional photo meets the students` natural curiosity, provides engaging elements to increase their interest in the content, which should be accurate and current. The instructional photos should also be a documentary photo that shows the students a certain reality, reflects the truth in their eyes and minds. It should confirm that the photo content actually exists. Some instructors prefer using photos that have emotional meaning because that has a powerful impact on the viewer's perspective (Buhamad, 2016).

Addressing the Needs of a Storyteller

Apart from learning how to deliver a story in a selected medium (using software or a code), you may also want to think about making a new addition to your portfolio and enhancing your résumé. You may want to visually program a set of 3D images, and then create your own story, and a storyline for animation, followed by animations. They will later on be added to the database for comparing codes and discussing them, and for critiques of the projects. You may also want to consider the current methods and techniques of hiring used by companies. All this calls for thinking about the outcome of visual solutions, the use of shortcuts, and securing the fun element. For example, if you feel tired of coding still having a good idea about the whole project, you can send parts of your project (or separate codes) to one of the video editing software platforms. They may be sent as a movie file or as still images. They would be stitched together in a video editing program (after finding online the video resources for free or paid video edited programs).

To prepare a quality portfolio, include (under a password) an item you are proud of it into your visual, still growing gallery. If you put your files on a shared school gallery, in addition to the convenient view of other solutions of projects you will have occasion to discuss them, get an advice from fellow students, and provide them with a positive feedback. When your quality portfolio comprises art products, projects may be designed as digital collages that mix programming with software for creating visual products.

Projects may be color coded or designed as grayscale (black-and-white) digital images where the value of each pixel, varying from black to white carries intensity information (Johnson, 2006).

Learning Project: Horse Gaits – Horse Steps in 3D

This project presents various ways in which horses can move. After gathering information about this theme you will create several steps that are needed for creating animation, film, or a web project. The task will consist of creating a storyline and then a storyboard for an animated project about the horse gaits.

The first task involves gathering the data. Examine various steps used by horses. Look at the photographs of horses and then create an outline for each horse. Later on, you will add points and lines to that outline to add the third dimension to your horse. You might want to Google some images created by Eadweard Muybridge for your artistic inspiration.

Familiarize yourself with basic horse gaits (Harris, 1994):

- The four-beat walk (about 4.0 mph, 6.4 km per hour);
- The two-beat trot or jog (8.1 to 11.8 mph, 13 to 19 km per hour);
- The three-beat canter or lope (12 to 15 mph, 19 to 24 km per hour).
- The gallop averages 25 to 40 mph, 40 to 48 km per hour.

A horse moving on the ground leaves impressions of its hoofs. Show horseshoe impressions of your galloping horse using a bird's eye view of these horseshoe prints. After drawing sketches write a program that generates an outcome of a visual presentation of horseshoe impressions made by a galloping horse, and then change this program to show other basic gaits of the horse that walks, trots or jogs, canters (between a trot and a gallop), and finally of a galloping horse's horseshoe impressions.

Then, change the bird's eye view into the orthographic projection of a galloping horse, where this animal is depicted with the use of parallel lines that project its shape on to a plane. You would see a three-dimensional horse on a two-dimensional plane (a side view). Draw a set of sketches of a horse, first when it walks, and then when it trots or jogs, canters, and finally make a sketch presenting your horse when galloping. These should be quick sketches, so do not bother whether you have enough drawing skills. You may also want to write a code for this task. For this purpose, use a three-dimensional wireframe model of the horse with x, y, and z coordinates, with a 0 originating in a lower left corner. If your system has other screen origin, write a program that would transfer the 0.0.0. into that corner. You may want to translate this program into another computer language.

Applying a Storytelling About Horse Steps to Animation

Now it's time to convert images of horses and their horseshoe impressions into an interesting story that would serve for creating the animated footage about a particular horse. Begin your storytelling by creating your storyline. Invent a story involving your horse and other characters. Describe your characters – it maybe not only a horse but also its owner and other characters, a person, animals, and other living beings. Invent a possible conflict, or an obstacle, and then find a dynamic solution leading to an ending. Create a situation when your horse (your main character) has to change its gait for some reason you will explain to the viewer, or when four horses have to go simultaneously, but for some reason using different gaits. Imagine how the horseshoe impressions may appear on the ground, and why they become an important source of information about what happened to your horse. What would be a moral of this story? Combine four-horse animation showing various gaits into a storytelling-based animation. This can be done with any video-editing program.

You may decide what kind of a container you can assign to the same story by changing specific settings and styles. Decide how your story should be retold depending on the medium you choose. Your digital storytelling may combine several modes of presenting visual material such as a graphic, a comic strip or a comic book, an animated cartoon, manga, an animated film, a theater performance, VR, a game, a movie, a radio show, etc. After choosing a container of your story you will define how the story will be delivered in the selected medium. It may require designing another setting. Who would be your audience?

After writing this short story you may rework it by assigning another visual container to your story for creating illustrations or animations. Perhaps you may decide your story would not be linear – it may shift or travel in time, flash forward or backward, change the point of view or even the narrating person, or it may have more than one outcome. For example, you may choose quite another approach to the theme by introducing an ant. For example, an ant might become annoyed because of the horseshoe impressions in the ground. Imagine how the horseshoe impressions may act as a part of the ground. Horses make big holes according to her perspective (there is a possible conflict). After a rainfall the holes are filled with water, so the ant could drink water, unless it wouldn't fall and drown in water (so there may be a solution or another possible conflict). Show a point of view and perspective of the horse and of the ant. Change the viewpoint to show an ant's view. How an ant would see a horse? Then imagine how a bird would see a horse. A bird might be interested in horse's food. When chased away by the horse, it jumps up in fright and flies away. Invent a story making a small creature the main character and making the horse (or its owner) a source of possible conflict.

While working on your storyline you may decide to transform your sketches by changing the look of a mouth of the horse or of the ant. Create personality and emotional expressions for these characters. Then, equip them with meaningful features in a simplest, most concise way, and add some props. Remember to show their moods when you will change the circumstances you put them in. Show reactions of your invented characters to changes in habitat or the individually created environment.

Create a storyboard for your animation. Your drawing or sketches will serve as frames for your visual storytelling. Pick one template that meets your aesthetic and intellectual needs. Define your key frames, the starting and ending points of transitions, and the timing of each movement. Then fill the remaining frames with in betweens – the remaining sketches. After your storyboard is completed you can convert your project into animation or a short movie. This can be done with any video-editing program.

Creating and Editing Animation or a Movie

Now you may want to record the story and then edit it, caring for economy and amount of details, adding transitions, titles, and a credit for your work. Your drawing or sketches will serve as frames for your visual storytelling. In video technology a frame is a coded image. If you would like to create animation, you will also define your key frames, which will present starting and ending points of transitions, the timing of the movement. The remaining frames will be filled as inbetweens. Pick a template that meets your aesthetic and intellectual needs. Insert your sketches of major key frames, and then insert your frames. Write captions under every change that will explain each dynamic action. All pictures or sentences created by others must be credited, or provide a Creative Commons license information.

It is time to check if the voice is audible; if you add music it should match the story line. Finally, you may want to save a story on a flash drive, post it on your website or on social network (Center for Digital Storytelling Cookbook, 2010), or you may still want to burn it to CD, or a DVD.

Interactive Movies

A movie's scenes can be controlled depending on individual users, with different responses in the form of specific scenes. If the user clicks a button, the movie plays a certain scene; if this user clicks another button it plays a different scene, but scenes are selected according to individual viewers. The cardinal directions (the four main points of the compass: north, south, east, and west) presented with the use of temperature and color may serve in a button-controlled animation where a text may be supported with images or animations depending on the use of a selected button. Maybe you would consider designing a virtual remote control with the use of Processing and Arduino.

CONCLUSION

Storytelling refers both to the archived oral tradition in storytelling in different cultures, times, and places, and to the digital storytelling using a variety of media formats not possible for various interfaces. A story needs to be told differently for each medium. Crafting a story is a challenging task because a story should be engaging both intellectually and visually. Story visualization technologies combine storytelling with multimedia formats. Storytelling Studies became an interdisciplinary field or a discipline unto itself. Visual-verbal and sound-based projects may take form of interactive collaboration and may often become narrative visualizations.

REFERENCES

27 ways to tell a story in VR. (2018). Retrieved from http://alookintolater.blogspot.com/2018/05/27-ways-to-tell-story-in-vr.html

Adobe Education White Paper. (2011). *Adobe Systems Incorporated*. Retrieved from https://www.adobe.com/content/dam/Adobe/en/education/pdfs/strategies-for-digital-communication-skills-across-disciplines-june-2011.pdf

Alexander, B. (2011). *The New Digital Storytelling: Creating Narratives with New Media*. Praeger.

Alexander, B., & Levine, A. (2008). *Web 2.0 Storytelling: Emergence of a New Genre*. Retrieved from http://www.educause.edu/EDUCAUSE+Review/EDUCAUSEReviewMagazineVolume43/Web20StorytellingEmergenceofaN/163262

Baker, F. W. (2013). Teaching media literacy with technology. *Learning and Leading with Technology*, *40*(7), 32.

Bloop Animation Studios. 2017). *How to Make an Animatic (Making an Animated Movie)*. Retrieved from https://www.bloopanimation.com/animatic/

Buhamad, A. (2016). *Visual Approach and Design: the Appropriate Characteristics of Instructional Photos as a Tool to Support Elementary Setting in Kuwait.* Doctoral Dissertations, Paper 323. Retrieved April 25, 2017, from http://digscholarship.unco.edu/dissertations/

Buzan, T. (1976). *Use both sides of your brain.* New York: E. P. Dutton & Co.

Caputo, A. C., Ellison, H., & Steranko, J. (2011). *Visual Storytelling.* Watson-Guptill/Random House.

Create your storyboard in Microsoft Word. (2017). Retrieved from http://digitalstorytelling.coe.uh.edu/pdfs/How-to-Create-Storyboard.pdf

Davies, M. (2011). Concept mapping, mind mapping and argument mapping: What are the differences and do they matter? *Higher Education, 62*(3), 279–301. doi:10.100710734-010-9387-6

Download a storyboard template as PDF. (2018). Retrieved from http://digitalstorytelling.coe.uh.edu/storyboard-templates/PDF-storyboard.pdf

Educational Uses of Digital Storytelling. (2017). Retrieved from (http://digitalstorytelling.coe.uh.edu/page.cfm?id=23&cid=23&sublinkid=37

Essley, R., Rief, L., & Rocci, A. l. (2017). Visual Tools for Differentiating Reading & Writing Instruction. Strategies to Help Students Make Abstract Ideas Concrete & Accessible. *Scholastic.*

Hensel, J. (2010). Once Upon a Time. *Meeting Professionals International.* Retrieved from http://www.mpiweb.org/Magazine/Archive/US/February2010/OnceUponATime

Holm, G. (2008). Photography as a performance. *Forum Qualitative Social Research, 9*(2), 38. Retrieved from http://www.qualitative-research.net/index.php/fqs/article/viewArticle/394/856

Jackson, S. (1981/2018). *Killer: The Game of Assassination.* Retrieved from http://www.sjgames.com/killer/

Jenkins, H. (2011). Transmedia 202: Further Reflections. *The Official Weblog of Henry Jenkins.* Retrieved from http://henryjenkins.org/blog/2011/08/defining_transmedia_further_re.html

Johnson, S. (2006). *Stephen Johnson on Digital Photography.* O'Reilly.

Johnstone, A. H., & Selepeng, D. (2001). A language problem revisited. *Chemistry Education: Research and Practice in Europe, 2*(1), 19–29.

Knödel, S., Hachet, M., & Guitton, P. (2009). Interactive Generation and Modification of Cutaway Illustrations for Polygonal Models. In *Proceedings of the 10th International Symposium on Smart Graphics* (pp. 140-151). Berlin: Springer-Verlag. 10.1007/978-3-642-02115-2_12

Leopold, C., & Leutner, D. (2012). Science text comprehension: Drawing, main idea selection, and summarizing as learning strategies. *Learning and Instruction, 22*(1), 16–26. doi:10.1016/j.learninstruc.2011.05.005

McCloud, S. (2006). *Making Comics: Storytelling Secrets of Comics, Manga and Graphic Novels*. William Morrow Paperbacks.

McKenzie, B., Mims, N., & Ozkan, B. (2010). Identifying the characteristics of photo bloggers: An exploratory study. In D. Gibson, & B. Dodge (Eds.), *Proceedings of Society for Information Technology and Teacher Education International Conference 2010* (pp. 1539-1545). Chesapeake, VA: Association for the Advancement of Computing in Education (AACE).

Moreno, R., & Mayer, R. E. (1999). Cognitive principles of multimedia learning: The role of modality and contiguity. *Journal of Educational Psychology, 91*(2), 358–368. doi:10.1037/0022-0663.91.2.358

National Education Association (NEA). (1920). *Reorganization of science in secondary schools: A report of the commission on the reorganization of secondary education (U.S. Bureau of Education, Bulletin No. 26)*. Washington, DC: U.S. Government Printing Office.

Ohler, J. (2012a). *Digital Storytelling Storyboard Templates*. Retrieved from http://www.jasonohler.com/pdfs/digitalStorytellingStoryBoard-adv.pdf

Ostashewski, N., & Reid, D. (2012). Digital Storytelling on the iPad: apps, activities, and processes for successful 21st century story creations. In T. Amiel & B. Wilson (Eds.), *Proceedings of EdMedia: World Conference on Educational Media and Technology 2012* (pp. 1823-1827). Association for the Advancement of Computing in Education (AACE).

Pantaleo, S. (2015). Language, literacy, and visual texts. *English in Education, 49*(2), 113–129. doi:10.1111/eie.12053

Park, I., & Hannafin, M. (1993). Empirically based guidelines for the design of interactive multimedia. *Educational Technology Research and Development, 41*(3), 65–85. doi:10.1007/BF02297358

Park, J. (2004). The value of images in science instruction. In R. Ferdig, C. Crawford, R. Carlsen, N. Davis, J. Price, R. Weber, & D. Willis (Eds.), *Proceedings of Society for Information Technology and Teacher Education International Conference 2004* (pp. 4591-4594). Chesapeake, VA: Association for the Advancement of Computing in Education (AACE).

Perrault, C. (2012). *The Fairy Tales Of Charles Perrault*. CreateSpace Independent Publishing Platform.

Processing. (2018). Retrieved from https://processing.org/ https://processing.org/download

Ricou, J., & Pollock, J. A. (2012). The Tree, the Spiral and the Web of Life: A Visual Exploration of Biological Evolution for Public Murals. *Leonardo, 45*(1), 18-25.

Siler, T. (2012). The ArtScience Program for Realizing Human Potential. *Leonardo, 44*(5), 417–424. doi:10.1162/LEON_a_00242

Sterling, C. H. (2009). Encyclopedia of Journalism. SAGE Publications, Inc. doi:10.4135/9781412972048

Storyboard. (2017). Retrieved from http://www.wikihow.com/Create-a-Storyboard

Storyboarding. (2016). UC Berkeley, Advance Media Institute. Retrieved March 26, 2017, from https://multimedia.journalism.berkeley.edu/tutorials/starttofinish-storyboarding/#sf_form_salesforce_w2l_lead_7_sidebar

Storycenter. (2018). Retrieved from https://www.storycenter.org/

Tippett, C. D. (2016). What recent research on diagrams suggests about learning *with* rather than learning *from* visual representations in science. *International Journal of Science Education*, *38*(5), 725–746. doi:10.1080/09500693.2016.1158435

Video. (2013). *Video: An Insider Look at Storyboarding with the Coen Brothers' Storyboard Artist.* Retrieved March 27, 2017, from http://nofilmschool.com/2013/08/storyboarding-with-coen-brothers-storyboard-artist

Ward, M. O., Grinstein, G., & Keim, D. (2015). Interactive Data Visualization: Foundations, Techniques, and Applications (2nd ed.). A. K. Peters/CRC Press.

Wiles, A. M. (2016). Figure analysis: A teaching technique to promote visual literacy and active Learning. *Biochemistry and Molecular Biology Education*, *44*(4), 336–344. doi:10.1002/bmb.20953 PMID:26891952

Wilson, K., Copeland-Solas, E., & Guthrie-Dixon, N. (2016). A Preliminary Study on the use of Mind Mapping as a Visual Learning Strategy in General Education Science classes for Arabic speakers in the United Arab Emirates. *The Journal of Scholarship of Teaching and Learning*, *16*(1), 31–52. doi:10.14434/josotl.v16i1.19181

Wirth, K. R. (2008). *Learning About Thinking and Thinking About Learning: Metacognitive Knowledge and Skills for Intentional Learners.* Retrieved April 25, 2017, from http://serc.carleton.edu/NAGTWorkshops/metacognition/workshop08/participants/wirth.html

Wirth, K. R., & Perkins, D. (2008). *Learning to learn.* Retrieved April 25, 2017, from https://www.macalester.edu/academics/geology/wirth/learning.pdf

Wu, W. C., & Yang, Y. T. C. (2009). Using a Multimedia Storytelling to Improve Students' Learning Performance. In G. Siemens & C. Fulford (Eds.), *Proceedings of EdMedia: World Conference on Educational Media and Technology 2009* (pp. 3159-3166). Association for the Advancement of Computing in Education (AACE).

Zeng, X., Mehdi, Q. H., & Gough, N. E. (2003). Shape the Story: Story Visualization Techniques. *Proceedings of the 7th International Conference on Information Visualization*, 144-149. 10.1109/IV.2003.1217971

ADDITIONAL READING

Boden, M. A. (2010). *Creativity and Art: Three Roads to Surprise.* Oxford, UK: Oxford University Press.

Boden, M. A. (2016). *AI: Its nature and future.* Oxford, UK: Oxford University Press.

Borges, J. L. (with Guerrero, M.) (2006). The Book of Imaginary Beings. Translated by A. Hurley. Westminster, UK: Penguin Books. ISBN 978-0-14-303993-8.

Christian, B., & Griffiths, T. (2016). *Algorithms to Live By: The Computer Science of Human Decisions.* New York: Henry Holt and Company.

Damasio, A. (2010). Self Comes to Mind. New York, New York: Pantheon. Reprint: Vintage. ISBN 030747495X.

Editors of Phaidon (Author). (2012). *The Art Book*. London, UK: Phaidon Press.

Hanson, R. (2016). *The Age of EM: Work, Love, and Life when Robots Rule the Earth*. Oxford, UK: Oxford University Press.

Lima, M. (2011). Visual Complexity: Mapping Patterns of Information. New York: Princeton Architectural Press. ISBN 978 1 56898 936 5.

Lima, M. (2014). *The Book of Trees: Visualizing the Branches of Knowledge*. New York: Princeton Architectural Press.

Tufte, E. R. (2001). *The Visual Display of Quantitative Information* (2nd ed.). Cheshire, CT: Graphics Press. (Original work published 1983)

Tufte, E. R. (2005). *Envisioning Information*. Cheshire, CT: Graphics Press. Third printing with revision. (Original work published 1992)

Yau, N. (2011). *Visualize this: The flowing data guide to design visualization and statistics*. Hoboken, NJ: Wiley.

Yau, N. (2013). *Data Points: Visualization That Means Something*. Hoboken, NJ: Wiley.

KEY TERMS AND DEFINITIONS

Animatic: A simplified mock-up, a series of still images as an initial version of animation, video, or film containing successive sections of a storyboard and a soundtrack with rough dialogues. Storyboards and animatics allow pre-visualizing a project to get an insight about how the motion, soundtrack, and timing will work together before beginning the production.

Avatar: A representation of a person (a user) or a character created by this person in a form of a figure or an icon, used in video games, motion pictures, online forums, virtual reality, etc.

Horse Steps: The four-beat walk (about 4.0 mph, 6.4 km per hour); the two-beat trot or jog (8.1 to 11.8 mph, 13 to 19 km per hour); the three-beat canter or lope (12 to 15 mph, 19 to 24 km per hour); the gallop averages 25 to 40 mph, 40 to 48 km per hour (Harris, 1994). Basic horse steps are natural; they do not require any special training.

Icon: Icon represents a thing or refers to something by resembling or imitating it; thus, a picture, a photograph, a mathematical expression, or an old-style telephone may be regarded as iconic objects. Thus, an iconic object has some qualities common with things it represents, by looking, sounding, feeling, tasting, or smelling alike.

Motion Graphics: A sequence of abstract or thematic electronic images – parts of a film, animation, a multimedia project, or a trademark, supported by fragments of soundtrack; motion graphics provide illusion of motion or rotation but usually do not tell a story.

Pictograph: A symbolic image representing a word or a sentence wide used in ancient cultures such as in Egypt, Mesopotamia, or Indian pictographs and petroglyphs. Also, a pictorial representation (an icon, a symbol, or a picture) presented on a computer screen, or a chart, showing the value of the data or comparing the sets of the data; pictographs are used to replace or enhance graphs that present the data as lines, curves, or bars.

Chapter 5
How We Hear and Experience Classical, Computer, and Virtual Music

Robert C. Ehle
University of Northern Colorado, USA

ABSTRACT

This chapter examines occurrences and events associated with the experience of composing, playing, or listening to music. Discussion of popular music and computer music begins the chapter, including issues pertaining the tuning systems, digital interfaces, and software for music. It then recounts an experiment on the nature of pitch and psychoacoustics of resultant tones.

INTRODUCTION

It is typical of us to assume that when we perceive things with our senses, we just take in things as they are, and we understand them using their nature as a basis. We just perceive things as they are and then we work with them, and lead our lives with them. The problem with this concept is that the nature of the things we perceive never reaches our brains. Our senses convert incoming sensations into neural impulses and then the neural impulses carry information about the world to our brains. There are various codes that stand for the characteristics of things, and the neurons are set up to detect things and then send information to our brains by means of these various codes. Neural impulses that travel up to our brains resemble the pulses that travel around in computers. They are not the same, however, because they are not digital in the sense that they do not code for numbers. They code for various things: edges, shapes, colors, pitch, loudness, saltiness, etc.

Learning before birth and also immediately after birth is traditionally called Imprinting, to distinguish it from the intellectual type of learning that will take place years later. Imprinting has been extensively studied in animals and birds and has been extensively documented. Konrad Lorenz (1937), probably the best-known researcher on imprinting, defined imprinting in his classic studies on graylag geese and other animals as the rapid learning occurring in early stales of life. Obviously, animals, and humans too,

DOI: 10.4018/978-1-5225-7371-5.ch005

are capable of learning some things around the time of birth and before. This type of learning is usually said to be subcortical because it takes place in lower parts of the brain than the cerebral cortex, which is rather undeveloped at this stage of life.

This chapter tells about the ways we experience music, how our brain perceives pitch, and discusses the role of its early development in the perinatal period.

CREATING POPULAR MUSIC WITH COMPUTERS

The new generation of popular music (that teenagers listen to) is not guitar-based, as young people no longer desire to play guitar. The new popular music features a young generation of singers, but the accompaniments is created in recording studios with keyboards, workstations, and various types of MIDI controllers capable of producing a wide variety of electronic sounds. All of these devices are, in fact, computers. Thus, the music they are creating is computer music. Figure 1 presents a studio comprising old and new music technologies.

Computer music has been around for 50 years but the popular musicians have generally resisted it. Possibly, the change at this time has to do with intonation – the general pervasive adoption of equal temperament tuning. The change seems to have been initiated by the extensive use of auto-tune software that made it possible to correct the intonation of singers or instruments. Such software made it possible for all vocal and instrumental intonation to be corrected to precise equal temperament, something that can only be accomplished with computers.

Figure 1. The author's studio with a collection of hardware, software, and interfaces for creating music (2015, © A. Ursyn. Used with permission)

This series of events is totally unexpected, remarkable, and surprising. It is a generational shift comparable to the rock and roll revolution of the '60s. But so far it seems to have largely gone unnoticed by the writers and commentators on popular music, probably because they all focus on the singers and ignore the backup musicians. Attempting to explain why and how it happened will require a considerable amount of studying history and music theory. Some beginnings of this work are provided below.

The New Pop Music

By pop music, of course, I do not mean any style or genre but simply the music that a particular generation likes to listen to and listens to continually. It should be stressed that there is a particular generation involved here: most people under 25; the older generations are often not involved and probably not interested what is going on. How does this music get recorded? I'm not sure, but my guess is that the singers write their songs and then sing them for local people. Someone says, "You should record that," so they go to a recording studio and record it. Then the musicians affiliated with a particular studio proceed to construct computer orchestrations around the song.

It is interesting to note a couple of things:

1. The accompaniment is probably not performed at the same time as the singer,
2. The final arrangement has probably never been performed live,
3. The resultant arrangement cannot be performed live as it sounds,
4. The final orchestration will probably be played in a concert (with the singer deleted) but the singer can sing along with it,
5. The stigma attached to "tracking" in live performance seems not to apply in this case,
6. The resulting recording will probably be presented in a theatrical type of situation showing the singer(s) acting out numerous routines (like MTV),
7. The final result is the product of much work done in the computer/music studio.

This new pop music is probably the first pop music in several generations that is not band-based. The computer musicians who provide the backing tracks are not a part of a band, group or ensemble. They are truly anonymous and do not receive label credits. Typically, they are recording studio personnel who knew enough about both music and technology to be able to offer to enhance a recording. This new pop music probably comes out of "The Voice," or "America's Got Talent" traditions, where the singer is the only important person. It is only by listening to the recordings that you can tell that the accompaniments are computer music. This is never acknowledged. The thing you hear, though, is that there are usually no rock guitars in the mix. Often there will be a piano sound, but it is obviously a computerized piano sound because of the effects that are a part of the sound. These are usually space-enhancing effects that defy simple characterization. They may involve resonance peaking effects that swell on each note or chord or that swirl around. There may be ambient space effects added, too, of the sort that have become common in computer music. There are probably no analog electronic instruments being used simply because of the need for perfect equal temperament, something that was never possible with analog synthesizers. The decision to apply auto tune to the singer is probably made in the studio as well, at least if a producer becomes involved. It remains surprising how intolerant of pitch errors this new type of music has become.

Precise Intonation of Computer Notes Encoded in Numerical Form vs. Limitations in Producing Pure Intonation of Analog Musical Instruments

The growing attractiveness of modern computer music may result from the fact that digital instruments will always produce a precise intonation every time, probably with a degree of precision way beyond that of analog instruments. This precise intonation is alluring to listeners, sneaks up on them and captivates them, so that they find themselves going back to it without knowing exactly why.

Computer music offers a new and totally different approach to intonation than those offered by all the music instruments of the past. In the past all musical instruments were analog, meaning that the pitches produced were analogous to some physical dimension of the instrument: length, width, density of materials, etc. Computer musical instruments, on the other hand, are digital, meaning that the notes are encoded in numerical form and are produced by mathematical calculations. The computer will calculate the wave shape desired, and produce it in a string of samples at exactly the rate needed to produce the pitch desired. Thus, digital instruments never have to be tuned, whereas analog instruments were tuned by the player, by a specialized tuner, at the factory, or perhaps by all three. There have been hundreds of tuning systems proposed and used over the centuries, gradually replaced by another system after several generations. Maybe, hearing a tuning system as infants, people created templates in their brains and have been conditioned to like it.

While I do not intend to review the entire history of intonation theory, I wish to point out that the guitar is tuned in an approximate equal temperament. Thus, a prolonged exposure to guitar-based music reinforces a liking for equal temperament. Other musical instrument families, famously, do not use equal temperament. The bowed string instrument family (violins, violas, cellos and string bases) is usually played in what is called a Pythagorean tuning system where notes are played high or low based on their resolution. Since this family of instruments has no frets (raised elements), the players are free to choose their own tunings. Tuning sharp or flat, in the direction of resolution is said to enhance the expressiveness of this style of playing. Guitarists and players of other fretted string instruments (banjo, mandolin, dobro, etc.) do not have this option, and they are largely locked in to approximate equal temperament by their frets. Thus, several generations of pop music listeners have been conditioned to like equal temperament.

Fretted string instruments approximate equal temperament but there are always little factors with the frets that keep the intonation from being pure. The fact that the same set of frets must be used on all of the strings is one of these. Another is the fact that all strings have a degree of stiffness that tends to make them go sharp on their high notes. Computer music has none of these limitations.

The family of brass instruments (trumpet, trombone, horn and tuba) is usually said to use the tuning system called Just, a system that draws its intervals from the harmonic series. These intervals are the smoothest tunings, and brass instruments, belonging to the loudest family, benefit most from smooth sounding intervals. Computer music largely overcomes this limitation because electronically produced music is compressed. The louds are less loud and the softs less soft, so these effects are reduced greatly.

The pop music of the first half of the 20th century employed lots of orchestral instruments; jazz, too, employed lots of wind instruments. With the advent of rock and roll and subsequently rock, only the guitar and the guitar bass were widely used, making equal temperament pervasive, if imperfect. Now, computers have perfected it. Anyone wondering why other families of instruments almost never made their way into the rock music, can now see that intonation is the reason. The other families of instruments just don't play the same notes as electric guitars.

The things that an infant experiences, usually from the mother, are imprinted and create templates in the brain that last a lifetime and are able to trigger the release of neurotransmitters that provide pleasure (or pain, as the case may be). In this way the mother is able to have extended control over the infant's behavior, which is adaptive and beneficial. It also explains why any culture can be transmitted across multiple generations, and why members of any generation tend to have similar tastes.

In this case, it is a liking for pure equal temperament that has been learned and imprinted. It is interesting to note that musical intervals, even subtle variations in musical intervals, can be carried across generations. In the history of intonation there are many instances where this sort of thing happened.

The Medieval period tended to use Pythagorean tuning with its good fifths and fourths. In the Renaissance the Just diatonic scale with pure triads was used for harpsichord tuning, yet hold outs continued to use Pythagorean tuning for wind instruments, and choirs probably sang Just intervals when they sang unaccompanied, just as they do today.

The Baroque period adopted a type of tuning known as Meantone. Then in the Romantic period, composers such as Wagner wanted universal modulation and so started using equal temperament. There was a lot of resistance, as the sounds of the 3rds and 6ths is not nearly as consonant in equal temperament than it is in Meantone tuning.

The type of pure equal temperament that we like today is actually impossible to produce except with computers. Even the best achievable equal temperament put on the analog instruments of music history is only approximate and will have deviations that are obviously audible. The semitone of equal temperament in ratio form is the twelfth root of two to one and in decimal form produces an irrational number: 1.05946...to 1, with digits extending into infinity. A computer can handle this type of math. On an analog instrument, it is done by ear, producing an approximation that is never perfect.

A piano tuner learns systems for producing these approximations. One of the best tuners I have met used a machine, their way of saying they have a tone generator that produces the notes of equal temperament; then the tuner matches the machine on the piano by ear. Thus, it is actually computer music that provides the standard.

Psychoacoustics of Tuning Systems

Many years ago I read a comment in an Electronic Musician Magazine that said, it was the unfortunate thing about computer music that was that it was all equal tempered. Apparently, the writer grew up in the era when orchestras used mixed tuning systems: the strings played in Pythagorean tuning, the woodwinds played in approximate equal temperament, and the brass played in a Just tuning system. For years, brass players in colleges have been taught how to play in the Just system, with the understanding that it enabled them to get greater power and impact. Having worked with brass sections over the years I can attest that beats are particularly annoying when produced by loud brass sections, and clean Just intonation is very effective. Of course, this is true for live performances in concert halls where there might be at least an 80-decibel dynamic range (30-110) at the front seats and on stage. Computer music, on the other had, must come from loudspeakers, which means there is ample opportunity to compress the dynamics.

Over several generations, people might adjust, and today people are more accepting the total and pure equal temperament of the sort produced by computer music. In addition, in pop music, the singer or singers are the lead parts, and all the rest have to be placed under them dynamically. Beats are not the problem when they are in concert hall performances on acoustical brass instruments.

DIGITAL INTERFACES AND SOFTWARE FOR MUSIC

Musical Instrument Digital Interface: MIDI

MIDI – Musical Instrument Digital Interface is a standard used to bring musical instruments, computers, software, and hardware together into a functioning whole. It enables traditional analog musicians to make computer music. It is the force that is powering the new computer pop music revolution. Essentially, no matter what musical instrument you happen to have spent years learning to play, there is a MIDI controller that will take your musical performance and turn it into digital code that can be saved in a computer program and used to make all sorts of electronic sounds. In actuality, it makes you a master of electronic music; that is, if you know how to hook it up and make it work. This is where the new recording studios come in. They have people who have mastered MIDI interface processing and they can turn your performance into computer tracks giving you access to the world of electronic sounds.

MIDI is available for pianos, pipe organs, guitars, woodwind instruments, brass instruments, drums and specialized devices that can attach to your toe shoes or your arms, and turn body movements into computer music. The sounds that can be used with MIDI include all the sounds made by synthesizers and also any sound from the world of sound. These sounds are captured by a process called sampling and then the samples can be transposed across the keyboard to give you the entire scale in any particular sound. Most of these sampled sounds have already been recorded and transposed and are available in the keyboards and workstations available at general stores like Walmart or music stores. Because most musicians have had some experience working with these common instruments, they have enough knowledge to be able to request certain sounds for their recordings. Thus a songwriter who sings her own songs will come in to a recording studio with the idea for a variety of sounds she wants to have behind her voice in her recording and the studio will have technically qualified personnel who can play the MIDI instruments, select the sounds and help the singer create the final recording.

MIDI can be used to synthesize an entire orchestra to a degree that an expert might not be able to tell the difference from a real orchestra. This is the area known as electronic orchestration. When you hear orchestral music behind the news shows on TV, there is a good chance they are computer orchestras and that no one actually performed those pieces but that they were made on a computer – in pure equal temperament. The NBC news theme is performed by a real orchestra. It was composed by John Williams and recorded in a Hollywood studio, but it the major exception.

Most of these themes are not new. MIDI has been around for 30 years, but having people who are qualified to integrate all parts of the process, from performing to composing, to wiring, programming, and recording is pretty new. It is my opinion that the change is being driven by the singers, who no longer want thrash guitars behind their vocals. The singer is generally the focus of a piece of pop music and the vocal track has been called the money track because it is what sells the recording. So the new computerized pop music movement is being driven by singer/songwriters and their managers.

Software for Music

There are very few pieces of software that will allow composing orchestral scores and parts for live performance. *Finale* is a deep program and one has to spend a lot of time learning to use it. Finale is very good music notation software that is basically Microsoft Word but for musicians: it allows you to write your own scores, and you can also record them when playing via a midi keyboard or controller. Overall it's a great program for not only teaching and learning, but for sharing as well. I did chamber music in Finale and I could not have had my successes without it.

When music is performed someone will use recording software to create sound files. Some use *Pro Tools* for this, but *Audacity* is a free program that does what I need. I have been using Audacity to make mp3 files of my recordings so that I can post them and so everyone can listen. Audacity is great program to use for sound editing and recording for example, from a microphone, but using it with a midi keyboard can be difficult when making sounds in *FL* and *Ableton*, and to transfer sounds from one program to the other. Like all free things there's a catch, but as far as free programs go Audacity is probably the best.

- **Ableton Live:** A program commonly used to record and edit audio through plug-ins similar to massive, groove machine (GMS) and *Sytrus*. I hear good things about Ableton live software. Unlike FL studios, Ableton live allows you to edit sounds in almost every way, and is far more complex than programs like FL studios. However, because of this it's user interface can be quite confusing to those who have never used an audio editing program. Another plus side though is that it supports all kinds of different midi keyboards, and launchpads. This means that more specialized midi controllers, as well as scratch tables are supported by this software.
- **FL Studios:** A program very similar to Ableton live, in fact they provide about the same amount of plug-ins. However, the difference between Ableton and FL studios includes the preset sounds that come with the application as well as the simple user interface. Those who are still fairly new and learning all the ins and outs would enjoy FL, as with FL's simple user interface they can easily figure out what needs to be done and where.
- **Digital Performer:** A program similar to Ableton live and FL studios, and it's the best of both worlds. The user interface is friendly like FL studios, and has Abletons complexity as well. Aside from the user interface and available mechanics, Digital performer seems to be your average plug in processor.
- **Absynth:** A plugin that can be used with programs such as FL studios and Ableton live. This plug in has many different osculators and is seen as a powerful synth creator capable of generating outstanding sounds. It also comes with 1,800 preset sounds as well as sound filters like *Aetherizer, Cloud Filter*, and *Supercomb*. The program seems awfully simple to use as well, and the cooler aspect is the program's ability to merge two sounds together smoothly.
- **Hydrogen:** A pretty straightforward drum machine. It's a free program with no catches, and works well with FL and Ableton. The cool thing about it though is the availability. Linux doesn't have many available plug-ins, let alone plug in processors, yet Hydrogen is available for all platforms. It works great on FL studios, and can produce a variety of nice sounding beats.
- **Kapling Strong**: A nice tool but the problem is in its availability and the fact that it's standalone. A PC user can't really use it; the standalone plug-ins may often cause trouble when trying to make music through plug in processors like Ableton. It makes hard to transfer work. With patience, it can be an effective tool and be great with modeling synthesizers. It does an average job, which is more than what most would expect from a free product.

What I think most people want, though, is what I might call improvisation software. Many people want to improvise on one or more instruments and create music soundtracks from that. They do not want to write down musical notes and do not want to do anything on paper. They need to record MIDI tracks and they need a lot of editing and processing options.

- **Max Software:** A music programming language for developing interactive multimedia. It is used for instance, as a music performance software.
- **Autotune Software:** Is used a lot, too. Even though it was originally intended to fix bad notes, people started to like the effect it produces and use it for that.

Experimental Music is another big category. This might be analog using analog synthesizers or a mix of the analog and digital gear. The whole idea is to do something new and different, so you can't be very specific about what will work. It often involves re-purposing everything you use.

SoundCloud is like the Pintrest of songs. Many artists use SoundCloud to showcase their music in the same way as visual experts or digital artists would use Pintrest. Anyone can post songs or sounds that they have created, making it a fair way to get recognized amongst listeners. One can also comment on a specific part of the song, letting the artist know whether you like it or not. Overall, SoundCloud is closer to a multi media website than a sound software, but is a useful tool none the less.

Sampla is another audio editing plug in, that is generally used for hip hop, but its applications extend beyond just that. The slice features can be useful in the many different genres of house, and other kinds of electronic music. It also comes with built in support for many of today's midi controllers and keyboards. Aside from having a small library of presets to choose from, Sampla makes up for it by adding additional LFO's and envelopes making sound creation simple and easy.

Iris/izotope is a very interesting plug because it introduces many new ways to edit synthesized sounds. The big difference Iris has from other programs is the accuracy it has with adjusting sounds. A good example would be the sonic sound selector in which you can select sounds in a way similar to the quick selection tool in Adobe Photoshop. The plug in also comes with 11 gigabytes of audio samples, which is absolutely outstanding, and is not common among plug-ins.

Karplus stray is not a program as much as it is the science behind synthesizers. Essentially a synth starts out as white noise, but after including a wide band signal like a sawtooth wave the excitation is output and fed back into a delay line. After the delay line makes an output it's then fed through a filter. The filters output is the mixed back into the output and delay line at the same time.

Copyright Issues and Marketing

The music industry has matured to the extent that most musicians understand that anything they create, songs, lyrics, pieces of instrumental music, dialog, etc., is automatically copyrighted at the moment of creation. This includes both paper creations and recordings. Visual artists and photographers understand, also, that a bundle of rights are available to them for their creations. When it comes to a piece of pop music, there may be six or more copyrights attached to any one piece. If a team of songwriters works together, each of them owns a share in the piece and the duration of the copyright is determined from the death date of the last surviving writer. The words, too, have copyrights and they can be diverse. If the words are a reworking of an old song there might be the original copyright plus the copyright pertaining to new material that has been added. Theatrical works have a separate copyright process.

Because of the complexity of the copyright process, big corporations that use music often make contracts with musicians, producers, agencies and agents to produce their own in house music stream. I was in my usual grocery store the other day when an announcement came on saying, "the music you are hearing was created by the In Store Music Service." In other words, the Kroger company had worked with a customer service to create the collection of Christmas Carol recordings that I had been hearing.

In addition to the copyright that attaches to any creation, there are separate performance rights, usually managed by performing rights organizations (ASCAP, BMI, SESAC, and others). Getting performance rights to songs can be complex, so there is an opportunity for songwriters to create custom songs for the large corporations.

These days, when a recording studio might include marketing services, the singer can have complete production service from digital computer music back-ups to recording, marketing, and legal protection, all under one roof. My gym (VASA) seems to have such a system at work and the standardized music tracks are distributed across the system of gym.

VIRTUAL MUSIC

Perhaps not everybody knows that in addition to the usual world of music that we study every day and teach in music theory classes, there is a second world of music, a virtual world. Like a reflection of a mountain range in a lake, the virtual world is generated from and depends upon the real world of music, yet it is separate, different, and affects us differently. It can be independently controlled and employed, too.

The world of virtual music is somewhat evident to us in acoustic phenomena. A composer and music theorist Georg Andreas Sorge, who was a fiend of Johann Sebastian Bach described first the psychoacoustic phenomenon of combination tones, which are perceived when two real tones are played at the same time. However, combination tones are usually ascribed to the famous 17th century violinist Giuseppe Tartini, and a manifestation of this phenomenon in difference tones have come to be called "Tartini Tones." The combined tones are usually called difference tones because their frequencies are the difference between two sounding notes.

As described by the Encyclopedia Britannica (2015), "Combination tones are heard when two pure tones (i.e., tones produced by simple harmonic sound waves having no overtones), differing in frequency by about 50 cycles per second or more, sound together at sufficient intensity." Two varieties of the combination tones are the difference tones whose frequencies result from the difference between the frequencies of real tones, and the sum tones whose frequencies can be found by adding the frequencies of two real tones. There has been some speculation about summation tones too but little confirming evidence. However, there is little confirming evidence about sum tones.

Periodicity pitches are the resultant tones that arise from the linear mixing of acoustic waves. They are phantom pitches in that they have no energy at their frequencies, but many writers claim that we can hear them, anyway. They are the result of additive and subtractive interference between pairs of sound waves. The equivalent in water waves may be seen when the wakes of two boats interact on the surface of a river. Where the wakes cross, new wave patterns will arise, relatively permanent and static.

Brass players and also didgeridoo players use difference tones to generate complex chords. They can play triads, even whole chorale chord progressions, or, in the case of the didgeridoo, the sounds of wild animals. The French 18th century composer Jean-Philippe Rameau used them to show the true roots of chords in inversion. Guitarists and other musicians use similar difference tones when they overdrive an amplifier producing distortion or when they leave out the root of a chord. Many players use beats, a difference tone phenomenon to play in tune.

Acoustical phenomena as listed above are some of the well-known parts of virtual music. The less known parts of this phenomenon relate to psychoacoustics, as they occurr in the inner ear and the brain. These events include virtual pitches (Terhardt, 1974), subjective tones (Lewis, & Larsen, 1927), missing fundamentals (Schnupp, Nelken, & King, 2011), Schouten's residue pitches (Schouten 1940; Schouten, Ritsma, & Cardozo, 1962), and others.

In the realm of the psychoacoustics, we have rootless voicings of jazz musicians. We also have quartal chords such as Aleksandr Nikolaevich Scriabin's *Mystic* chord, and Ferde Grofe's Painted Dessert music in the *Grand Canyon Suite* that seem to have virtual chord functions.

This entire arena has been somewhat known for centuries, but has been dismissed as the junk of music for most of that time. Recently though, experiments with the new medical technology machines (MRI, fMRI, PET, MGG, MEG, CAT, etc.) have implicated the presence of these phenomena in musical emotion. Showing that the amygdala, the brainstem, the cerebellum, and other lower parts of the brain light up in scans is an evidence of emotional response in the centers of emotion in the brain. The implication is that these parts of the brain are emitting neurotransmitters into the nervous system and thus changing states of feeling. Most of this takes place subliminally, subconsciously, and unknowingly to musicians.

Today, several European music theorists use the term Virtual Pitch for such phenomena, for example Ernst Terhard (1974) and Richard Parncutt (2011). Americans (John R. Pierce (1990), Max Mathews (Mathews, & Moore, 1970), John Backus (1969) seem to prefer the term Periodicity Pitch. I would suggest that there is a wide range of phenomena and experiences, some of which are acoustical and some psychoacoustical, yet the key component is the ability of these phenomena to modulate emotion. There is a deep emotional component in the music of some composers that results from these unwritten and unaccounted-for pitch phenomena, both acoustical and psychoacoustical.

The subjective emotional charges that some pitch collections and voicings are able to carry comes from primitive voice recognition functions in the brain. The brain has mechanisms for monitoring the moods of other people: major means calm, minor means sad or distraught, and dissonant (containing tritones and seconds) means angry. There is also a mechanism for memorizing people's voiceprints that we use every day on the telephone. We recognize people from their voices. This is similar to the mechanism that allows us to recognize musical instruments from their tone colors. The Pavlovian conditioning psychology can be referring to these identifications, so we experience a learned emotional response every time we hear certain voices or sounds.

Human beings or, earlier, quasi-human beings have existed on this planet for hundreds of thousands or even millions of years without metal tools, living in similar conditions as the ancient Native Americans, the Yannomamo of Brazil, or the tribes of central Borneo. They could not modify their environment very much but had to learn to live within it. The sense of vision might be dominant, so they would deal with the things they saw, but the auditory sense was supportive, doing what is called auditory scene analysis Bregman, 1990). These people would be constantly analyzing their environment with the auditory sense looking for threats or opportunities. Thus, the auditory sense would become finely honed. Such people would be able to recognize friend or foe, family member, voracious animal, or other important things a mile away, from a wisp of sound carried on the wind. These things carried strong emotional meanings, because they indicated life or death matters. Such is the legacy we own and deal with. It is mostly out of place in our modern world where we have modified our environment to make it more comfortable and safer, and where danger can come so fast that you never see or hear it coming, but we were not designed for the modern world, we are products of the primitive world.

I have always thought and felt that concerts, recitals, performances, etc. are fine, but that the meaning of music is not contained in them. The meaning of music comes from primitive responses to primitive sounds that can be embodied in various musical compositions. Such music is powerfully meaningful, no matter how you hear it. By contrast, other music may lack meaning, no matter how it is performed or presented.

How to Play or Write Virtual Music

To be sure, this is mysterious stuff. This is a fertile territory for composers, arrangers, and improvisers, and it works spectacularly well on the piano. Here are some rules or at least suggestions:

1. Leave out the roots and most of the bass notes.
2. Use one tritone in some sonorities. A tritone implies 3 up to b7, or 8 up to #11, and can generate a subjective root in your inner ear.
3. Use one or two minor seconds in a chord. These imply #11 up to 12, or 6 up to b7 in a chord, and can generate subjective roots, too.
4. Use several whole steps in a row. These imply b7, 8, 9, 10, and #11, and will generate subjective roots.
5. Play or write for piano with the middle pedal depressed. On most pianos the lower strings will pick up resonances from the notes you play. (On a few concert grand pianos, capture a thirteenth chord in the key in which you are playing.) These resonances can provide bass notes and roots.
6. Practice imitating various natural sounds with your voice, on the piano, or in compositions.
7. Most of all, be aware that like the reflection of the mountain in the lake, there are notes being produced by these processes. If you write or play the root and/or bass, your played notes will dominate. It is only by leaving these notes out that you can hear the virtual ones provided by nature.

THE NATURE OF PITCH: PSYCHOACOUSTICS OF RESULTANT TONES

Interactions of Tones

When two musicians perform together on stage (playing a flute and a clarinet, for instance) their notes may sometimes interact, but usually they do not audibly interact. Brass instrumentalists frequently play one note, sing another, and complete the chord by the resultant tone. There are three places where tones might interact: in the instruments themselves, in the air or other transmission medium such as an audio system, and in the human auditory system.

Musical acoustician John Backus (1969) described three types of interactions: difference tones, subjective tones, and beats. For example, resultant tones (difference tones, subjective tones, and beats) are all a part of the sound of the Australian didgeridoo. Musical instruments produce an audible difference tone, which might be incorporated into the harmony. Jazz musicians often play rootless voicings in which the root or bass note is a subjective resultant tone. Sometimes two players will use beats to help them tune.

Interferences of Tones

Physics and acoustics books frequently discuss interference. The two categories of interference are the additive and subtractive interference, and the resultant wave patterns are called interference patterns or interference waves. The wave interference patterns are frequently displayed as diagrams and photographs presenting water waves, light waves, as well as sound waves.

However, many aspects of the complex subject of interference remain controversial, and discussions that give frequencies and calculate difference or sum frequencies are rare. Studies on musical acoustics usually include frequencies because we hear these frequencies as musical tones and under some circumstances we can hear difference tones. This leads us to pay attention to the frequencies. There are two or more types of difference tones, one being f1-f2, and the second one being 2f1-f2, in both cases f1>f2. These are sometimes called quadratic and cubic difference tones. Sum tones (f1+f2) might be also included, although their existence has been debated in musical acoustics. Some musicians claim to be able to hear sum tones as the resultant tones.

How We Hear Pitch

Over the years, many people have speculated about how human beings and other animals hear pitch. Suggested answers have included genetic factors, harmonic series factors, learning theories, environmental concepts, and no doubt other approaches, as well (Stevens, & Warshofsky, 1981). Speculations have included Fourier analysis by the Place process, autocorrelation analysis in the auditory system, time-based analysis, harmonic templates, volley processes, and many others. The 1961 Nobel Prize laureate Georg von Bekesy explored the Place process. He detected under the microscope an undulation sweep over the basilar membrane when a sound was introduced into the cochlea. Von Bekesy found that the high-frequency tones were perceived near the base of the cochlea and the lower frequencies toward the apex.

One may ask, what if the brain does not really hear pitch at all. The inner ear detects pitches, but immediately converts them into neural impulses that travel up the auditory nerve system to the primary auditory cortex (PAC) in the middle level of the brain. What if the PAC records not the pitches but the nerve activity on which the impulses arrive? The auditory nerve system is tonotopically organized, meaning that the basilar membrane in the cochlea in the inner ear always sends an impulse to the PAC on the same nerve when it receives a specific frequency. Thus, when the PAC receives an impulse on a particular nerve, that nerve represents a particular pitch even though no remnant of the pitch itself might ever be received in the brain.

It is helpful to think of the auditory system as a survival mechanism that evolved according to the Darwinian survival strategies. Its task is to recognize danger and safe havens. This is done by creating templates in the brain that correspond to the voice elements of the mother's voice, other family members voices, and familiar domestic sounds that represent safety for the young child. Also, it is necessary when encountering danger to create templates in the brain representing that danger so it can be avoided in the future. However, these templates might represent only the nerve on which a neural impulse was received. They are not necessarily harmonic templates, and the brain knows nothing of harmonics as such. If the young child is bombarded with harmonic sounds, the child will appear to have imprinted the harmonic series, but actually it only imprinted the neurons that were stimulated by sounds that had a harmonic series aspect to them.

Because, according to Ernst Haeckel, Charles Darwin, and others, ontology recapitulates phylogeny, the development of the brain takes a course that parallels the evolution of previously existing brains: upward from the brainstem to the mid brain and finally to the upper or cerebral part of the brain. Thus, in a very young child the mid brain may be mature enough to function, while the upper or cerebral part of the brain is too immature to do so. Thus, the mid brain can imprint sounds heard before birth and immediately after birth by creating templates in the PAC. However, it cannot analyze the structures of sound patterns because it does not have that capacity. The analysis of sound patterns must await the cerebral development that makes it possible, and that initiates the natural language learning phase of human development. This takes place after a year or more and phases out the sound-imprinting phase that took place in the perinatal period.

The templates that are created represent the nerve patterns that are stimulated by each of these sounds, perhaps along with visual and other (tactile, odor, taste, etc.) sensations. It is important to note that the pitch need never be recorded or experienced. There are 30 to 50 thousand nerves in the auditory nerve system and so the frequency scale is divided into 30 to 50 thousand small steps. These represent the frequencies detected by the Place process in the inner ear but do not carry any vestige of pitch representation with them. In fact, by the time the nerve impulses reach the PAC, all vestige of pitch can be discarded and forgotten. The PAC looks at these nerve impulses solely as a pattern that represents danger or safety. If danger is encoded then the PAC sends messages of fight or flight to the appropriate brain centers. If safety is detected, the PAC sends messages of pleasure and contentment to other brain centers.

The consequences to this imprinting process are that we will always like and prefer sounds like the ones we heard in our mother's voice and our prenatal and perinatal environment and that these preferences will stay with us for life. Also, people living in a close-knit group will share certain vocal sounds that everyone will know in that area (accents, dialects, pidgins, Gullah language, etc.). Thus, there will be auditory communities that share certain vocal sounds. Everyone from another community will automatically be identified as a stranger and a potential source of danger. Note that the voices themselves are not recorded in the PAC, only the pattern of nerve endings sending impulses when a certain sound is heard is recorded. Because the PAC's operations are largely subconscious, we have little knowledge of this taking place. Note that this sound imprinting takes place in the middle brain and that the cerebral cortex is so undeveloped at this period as to be incapable of involvement. Also note that only isolated sounds are imprinted. The learning of sound structures will come later in the natural language learning phase, which this period precedes. For this reason, I like to refer to this phase as the phonological learning phase.

It should be apparent now that all sound is relative. Only the nerve patterns are recorded. Nature knows no number system, so the nerves are not numbered. The nerves are known only by their order from low to high. Nature has no need to record the sounds themselves, nor any need to know the specific pitches (or frequencies) involved. Nature's sole need is to establish a basis for safe conduct for the yet-to-be-born child. To do this, it needs a sound detection and analysis system, an emotional and behavioral control system, and a simple system of values (or weightings) to connect the detection system to the control systems.

The most mysterious part of the system is the illusion that we are actually hearing sounds. This illusion is generated in the PAC and is sent to consciousness, that means to the cerebral cortex. Eric Heller (2012) refers to the sounds we hear as "executive summaries;" they are illusions created by the brain but they are related to experience in a convoluted way. We hear what we expect to hear, the brain provides a maximum amount of useful information (in a survival context) for us to make successful choices in dangerous situations. Thus, sounds that are outside of our life experience are not heard. This seems absolutely bizarre and impossible. It is most likely that colors, scents, tastes, and other world qualities are similarly synthesized for us in our brains!

This is the mysterious part of the process and no one seems to have much knowledge of how it works. We do know that our experiences of sense data do not correspond with the realities of the sensory data received. For example, the sounds of musical instruments are single gestalts that have very little to do with the harmonic construction or non-harmonic construction received by the ear. A violin is "warm," an oboe is "spicy." A clarinet is "hollow." Chili is "hot." To some extent, there is logic and a general agreement to this, but it also seems to reinforce the idea that we hear or experience what we expect to hear or experience. This suggests that we are unlikely to experience sensory patterns that are completely new. It is as if an agency in the brain looks at what we know and what we expect, and then gives us that thing as a sensation. The experiences we had in the perinatal period from several months before birth up to several years after being born are all likely contributors to this experience.

During the period when the nervous system is growing it is capable of configuring itself in conformity with incoming nervous system patterns. Once it is completed there is no possibility to do this anymore, and learning takes place through the acquisition of weightings in neural networks. Thus we reach the stage of learning that we all know and use. It is fundamentally different from the system of learning (imprinting) that takes place in the earliest months or years of life.

Otoacoustic emission (OAE) is a sound produced by the outer hair cells in the cochlea. Otoacoustic occur spontaneously or can be evoked by acoustic stimuli (Farlex, 2012) indicating that this capacity exists in the cochlea. Low-intensity sounds are transmitted through the middle ear apparatus to the ear canal (Glattke, & Kujawa, 1991). Research into otoacoustic emissions has identified a category called distortion product otoacoustic emission (DPOAE) that do this process of creating difference tones. Research results suggested that DPOAEs might serve as an objective indicator of frequency discrimination. The difference tones are generated, it is said, due to non-linearities in the alignment of frequency across the basilar membrane. Once they are generated they travel to their proper place on the basilar membrane where they might be heard, and then feedback through a process called the cochlear amplifier causes them to be regenerated by the outer hair cells and then they can be picked up by ultra-sensitive microphones placed in the auditory canal. Two major categories are quadratic difference tones: $f2-f1$, and cubic difference tones: $2f2-f1$.

What all of this suggests is that if you were not exposed to difference tone effects as periodicity pitch waves in the perinatal years, you will be unable to hear them as an adult because consciousness has no experience on which to base its synthetic sensory experience. As a result, a percentage of the population will hear them and another percentage will not. If no templates have been created in the PAC for neural patterns representing a certain experience, then that experience does not exist for that person. Later in life, the synthesis process depends on pattern templates to create its version of reality. A good example is that of absolute pitch (or perfect pitch) – the rare ability to name or produce a note of given pitch in the absence of a reference note (Deutsch, 2013). This ability may be related to the critical periods in perceptual and cognitive development, the brain substrates of specialized abilities, and the role of genetic factors in perception and cognition. Later in life the conscious brain can create specific pitch experiences with names only if an earlier process imprinted neural patterns representing pitch effects with an unambiguous identity. That imprint does not have to be a musical one, but it must be strong and unambiguous as a result of having been reinforced a great many times in early life. Once that has been done, the brain will have acquired a neural pattern representing a specific pitch and then later, consciousness can use that template to create additional specific pitch experiences.

The current thinking is that you learn pitches from aural experience before or immediately after birth probably identified by the emotions accompanying them, and then these pitches acquire musical or other meanings later in life, mostly by association. In other words, there is nothing intellectual about acquiring perfect pitch because it happens before the intellectual portions of your brain develop. In later years the assigning of names to pitches can be intellectual and can be carried out in a complex way that introduces other elements: transposing instruments, movable clef signs, Baroque pitch and so on.

Sometimes this can become so complex that the perfect pitch breaks down. You may hear people say that playing Baroque violin killed their perfect pitch. This is because Baroque pitch is usually about a half step lower than modern pitch but it can also have different pitches altogether, and some Baroque players played higher than modern pitch. The violinist Franz Biber apparently did so, and he must have used a particularly short violin to get these higher pitches tuned on the open strings.

An Experiment on the Nature of Pitch

This experiment is derived from the musical experience but is not typical of physics. We are specifically interested in the musical results that we can hear. The experiment that I ran in my laboratory at the University of Northern Colorado had to do with the nature of periodicity pitch and by extension, pitch in general.

If the instruments are playing high notes rather loudly an audible difference tone can often be heard. For example, if the flute is playing 1200 Hz (close to Eb 6) and the clarinet is playing 1000 Hz (close to C6) a difference tone (1200-1000) of 200 Hz (close to Ab3) will often be heard. As such, the question often arises: is the resultant tone is generated in the instruments, in the transmission medium or in the auditory system, or perhaps in more than one of these places.

This research project is intended to answer this question. I connected three sin wave generators to a mixer, an oscilloscope, an amplifier, and a loudspeaker. Two sinusoidal frequencies were generated by electronic oscillators and then fed to an oscilloscope and a spectrum analyzer (iSpectrum running on an Intel Macintosh computer). First, in the two-frequency experiment I generated frequencies A3 at 220 Hz and D4 at 293.3333 Hz. The oscilloscope was adjusted to show a single trace synced to sub-multiple of the frequency 220 Hz. On the oscilloscope screen a wave was shown, which was the composite of the two waves: a 220 Hz wave with an amplitude change at the frequency of the largest common factor: 73.3333 Hz (D2). This is a periodicity pitch; it can be shown on the face of an oscilloscope, thereby proving that periodicity pitch has a physical basis and is not just an artifact of the hearing process. The result was as follows: the periodicity pitch difference tone was visible on the face of the oscilloscope, but its frequency could not be found by the spectrum analyzer.

The indications are that there are two classes of acoustic waves: (1) those that have power at their specific frequency in the power spectrum and (2) acoustic waves that are the interference products of two other powered waves but do not have power at their specific frequency in the power spectrum. The latter waves are usually called resultant tones and are widely displayed and discussed in the literature. Resultant tones might be produced in the instruments themselves, in the transmission medium and/or in the auditory system, but because they have no power at their characteristic frequency they will not appear on a spectrum analyzer and might be heard only under certain specific conditions.

In the three-pitch experiment, I used the previous two frequencies and added the frequency E3 at 165 Hz. The objective was to see if a stable display on the oscilloscope could be achieved with each combination. I consider a stable display to be indicative of the existence of a common denominator to the frequencies. The common denominator is the sweep frequency to which the oscilloscope must synchronize, if a stable single-trace display is to be achieved.

I then played the tone pair into a spectrum analyzer (iSpectrum running on a Macintosh computer). The original pair of tones shows up very nicely on the screen, but the periodicity pitch at the frequency of the largest common factor is not seen on the screen of the spectrum analyzer. I take this result to indicate the following: a periodicity pitch, as it is commonly called, is an acoustical phenomenon but it differs from the waves produced by oscillators (and musical instruments) in that there is no power at that frequency. The periodicity pitch is a wave phenomenon produced by the additive and the subtractive interference. It appears that any time two waves are linearly mixed in a common medium (like the air, electrical waves in a wire or air in the middle ear), the periodicity pitch will appear, and it can be displayed on an oscilloscope screen.

An implied result is that when the two test frequencies are mixed in the perilymph of the inner ear, the periodicity pitch interference frequency will also appear, and that it might be audible, at least to a listener who has been trained to hear it.

For the three-pitch experiment, I added a third oscillator running at the frequency of E3. This three-oscillator group produces what is commonly called a quartal chord of E3, A3, and D4. The smallest common factor is C minus 1 at about 8 Hz. A slightly higher common factor is D minus 1 at about 9 Hz. This is a common chord existing in the 20ᵗʰ century classical music, and it is a widely used left hand jazz piano chord in modern jazz. I wanted to hear if this chord would be heard as a D chord or a C chord. What I perceived was that I could hear it either way depending on context. I think that this is a common experience in hearing periodicity pitches. They can be heard, but they can be heard in different ways depending on context.

If C is the root, D is the ninth of the chord, A is the thirteenth, and E is the third. If D is the root, E is the ninth, A is the fifth, and D is an octave; of course, all at multiple octaves up. But I really wanted to see if I could get a stable single-trace oscilloscope display for this 3-frequency-quartal chord. I found that I could do so with a sweep frequency of around 18 Hz. Because my oscilloscope has a lowest sweep frequency of 14 Hz, I must conclude that I was sweeping the wave at twice the fundamental frequency. The display did stabilize but did not show a simple waveform. By adjusting each of the frequencies very carefully I could get an unchanging, stable single-trace display indication of a common factor on which the oscilloscope could synchronize.

My point in running these experiments has been twofold: first, I wished to show that periodicity pitches are a natural acoustical phenomenon, not just a psychological one; and second, I wished to show that there was no power present in the periodicity pitches, but that they were produced by a natural additive and subtractive wave interference process. I am speculating that if such process takes place in the air or electrically in a wire, than it will occur naturally in the perilymph of the cochlea as well, and that it might be perceived, at least with the proper training or experience. The research published in the Heidelberg University article suggests that some people do hear such periodicities and others do not, hearing instead, the present frequencies separately.

Conclusions About Pitch

If my hypothesis that the only pitch receiving process is the Place process occurring in the cochlea, then it is necessary to consider the various pitch phenomena that have been reported, to see if they can be performed by the Place process in the cochlea. Such phenomena include periodicity pitch, phantom tones, residue pitch, some sort of autocorrelation-like sorting of pitches into more and less commonly recurring categories, missing fundamentals, rippled noise and pitch sensations from noises such as staircase pitch, and fast echo effect pitches. The cochlea is a transducer like no other and its full capabilities are not known. I think it is fair to say that there is a good chance that the cochlea can produce all of these effects without invoking any additional nervous system or brain system of processing. A point to be made is that while all sounds differ from each other in small or large ways, all sin waves are, by definition, the same.

Again, all sin waves having the same frequency and amplitude are exactly the same. Thus a neural impulse representing that frequency and amplitude carries all the information that is necessary for a complete description of that sin wave. If all sounds can be represented by sin waves, the neural patterns are capable of carrying all the required information for all sounds. The auditory neurons are said to have a refractory period (recovery time after firing) of around 3 milliseconds before they can fire again. Thus they cannot fire on every period of common pitches for sin wave frequencies above about 350 Hz. An advantage to vibrato, tremolo, reverberation, early reflections in the reverberant field, echo, pitch spreading (as in violin jitter), chorus effect, and other effects is that they can recruit more neurons and thus produce a stronger sensation because more neurons will be coaxed to fire.

A critical stage in the processing is the early childhood (the perinatal period) stage of imprinting neural impulse patterns in the PAC. If the child should be extensively exposed to harmonic sounds at this time, the impulse patterns that get reinforced will be harmonic and it will appear that the person has harmonic templates. If the reinforced experiences are specific pitches (as with native Mandarin Chinese speakers) then the templates will appear to be of specific pitches. If the reinforced experiences are a specific type of intonation, specific noises, specific linguistic intonations, or any other sonic phenomena, then it will appear that the person has acquired templates for that phenomenon. In actuality, according to my theory, all that has been recorded by the memory section of the PAC is that the nerve-ending pattern of the auditory nerve from the cochlea has been recorded and reinforced. Thus it is totally non-sound specific and may be redirected to other sonic activities at any time.

It is widely agreed that different people hear sound and particularly music in different ways and that they have different preferences. This research suggests that the executive summaries of sounds that we hear are based on early experiences that are replicated in current experience. In other words, if one was not exposed to a certain sound or sound producing process in early life (the perinatal period) the executive summary process will have no way of synthesizing it later in life. There will be no basis for it. Specifically in the context of this chapter, if one was not exposed repeatedly to periodicity-pitch producing sonorities early in life, one will have no mechanism for the executive summary process to create them for you to hear later in life. The same applies to absolute pitch, complex harmony (like quartal chords) and even the experience of pitch, itself. One has to have created neural templates in the PAC that can represent an auditory phenomenon or one will be unable to perceive it later in life. The executive summary process will have nothing to work with. Most likely, this applies to all percepts.

Since there are two classes of acoustic waves: powered waves and resultant tones that have no power at their characteristic frequency, then perhaps other types of wave energy would exhibit this duality as well: water wave, light waves, and esoteric forms of waves such as quantum wave or gravity wave. Researchers should look for non-powered resultant waves of these types.

ACKNOWLEDGMENT

Most of the ideas contained in this chapter are not available in books but were gleaned from many years of reading professional trade magazines and publications including:

1. ASCAP Daily Brief (an on-line daily newsletter for members only)
2. Many transcripts of ASCAP court proceedings (I am both a writer and publisher member of ASCAP, a writer since 1968).
3. Composer USA
4. Computer Music Journal
5. Contact List for Electronic Music (CLEM), published in Canada
6. Electronic Musician Magazine
7. Electronic Music Review
8. Keyboard Magazine
9. Mix Magazine
10. Pro Sound News
11. Synthesis Magazine

REFERENCES

Backus, J. G. (1969). The Acoustical Foundations of Music – Musical Sound: a Lucid Account of its Properties, Production, Behavior, and Reproduction. W. W. Norton.

Bregman, A. S. (1990). *Auditory scene analysis*. Cambridge, MA: MIT Press.

Deutsch, D. (2013). *The Psychology of Music* (3rd ed.). Elsevier Inc.

Encyclopedia Britannica. (2018). *Combination tone*. Retrieved from http://www.britannica.com/science/combination-tone

Farlex. (2012). *Otoacoustic emission*. Farlex Partner Medical Dictionary.

Glattke, T. J., & Kujawa, S. G. (1991). Otoacoustic Emissions. *American Journal of Audiology*, *1*(1), 29–40. doi:10.1044/1059-0889.0101.29 PMID:26659426

Heller, E. J. (2012). *Why You Hear What You Hear: An Experiential Approach to Sound, Music, and Psychoacoustics*. Princeton University Press.

Lewis, D., & Larsen, M. J. (1927). The Cancellation, Reinforcement, and Measurement of Subjective Tones. *Proceedings of N.A.S.*, *23*(7), 415–421. doi:10.1073/pnas.23.7.415 PMID:16588176

Lorenz, K. (1937). The Companion in the Bird'. *The Auk*, *54*(3), 245–273. doi:10.2307/4078077

Mathews, M. M., & Moore, F. R. (1970). GROOVE – a program to compose, store, and edit functions of time. *Communications of the ACM*, *13*(12), 715–721. doi:10.1145/362814.362817

Pierce, J. R. (1990). *Telstar, A History*. SMEC Vintage Electrics.

Schnupp, J., Nelken, I., & King, A. (2011). *Auditory Neuroscience*. MIT Press.

Schouten, J. F. (1940). The residue and the mechanism of hearing. *Proceedings of the Koninklijke Akademie van Wetenschap, 43*, 991–999.

Schouten, J. F., Ritsma, R. J., & Cardozo, B. L. (1962). Pitch of the residue. *The Journal of the Acoustical Society of America, 34*(9B), 1418–1424. doi:10.1121/1.1918360

Stevens, S. S., & Warshofsky, F. (1981). *Sound and Hearing* (Revised Edition). Time Life Education.

Terhardt, E. (1974). Pitch, consonance, and harmony. *The Journal of the Acoustical Society of America, 55*(5), 1061–1069. doi:10.1121/1.1914648 PMID:4833699

KEY TERMS AND DEFINITIONS

Acoustic Waves: Longitudinal waves with the same direction of vibration as the direction of their traveling in a medium such as air or water. Linear mixing of acoustic waves results in forming periodicity pitches of the resultant tones.

Pitch: A sound quality describing the highness or lowness of a tone, defined by the rate of vibration that produces it.

Sound Waves: Sinusoidal waves characterized by their frequency, amplitude, intensity (sound pressure), speed, and direction. Pairs of sound waves may reveal additive and subtractive interference.

Tonotopic: Organization means the arrangement of spaces in auditory cortex where sounds of different frequency are processed in the brain. Tones close to each other frequency are represented in topologically near regions in the brain.

Tritone: An interval of three whole tones with an augmented fourth. For example, between C and F sharp.

Chapter 6
Dialogue With Interfaces:
Beyond the Visual Towards Socio-Spatial Engagement

Ana Paula Baltazar dos Santos
Universidade Federal de Minas Gerais, Brazil

Guilherme Ferreira de Arruda
Universidade Federal de Ouro Preto, Brazil

José dos Santos Cabral Filho
Universidade Federal de Minas Gerais, Brazil

Lorena Melgaço Silva Marques
University of Birmingham, UK

Marcela Alves de Almeida
Universidade Federal de São João del-Rei, Brazil

ABSTRACT

This chapter grapples with the hegemony of the visual and its pervasiveness in current urban installations. It discusses how technology and the visual are fetishized instead of used in their dialogical potential to engage people in socio-spatial transformation. This chapter presents the trajectory of the Graphics Laboratory for Architectural Experience at Universidade Federal de Minas Gerais, Brazil (LAGEAR) in its theoretical and practical development. This chapter then discusses LAGEAR's main drives, which are the playful interaction, the distinction between interface, and interaction and dialogue, in order to create interactive interfaces that actually engage people in socio-spatial transformation. It presents examples of the authors' works, drawing from visually based to bodily engaging and socio-political installations. Discussion concerns the problematization that leads to the need of engagement rather than the bodily engagement. Emphasis was put on working with the socio-spatial context and proposing interfaces that take into account the process in its openness and indeterminacy instead of prescribing a product (even if an interface-product).

DOI: 10.4018/978-1-5225-7371-5.ch006

INTRODUCTION

This chapter discusses urban interactive installations as important means to engage people in socio-spatial transformation of cities. It proposes a critical view of their usual drive, which is highly dependent on digital technology and overemphasises the visual. Since the beginning of the century we have been witnessing a period of enthusiasm related to the emerging digital technologies, which is clearly exemplified in a group of texts by different authors (Graham, 2004) discussing the overcome of physical space by information and communication technology. In such a view, digital technologies overcome the gap between space and time, being omnipresent and granting a remote access to the world in real time. However, we cannot ignore that these technologies make also a fragment our aesthetic experience by overemphasising the visual. In this way, most interactive urban installations are strongly based on digital technology and are also spectacular (Baltazar, 2009; Baltazar, Cabral Filho, Melgaço, Almeida, & Arruda, 2012; Baltazar, Arruda, Cabral Filho, Melgaço, & Almeida, 2014).

This chapter revisits two papers by the authors (Baltazar et al, 2012; Baltazar et al, 2014) and updates the discussions taking place at the Graphics Laboratory for Architectural Experience at Universidade Federal de Minas Gerais, Brazil (LAGEAR). Up to 2014, when we published "Beyond the visual in urban interactive installations: dialogue and social transformation" (Baltazar et al, 2014), the critique of the visual was systematised in two main directions in the development of interfaces, developed first from 2006 and then from 2010. First, since 2006 we have been developing interfaces to connect remote communities by spatialising information and communication. This meant that interfaces were programmed to engage people in dialogue; that is, interaction is dialogical not the interface. Even if this seemed to advance the current research on urban interactive installations, people's engagement was not enduring. Assessing the interfaces produced, the prevalence of the visual was seen as one of the main problems. The spectacle produced when people interacted with each other by means of the interfaces would catch people's attention for a short period, but was not enough to promote people's bodily engagement with the city by means of the interfaces. So, in 2010 our approach started to concern the development of interfaces to enable remote physical actuation by means of physical computing, moving beyond visual towards bodily interaction. This meant that the interface could also be dialogical, not only the interaction. Dialogue was present in both early developments of urban interactive installations by LAGEAR. In the first case the interfaces are visually based but trigger dialogue between people. In the second case the interface, besides having a visually based output, is strongly based on action: the input of people in one place triggers actions of people in another place. In this case the interface works dialogically regardless of the interaction of people (which most times is also dialogical).

Nevertheless, the persistent ephemerality of the interfaces was overwhelming, and there was no actual socio-spatial transformation. Even if there was a more sophisticated interaction, as people were not only interacting with each other but also with the interface, the dialogue prompted had no impact on people's engagement with the city, even in short term. As the main assessment of this stage, the LAGEAR research group questioned the complexification of the interfaces assuming a prevalence of digital technology, and started thinking of other means to engage people in socio-spatial transformation. The main challenge, then, is to propose interfaces that avoid both visual and technological fetishisms, working towards a broader concept of dialogue, drawing from Hannah Arendt's provocation for the resumption of the public sphere, taking into account plural interaction amongst people from different classes and social backgrounds (Arendt, 1998).

Such a discussion is the main purpose of this chapter, while it is not present in the former papers (Baltazar et al, 2012; Baltazar et al, 2014), which is organized as follows. First, the discussion of the prevalence of the visual in architecture and the possibility of surpassing such a 'logic of the visual' if working with its dialectical relation with experience is presented (Baltazar et al, 2012; Baltazar et al, 2014). It then discusses the 'logic of the visual' in urban interactive installations and the emphasis on technological development prior to contextual problematisations of the urban spaces. From that it introduces playful interaction, the distinction between interface and interaction in dialogue, which are the main drives for LAGEAR's production. Then it presents a selection of LAGEAR's urban interactive works bringing the cumulative experience and criticism that led to interfaces to trigger socio-spatial transformation.

The works presented are the Ocupar Espaços (Occupy Spaces – a visually based, triggering dialogue between people), Long Distance Voodoo (action-based interface proposing a dialogical interaction), Ituita (which works towards the dialectics of a spectacle and an experience but fails to escape the fetishism of digital technology; it does not engage citizens with the everyday input necessary to enable the socio-spatial transformation foreseen by the technical team), and CANI (which puts the problematisation of the socio-spatial context before any digital technological development, and manages to engage people in a dialogical and plural interface directed to engage them in a discussion towards the resumption of the public sphere).

BACKGROUND

Before discussing LAGEAR's critical path towards the socio-spatial transformation, it is important to point out the two main discussions regarding the 'logic of the visual' (and the possibility of a dialectics of spectacle and experience) and the fetish of digital technology.

The 'Logic of the Visual' in Architecture

Hegel stated that vision and hearing are the two superior senses, as they do not consume their objects; what is seen and what is heard remain the same, while what is eaten, for example, finishes. According to Alberto Pérez-Gómez and Louise Pelletier (1997) the privilege of vision and hearing over other senses dates back to classical Greece, when the 'distance' that has marked Western science and art was established, and when Greek Tragedy separated a stage and an orchestra from spectators in the amphitheater.

The 'logic of the visual'– to use Henri Lefebvre's term (1991) has its impact on space first as a 'spatial practice,' as that of the theatre displacing the 'lived space' of the ritual, and only later, in the Renaissance, as the dominant means for the production of space, which Lefebvre calls 'representations of space' or a 'conceived space.' Such an impact means a clear distancing from the lived space, the space in which people are bodily engaged in its simultaneous design, building, and use, towards the conceived space in which design, building, and its use happen separately.

The hegemony of vision is not usually acknowledged by historians of architecture and urban space. According to Lefebvre, even Sigfried Giedion, the first historian who put "space, and not some creative genius, not the 'spirit of times,' and not even technological progress, at the centre of history" (Lefebvre, 1991, p. 126), failed "to show up the growing ascendancy of the abstract and the visual, as well as the internal connection between them; and to expose the genesis and meaning of a 'logic of the visual'."

(Lefebvre, 1991, p. 128). However, Pérez-Gómez and Pelletier (1997) in their history of architectural representation point out that such hegemony of vision culminates with the shift from embodied to visual spatial practice. For the user this means a contemplative practice and for the designer it means that perspective and projections are used to foresee space as an object. Moreover, Sérgio Ferro (2006) shows that as well as representing space as an object, this design process serves to make space into a commodity.

The privileging of the visual is questioned in some of Pérez-Gómez's works. For instance, he introduces the 'erotic paradigm' as an alternative to the perspectival paradigm, a means to 'retrieve a new depth, a true depth of experience' (Pérez-Gómez, 1994, p. 21), a return to embodied participation, even in visual representations such as paintings. The problem is that it presupposes space and its meaning as representation. And even if the erotic paradigm escapes the hegemony of vision, it is only an illusory escape: the result is still a finished painting or building that contributes nothing to change the tradition of the visually based production of space.

Nevertheless, we might not forget that the erotic paradigm proposed by Pérez-Gómez draws from Poliphilo (Colonna, 1999), which narrative is useful as an example of a dialectic attitude, using images not to reproduce or simulate the realm of imagination in the realm of experience, nor even to bridge both, but to enrich experience itself; to enlarge the possibility of pleasure in the process without envisaging a closed, finished future product; to acknowledge the indeterminacy of the process to trigger different actions, instead of reproducing previously set behaviours (Arendt, 1998). Despite such an erotic path for the production of space being formulated in the Renaissance, it was not enough to fight the perspectival paradigm based on representation and the hegemony of the visual. The latter prevails in the production of space – mainly extraordinary, not everyday spaces, which instead of being designed as open interfaces reinforcing use value, transforms spaces into commodities.

The 'Logic of the Visual' in Current Urban Interactive Installations

Most urban interactive installations follow the same logic of the visual, becoming product–commodities rather than interfaces that privilege processes of production of space open to people's engagement. They highlight three main points. First, most of these installations still rely on the spectacle and propose contemplative experiences, even if collective. Second, since most of them are ephemeral, they tend towards forgettable experiences, fostering little social awareness, let alone socio-spatial transformation. Third, they rely on the 'magic by ignorance' (Baltazar & Cabral Filho, 2010), which means that the illusion resulting from the interaction is sustained only by ignorance of the system, the 'black box.' As soon as the system is revealed, the spectacle's magic is gone.

We have elaborated on these three points (Baltazar et al, 2014) when analysing the urban installations: Gravity (by 2Roqs, 2009), Solar Equation (by Rafael Lozano-Hemmer, 2010), and D-Tower (by Q. Serafijn and Lars Spuybroek, 2003), showing that on the one hand they were visually based, but on the other their intentions were subjective and artistic, with no purpose of engaging people in any sort of social transformation (Baltazar et al, 2014).

However, in the last decade the Arab Spring has marked a wave of protests and uprisings worldwide. Words such as democracy, participation, and empowerment, fruits of such a socio-political mood, became central in a variety of fields, including architecture and art. Different from the early assumed visually based and spectacular urban interactive installations, we have started to witness urban installations that base their discourses on socio-political transformation, but not actually proposing a change in their visual bases (Baltazar, 2017). An example is the urban installation VoiceOver (Umbrellium group,

Haque, 2016-2018), which is presented as a participatory platform that aims to "re-establish community engagement" (Haque, 2017, p. 87) facing our constant loss of collective power of decision-making to automated processes. What the interface actually proposes is a disguised spectacle with a discourse of experience, not even getting close to promote the dialectics of spectacle and experience.

This installation, already tested in the British village of Horden and also in London, creates a temporary communication network between neighbours by means of a light antenna, which is installed in the houses' front window, and a radio box. People are invited to record a short broadcast about their life using the radio box, so the narratives are transmitted from house to house, connecting the residents while the sounds are translated simultaneously into beams of light, making the antennas light up creating a visual urban spectacle.

As people can speak what they want, at a first glance VoiceOver seems to offer an indeterminate experience that induces people's engagement and participation. But there is a clear problem concerning the logic of the visual. The potential to reverberate ideas in the public space is reduced to a display of colored lights without any meaning at all, that is, people on the street cannot hear the speeches, just contemplate the spectacular show of lights, which cannot be seen as anything other than random from their point of view.

This leads us to our next point by joining the prevalence of the visual and the fetish of digital technology, which in this installation is expressed by means of a blind belief that digital technology and the spectacle are enough to trigger transformation and engage people into dialogue. Although the installation's goal to connect people in communication networks is an important step towards social transformation, there is a greater emphasis on the visual and the spectacle (on the interface) rather than on the content of communication itself. In this sense, to give voice by transforming it into unintelligible lights is not enough. A truly responsible interface would focus on the potential to engage people in dialogical interactions, otherwise it will only reproduce a one-hand communication, without opening for new information to come out.

The Fetish of Digital Technology

Technology exerts a fascination on people's mind that very often it reaches the level of a fetish, in the sense that people demonstrate an almost irrational interest in any technological objects. To understand such a fetish we have to understand two different things: the magical aspects surreptitiously concealed in technological artefacts; and the fragmentation of our experience that is at the core of our use of technology.

The magical perception of digital and computational technology comes from the fact that from a layperson's perspective their functionality defies the causality of the natural world. These technologies apparently present a split between the action that triggers an event and the effect resulting from that event. To a certain extent, this is the description of the black box concept used in Cybernetics. Seen as a black box, technology becomes magical and seductive, leading to a widespread fetishism.

The fragmentation of our experience – focusing on one body sense at the expense of the others – not only abolishes the synergy and synaesthesia of our senses but imposes a bodily disengagement that became a characteristic of our living with technologies. This bodily disengagement, coupled with the illusory disembodiment of information, allows for a recursive increase of technology development. In fact, one of the hallmarks of digital and computational technologies is that their development allows and promotes further development of the technologies themselves. This recursivity ends up accelerating the technological progress in a linear fashion, where a new model substitute the old one, be it an artefact or a piece of software.

The fetish of technology leads to the acceleration of its development as its sole purpose. As if we were enchanted by the possibility of competing with gods or supernatural forces. Thus, we frequently have huge advances in technologies that do not respond to necessity, or even that is not desired at all. That turns into progress for the sake of progress. Thus, we often see high technologies used with the mere purpose of amusement (distraction), in the sense of empty spectacle, without reaching the fulfilling recreation of proper play, without moving towards the dialectics of spectacle and experience.

LAGEAR'S MAIN DEVELOPMENTS QUESTIONING THE FETISH OF THE VISUAL AND OF DIGITAL TECHNOLOGY

The main drives of LAGEAR's investigations are the playful interaction, the distinction between the interface and the interaction and dialogue.

As urban interactive installations draw from digital technology, it is important not only to understand the state of art of technology, but also discuss interaction and its possible development. Therefore, we might envisage two stages of interaction. First, when interacting with an interface to access a prede-termined content; second when interacting with content through an interface. When interacting with a music box, for example, by winding the crank, one is interacting with the interface, not with content – the music –which is a predetermined output. On the other hand, when playing the piano, the musician creates music, an indeterminate content, accessing predetermined notes through the keys. While in the first case those interacting tend to become functionaries of the 'apparatus' acting as expected, in the second they might use the apparatus to engage playfully with content.

According to Vilém Flusser (2000), 'play' is a means to overcome a functional relationship with the apparatus. A playful interaction means using the apparatus beyond its prescriptions, engaging with content and not only with the interface (Baltazar and Cabral Filho, 2010). Certainly, a music box might be used in a playful way, but its prescriptions are much more limiting than those of the piano. On the other hand, who plays the piano might become a functionary when struggling with the interface – keys and notes – or merely reproducing a song. As the piano, current technology, such as that of video games has a potential for playful interaction, but paradoxically, it has been mostly used in a functional way, as the output of interaction brings no novelty, let aside social transformation. It might be said that the 'magic by ignorance' is no longer an issue for video game users, as the pervasiveness of technologies leads them to lose interest in unveiling the 'black box.' In fact, there is no magic at all: users become functionaries of the games they consume.

Urban installations are often designed for people to interact with the interface, not with content. They are not playful in Flusser's sense, but only to the extent that the 'magic by ignorance' prevails. More-over, as discussed above, even a bodily engagement is predominantly mediated by images. If the visual facilitates people's immediate grasp of ephemeral installations, leading to a lack of a more enduring engagement of people with each other and with the space. In order to overcome the stasis prompted by image-based interaction with the interfaces, is needed to increase people's feeling of belonging. This might be achieved when people are encouraged to negotiate and physically act in a playful interaction with content by means of an interface that enables communication.

For that, instead of discussing the production of an interface-product – which might be reactive, proactive or dialogical – we propose to firstly discuss the interaction one is willing to promote by means of the interface. As already discussed (Baltazar et al, 2014) both interface and interaction might be reactive, proactive, or dialogical. By reactive we mean that which programmatically reacts to input given by participants (Dubberly, Haque, & Pangaro, 2009). Proactive means not only reaction but a contribution to present-time changes that take people by surprise (Oosterhuis, 2002). According to Vilém Flusser (1999a), the dialogue or intersubjectivity is the main characteristic of a responsible design. Responsibility in Flusser's sense means the openness of the design to others.

A good example of LAGEAR's experiment that made us learn to separate between interface and interaction, and value more a dialogical interaction rather than a dialogical interface, was Ocupar Espaços (Occupy Spaces). This project was a partnership of LAGEAR with the NGO Oficina de Imagens in 2006, connecting two favelas – shanty towns in Belo Horizonte – Aglomerado da Serra and Barragem Santa Lúcia. It aimed to connect people, usually socially excluded, in these two remote favelas by means of the Internet, web cameras and collaborative interactive projections. A few interfaces were programmed to be interacted with by means of gesture, being some of them puzzle based (Figure 1, right image), requiring two users to collaborate in order to move the pieces of the puzzle to form an image, and others were programmed to enable a more creative and free interaction of people with content, such as the digital graffiti. Besides being playful and not merely functional, these interfaces were not the most successful. People were much more interested in playing with pre-recorded images of their context projected in 1:1 scale in different surfaces such as the floor and the ravine (Figure 1, central and left images). Such unprogrammed interfaces triggered a much more engaging experience for the participants than the overprogrammed interfaces. This indicated that the spatialisation of information and communication, and moreover the spatialisation of the interface, is much more important to create an event for playful interaction than the programming of the interface. That is, the events created are more important to promote the feelings of belonging and presence than the interfaces designed. In other words, the interaction in this case was dialogical, not the interface.

The emphasis on promoting dialogue between people became the research group's most important drive meaning that we must avoid reproducing the fetish of the visual and of technology in the interfaces we produced. With time we have developed different experiments that have indicated that the priority is to understand the context and help promoting socio-spatial transformation, instead of starting from the discourse of social transformation and fall into the trap of representation, by prioritising the visual and the technological development. We have learned that perhaps an analogical game might be more effective

Figure 1. LAGEAR and Oficina de Imagens. Ocupar Espaços (Occupy Spaces) (Copyleft 2006, LAGEAR. Used with permission)

in engaging people than a very sophisticated interface based on the spectacle and digital technology. The most important is that the interface enables new information to arise, opening up people's imaginary and engaging them in dialogue with each other and with the interface. Now that we have presented Ocupar Espaços, a visually based interface triggering dialogue between people, we will present other projects developed in LAGEAR drawing from the main drives discussed above: Long Distance Voodoo, Ituita and CANI.

The next sub-items present a few examples of LAGEAR's developments drawing from the main drives discussed above. We have already presented Ocupar Espaços, a visually based interface triggering dialogue between people and will now discuss Long Distance Voodoo – an action-based interface, proposing a dialogical interface – Ituita (Stralen, Baltazar, Melgaço, & Arruda, 2012) – an interface working towards the dialectics of spectacle and experience but failing to escape the fetishism of digital technology, not engaging citizens with the everyday input necessary to enable the socio-spatial transformation foreseen by the technical team, and CANI – putting the problematisation of the socio-spatial context before any digital technological development and managing to engage people in a dialogical and plural interface directed to engage them in a discussion towards the resumption of the public sphere.

Long Distance Voodoo

LAGEAR has experimented with an interface to promote remote actuation in 2011. It was an event called *Long Distance Voodoo*, connecting people located in different public spaces and the Internet. Its main goal was to develop and test tools, using off-the-shelf hardware and software, to promote remote communication beyond the visual, such as a wearable that allowed people to be remotely touched.

Long Distance Voodoo connected people from different countries – Brazil and Germany, putting in evidence cultural contrasts, as people in one country stimulated dancers on the other by means of signals sent through the Internet. It must be said that the dancers are part of a group that usually start their improvised movement when another dancer touches them. Therefore, the signal sent through the Internet directly stimulates one dancer but, indirectly, affects the whole group. In all cases this hybrid experiment – connecting groups in two physical spaces and the Internet – promoted negotiation by means of remote actuation, enhancing people's feeling of belonging and presence.

This ephemeral event happened physically in two remote public spaces: in Germany, in the Oderberger Straße in Berlin, in front of the *Kauf Dich Glücklich Café*; and in Brazil, at the Raul Soares Square in Belo Horizonte, using the Internet to create a dialogue between both spaces and to broadcast the event (Figure 2). Berlin was equipped with a projector displaying images from Belo Horizonte, a physical doll equipped with sensors and a computer connected to the Internet sending the output of the doll's sensors and images from Oderberger Straße to Raul Soares Square. The latter hosted the dancers, one of whom dressing a wearable (equipped with actuators) and two computers connected to the Internet: one sending images from the Square to Oderberger Straße and the other receiving signals from the sensors in Berlin and activating the wearable.

The doll had five pressure sensors: on the head, each arm, and each leg, which captured people's touch. The doll was wirily connected to a microcontroller Arduino that received the sensor's output starting a Processing program in the computer at the Café sending the sensor's data through the Internet to a computer in Belo Horizonte. The signal was then received in a Processing program and was transmitted to a wireless radial module Xbee mounted in another Arduino placed in the wearable (Igoe, 2007). Thus, the output of Berlin became the input of the wearable triggering small vibrators producing

Figure 2. Sensor to actuator transmission and image exchange between spaces A and B (Copyleft 2011, LAGEAR. Used with permission)

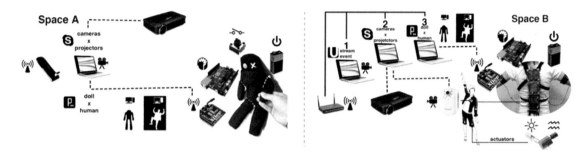

physical stimuli on who wore it. In this way, the performer in the public square was remotely touched by the person playing with the doll in the cafe. There was a LED near the vibrator that turned on at the same time the vibrator became active, i.e., if the right arm of the doll was touched, the vibrator and the LED display on the right arm of the performer became active. So there was a correspondence between the action upon the doll in Berlin, and the stimulus produced in the dancer in Belo Horizonte (Figure 3).

As a technical experiment, *Long Distance Voodoo* successfully connected two remote spaces. Its tactile interface, between doll and wearable, between both spaces, pointed possibilities of remote negotiation by exploring the feeling of presence beyond representation as people established a bodily connection by means of physical remote actuation. This connection triggered spatialised communication, as people playing with the doll gradually realised they could remotely touch the dancer initiating a more lasting and meaningful interaction which was based on physical actuation instead of representation. The dancer participated in this conversation by reacting to the remote touch, influencing the rest of the group by reverberating the stimulus received. Nevertheless, the most important contribution of *Long Distance Voodoo* is the further discussion it fosters regarding both the achievements and their limits related to the theoretical approach that inspired it, especially those relating to the engagement of people in both spaces.

Figure 3. Electronic equipments and their role in Berlin (space A) and Belo Horizonte (space B) (Copyright 2011, LAGEAR. Used with permission)

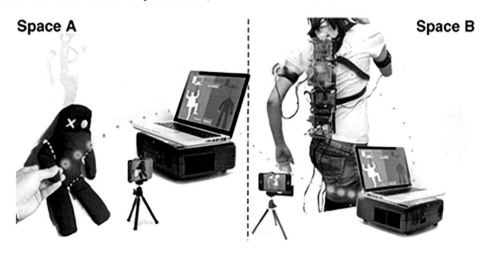

In Berlin, it was identified that people were mostly interested in the 'magic' of the remote touch, not realising its potential for negotiation and dialogue (Figure 4). The interest in the interface—the 'magic by ignorance' – was reinforced by three main features of the installation. First, the need to look at the projection to understand what happened in the other space and therefore give meaning to one's own action, reinforcing the logic of the visual; second, the static position of the doll, hindering the bodily engagement; and third, a technical constraint leading to a delay between the action of poking the doll and the answer from the dancer, making remote negotiation difficult.

These three aspects contribute to a more functional than playful interaction in Berlin. Even though Flusser states a possibility to 'play' by overcoming the apparatus' prescriptions, that is, engaging with content and not only with the interface, the doll eventually worked more as the music box than as the piano, limiting people's interaction with the content and reinforcing the difficulties to avoid the hegemony of the visual.

In Belo Horizonte, however, the dancers were much more involved in the experience, focused on the interface's possibilities to promote conversations by engaging with people in Berlin – leading to a 'magic by experience'. Even though the interface – the wearable was limited, for it provided an individual and reactive experience, it allowed the dancers to more freely interact among themselves and with the space. They were prone to bodily engage in the experiment, since they are already comfortable with performing in public spaces (Figure 5). They also knew beforehand the mechanisms of the wearable and used it to tease people in Berlin to further interact with them. Nevertheless, the experiment did not integrate other people in Raul Soares Square, since passers-by still perceived it as a performance to watch and not to participate, reducing the experience for those in Belo Horizonte again to the 'logic of the visual'. Therefore, despite the possibility of actual playful interactions between those remotely connected noticed in the interaction of the dancers with the wearable, the experience ended up highlighting a functional relationship to technology, hindering any possibility of social awareness, let alone transformation.

Figure 4. People interacting in Berlin with the doll having as visual feedback the image of the dancers in Brazil and the dancers in Brazil stimulated by people touching the doll in Berlin (Copyright 2011, LAGEAR. Used with permission)

Figure 5. The dancers in Brazil wearing the Voodoo device being stimulated by people in Berlin (Copyright 2011, LAGEAR. Used with permission)

Despite the problems above discussed *Long Distance Voodoo* has fulfilled its main objective: to develop and test an interface that allows remote touch by using low-tech and low-cost devices. However, these were not enough to trigger socio-spatial transformation. It is important to say that the fetish of technology has clouded our judgment in this specific installation. Even if we can foresee possible future developments of remote actuation to overcome the fetishism of the visual, this might not be done taking technological development as all there is. We have discussed this experiment in a more optimistic tone (Baltazar et al, 2014), believing that "exploring negotiation beyond the 'logic of the visual' by means of remote actuation is a way to enhance the feeling of belonging and presence." However, we have learned that socio-spatial context needs closer attention and for that an endurable and dialogical interaction needs attention. This leads us to *Ituita*.

Ituita

Ituita (a name derived from the Indian Guarani language meaning stone cascade) is an interface developed by Opera Studio in partnership with LAGEAR in 2012/2013. It is composed of an interactive urban LED display connected to a website, placed in the cascade at the central square of the Baroque city of Congonhas, Minas Gerais, Brazil (Figures 6 and 7). *Ituita* was designed to engage people with their city issues in two different ways. First by means of the website in which people answer questions regarding different monthly themes related to the city (waste, health, transport etc); and second by playfully interacting in the square with graphics that summarize the results of the online questionnaire—such graphics are animated responding to people's movement in the square captured by Kinect sensor.

As a reactive interface, *Ituita* enables a reactive interaction, when the users respond the questionnaire and graphics are automatically shown in the LED displays in the square. As a proactive interface, *Ituita* enables a proactive interaction, when people are interacting with the graphics in the square and suddenly different graphics appears on the LED displays (output of online answered questions). Nevertheless, even if the interface is reactive and proactive triggering reactive and proactive interactions, there is also a dialogical interaction promoted by the openness of the project to people's engagement.

Figure 6. How Ituita works (Copyright 2012, LAGEAR. Used with permission)

Figure 7. The inauguration of the central square in Congonhas, with Ituita working (Copyright 2013, LAGEAR. Used with permission)

Ituita is a kind of thermometer of the city, and proposes a circularity of actions implied by the present-time feedback between the website and the LED displays. The given answers to the online questionnaire generates the graphics shown in the square. At the same time the interpreted graphics trigger discussions in the online forum, which in a feedback system influence the answers shown in the square. Such a circularity is not limited to the Internet but might reverberate in the city if people really engage in a direct democracy proposed by the interface.

In the case of *Ituita* interaction is dialogical not the interface. The interface by itself does not enable the enhancement of the feeling of belonging and presence, it only stimulates people to engage in discussions about the city. The interface works only as a catalyst of socio-spatial engagement and transformation. However, such a feeling of belonging and presence is very difficult to be directly connected to any interface or space. It is much more a question of the way people interact with the interface and with each other by means of the interface.

If on one hand *Ituita* moves towards the dialectics of the spectacle and experience, as it proposes an open and indeterminate experience beyond mere contemplation, on the other it was not enough to engage citizens in dialogue with themselves regarding the city. The main problem was the belief that an interface that is open to dialogical interaction would be enough to trigger dialogue between people without a strong political support to make it knowledgeable by all the citizens. A possible solution for that would be to make the design process itself dialogical.

Once people are included in the process, they might understand the potential of the interface and, in the case o *Ituita*, might be compelled to feed the questionnaires with more contextual issues, more dear to them, instead of the generic prescribed issues we have programmed. This has led us to our next development.

CANI (Catas Altas Network of Ideas)

Ituita was essential to rethink the processes when proposing an urban intervention for socio-spatial transformation. While on the one hand *Ituita* has shown technology's potential to provide a hybrid dialogical interface (between the panels in the central square and the website), on the other hand it has proven its failure to engage residents in dialogue. The main weakness of the interface lies in the lack of dialogue between the proponents and the population, both during the design process and the disclosure and dissemination process. In addition to requiring a certain complexity of interaction, the subjects covered by the interface did not encourage dialogue. *Ituita*, therefore, relied heavily on technology while leaving everyday (and socio-spatial) issues in the background.

In this way, the urban interface CANI, developed in Cata Altas, also a small town in Minas Gerais, had as its main focus the problematisation of the socio-spatial context before any digital technological development. In addition to the previous experiences already mentioned, the process was inspired by Hannah Arendt's concepts of public sphere and political action (Arendt, 1998) that approached the idea of social transformation. For the philosopher, there are three human conditions: work, labour, and action, the last being the political activity *par excellence*, corresponding to the human capacity to unleash the new. While work and labor do not necessarily depend on the relationship between people, action responds to human plurality and has an adequate space in the public sphere. However, for Arendt, the collection of individual wishes on the public domain – she sees it as (one of the causes of) the rise of the social – is one of the main causes of the decline of the public sphere, while the blurring between the public which is the domain of the citizens, and the private which is the domain of the individual prevents political action, that is, social transformation.

So, we can say that CANI aims to engage people into the direction of the resumption of the public sphere, this means to open possibilities of dialogical interactions between plural individuals coming from different classes and social backgrounds about common issues, so they can act politically as citizens.

Catas Altas, a small town in Minas Gerais (about 4,000 inhabitants) was chosen for the experiment because of the patent need for citizens to articulate themselves, once they suffer from the presence of two of Brazil's biggest mining companies: Vale and Samarco. It is a critical situation, because while the population depends on the jobs created, the mining companies consume the natural wealth of the region from which the city depends to boost tourism and generate independent jobs, among other things. So, Catas Altas is a good example of a community where the disconnection between the residents prevents political action (or social transformation).

CANI's main strategy to incite social transformation was to encourage a dialogue between citizens based on the socio-spatial complexities of the place. And for this, the first step was to gain knowledge about such complexities under the watchful eyes of those who know most about the daily life of Catas Altas: the residents themselves.

During ten months, participatory activities were carried out in order to articulate the residents in their plurality since the beginning of the process, and to know the most of the community's socio-spatial complexities. In this way, the inhabitants of Catas Altas were not mere objects of study, but the main characters, since it was the interaction with them (and between them) that defined each subsequent step of the process. So, as we aimed to build a dialogical interface that incites dialogical interactions, the process itself was dialogical, that is, uncertain but always contextualized.

The first proposed activity was a photography workshop that had two goals: to enable an initial approach to the daily life of the city and to set in motion a group formed by young people interested in discussing and changing the city. We focused on this group because youngsters may have spare time to engage with such a project and because they may also potentially expand the discussion within their own family and friends circles. A young female inhabitant, whom we met previously and who was very interested in discussing the city she lived on, became our local expert and helped us articulate this group. By means of a pamphlet distributed by us at the end of a school session, we advertised the workshop, and it was clear that her involvement enthused students to participate because they already knew her. Thus, she became an important link between the researchers and the participants, specially in the early stages of the research. At the workshop day, there were 10 participants. They took pictures of places or situations that they found interesting and, later, the images were projected into a wall. The participants were asked to make comments and to relate the pictures to a fabric map laid out on the floor and a discussion about their city followed. They were then invited to formalize a group interested not only in discussing, but also changing the city. All upcoming activities resulted from decisions of the group members themselves. Over the next months out activities were carried out, such as a video workshop to film interviews with the older residents to remember the stories of the city, manufacturing flyers questioning the relations in the city, and even an open air cinema club. The researchers' job was to do the logistics for the activities that are happening and to observe people interaction. Unlike interviews and surveys, all these activities revealed the important issues that sometimes people themselves can not express formally.

The open air cinema club has proved to be an important interface both to articulate people and to let us know more about the dynamics of the city. Altogether there were seven sessions (some with more than 100 spectators), always in the public space. The movie and the place where it would be displayed were chosen by the residents themselves via Facebook.

From the dialogical process, we had three main guidelines for the design of the interface. First, it should be based on the city map because a very simple map proved to be a great articulator of people's ideas. Second, it should be designed as a portable urban interface that might easily travel to different neighborhoods, in order to articulate the maximum of residents in their plurality. And finally, the interface should return to the residents the main socio-spatial complexities that came to light during the process in order to incite dialogues.

After ten months of dialogical process between the researchers and inhabitants, we built CANI. It may be said that even though CANI's design was a top-down process, in terms of the interaction it enables, empowerment happens in a bottom-up fashion, starting from the users. As such, CANI is a result of bringing together our knowledge – technical, methodological, and theoretical – and the residents' knowledge about their everyday life. The interface, made of simple and cheap materials, is an ambulant structure composed of an acrylic display of the map of the city that can have its parts illuminated according to people's responses to the proposed questions. These questions were created based on all the information about the relations in the city collected throughout the process. After answering what is suggested on the LED illuminated panel, such as highlighting an area they feel is the most neglected in the city, the person must press a button that triggers a webcam, located on top of the interface. All answers are recorded and then a synthesis map is made available at the Internet. Figures 8, 9, 10 and 11 present the design, interface, the setup, and the synthesis of the interactions.

Each action informed about the reality of that place and allowed citizens to articulate themselves and rethink the socio-spatial complexities of Catas Altas.

CANI has been used by over a hundred residents for five days, and we witnessed clever dialogues on the issues of the city, among people who sometimes did not even know each other. It was a surprise to note that the discussion did not took place on the Internet but live, when people were interacting with the map. So people do not only interact with the interface but interact with each other. The technology served more to 'attract attention' than as a basis for dialogue. What most 'kept the eye' were the map and the related issues. These simple but contextualized questions were enough to promote dialogue around the subjects of the public but not private interests. People were talking as citizens

Figure 8. The general design of the urban interface CANI (Catas Altas Network of Ideas) (Copyright 2014, LAGEAR. Used with permission)

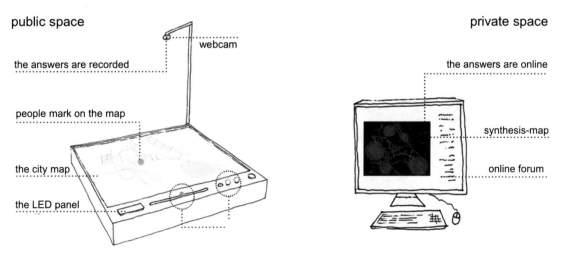

Figure 9. The drawing of the arrangement of CANI elements (Copyleft 2014, LAGEAR. Used with permission)

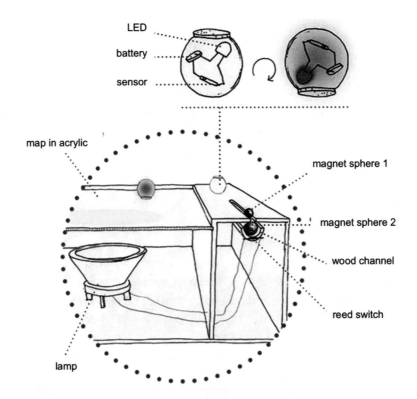

Figure 10. The arrangement of CANI elements (Copyright 2014, LAGEAR. Used with permission)

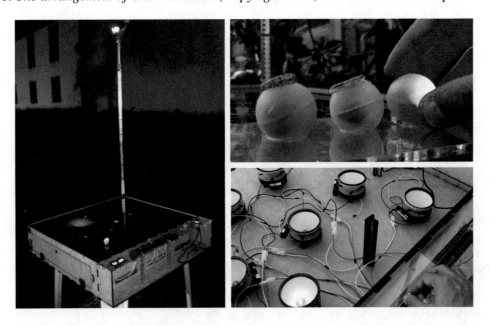

Figure 11. Systematisation of people's responses to the proposed questions displayed in a website (Copyright 2014, LAGEAR. Used with permission)

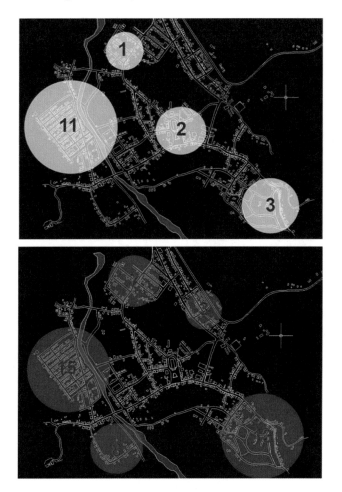

CONCLUSION

This paper discusses LAGEAR's main drives, which are playful interaction, the distinction between the interface and interaction and dialogue, in order to create interactive interfaces that actually engage people in socio-spatial transformation. Examples of the authors' works were presented, from visually based to bodily engaging and socio-political installations.

The current popularisation of discourses on social transformation has contributed to cultivate the fetish of the visual and of digital technology, as instead of focusing on socio-spatial contexts most urban installations are using the social discourse as a source of inspiration to create a spectacle based on technological development. Even if we were aware of the fetish of the visual, the dialectics of spectacle and experience was still clouding our perspective of the fetish of digital technology. To mention Cedric Price (2003), we were accepting that technology was the answer, even without asking the question. The main question we started to ask concerns how people might engage in socio-spatial transformation by means of our projects. This leads to a need to seriously problematising the contexts for which we are developing urban interfaces and avoiding the visual and technological spectacles disguised behind empty discourses of social transformation. The most important discussion did not concern the bodily engagement but the problematisation leading to the need of engagement. This means, the need to work with the socio-spatial context and propose interfaces that take into account the process in its openness and indeterminacy, instead of prescribing a product (even if an interface-product). For that, instead of discussing the production of an interface-product – which might be reactive, proactive, or dialogical – we propose to discuss first the interaction one is willing to promote by means of the interface.

ACKNOWLEDGMENT

We would like to thank the Brazilian Agencies Fapemig, CNPq, CAPES, and FINEP that funded the research projects taking place at LAGEAR. We also thank Mateus Stralen from Opera Studio for the partnership in the development of *Ituita*.

REFERENCES

Arendt, H. (1998). *The human condition*. Chicago: University of Chicago Press. doi:10.7208/chicago/9780226924571.001.0001

Baltazar, A. P. (2009). *Cyberarchitecture: the virtualisation of architecture beyond representation towards interactivity* (Unpublished doctoral dissertation). The Bartlett School of Architecture, University College London.

Baltazar, A. P. (2012). Beyond representation: possible uses of new media in architecture. In *V!RUS 8: RE:PRE:SENTAR*. São Carlos: Nomads. Retrieved from http://www.nomads.usp.br/virus/virus08/?sec=4&item=1&lang=en

Baltazar, A. P. (2017). Architecture as interface: a constructive method for spatial articulation in architectural education. In *Architectural Research Addressing Societal Challenges*. London: Taylor & Francis. Retrieved from http://www.mom.arq.ufmg.br/mom/arq_interface/3a_aula/2016_06_16_eaae_baltazar.pdf

Baltazar, A. P., Arruda, G. F., Cabral Filho, J. S., Melgaço, L. M. S., & Almeida, M. A. (2014). Beyond the visual in urban interactive interfaces: Dialogue and social transformation. *International Journal of Creative Interfaces and Computer Graphics*, 5(2), 1–15. doi:10.4018/ijcicg.2014070101

Baltazar, A. P., & Cabral Filho, J. S. (2010). Magic beyond ignorance: virtualising the black box. In H. Roscoe, P. Moran, & T. Mucelli (Eds.), *FAD—Festival de Arte Digital 2010* (pp. 19–23). Belo Horizonte: Instituto Cidades Criativas.

Baltazar, A. P., Cabral Filho, J. S., Melgaço, L. M. S., Almeida, M. A., & Arruda, G. F. (2012). Towards socially engaging and transformative urban interactive interfaces. *Proceedings of Artech 2012 – 6th International Conference on Digital Arts*, 279–285.

Colonna, F. (1999). *Hypnerotomachia Poliphili: the strife of love in a dream*. London: Thames and Hudson.

Dubberly, H., Haque, U., & Pangaro, P. (2009). What is interaction? Are there different types? *Interactions Magazine, 16*(1). Retrieved from http://www.dubberly.com/articles/what-is-interaction.html

Ferro, S. (2006). *Arquitetura e trabalho livre*. Belo Horizonte: Cosac Naify.

Flusser, V. (1999a). Design: obstacle for/to the removal of obstacles. In V. Flusser (Ed.), *The shape of things: a philosophy of design* (pp. 58–61). London: Reaktion.

Flusser, V. (2000). *Towards a Philosophy of Photography*. London: Reaktion Books.

Graham, S. (2004). *The Cybercities Reader*. New York: Routledge.

Haque, U. (2017). VoiceOver: Citizen Empowerment Through Cultural Infrastructure. *Architectural Design, 87*(1), 86–91. doi:10.1002/ad.2136

Haque, U. (2016-2018). *Umbrellium Group, VoiceOver*. Retrieved from <http://umbrellium.co.uk/initiatives/voiceover/>

Igoe, T. (2007). *Making things talk: practical methods for connecting physical objects*. Beijing: O'Reilly.

Lefebvre, H. (1991). *The production of space*. London: Blackwell.

Lozano-Hemmer, R. (2010). *Summer equation, Relational Architecture 16*. Retrieved December 03, 2013 from http://www.lozano-hemmer.com/solar_equation.php

Oosterhuis, K. (2002). Lecture at the Building Centre. London: Academic Press.

Pérez-Gómez, A. (1994, July). The space of architecture: meaning as presence and representation. In S. Holl, J. Pallasmaa, & A. Pérez-Gómez (Eds.), Questions of perception: phenomenology of architecture, a+u, Architecture and Urbanism special issue (pp. 7–25). Tokyo: Academic Press.

Pérez-Gómez, A., & Pelletier, L. (1997). *Architectural representation and the perspective hinge*. Cambridge, MA: MIT Press.

Price, C. (n.d.). *The Square Book*. Academy Press.

Stralen, M., Baltazar, A. P., Melgaço, L., & Arruda, G. (2012). Congonhas Media Cascade – Ituita: a permanent urban interactive interface for citizenship. In *Proceedings of eCAADe 2012*. Praga: Cumincad. Retrieved from http://www.mom.arq.ufmg.br/mom/arq_interface/3a_aula/stralen_baltazar_ecaade.pdf

KEY TERMS AND DEFINITIONS

Dialectics of Spectacle and Experience: The visual is not taken as merely contemplative and experience is not taken as merely active, they work in a dialectic relation, enriching each other, avoiding a contemplative finished product and promoting a seductive and enduring interaction of people with each other and with the space.

Dialogue: Exchange of pieces of information to synthesize new information as proposed by Vilém Flusser.

Engagement: Active and continuous participation.

Fetish of Digital Technology: The assumption that the use of digital technology is an end in itself, and in the context or urban installations, enough to accomplish socio-spatial transformation, but in fact it contributes to fragment people's experience.

Interaction: The way people relate to each other or how people relate themselves to interfaces and objects.

Interface: Digital-physical devices that enable human-machine or human-human interaction.

Logic of the Visual: The privileging of the visual over lived experiences, which ultimately leads to the commodification of space.

Playful Interaction: A form of interaction when one uses an apparatus beyond its prescriptions, engaging with content and not only with its interface.

Socio-Spatial Transformation: A political transformation of space having social emancipation at the horizon, acknowledging that space is a social product and that society is formed and transformed by the space it forges.

Section 2
Interfaces That Support Art

Chapter 7
The Forking Paths Revisited:
Experimenting on Interactive Film

Bruno Mendes da Silva
Centro de Investigação em Artes e Comunicação, Portugal

Mirian Nogueira Tavares
University of Algarve, Portugal

Vítor Reia-Batista
Centro de Investigação em Artes e Comunicação, Portugal

Rui António
Centro de Investigação em Artes e Comunicação, Portugal

ABSTRACT

Based on the triad, film-interactivity-experimentation, the applied research project, The Forking Paths, developed at the Centre for Research in Arts and Communication (CIAC) endeavors to find alternative narrative forms in the field of cinema and, more specifically, in the subfield of interactive cinema. The films in the project invest in the interconnectivity between the film narrative and the viewer, who is given the possibility to be more active and engaged. At same time, the films undertake a research on the development of audio-visual language. The project is available at an online platform, which aims to foster the creation and web hosting of other interactive cinema projects in its different variables. This chapter focuses on the three films completed up to the moment: Haze, The Book of the Dead, and Waltz.

INTRODUCTION

The Forking Paths project began in January 2013 and is available at an online platform (oscaminhosque-sebifurcam.ciac.pt) dedicated to interactive film experiences. In addition to other productions, all the films included in the project can be found at the platform: *Waltz* (2016), *The Book of the Dead* (2015) and *Haze* (2014). Seeking to align applied research with experimental development, this project comprised the following purposes at an early stage: the production of interactive film narratives that aim to take the viewer from an extradiegetic level to an intradiegetic level through a process of immersion;

DOI: 10.4018/978-1-5225-7371-5.ch007

the reflection and the experimentation on the concept of time in cinema; the creation of a platform for hosting films and interactive film projects.

This chapter begins with a visit to the most significant moments in the history of interactive cinema, both at a purely technological level and at an aesthetic level, which is the result of a balanced combination between creative content and technology. Then, the central issue of this project, time in cinema, is developed, relating it to the theme and form of the tales chosen for adaptation. The methodology used and the interactive films produced or invited within the scope of the project will also be given special attention. Finally, the platform, the virtual place to where all content related to the project (from news to scientific articles) converges, will also be analysed in this article.

INTERACTIVE CINEMA

Several filmmakers and artists have ventured upon film productions which rely on multiple narratives, such as *Glimpses of the USA*, a 1959 film by Charles and Ray Eames (Glimpses of the USA, 1959).

This film consists of seven images projected simultaneously, giving the viewer the freedom to combine the images as he/she so chooses. Multiple narratives usually consist of several closed narratives and use multiple events that may intersect and complement each other, giving meaning to the story as a whole. These characteristics bear some resemblance to the aesthetics of hypertext on the internet.

Back in 1927, film director Abel Gance released *Napoleon*, an epic film with multiple projection on three adjacent screens, building an enormous triptych, a technique which became known as Polyvision. Filming with three cameras, Gance intended to create widescreen panoramas and, in this way, enhance realism (see picture 2.17). While editing, Gance realized that the use of different images, side by side, had as great an impact as the panoramas, and, for that reason, he ended up using both the widescreen panoramas and the tryptich montages in the film *Napoleon*. The initial intention of achieving an increase in realism eventually led to an increase in abstraction.

In 1961, the horror film *Mr. Sardonicus* was realeased in movie theatres. Near the end of the film, there was a poll to punish the bad guy (Mr. Sardonicus, 1961). Using glow-in-the-dark cards, the audience would choose if this character would die at the end of the film. Luckily, the audience always voted for Sardonicus's death, as producer William Castle never shot the scene where Sardonicus did not die (Waters, 2007).

The first interactive film narrative installed in a custom-built projection room was released in 1967: the *Kinoautomat: One man and his House* by the Czech filmmaker Radúz Činčera (Kinoautomat, 1967).

The movie stopped at certain points to give the audience the possibility to interact with the narrative, using buttons installed on their seats. Given the two options, the audience voted by pressing one of the buttons, either red or green, and, according to their choice, the most voted option would dictate the scene to be played. Seeing that the possibility of choice given to the audience resulted in a certain form of empowerment regarding the unfolding of the narrative made this film a success at the International and Universal Exhibition held in the city of Montreal, Canada.

In the 80s and 90s, an interactive program called *Agora Escolha* [*Now You Choose*] was broadcasted on Portuguese television. The audience was given the opportunity to choose the program to be broadcast at a certain time, between two possible options, through real-time voting and by telephone. There was a similar program in Brazil broadcasted by Rede Globo, in the 90s, named *Você decide* [*You Decide*]. The difference lay in the fact that, instead of having two different programs to choose from, this one allowed to choose between two different endings for the same program.

In 1991, two German television stations (ARD and ZDF) produced *Mörderische Entscheidung* [*A Murderous Decision*], directed by Oliver Hirschbiegel, a film that presents two versions simultaneously: one from the perspective of a woman, the other from that of a man. The films intersect in some scenes in which both the woman and the man perform together. The audience follows both perspectives by zapping in a story where neither the Aristotelian unity of space and time nor the narration can be altered.

In 1992, the cinema company Interfilm, in joint partnership with Sony, began conducting interactive cinema experiments, but, due to their very limited forms, they did not receive due attention for pioneering cinema interactivity. According to Lunenfeld (2005), one of the first to claim the title of interactive film (there were several who claimed this title) was Bob Bejan, in 1992, with *I'm your man* (Graham & Bejan, 1992). In this film, the audience used a seat-mounted joystick to vote between three narrative options, at six different points throughout the film. The film followed an arborescent structure and stopped at the different intersection points to allow public interaction.

The film lasted twenty minutes, but the ticket that the spectator bought allowed him/her to watch the film as many times as desired. Although the film version was not very successful, six years later, the DVD version would be released. One of the problems with the screening in movie theaters with a voting system is that a part of the audience, those with the least votes, can not enjoy their choices. This problem has been overcome with the DVD version.

Currently, with the consumption habits and the possibilities of network communication technology, this obstacle has become less relevant, allowing the creation of interactive products for individual use. Interactivity with voting system by the audience was adapted by some television programs, usually using telephone voting.

However, several scholars consider the film *Smoking/No Smoking*, by Alain Resnais, 1993, the first film to be internationally regarded as an example of interactive cinema. *Smoking/No Smoking* deals with choice. The audience is given the choice between two opposing situations: smoking or not smoking. In addition to the initial separation of the two films, each film also contains six bifurcations resulting in six different stories within the same narrative. Each film is projected simultaneously in different rooms. This way, the audience chooses the initial action of the plot by choosing the room.

In 2002, Lev Manovich conceived *Soft Cinema*, software that randomly displays sequences of images and music stored in a database. Although the montage technique can be found here, the intrigue in the narrative is non-existent. The montage sequence is pre-programed by the viewer's interaction with a keyboard. The narrative is generated by the database. According to Manovich (2010), the database is the counterpart of the traditional narrative form.

In 2003, Peter Greenaway releases an ambitious transmedia project entitled *Tulse Luper Suitcases*, which includes four films, a 16-episode television series, a set of 92 DVDs, CD-ROMs, books, exhibitions, installations, concerts, a play, web sites and an online game entitled *The Tulse Luper Journey* (Greenaway, 2003). This game offers the player the possibility of exploring a puzzle that is unveiled with the visualization of each of the 92 fragments that make up the film. These fragments represent the life of the character Tulse Henry Purcell Luper, who packed his life in 92 suitcases distributed throughout the world. It is up to the player to put together the character's life using the evidence found in the suitcases.

Greenaway thus tries to break with Griffith's model of narrative cinema, based on the settings and on the actors, to venture into a project that expands itself, dadaistically, through diverse media and diverse spaces, with tenuously defined contours, where the limits between cinema, performance, visual arts and digital media dissolve. Like Joseph Kosuth's *One and Three Chairs*, which features a chair, the photograph of that chair, and a definition of of the word "chair" taken from a dictionary, Greenaway also works around the object, the picture, and the concept, but on a larger interactive scale and using different perspectives. While Kosuth is interested in problematizing the relation between object, picture and concept, Greenaway uses the three elements with the purpose of self-reinforcement. With his project, Greenaway seeks to challenge not only traditional cinema technology, but also its structure, which, according to the author, has not gone beyond illustrated text.

Greenaway is rather critical about cinema, stating that cinema is passive and therefore does not evolve with digital technology. The author goes even further and announces that the death of cinema took place on September 31st, 1983, with the introduction of the remote control in domestic households (Greenaway, 2007). Greenaway's project invites the viewer to participate actively in his work, by taking him/her to different environments such as cinema rooms, television, theaters, streets, art galleries and the internet. The contents and the mediums are an unfinished and constantly growing network structure. Like most of Greenaway's work, this project has no emphasis on narrative and is an encyclopedic cluster that explores the dialogue between art and technology. The viewer is given the opportunity to immerse himself/herself in the work exploring various means and senses. The viewer sees, hears, touches, accesses and participates in the process of creation.

In 2009, director James Cameron releases the interactive trailer for the film *Avatar*. This trailer may be downloaded from the official website [www.avatarmovie.com/air/] and installed on the computer. The viewer has the option of watching the trailer without interruptions or relishing the interactive possibilities. The interactivity lies in the possibility of the viewer deciding whether to receive additional content on the film. The timebar includes eleven points that correspond to small stops, during which the viewer has access to one of the characters. These links allow the viewer to watch more details on an additional video.

The trailer has 3'32'' minutes, but, with the additional videos, it reaches 18'45''. There is also the option to check out the latest Twitter posts related to the movie and to download other content, such as the soundtrack of the film.

In 2010, Jung Von Matt produces *Last Call* (Jung Von Matt, 2010), an interactive film project, created as a commercial piece for a channel owned by NBCUniversal. It is a short film that was played in German movie theatres. The film tells the story of a female character stalked by a Serial Killer. While trying to escape, she finds a cell phone, which she uses to establish contact with the members of the audience. These may help her with the decisions she has to make during the narrative. Upon entering the room, the viewers receive an invitation to submit their mobile phone number on a specific digital platform, which will enable them to receive calls from the protagonist, at any time. At certain points in the movie, the main character randomly calls someone in the audience and asks a question about the path to take or the decision to make. A voice recognition software captures the viewer's decision. Based on the answer, the protagonist will take the path suggested by the viewer, following a specific sequence of the story. *Last Call* includes a series of paths and possible endings based on the interaction of the viewers, who determine changes in the narrative, giving them the feeling of control over the story.

In the same year 2010, *Scenario*, a 3D interactive film, was released (Scenario, 2010; Couts, 2011). The film was developed at the iCinema Centre for Interactive Cinema Research, at the University of New South Wales.

The film is projected onto a 360° widescreen with motion sensors which track the audience. The interaction happens between the human participants and the humanoid creatures on the screen controlled by the artificial intelligence mechanism of the film. The narrative unfolds depending on how the audience interacts with the film.

Sufferrosa, a project by the multimedia artist Dawid Marcinkowski, was released in 2010 and is an interactive, non-linear narrative that combines music, film, photography and the internet (Sufferrosa, 2010). *Sufferrosa* was screened at various festivals and exhibitions, such as MOVES International Film Festival and OFFF Post-Digital Culture Festival. The plot of the film centers on the protagonist, the detective Ivan Johnson, who is searching for a missing woman. The spectator becomes the protagonist, and immerses himself/herself deeply in the narrative meeting several characters along the way and finding links that help to unravel the mystery. The film is based on the premise "What happens in the film depends entirely on the viewer's choice."

The film consists of 110 scenes, 3 alternate endings and 4 Levels -1, 0, 1 and 2. Interactivity is accomplished when the viewer hovers the pointer of the mouse over the pictures, movie clips, and links that provide the necessary information for the progression in the film sequence. At any moment, the viewer is able to see the map of the clinic where the action takes place, which offers an overview of the all the optional links and their location.

The links only become visible when the viewer moves the pointer of the mouse over certain areas of the screen, which implies exploring and discovering the different options available. Although the viewer chooses the links, finding them happens randomly, as it results from the exploration of the movement of the mouse over the screen. Therefore, the sequence of the film is also random.

In 2014, the production company Filmstrip started the project *Biosuite* (Filmstrip, 2014) in collaboration with the Sonic Arts Research Center (SARC), at the University of Queensland. In order to control how the film narrative unfolds, this project explores the emotional reactions from the audience, using Electrocardiogram (ECG) signals and Galvanic Skin Response (GSR), which measures a person's skin conductance levels. These signals are interpreted by a computer-run software and determine the changes in the film narrative, as well as the creation of sound effects.

There are very few examples of film interactivity with mobile devices; one of them is by Häkkilä et al. (2014), who enables interacting with the content of the 3D film in movie theaters using a mobile phone. Viewers can use their personal devices to access different pieces of information, such as additional data about the producer of the soundtrack being played or or a discount voucher for some of the accessories worn by the main actor. However, this project is quite different from the one set out in this study.

Given the above information, there a number of ways to develop interaction. One of the paradigms of human-computer interaction are 3D sensors, such as Microsoft Kinect (Kinect, 2014), Asus Xtion (Xtion, 2014), Leap Motion (Leap, 2014) or Structure Sensor (Struture, 2014). Those sensors can be used to interpret specific human gestures, enabling a hands-free control of electronic devices, manipulating objects in a virtual world, or interacting with augmented reality applications. Many of those tracking and gesture recognition sensors are extremely important in the video game industry. With the appropriate software, the sensors also have the ability of tracking the user's skeleton and/or tracking a single user or multiple users. The sensors are able to accurately replicate the user's hand gestures and movements in a three-dimensional manner.

Several research centers have emerged in the area of interactive cinema, among which two stand out: the Interactive Cinema Group, directed by Glorianna Davenport, founded in 1987 by the MIT Media Laboratory in Cambridge, Massachusetts, and the iCinema Center for Interactive Cinema Research, led by Jeffrey Shaw, founded in 2002 by the University of New South Wales, Australia. While the first one (in the meantime inactive) had as its main focus on the investigation of formal structures, construction methods and the social impact of the distribution of interactive films, the second embraced a wider scope, exploring the technological development of immersive systems.

MODELS

We now need to classify the above-mentioned experiences. Therefore, we tried to find a set of models capable of including all interactive films: (a) the arborescent model, based on a simple one-off choice made at certain moments in the narrative, where the viewer can choose paths A or B, for which we may use the film *Last Call* as an example; (b) the constructive model, which involves multiple interpretation, according to the options offered by the project, where we can include the experimental film *Haze*; (c) the paired model, which allows the incorporation of content external to the narrative, as in the film *Take This Lollipop*; and (d) the fertile model, whose process of interaction between spectator and film entails the creation of new content, although such a film does not yet exist.

The last model (fertile model) is presented as the possibility of rupture with the sequence of experiences that have been carried out since the middle of the last century. The interactivity of these films has always been limited to the possibilities of choice offered by each project. possibility of generating new content that is not predefined. This possibility of effective image, captured in the real world and, therefore, dependent on previously made footage. However, if we think about animated films, the creation of new narrative continuities may be a reality in the near future.

TIME AND THE TALES

A key issue in this project is time: time at cinema. First of all, it is important the temporal experience of the film narrative by the conventional viewer, as well as by the spectator-protagonist. In the first film, *Haze*, this issue has been developed through the spectator-protagonist, who experiences the same moment more than once, until that very moment becomes something else: a moment that is both the same and another. Thus, the space-time relation becomes a space-times relation. In the second film of *The Forking Paths, The Book of the Dead*, the time issue focuses mainly on the interpretation of the film, offering the spectator the possibility to read at his/her own pace, as if he/she were reading a book. As theoretical basis (Silva, 2013), the notions of movement-image, time-image and crystal-image, proposed by Deleuze (1995), serve as structural basis for this work. By appealing to viewer immersion, they cause a reaction contrary to the usual passive-submissive reaction.

According to Deleuze (1990: 29), the sensory-motor sensations, indirect representations of time, tend to be replaced by exclusively visual and audible conjunctures, namely the opsign[1] and the sonsign[2], direct representations of time. Through this theoretical background, *The Forking Paths* uses eminently visual situations in the film *Haze*, by means of a subjective camera and the exhaustive repetition of images, endeavouring to meet the opsign concept. It is also related to the concept of sonsign in sound situations that arise without any corresponding or related images. In the film *The Book of the Dead*, the concept of opsign is closely related to moments where two parallel planes, connected by the same sound, occur simultaneously (according to the spectator's choices). These moments (always referring to the present) take place simultaneously in two different spaces, by changing the space-time relation to a space-space-time relation.

We found the indicated features in the work of Italo Calvino (2002), taking into account (the tale) and the background theme (time) to convert the literary text into film text in the films *Haze* and *The Book of the Dead*. These choices were made on an experimental perspective and, although in formal and conceptual terms they coincide with the structural lines of the project *The Forking Paths*, they are admittedly a personal choice. In these tales, the idea of interactivity is present through the game[3] that the author develops between the narrator and the narratee, as well as the idea of virtuality. According to Lévy (Lévy, 1995), imagination, memory, knowledge, and religion are factors of virtualization that made us abandon the physical presence long before the arrival of digital networks. Another author whose work addresses the question of time (of the time that is parallel, multiple, which forks and simultaneously crystallizes at the present) is Jorge Luis Borges (2000). The name of this project pays homage to the tale *The Garden of Forking Paths*, which addresses issues related to the possibility of multiple choices and, especially, of multiple experiences, such as the ones in the interactive films we have produced.

THE FILM

An original script was written for the film *Waltz*, while *Haze* and *The Book of the Dead* are based on stories written by Italo Calvino (2002), however, all three rely on an experimental dimension, both at formal and aesthetic levels. Therefore, the following parameters were taken into account: (a) narrativity – the search for new relations between the narrative and the spectator; (b) cinematography – the search for filmmaking processes suitable to the interactive models; and (c) interactivity – the search for interactive technologies suitable for cinema.

Within this framework of thought (Figure 1), which tries to find solutions simultaneouly creative and functional, we can still find the following interceptions:

1. At the intersection between Narrativity and Cinematography, we chose a tale that would enable the convergence of these two parameters.
2. At the intersection between Narrativity and Interaction, the audiovisual Genre of the narratives was taken into account, so that the choices regarding the interactive technologies were safely made.
3. Finally, at the intersection between Narrativity, Cinematography and Interaction, we can find the Form through which the film is presented to the spectator and devoloped with him.

The interactive film *The Book of the Dead* (Figure 2), from 2015, tries to interact with the viewer at two levels: by controlling certain actions of the characters and by controlling the narrative time, allowing the spectator his/her own reading pace. When we read, we use our own reading pace, we can read slower or faster, but when we hear someone else reading, we depend on a reading pace that is not our own and to which we must adapt. The same happens when we watch a film: the viewing time is imposed by the pace of the film editing, which can be faster or more contemplative. In *The Book of the Dead* the viewers are the ones who choose the length of each plan. Therefore, the film offers an opportunity never experi-

Figure 1. Framework of conceptual interceptions (© 2014, B. Silva. Used with permission)

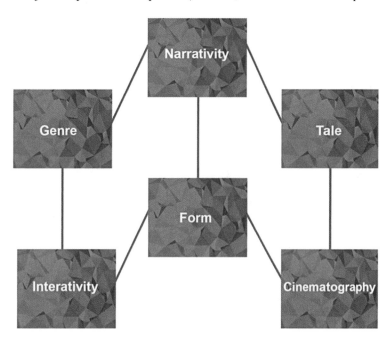

enced before: the viewer has control over the film narrative pace. This possibility enables the spectator to adapt the reading time of the moving images to his/her personal pace. This control works in a very simple way, by clicking on the image. After perceiving the action inherent to each plan[4], the viewer can move to the next level or, if he/she so chooses, he/she can remain in the same plane and get to know its content better, both aesthetically and narratively. On the other hand, the viewer is also given some choices at certain points in the narrative. This possibility takes place within the scope of an arborescent structure, where it is possible to choose between paths. Those choices are confined to key moments in the narrative and are made by clicking in certain areas of the screen. These choices function as paths parallel to the central narrative and do not alter its predefined course. *The Book of the Dead* takes place in the 20s, when two ladies are trying to get rid of a corpse in a spring evening. This is the premise for a series of adventures that invariably end badly. This interactive film is designed to be viewed both on the internet and on mobile devices. It is therefore a movie prepared to be viewed individually. The trailer is available at https://vimeo.com/127651062 and the full version of the film at http://oscaminhosquesebi-furcam.ciac.pt/livros-dos-mortos.html.

Technically, *The Book of the Dead* was filmed with a Canon EOS camera. Several technical resources were used when filming, such as cranes and distinct lighting systems. Particular attention was given to colour relations between the different pictorial elements. It is also important to point out that the movie was shot entirely at night. Among the film settings, the most particular is perhaps the Estoi Palace (Figure 3), an 1840 building, famous for its tiles and its garden sculptures[5]. Five semi-professional actors and a former star of the Portuguese television, Luís Pereira de Sousa, were chosen to play the characters, so that the viewer could identify the actors more easily. With regard to the technical staff, the team that directed and produced the interactive film *Haze* remained roughly the same, as it can be attested in the closing credits of both films.

Figure 2. A film scene picture by Jorge Jubilot, Chão Limpo, Quatrim Norte (© 2015, J. Jubilot. Used with permission)

Figure 3. A film scene picture by Pedro Jubilot (Estoi Palace), (© 2015, J. Jubilot. Used with permission)

The Interactive film *Haze*, 2014, was released to the public between June 16th and July 16th at the International Electronic Art Festival – FILE 2015[6]. It dismounts the tale *If on a winter's night a traveller*, by Italo Calvino, into sound and visual fragments which repeat themselves until they lose meaning (or gain new meaning, as we will see below). That process intends to offer the viewer the status of specta-tor-protagonist. By means of distinct morphologic resources, it allows the viewer to become the main character in the narrative, i.e. it enables the spectator to transit from a passive role (extradiegetic) to an active role (intradiegetic). A voice-over establishes a dialogue with the viewer to achieve that transition. We call it Polish narrator (as we have seen, it is a narrator who dubs the dialogues of all the characters).

The Polish narrator is the first contact that the spectator has with narrative and he guides the viewer in the immersion process through pieces of advice and confidences. With the unfolding of the narrative, the distinction between the Polish narrator and the spectator-protagonist becomes increasingly blurred, helping to deepen the dark and mysterious atmosphere. Moreover, given that the film is divided into three distinct image flow (Figure 4), sometimes with changes in character gender between the flows, the Polish narrator dubs all the lines of the characters in the film (including the cues of the spectator-protagonist). The narrative structure cannot be altered; however, the filmic experience depends on the choices made by the spectator-protagonist for the previously mentioned flows. These flows (Figure 5) are divided into central, lateral-right and lateral-left, and the path between them is the responsibility of the spectator-protagonist. Navigation between flows is achieved by hovering the pointer of the mouse over both sides of the image.

As for the experimentation with the idea of time in cinema, *Haze* repeats all planes three times, interspersing them and attempting to interfere with the time perception of the spectator-protagonist. The plan repetition can cause three types of reading (Silva, 2014a): (a) emptying the meaning of the image, through the loss of the seduction aroused by the first viewing; (b) enhancing the image, by discovering details which may not have been perceived at the first viewings but may become important as the narrative unfolds; (c) enhancing the image, by discovering details that did not exist in the first viewings.

As already mentioned, the film can be viewed both individually as well as collectively. Individually, through devices with internet access. Collectively, it can be viewed in physical screens. In the second option, the central flow is projected and the lateral flow may be accessed on synchronised devices. Thus, several spectators-protagonists may coexist in the same viewing. A Canon EOS camera was also used in the production of this film. The shooting took place in a black box (the theatre lab of CIAC at UAlg). In addition, a smoke machine was used to create an environment suitable for the unfolding of the narrative (picture 5), enhanced by the absence of colour throughout the film. The result was the absence of the spatial dimension of the story. Although the Polish narrator (voice-over) makes numerous references to an urban area involving a train station, that physical space is never explicit. There is nothing. Neither in nor out of the station. It was thus intended that the space-time relation in the film was entirely dominated by the time dimension.

Figure 4. A structure of the narrative in three flows (© 2014, B. Silva. Used with permission)

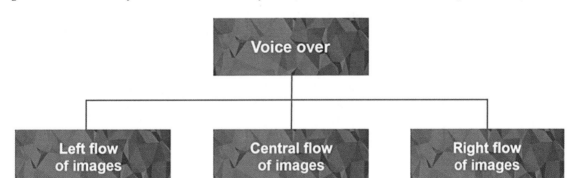

Figure 5. A frame shot 36 B (right flow), (© 2014, B. Silva. Used with permission)

Waltz (Figure 6), produced by Rui António, is a film composed of five intersecting narratives. Each of these narratives can be viewed independently; however, the five narratives together build up a film footage. The action of all narratives unfolds in the same chronological space. Through the montage, the viewer can switch between the characters and choose the sequence of the film. Each of the five characters has its own story, which is somehow connected to at least one of the other characters. Thus, these characters share anguish, betrayal, love, disappointments and hope, in a film structured in layers, which unfold and complement each other as the different plots and intrigues interweave.

Despite being an experimental film, an attempt was made to include in the narratives some elements that made them accessible to the audience. The narratives intend to involve and capture the viewer's attention through emotional moments, which embrace various film genres, such as suspense, drama and comedy.

The plot has a closed ending, as in the classical model, and it has a linear time structure.

Depending on the interaction of the viewer, we obtain different film footage. The conceivable layouts correspond to the different possible sequences resulting from the different interactive choices made by the viewer. The film *Waltz* lasts 6 minutes and 30 seconds and has 25 alternative flows for each moment. Taking into account that the viewer may interact every 5 seconds (empirical value, since the viewer may, in fact, interact more often, though such use of the film would prevent the viewer from fully enjoying the narrative), we can calculate the number of interactive moments as follows: $d \times 60 / i$, where d = film duration in minutes, and i = frequency of interaction in seconds. We therefore have 78 possible interactive moments in the film (6.5 x 60 / 5 = 78).

We may calculate the arrangements as follows:

$$A! = n!,$$

where $n = 25$ and $p = 78$, with $A! = 25!$".

This number corresponds to the total amount of possible arrangements, i.e. different film sequences, for a 5-second interaction with the viewer. If the viewer interacts less often, there will still be a very large number of possible different sequences. As an example, if the viewer interacts only 6 times throughout the entire movie, there will still be 244,140,625 different possible montage sequences. Thus, it becomes clear that the possibility of viewing the exact same film sequence becomes exceptionally small. There are two versions of this film: (a) a Kinect sensor version – the image is projected by a video projector onto a wall or screen and the film montage is made by the viewer's lateral and longitudinal body movement; (b) a version for mobile devices – this version enables the viewer to watch the film on different devices, such as smartphones and tablets, and the interaction is made by touching and combining finger touches on the screen.

THE PLATFORM

The Arts and Communication Research Centre (CIAC) of the University of Algarve has been producing digital artefacts (Silva 2014; Silva, Rodrigues, Alves, Madeira, Ferrer, Casta & Martins, 2014; Silva & Dominguez, 2014) which promote the interconnection between arts and technology, and part of the developed products are the result of projects in the area of interactive cinema (Silva, 2014; Silva, António & Rodrigues, 2015). These applied research lines, whose guidelines have served as a starting point for the emergence of several doctoral projects (Tavares, Cruz & Paulino, 2014; Silva, António &

Figure 6. A photogram of the film Waltz (© 2016, R. António. Used with permission)

Rodrigues, 2015), are based on the development and evolution of audio-visual language. On the other hand, the production of platforms (Silva & Costa, 2014), whose objective focuses on creating, fostering and expanding networks of excellence in the areas of culture and digital art, has been the area where CIAC has greater visibility. It is also important to remember that we live in a benjaminian (Benjamin, 1985) post-aura time (or perhaps neo-aura), where the relation between author-work-public has undergone a paradigm shift. This new interconnectivity also includes cinema and offers the viwer an active co-authorship role regarding the ending of the film.

It is in this context that platform *The Forking Paths* emerges, prepared to support and/or host films for collective or individual viewing. The platform (Figure 7) is hosted at http://oscaminhosquesebifurcam. ciac and despite working through scroll down it is divided as follows:

1. **Home:** Where the menu of the platform is displayed. The background image visually explains the idea of forking paths and the chromatic gradient, which begins with cool colours and ends with warm colours, takes us to the beginning of a journey that promises to be intense.
2. About the project: it is introductory page of the project (Figure 8), featuring a small synthesis, as well as the logo: a stylized cat. The cat appears in the film *Haze* with a realistic look and in the film *The Book of the Dead* with the same appearance as in the platform. When we get to this page, the cat, which is initially sitting, gets up (as a warning sign) through an animation.
3. **Films:** It is the presentation page for the films (Figure 9) that can be viewed or to which you can be redirected by selecting the one you choose. The film *Haze* includes two display options besides the explanation on the interactive method: collective viewing, in movie theatres, and individual viewing, on devices with internet access.
4. **News:** Page where news about the project and the films is disclosed (Figure 10).
5. **Support, Publications and Contacts:** Pages disclosing project support, scientific publications related to the project (Figure 11) and, finally, the contact information (e-mail, skype and personal page) of the person responsible for project.

Figure 7. A homepage of the platform (© 2014, B. Silva. Used with permission)

Figure 8. A page About the project (© 2014, B. Silva. Used with permission)

Figure 9. The presentation page for the films (© 2014, B. Silva. Used with permission)

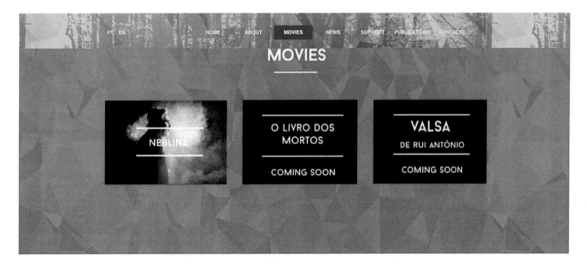

CONCLUSION

The fascination for the issue of time and its relation with cinema was the *leitmotif* of the project *The Forking Paths*. Psychosomatic processes, which can create different sensations and, consequently, different perceptions regarding its passage (so many times divergent from the measuring devices – watches), acquire in cinema an impending experimentation potential. It was that potential, which had already been addressed in literature (in particular through tale) by authors such as Jorge Luis Borges (2000) and Italo Calvino (2002) that we have tried to bring into the project. We think we can find in *The Forking Paths* a certain evolutionary trend (Reia-Batista, 2006; Murray, 1997) regarding audio-visual language. Therefore, although the morphological issues remain unchanged, we found signs that appear to indicate

Figure 10. News section (© 2014, B. Silva. Used with permission)

Figure 11. Pages related to project support, publications and contact information (© 2014, B. Silva. Used with permission)

a possible evolution within the audio-visual syntax. Namely the relativity of the concept of plan, which alternates from an objective into a subjective stance, taking into account the possibility of multiple choices, as well as the multiple interpretation possibilities of the idea of sequence, following the same principle. It is important to remember the role of the viewer, who not only becomes an active part in the narrative but can also undertake the task of co-authoring, taking into account the possibilities of choice he/she is offered and the substantial changes in the narrative structure those choices inevitably bring to the viewing of the films. It is also necessary to underline the importance of academic experimentation, which should, whenever possible, go beyond theorizing and involve a praxis through a demonstration of the developed theories. Within the scope of the models found (arborescent model, constructive model, paired model and fertile model), the possibility of generating new content (fertile model) through the interaction man-machine is regarded as the most likely possibility of rupture and the development of a new generation of interactive movies. The viewer acquires creative powers that are beyond his/her control (as well as beyond the author's control): the creation of content that was not foreseen. This will certainly be a rupture in the logical sequence of the history of cinema, where the film will become something that has never been so far: a complete audio-visual experience. This is hence a limitless project, which has taken on a life of its own and wanders around.

REFERENCES

Benjamin, W. (1985). A Obra de Arte na Era da sua Reprodução técnica. In E. Geada (Ed.), *Org.). Estéticas do Cinema*. Lisboa: Publicações Dom Quixote.

Borges, J. L. (2000). *Ficções*. Lisboa: Visão.

Calvino, I. (2002). *Se numa noite de Inverno um viajante*. Lisboa: Editorial Teorema.

Deleuze, G. (1985). *A Imagem-Movimento*. São Paulo: Brasiliense.

Deleuze, G. (1990). *A Imagem-Tempo*. São Paulo: Brasiliense.

Graham, J. (Producer), Bejan, Bob (Director). (1992). *I'm your Man*. [Motion picture]. New York: ChoicePoint Films.

Greenaway, P. (2003). *Tulse Luper Suitcases*. Delux Productions.

Greenaway, P. (2007). O cinema está morto, vida longa ao cinema. *Caderno SESC Videobrasil*, *3*, 3.

Häkkilä, J. R., Posti, M., Schneegass, S., Alt, F., Gultekin, K., & Schmidt, A. (2014, April). Let me catch this!: experiencing interactive 3D cinema through collecting content with a mobile phone. In *Proceedings of the SIGCHI Conference on Human Factors in Computing Systems* (pp. 1011-1020). ACM.

Huizinga, J. (1992). *Homo ludens: o jogo como elemento da cultura*. São Paulo: Perspectiva.

Lévy, P. (1995). *O que é o Virtual?* São Paulo: Editora 34.

Lunenfeld, P. (2005). Os mitos do cinema interativo. In *O chip e o caleidoscópio: reflexões sobre as novas mídias*. São Paulo: SENAC.

Manovich, L. (2010). *Software take command*. Olivares Edition.

Manovich, L. (2011). *The language of new media*. The MIT Press.

Murray, J. (1997). *The Future of Narrative in Cybersapce*. New York: The Free Press.

Reia-Baptista, V. (2006). New Environments of Media Exposure - Internet and Narrative Structures: From Media Education to Media Pedagogy and Media Literacy. In U. Carlsson & C. von Feilitzen (Eds.), *The Service of Young People?* Studies and Reflections on Media in the Digital Age.

Silva, B. (2013). The Forking Paths: a experiência temporal na narrativa fílmica. Ibercom 2013, Santiago de Compostela.

Silva, B. (2014a). The Forking Paths: An Interactive Cinema Experience. *International Journal of Creative Interfaces and Computer Graphics*.

Silva, B., António, R., & Rodrigues, J. (2015). Dialectical Polyptych: an interactive movie. *Third International Conference on Advances in Computing, Communication and Information Technology*.

Silva, B., & Dominguez, M. (2014). Between the Sacred and the Profane in the S. João d'Arga's Festivities: A Digital Art Installation. *International Journal of Creative Interfaces and Computer Graphics*, *5*(1), 1–20. doi:10.4018/ijcicg.2014010101

Silva, B., Rodrigues, J., Alves, R., Madeira, M., Ferrer, J., Casta, S., & Martins, R. (2014). Fátima Revisited: An Interactive Installation. *SGEM Proceedings*.

Silva, B. M. (2014b). *Haze em Avanca: apresentação pública do primeiro filme interativo da trilogia The Forking Paths*. Avanca: Avanca Cinema.

Silva, B. M., & Costa, S. (2014). Rede de Cultura e Arte Digital: O projeto Recardi. *INUAF Studia, 16*(9).

Tavares, M., Cruz, T., & Paulino, F. (2014). CulturalNature Arga#2. *International Journal of Creative Interfaces and Computer Graphics*, *5*(1), 21–31. doi:10.4018/ijcicg.2014010102

ENDNOTES

[1]   Purely optical description, where the spectator (the one who watches) replaces the protagonist (the one who acts).

[2]   Purely auditory description, the same principle of opsign.

[3]   Johan Huizinga (1992) sees the game as a piece of the time narrative where the player plays another parallel life and points out in his book *Homo Ludens: The Play Element of Culture*, the essential importance of the game in building the culture of any society.

[4]   A plan is a part of the film between two cuts. However, in this specific case, the viewer is the one who redefines the plan according to his/her choice regarding the second cut.

[5]   In the film, it becomes difficult to perceive the existence of one of the characters because we may confuse him with garden sculptures. The tiles also have an important role in the pictorial composition of the setting.

[6]   http://file.org.br/videoarte_sp_2015/file-sao-paulo-2015-video-art-53/

Chapter 8
CulturalNature Arga#2

Tiago Cruz
Instituto Universitário da Maia, Portugal

Fernando Faria Paulino
Instituto Universitário da Maia, Portugal

Mirian Tavares
University of Algarve, Portugal

ABSTRACT

CulturalNature Arga#2 is an interactive audio-visual installation intended to explore the concept of landscape as a verb (to landscape) questioning and reflecting about the semiotic discourses associated with this concept. The landscape as something natural, static, peaceful, silent, etc. is a semiotic discourse with roots in a past related with the representation of a point of view, not only perceptual but also conceptual, ideological. These representations informed the visual culture leading to a particular discourse. The installation proposes a reflexion about the way different elements associated with a particular territory shape this territory's landscape, giving it a dynamic existence, a product of cultural activity.

INTRODUCTION

Landscape is an extremely complex and subjective concept, being approached from a wide range of perspectives. Many disciplines, like geography, anthropology, history, architecture, ecology, art, design, etc., study and reflect about landscape. Through their studies we find different definitions and perspectives related to what we understand as landscape. The concept is polysemic and, according to Ribeiro (2007, p.13), some scholars put in question its conceptual value precisely because it's associated to a wide range of interpretations and subjectivity.

Historically, the landscape genre, in occidental art, emerges in the fifteenth century related with the representation of a point of view. These representations are strongly connected with a particular ideological or romantic view of the world, directly related with a particular visual culture. Connected with painting and drawing, the artistic landscape genre, in the nineteenth century started to decline dramatically, particularly with the upcoming of the emerging vanguards. Although there are authors that talk

DOI: 10.4018/978-1-5225-7371-5.ch008

about the death of this genre associated with the death of the painting, the landscape never really stopped being researched and reflected by the artistic community.

Today we see several artworks that explore the landscape concept. From representing a piece of territory, figuratively, on a canvas with paint, we went to representing the landscape in terms of media, artefact, system, ideology, place, static, power, sublime, picturesque, idyllic, decline, identity, etc.

The landscape genre is intimately related with the sublime, where it is objectified by nature - the most scary aspects can be appreciated by creating a distance -, and the picturesque, where subjectivity emerges through art - a romantic and subjective image. According to Fowkes (2010), contemporaneity shakes the picturesque by portraying landscapes that do not correspond to the conventional categories of this or calling the attention, deliberately, to these particular categories.

I would like to bring here some examples of artworks that explore the concept in other terms besides the figurative representation. The first one is Tree (2004), by Simon Heijdens Studio (Figures 1). According to the authors, "Ripples on a puddle of water, footsteps in the sand and slowly gathering grime. Natural processes are existent though becoming rare in our increasingly planned surrounding. While the trees on the streets are no longer nature but carefully controlled and managed, the wind that is moving its branches still is. An installation that traces and amplifies the leftovers of nature in the urban surrounding." (2004)

Eight meters tall computer synthesised trees were projected in several buildings. These trees balance with more or less velocity according to the intensity of the wind presented in that specific moment.

These trees appear full of leafs. But, when someone passes, one leaf falls on the floor. This process creates a pile of leafs that, with time, illuminate the place as a consequence of its increased projected light. These leafs projected on the floor move in reaction to the individual that passes walking.

Figure 1. Simon Heijdens, Installation tree (© 2004, images collected from the author's website. Used with permission)

The exploration of the relationship between nature and culture is worked in the sense that culture dominates nature. Itself, nature suffers a process of acculturation as a culturally programmed element. The author, in this reflexion, detects that the wind is still natural and, with this, he explores the cause/effect of this natural process over these cultural elements (planted trees, kept, and culturally controlled).

I would like to underline the tendency of the individual to dominate nature, running away from its chaotic, random and mysterious character. Nature (abstract) is represented through the tree (concrete) and, through a cause/effect metonym, the author explores the relation between nature and culture in a game of oppositions with semiotic potentials related with the myth of nature and culture. Here, the cultural activity finishes with the natural element. Each time someone walks by a leaf falls and all the others, that are on the floor, react to this individual by moving with his/her movement.

The discourse of the nature as something fragile and sensitive is explored with the intention of sensitise, in the same way, the individual. Although he/she can react (or not) to the artwork, the installation always react to the presence of the individual. In this sense there is a distinction about how the art piece sees the relation between nature and culture. We are in the presence of a relation of power, dominance, of exploration of resources.

The next artwork I would like to bring here is Bitscapes (2006), by Quayola (Figures 2). According to the author "Bitscapes is a multi-sceen installation exploring and challenging the ambiguity of realism in the digital realm. Natural landscapes from the wilderness of western Australia slowly deconstruct. By loosing their 'photographic skin', the illusion behind their realistic appearance is revealed." (2006).

Bitscapes questions the objective related with the realism of synthesised images. These are formed through a series of mathematical calculations and are presented, in this case, surrounded by a hiper-realism that will be a target of an algorithmic manipulation. This manipulation is related with a process of revealing the "true" nature of these images, questioning like this its value of truth, objectivity and authenticity.

Figures 2. Quayola, Artwork Bitscapes (© 2006, images collected from the author's website. Used with permission)

As a representation, the landscape is related with an eye enformed by several factors, in particular, the technology. In the context of this installation, the question the arises, once again, is a very old question: the representation. Here, not related with landscape painting, but instead with the landscape representation in the context of the bitmap images.

The mimicry and similarity are intimately related with the truth and objectivity by being similar representations to what our eyes perceive. The mimetic representation of landscape is a representation enformed by social rules and conventions that define a way of seeing and interpreting the world. The author questions the landcape-representation through an algorithmic deconstruction that brings to the surface its rules and consequences represented through the graphical distortions of the image.

It is not just the discourse of the landscape as a representation that emerges in this project but also the truth and objective nature of these representations. For this, the author also explores the landscape-representation as a system, artefact and culture. The nature/culture and real/imaginary are here presented in a steady game of oppositions with the intension of underline the fragility of the value of truth related with these representations, products of technological equipments.

The discourse of the image as something that tricks our senses has a long tradition that takes us to Aristotle and Plato. It is interesting to think about the landscape-representation in these two sides. On one side, the author underlines a landscape that is misleading and illusory and, on the other, this landscape, revealing its underlying system, assumes itself with an educational character about these same systems.

The third and last installation that we would like to bring here is called Untitled Landscape #5 (2009), by Leila Nadir and Cary Peppermint. According to the authors, "Commissioned in 2009 by the Whitney Museum of American Art as part of its inaugural Sunrise/Sunset net art series, in 2009, Untitled Landscape #5 investigates the disruption of technologies by both human activity and natural phenomena. Fluctuating orbs of light disrupt the 'digital landscape' of the Whitney Museum of American Art's website" (2009).

The user, navigating through the website, suddenly, is presented with an animation composed by a group of semi-transparent yellow circles that move on top of the website's graphical interface. These circles intent to denote the sunset luminosity over the space. The installation is part of a series of net artworks entitled "Sunrise/Sunset". According to the authors, the artwork explores an interactivity between the human activity and the natural phenomenon where both interrupt each other mutually.

These lights are semiotic resources that intent to represent, metonymically, nature, the natural phenomenon and, with this, explore semiotic potentials like natural, pure, primitive and nostalgia. This discourse related with nature is very close to the myth of nature as something beautiful, healthy and pure.

On the other hand, the landscape where this sunset appears is the website of the museum. With this, the website transforms itself in a digital landscape, assuming the territory as something equivalent to the internet. It is interesting to point out that this digital landscape is not a view over a territory but, instead, over a place, a website. In this sense, the installation metaphorically works with the landscape-view discourse but, more specifically, with the landscape-place.

The landscape is cultural and interacts with the natural elements, although, here, this interaction presents itself as a tension between the two where the natural interrupts the cultural activity (the user browsing the website), covering this one.

The landscape is not related with the natural environment but, instead, with the digital. In this sense we talk about a digital landscape, in cyberspace, being shaken in its function and aesthetics through a simulated intervention of a natural phenomenon. Nature and culture enter in a conflict where technology is questioned through the intervention of the natural phenomenon and the human activity enforming that same phenomenon.

Figure 3. Leila Nadir and Cary Peppermint, Artwork Untitled Landscape #5 (© 2009, image collected from the author's website. Used with permission)

CulturalNature Arga#2 is a artwork that explores the landscape concept as a product of social and cultural practices pointing to the way particular aspects of the territory share and form the landscape. The conceptual point of view comes from the social semiotic theory, in particular, the discourse theory from Theo Van Leeuwen (2005). It is possible to identify a semiotic discourse, related to social and cultural practices, that contribute to the development of a particular visual culture regarding the landscape. Through the creative process associated with the installation and through the installation in itself, we intend to reflect about this phenomenon of the landscape as a product of social and cultural practices.

THE LANDSCAPE AND ITS SEMIOTIC DISCOURSE

Landscape, as a view, refers to a specific point of view over a scenery or specific area of a territory with particular natural and/or cultural characteristics. As a noun, it's related to a representation of this point of view. As a discipline, it refers to a particular field of disciplines like painting and photography, which deals with these representations. As a verb, it refers to the act of shaping a territory with the intent of making him more pleasant and useful. (Lorch, 2002)

We should pay particular attention to the role of the subject in this process. The Landscape, as a view, is defined by the subject. In many situations we create viewpoints specifically to appreciate these well defined views, we build highways where the landscape has an important role in defining the path the road should take, we orient houses and windows according to these views, etc.

The Landscape, as a noun, is produced in diverse formats by us. Whether a photograph taken by a tourist, a drawing made by a student, an art installation developed by an artist, they are all representations of a certain territory that the subject produces to communicate something about, and with, that view.

The Landscape, as a discipline, was created and is performed by the individual and targets the study of the concept in its various perspectives. As a view, a noun, a verb and the discipline in itself. Landscape, because we deal with it since immemorial times, is a topic so vast and complex that can be assumed as a field of study on its own.

Lastly, the Landscape, as a verb (to landscape), relates to cultural practices in which some are specifically intended to shape the territory but others just have, as a consequence, the transformation of the territory. Being a cultural practice, the individual is primarily responsible for this act and to landscape is an cultural activity enformed by social needs and interests.

The landscape is a social phenomenon that can be perceived according many different points of view and characteristics. It consists and it's formed by natural and cultural forces that can be studied and identified by a wide range of disciplines. In the context of the audio-visual interactive installation CulturalNature Arga#2, the landscape is thought as a verb (to landscape), as a social practice that acts over and transforms a particular space.

J. T. W. Mitchell (1994) identifies two ways of approaching the concept of landscape –as a representation and perception– and adds a third one –as a media in its own. The landscape, when it refers to a representation, on one side, may assume itself as a progressive movement in the direction of purification of the visual field and, on the other side, as perception, it can assume itself as a process of contemplation and naturalisation of cultural and social constructions. Besides these two, and in a postmodern perspective, Mitchell refers to landscape as an allegory to the social and psychological that needs to be deconstructed, underlining that the landscape is a media on its own that carries messages related with the space, the subject and the activities.

An important concept to bring here is the notion of semiotic resource. The term Social Semiotics emerges with the linguist Michael Halliday (1978) in the second half of the twentieth century. According to the author, the meaning is something that suffers transformations along time and, in this sense, language carries a "potential meaning" and presents itself as a resource used by the individual to communicate in a certain context. Robert Hodge and Gunther Kress (1988), moving away from the centrality in language and looking for the integration of other semiotic systems, talk about the uses of these systems inside the cultural practices and underline the process of interpretation as something central in the sense that a certain text fits in a certain speech. In this context, the notion of semiosis, for the author, influenced by the work of Charles Peirce, is a dynamic process where the meaning is not firstly defined in rigid structures or pre-defined cultural codes.

In the context of social semiotics, the notion of sign if substituted by the concept of semiotic resource avoiding, with this, the idea that a certain meaning is attached to a certain signifiant (Hodge and Kress, 1988; Leeuwen, 2005). This notion of semiotic resource has its roots, as mentioned before, in Halliday where the author defends that the grammar is not a code, or set of rules, but a resource used in the production of meaning (1978, p. 192).

According to Leeuwen (2005), semiotic resources are the actions and/or artefacts used to communicate, whether they are produced physiological (vocal system, muscles to create facial expressions or gestures, etc.) or technological (pen, ink and paper; hardware and software, with tissues, scissors and sewing machines, etc.). A semiotic resource is whatever it's used — or can be used — by the subject to communicate, to produce meaning, in a specific time and place. It's like a raw material that, through its manipulation associated with some communicative intention, and through a process of interpretation with the reader, inside a specific context with particular codes, rules and conventions, acquires meaning. However, it's important to underline that the sign is a resource used in the construction of the message and it has, in itself, a meaning potential when in interaction with a context and an interpretant.

In the context of this installation the landscape is assumed as a communication semiotic resource in the way that we can identify a semiotic discourse that characterises it as something natural. This discourse has its roots in the past associated to the notion of landscape as a view. According to Mitchell, this discourse emerges from the process of naturalisation. So, in the installation, the landscape is approached in a perspective that explores its formation. To landscape refers to a social activity that interferes, in a more or less profound way, in the landscape experience.

The discourse presents itself as a resource to the representation, a knowledge about a certain aspect of reality, that can be used to represent that same aspect. They don't determine what can be said about that aspect of reality, however, it is not possible to represent something without to call upon them. We need the discourses as a kind of framework to give meaning to reality. (Leeuwen, 2005) They shape the thought and behaviour of the individual that shapes other thoughts and behaviours by using the existent discourses and creating new ones. The semiotic discourse is a resource with a set of particular semiotic potentials.

Besides resources, the discourses are plural. There can exist several discourses that refer to a certain aspect of reality, normally related with certain interests and needs of their authors and the ones that use them. The information is filtered in the sense that certain aspects are represented in detriment of others according to the interests and social-cultural factors at stake.

Leeuwen (2005) believes that every semiotic discourse is moulded in social practices and that the knowledge is a product of doing. However, the discourses transform these social practices protecting some particular interests, in a specific social context. According to the author (2005), the discourses are never only about what we do, but, at the same time, always about the why we do it. In this sense, and given the plurality of discourses, the author establishes that these discourses are a version of a social practice, plus the ideas and attitudes relatively to that same practice. Referring to these "version" and putting the question of how a discourse transforms the reality in a version of itself, the author lists, first, the elements that are part of a particular social practice. These are the actions (what people do), the way (how they do it), the actors (who does), the presentation (with which presentation), the resources (with which resources), the time (in which time) and the space (in which space), Safeguarding the fact that some representation can contain only some of these elements and not all of them. Second, answering the question of how the reality transforms itself in discourse, the author refers four types of transformation: through exclusion (the discourses can exclude some elements of the social practice); the reordering (the discourses can reorder the elements); the addition (the discourses can add elements to the representation); and the substitution (the discourses can substitute the concrete over the abstract, the specific over the general, the do over the be).

Mitchell (1994), besides demystifying a series of preconceived ideas about the landscape theme, like its "beginning-middle-end" structure, the notion that it's a modern European western phenomenon and a new way of seeing, the author talks about an imperial landscape away from an idealised sight related with a group of social and economical values. The author moves deeper when he identifies the influence that the oriental genre landscape has in the occidental landscape, in particular associated with the British empire. According to the author, the landscape in the orient reaches its peak with the Chinese imperial power and enters in decline in the eighteenth century when China starts to be an object of fascination and appropriation by England, when this started to assume itself as an empire.

Landscape painting works with a series of myths like the Ideal, the Heroic, the Pastoral, the Bello, the Sublime, the Picturesque. In this sense, these representations serve specific political, economical and social purposes. The process of naturalisation in itself associated with these myths emerges surrounded by these same objectives. They not only define what should be represented and the way it's represented, but they are already representations of representations, of points of view.

In this context, the landscape is surrounded by semiotic discourses, while a media in itself, in the definition of the point of view and in its representation. The discourse can effectively begin to emerge in the space when this was a target of some social practice that transformed it. Cultural Nature Arga#2 intends to be a reflexion about this process and its consequences.

CULTURALNATURE ARGA#2

A dominant semiotic discourse surrounding the landscape is the one that represents it as something natural, virgin, and primitive. This discourse has roots in the past, connected with the landscape as a view, and naturalises the myth of nature. Taking this as a starting point, I was interested in exploring the formation of the landscape.

The landscape as a verb (to landscape) refers to a social activity that interferes, in a profound way, with the experience of the landscape. Putting it in better terms, the cultural landscape is created, largely, through social practices that transform the territory several times in a predetermined way taking into account the cultural codes and conventions that relates to what we commonly acknowledge as landscape.

In this context, landscape gets surrounded by semiotic discourses, in particular as a media on its own, in the definition of the point of view and in its representation. The semiotic discourse may effectively start to emerge in the territory when it was a target of some social practice that transformed it. CulturalNature Arga#2 (Figure 4) intents to be a reflection regarding this process and its consequences.

According to Simmel, "Our conscience, besides the elements, should enjoy from a new totality, from something unified, not connected to its particular meanings nor mechanically created by them — only that is landscape" (2009, p. 5).

Figure 4. Tiago Cruz, CulturalNature Arga #2 screenshot (© 2013, T. Cruz. Used with permission)

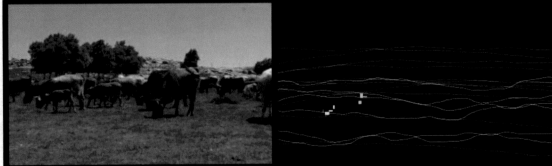

This idea of landscape as a whole, that is a product of small parts, was a central idea in the development of this installation. I was interested in working these two sides, this complementary opposition, part/whole. As such, I worked in a split-screen where the left side would be associated with the parts and the right with the whole.

On the right side, I wanted to build a landscape through the use of a generative algorithm. The introspection started by thinking which image and with which rules. Through several meetings in the territory of Serra de Arga, in the north of Portugal (Caminha), I observed, did several drawings, collected sounds and pictures, and I reflect upon this cultural landscape, product of a social activity. I realised that to perceive a certain view is a process highly conditioned not only by my individual culture, by my personal description of the world, but also by what presents itself to my senses. For example, there are several roads in the world that, by the time they were built, they were placed in strategic places in a way that the spectator could appreciate the landscape from a certain point of view. This way, the individual is immediately conditioned to perceive a particular aspect of the territory from a specific spot and, with this, building a mental image about what a landscape should be. This process goes even more far away when the territory is shaped according to these points of view and discourses. Here the parts make up a whole that presents itself to the senses of the one that perceives, in a particular way, according to the interests and needs of the agents involved in the related social practices. Despite this process being thought in an extremely conscious way by these social agents, the territory seems to be, most of the time, an unconscious result, not predicted, of all cultural activity. Observing the landscape of Serra de Arga, I see a space shaped by time. All the herd activity, through several years, shaped this territory. The same happened with the houses, the roads, the Garranos horses that run free in the mountains, etc. All the cultural activity is responsible for the transformation of the territory, in a conscious or unconscious way. Effectively, one of the important aspects in the creation of the landscape is precisely to transform this unconscious process in something conscious.

The landscape-representation created on the right side of the projection should be created from the cultural and natural activities presented in Serra de Arga. This way, this natural and cultural activity should come up on the left side of the split-screen. The parts and the whole should work together.

The semiotic resources selected to represent the elements that form the landscape and which are assumed as active agents in the process of creating the landscape were: (i) herd/grazing; (ii) agriculture; (iii) houses; (iv) water; (v) Garranos/horses; (vi) eolic fans. According to this, six videos were created to be presented in loop on the left side of the projection.

Figure 5. Tiago Cruz, screenshots: herd, agriculture and houses, (© 2013, T. Cruz. Used with permission)

Figure 6. Tiago Cruz, screenshots: water, horses and eolic (© 2013, T. Cruz. Used with permission)

To create a landscape through a generative algorithm having, as an input, these six videos was a complex conceptual task. Several experiments were made. From mixing the videos in an abstract image, to cut parts of these with the intent of forming a composition based on a collage process. The results didn't appeal to me. The user input was missing in the development of the narrative. The user should define the "what" and the "how" regarding how the left side (parts) affect the right (whole).

There was a need to think about the role of the individual in the development of the narrative. Thinking about what was developed in terms of the role of the subject in the construction of the landscape, the user should be responsible for the creation of this generative landscape. He should be the agent that would share the creation of the landscape-representation with the developed algorithm.

This algorithm needed an input and, in this moment, there were six possible inputs related with the presented videos. I wanted to work with Arduino, an open-source platform oriented to the development of electronic components/devices and, with this in mind, I started to think about some kind of interaction device. This object should allow the visualisation of each one of the six videos and make some kind of selection that could be used as an input for the algorithm.

This object should be something that, besides representing the territory, should be a part of this. A kind of synecdoche that represented, globally, the territory of Serra de Arga. The idea of a cube was an interesting one because I could relate each one of its facades with each one of the six videos. However, some time was necessary to think about its construction. The cube should be, in some way, in agreement with my point of view regarding Serra de Arga and, in this sense, semiotic potentials like rustic, rough, common, should be explored in the materials and presentation of this object. I see Serra de Arga as a territory that presents raw landscapes. Marked by a time that stopped existing long time ago.

Serra de Arga, in particular its north area, between *Arga de Cima*, *Arga de Baixo* and *Arga de São João*, is a territory occupied by a very aged population with, approximately, one hundred and fifty people. Talking with some of these individuals, I heard stories of abandonment. Young people that travelled to the big cities (mainly Lisbon) searching for jobs and only were coming back once in a while on weekends and vacations. This discourse always emerged in contrast with another one that talked about a past full of people, where the herding and agricultural activity was rich. Today, this aged population doesn't have the conditions to keep the herds or work the land.

The cube should be built in wood (Figure 7). An old wood, with scratches and marks that reflected the passage of time and the human activity. In the same way that all the territory is marked with these indexical signs of the past. I selected six different pieces of wood and I built a cube that was going to be the interaction device of the installation.

Figure 7. Tiago Cruz, Wiew of the cube (© 2013, T. Cruz. Used with permission)

The user, rotating the cube, was going to select one of the videos. This was possible through the implementation of a gyroscope connected through Arduino. With this electronic component was possible to know which face of the cube was facing up in the interaction moment and, with this, activate the visualisation of the corresponding video.

A selection mechanism was missing. The user should make some kind of action to trigger the connection of the selected video with the algorithm. The installed gyroscope worked also as an accelerometer and, through this resource, it was possible to use the cube's moving velocity, in conjunction with the selected video, as an input to be process by the algorithm.

To agitate the cube metaphorically reflected the social practice, the subject activity over the territory, making, with this, the bridge with the landscape-representation on the right side. The notion of direct manipulation carried by the user was much more intense and, with this, a more immersive interactive experience could be accomplished.

At the same time all these questions was being taken into consideration, the algorithm was being developed. The landscape as a whole is composed by different parts that emerge, in a more high or low degree, in the landscapes-view that we select. To create a landscape-representation from the elements selected by the user should be done by creating graphical elements that could represent those elements. Together, and thinking about Simmel's sentence, this landscape-representation should be perceived as a whole in a cause/effect metonymic relation with the actions of the user (Figures 8-13).

Six graphical elements were developed in relation to each one of the six videos:

Figure 8. Tiago Cruz, aspect of "herd / grazing" (© 2013, T. Cruz. Used with permission)

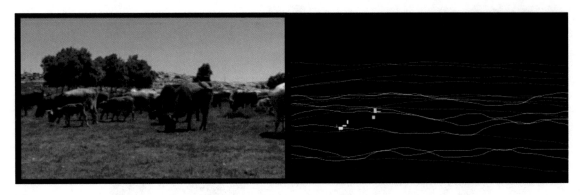

Figure 9. Tiago Cruz, aspect of "agricultural activity" (© 2013, T. Cruz. Used with permission)

Figure 10. Tiago Cruz, aspect of "dwellings" (© 2013, T. Cruz. Used with permission)

- **Water:** Blue lines that extend horizontally with a random undulation and position;
- **Oxen:** Red lines that extend horizontally with a random undulation and position;
- **Corral:** Two parallel lines that extend horizontally, with a random undulation and position, connected in the breaking points of the undulation;
- **Eolic:** Figurative representation of the eolic fan composed by four white lines in random positions;

Figure 11. Tiago Cruz, aspect of "water"(© 2013, T. Cruz. Used with permission)

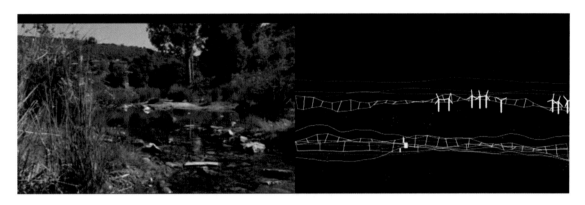

Figure 12. Tiago Cruz, aspect of "horses (Garranos)"(© 2013, T. Cruz. Used with permission)

Figure 13. Tiago Cruz, aspect of "wind fans"(© 2013, T. Cruz. Used with permission)

- **Horses:** Groups of little ellipses (random quantity) in which the colour varies randomly inside a colour gamut between reds and browns. The position and size also vary randomly within certain limits;
- **Houses:** Groups of little rectangles (random quantity) in which the colour varies randomly inside a colour gamut of greys. The position and size also vary randomly within certain limits;

By the time these elements were developed, I though in abstract shapes, created from a process of synthesis of the visualised shapes, that together could represent an interesting landscape in aesthetic terms. It was important to explore the contrast between shapes to accomplish this. Based on this premise, groups of lines are used for the water (flow of rivers) and for the oxen (paths left in the ground). In contrast with these lines, the Garranos (horses) and the houses share similarities. Both are groups of graphical objects although some are rectangles (denoting houses) and others ellipsis (denoting horses). At this point the visual result was not very satisfactory because of all the abstraction. The user could have a difficult time making the conceptual connection between the shapes and the video choices. In this sense, the corral and the eolic fans were approached in a more figurative way increasing even more the contrast between the shapes creating a more interesting image. With the corral, because of their shape and the way they mark the territory, the algorithm draws two broken parallel lines that are connected in the broken joints. Through this, in a more figurative way, this images represented the shapes that we see in the territory when viewed from the the top. Lastly, the eolic fans were the more figurative element and, in contrast with the others, animated. The intent was to reach a landscape-representation exploring semiotic potentials as dynamism, movement, transformation, process, construction, etc. The goal was that the landscape-representation was perceived as something that is in constant transformation as a result of the individual action.

Speaking about the sound, we have here two groups of sounds. On one side, each one of the videos is connected to a certain sound landscape that can be directly related with itself or related with the image. For example, visualising the empty and abandoned corral, we hear the sound of a cellphone ringing contrasting, with this, the human activity with the empty space. Visualising the houses, we hear the sound of a church bell, although there is no church in the visual field. The sound was worked in a process of complementary with the image with the intent of increasing the semiotic potential density. On the other side, we have glitch sounds triggered when the user agitates the cube. These glitches came from a conceptual exercise related with the gesture of agitating the cube. As I said, this cube intents to be a synecdoche that represents the space and agitating it is a metaphor of the subject action over the space. The landscape transforms itself by the second as a consequence of natural forces and, mostly, cultural. The cultural action interferes in this process in a decisive way shaping the landscape of the future. The cube should explore these notions and the glitch sounds emerge here to represent the intervention on the landscape that is being represented, metaphorically, as a machine-system. It was in a sleeping state and then, suddenly, by the intervention of the user, activates itself and changed to something else. In this sense, the glitch sound is a kind of metaphorical cut, incisive, on the territory. A cirurgical intervention with the intention of transforming/creating another thing.

The process runs *ad infinitum*. The user stops interacting with the cube and the image continues to be presented. When the user returns to the interaction process, the process return in the point where the last user left off. However, the elements that are added in the image of the right are not just added on top of the previews ones. Each time a user returns to an already seen video, the graphical elements related to that previews visualisation are substituted by new elements that result from the new interaction.

At stake is the production of a landscape, a whole, through the interaction with its particular elements. A landscape that is dynamic, mutable, a product of a series of interactions, social practices, rules, codes and social conventions. The activity of shaping the landscape will have irreversible consequences on the territory and in the way this is perceived and represented. In this sense, the landscape is always cultural and never natural. The landscape, in its definition, is always a point of view of a particular individual. A cultural "nature".

Technical and Technological Aspects

The installation is composed by a computer, a projector that projects the split-screen and the cube. The development was made with Processing, an open source library, and Arduino, the open source library and corresponding electronics. In terms of electronic components, inside the cube, I used an Arduino UNO, a gyroscope, an accelerometer and a bluetooth component to establish the communication with the computer Arduíno (Figure 14).

The library i2cdevlib (www.i2cdevlib.com), from J. Rowberg, was used to handle with the accelerometer and the gyroscope, and the SoftwareSerial (included with the Arduino distribution) to handle the communication with the Processing program. This way, only the code responsible for the transmission, in real-time, of the values related with the rotation and agitation of the cube (in XYZ axes) was created. The transmission is accomplished through the Bluetooth component JY-MCU (HC-06).

Figure 14. Tiago Cruz, Overview of the installation (© 2013, T. Cruz. Used with permission)

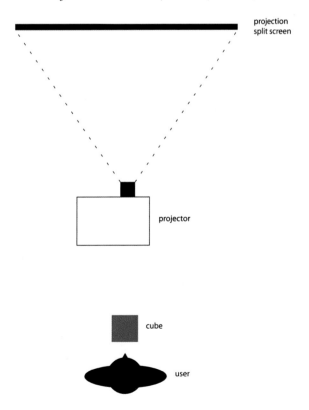

In terms of the Processing program, the following libraries were used: OpenCV for the video manipulation, Minim for the sound manipulation and Serial for the communication with Arduíno (Figure 16).

CONCLUSION

The installation is about the production of a landscape. A result that becomes a reality through the interaction of its particular elements. A landscape that is dynamic, changeable, a product social practices, rules, codes and social conventions. The activities that shape the landscape will have irreversible consequences in the way the landscape is perceived and represented. It is always cultural, always a point of view of the subject. To speak about landscape as "nature" is nonsense because we are talking about something that it's formed not only by natural phenomenon but, mainly, by cultural ones. A cultural "nature."

The installation addresses these issues and was a way of exploring these processes and concepts. Through its development, the interaction of micro (parts) and macro (landscape) was used to understand and communicate the notion of cultural landscape, shaped culturally by social and cultural practices.

The video and sound capture were made on location by Tiago Cruz and Fernando Paulino, the programming and development of the interaction device was made by Tiago Cruz and the glitch sounds used are from laptopnoise.com.

CulturalNature Arga#2 was exhibited in the Design Center of Óbidos (Portugal) during a Digital Media Art PhD students meeting in July (2013), and in Olhão (Portugal), at an European Researchers Meeting, in September (2013).

Figure 15. Tiago Cruz, Electronics schematics (© 2013, T. Cruz. Used with permission)

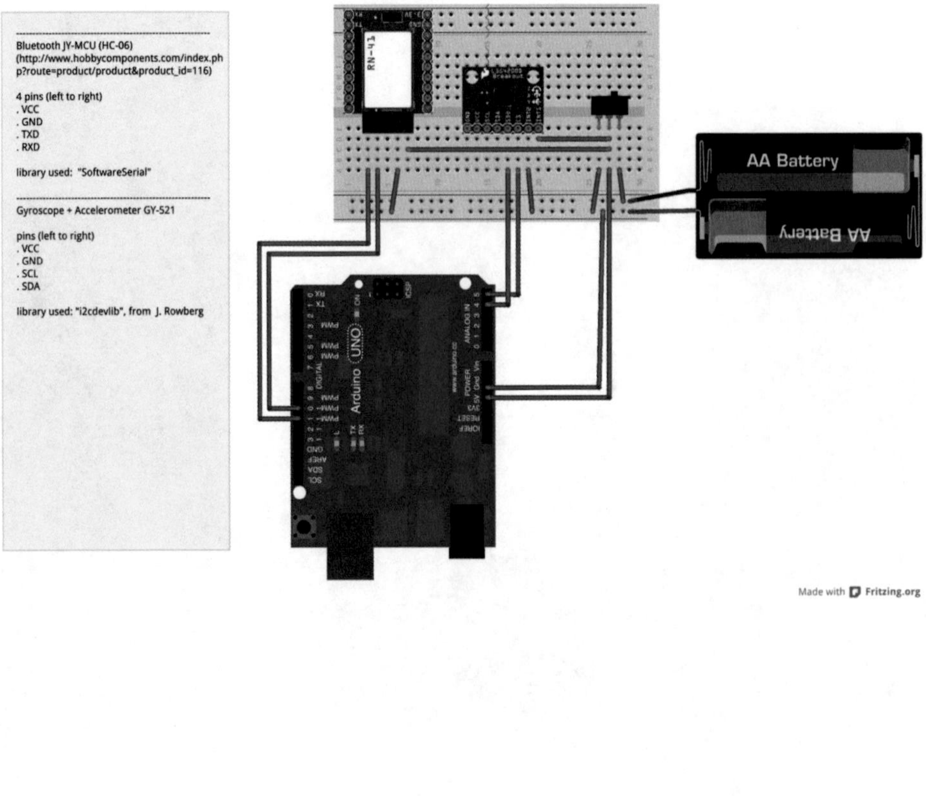

REFERENCES

Cruz, T. (2013). *CulturalNature Arga#2*. Retrieved March 30, 2018, from https://www.behance.net/gallery/10404419/CulturalNature-Arga2

Elkins, J., & DeLuc, R. (2008). *Landscape Theory*. New York: Routledge.

Flusser, V. (2011). *Into the Universe of Technical Images*. University of Minnesota Press. doi:10.5749/minnesota/9780816670208.001.0001

Fowkes, R., & Fowkes, M. (2010). *Unframed Landscapes: Nature in Contemporary Art*. Retrieved March 30, 2018, from http://www.neme.org/texts/unframed-landscapes

Galanter, P. (2003). *What is Generative Art?* NewYork: New York University.

Giannetti, C. (2006). *Estética Digital: Sintopia da arte, a ciência e a tecnologia*. Belo Horizonte: C/Arte.

Halliday, M. (1978). *Language as social semiotic: the social interpretation of language and meaning*. University Park Press.

Hodge, R., & Kress, G. (1988). *Social Semiotics*. Cambridge, UK: Polity Press.

King, A. E. (2010). *The Landscape in Art: Nature in the crosshairs of an age-old debate*. Retrieved March 30, 2018, from http://www.artesmagazine.com/?p=4744

Kress, G., & Leeuwen, T. (2001). *Multimodal Discourse: the Modes and Media of Contemporary Communication*. London: Arnold.

Leeuwen, T. (2005). *Introducing Social Semiotics*. New York: Routledge.

Leiderstam, M. (2006). *See and Seen: seeing landscape through artistic practice*. Lund University.

Lorch, B. (2002). *Landscape*. Retrieved March 30, 2018, from http://lucian.uchicago.edu/blogs/mediatheory/keywords/landscape/

Manovich, L. (2002). *The Language of New Media*. MIT Press.

Mitchell, W. J. T. (1994). Imperial Landscape. In W. J. T. Mitchell (Ed.), *Landscape and Power*. University of Chicago Press.

Paul, C. (2003). *Digital Art*. London: Thames & Hudson Ltd.

Ribeiro, R. W. (2007). *Paisagem Cultural e Património*. Rio de Janeiro: IPHAN.

Shama, S. (2004). *Landscape and Memory*. Harper Perennial.

Simmel, G. (2009). *A Filosofia da Paisagem*. Covilhã: LusoSofia.

KEY TERMS AND DEFINITIONS

Algorithmic Manipulation: Act of manipulating digital information through the use of computer algorithms.

Enformed: Something programmed, manipulated, shaped, educated by another entity.

Generative Art: Art created by an autonomous system, produced by one or more authors.

Glitch Sound: Sound produced by a failure in a system.

Installation: An artwork that uses different media to convey a concept (emotional and/or rational).

Landscape: Generally understood as a view over a territory. But can be the representation of this view, a discipline that studies this view, and the act of shaping the territory.

Social Semiotics: Is a branch of Semiotics that investigates meaning production in a social and cultural context, as something intimately connected with the related social practices.

Serra de Arga: Area of mountains located in the north of Portugal, between Viana do Castelo, Caminha and Ponte de Lima.

Vanguards: Artistic movements of the beginning of the XX century.

Chapter 9
Aesthetic Composition Indicator Based on Image Complexity

Adrian Carballal
University of A Coruña, Spain

Luz Castro
University of A Coruña, Spain

Carlos Fernandez-Lozano
University of A Coruña, Spain

Nereida Rodríguez-Fernández
University of A Coruña, Spain

Juan Romero
University of A Coruña, Spain

Penousal Machado
University of Coimbra, Portugal

ABSTRACT

Several systems and indicators for multimedia devices have appeared in recent years, with the goal of helping the final user to achieve better results. Said indicators aim at facilitating beginner and intermediate photographers in the creation of images or videos with more professional aesthetics. The chapter describes a series of metrics related to complexity which seem to be useful for the purpose of assessing the aesthetic composition of an image. All the presented metrics are fundamental parts of the prototype "ACIC" introduced here, which allows an assessment of the aesthetics in the composition of the various frames integrating a video.

DOI: 10.4018/978-1-5225-7371-5.ch009

INTRODUCTION

From image brightness indicators to facial recognition systems, multimedia devices in the home and commercial environments have gone through a revolution from the late 90s until the present day. These systems allow access to the images intrinsic information based on different phenomena, such as contrast, for instance, showing whether there is an under or over exposure at a given time.

Most of these indicators have the task of measuring objective phenomena, given that they can be clearly identifiable and quantified. Any system, which could be capable of measuring a relevant subjective phenomenon related to taking a picture or shooting a video would possess a high added value.

This paper proposes a system allowing the evaluation of the aesthetic composition of an image or the frames in a video (Liu, Chen, Wolf, & Cohen-Or, 2010). Thus, multimedia devices could help the user to identify in real time those framings with a certain aesthetic value. This would enable users without artistic background to take pictures and shoot videos of better appearance and with a more professional look.

Numerous papers (Machado & Cardoso, 2002; Rigau, Freixas, & Sbert, 2008; Ross, Ralph, & Zong, 2006; Machado, Romero, & Manaris, 2007) have appeared in recent years evaluating different elements of the aesthetic value of images and different ways to estimate it. This chapter introduces different metrics based on those works, based on the complexity of an image, which have already proven useful in experiments related to the ordering and classification based on stylistic and aesthetic criteria (Romero, Machado, Carballal, & Osorio, 2011; Machado, Romero, Nadal, Santos, Correia, & Carballal, 2015).

First, we will make a study of those metrics and their usefulness for calculating the aesthetic composition of a landscape. An experiment of image binary classification according to their aesthetic composition will be described for this purpose. Later on, we will present the design of a prototype system indicating the aesthetic composition of the frames integrating a video: **A**esthetic **C**omposition **I**ndicator based-on **I**mage **C**omplexity (a.k.a **ACIC**). This system will be used for the purpose of differentiating professional and amateur videos. Similarly, an example of functioning will be provided based on a professional video and the comments made by an expert on the results achieved.

We understand that the resulting prototype can be used for several tasks related to aesthetic composition: identification, classification, categorization, etc.; both in real-time multimedia devices and in stand-alone applications.

Next, the present paper is structured as follows: (i) a short description of the state of the art in composition systems is included; (ii) the hypothesis of the authors about possible metrics for evaluating the aesthetic composition of an image is presented; (iii) the features to be used in the study are described; (iv) the results obtained in an experiment of image classification according to their aesthetic composition are shown; (v) the design and functioning of a prototype will be detailed by means of a real example; (vi) and, finally, the conclusions and the upcoming research lines for improving the already presented prototype will be explained.

STATE OF THE ART

Santella, Agrawala, DeCarlo, Salesin, & Cohen (2006) presented a system which records user's eye movements for a few seconds to identify important image content. The given approach is capable of generate crops of any size or aspect ratio. The main disadvantage is that the system incurs on requiring user input, so it can't be considered a fully-computational approach. Once the important area of an image is detected, the crops are made considering three basics on photography: (i) include an entire subject and some context around, (ii) edges should pass through featureless areas whenever possible, (iii) the area of the subject matter should be maximized to increase clarity.

Santella et al. (2006) presented 50 images cropped using three different approaches: saliency-based (Suh, Ling, Bederson, & Jacobs, 2003), professional hand-crop, and gaze-crop to 8 different subjects. They obtained that their gaze-based approach was preferred to saliency-based cropping in 58.4% of trials and in 32.5% to professional cropping.

Liu, Chen, Wolf, & Cohen-Or (2010) have translated several basic composition guidelines into quantitative aesthetic scores, including the rule of thirds, diagonal, visual balance, and region size. Based on which, an automatic crop-and-retarget approach to producing a maximally-aesthetic version of the input image. Their approach searches for the optimal composition result in a 4D space, which contains all cropped windows with various widths and heights.

A dataset of 900 casual images arbitrarily collected from international websites in which skilled photographers rank photographs through them was employed to evaluate their score function. To evaluate the performance of their method generated a set of 30 triplets of images; the original image, one crop using Santella's method and one using theirs. These triplets were shown to 56 subjects, males and women, between 21 and 55 years old. In 44.1% of cases, the subjects preferred the cropped images provided by their approach. In addition, 81.8% were not able to distinguish whether the image was hand-cropped or computationally optimized.

Wang & Cohen (2007) propose an algorithm for composing foreground elements onto a new background by integrating matting and compositing into a single process. The system is able to compose more efficiently and with fewer artifacts compared with previous approaches. The matte is optimized in a sense that it will minimize the visual artifacts on the final composed image, although it may not be the true matte for the foreground. They determine the size and position that minimizes the difference between a small shell around the foreground and the new background, and then run the compositional matting. The developed algorithm not always gives satisfying compositions when the new background differs significantly from the original.

Zhang, Zhang, Sun, Feng, & Ma (2005) presented an auto-cropping model to obtain an optimal cropped image using the width and height of the original image, the conservative coefficient, the faces detected and the region of interest (ROI). The model consists of three sub models: (i) a composition sub model to describe how good the composition is, (ii) a conservative sub model to prevent the photograph from being cropped too aggressively and (iii) a penalty factor to prevent faces or ROIs being cut off. They used 100 pictures randomly selected from 600 home photographs. All the images were used into two studies. The first user study evaluated the auto cropping result in different aspect ratios. They obtained that the algorithm exhibits a satisfactory score on cropping. The second user study evaluated the improvement of the picture composition after cropping, in which observed the considering of the artistic rules leads to a good score of the improvement of the picture composition.

Suh, Ling, Bederson, & Jacobs (2003) proposed a set of fully automated image cropping techniques using a visual salience model based on low-level contrast measures. According to them, the more salient a portion of image, the more informative it is; and the visual search performance is increased as much recognizable the thumbnail is. They used their feature set on recognizing objects in small thumbnails (Recognition Task) and to measure how the thumbnail generation technique affects search performance (Visual Search Task). They ran an empirical study over 20 subjects, which were college or graduate students at the University of Maryland, and 500 filler images. In both tasks, the proposed set was capable to provide thumbnails substantially more recognizable and easier to find in the context of visual search.

HYPHOTESIS

The already described works focus on the search for metrics which show the composition quality or cropping methods which enhance the visual and aesthetic quality of a given image. Most of them use metrics related to Rule of Thirds (RoT), Region of Interest (ROI), or Saliency individually. RoT is a photographic framing technique, which divides the scene into 9 equally sized parts by means of three vertical and horizontal equidistant lines. This technique is based on placing the heaviest elements at the intersection among these lines. On the other hand, the use of ROI determines those image areas grouping the elements which attract the greatest interest. The saliency allows the differentiation of a foreground object from the background and to classify it as an interesting point.

Our hypothesis entails that the quality of aesthetic composition may be related to the visual complexity of the composition itself, as well as to the complexity derived from each of the elements represented in the same image. We assume that, inside the images, there are elements which attract the observer's attention, and their complexity must be taken into account when determining the composition aesthetics.

We propose the joint use of metrics allowing the determination of the complexity of an image as a whole, as well as of all the elements integrating it and, particularly, those which are its focus of attention. The proposed metrics are listed next.

Complexity

Machado & Cardoso (1998) based on previous works (Arnheim, 1956), proposes JPEG and Fractal Compression methods to estimate the image complexity. Forsythe et al. (2011) found a correlation between compression error and complexity of the image.

The error involved in the JPEG compression method, which affects mainly to high frequencies, depends on the variability of the pixels in the image. From this point of view, more variability involves more randomness and therefore more complexity. The fractal method tends to compress an image by filtering the self-similarities within. In this case, more self-similarities imply less variability, and therefore less complexity. Hence we considered applying JPEG and Fractal Compression methods as image complexity estimatives (Romero, Machado, Carballal, & Santos, 2012).

Subject Salience

Saliency is the quality that stands out one or multiple important objects from those that surrounds it/them. Somehow, saliency facilitates to focus the perception of the viewer on the most pertinent item or items on a scene. The saliency algorithm chosen to implement was the subject saliency algorithm also known as subject region extraction (Luo & Tang, 2008). Based on the idea that the subject in a photograph would be clearer and the background would be blurred, the algorithm extracts the clear region of an image, which theoretically holds the subject. This algorithm uses images statistics to detect 2D blurred regions in an image, based on a modification of (Levin, 2006). Subject Salience will be used to detect the foreground item/s, which should get the focus of attention.

Sobel Filter

The Sobel filter calculates the gradient of the image intensity at each point, giving the direction of the greater variation from light to dark and the amount of variation in that same direction. This gives us an idea of the variation of brightness at each point, from smooth to sharp differences. With this filter it is estimated the presence of the light–dark transitions and how they are oriented. With these light–dark variations corresponding to the intense and well-defined boundaries between objects, it is possible to obtain edge detection.

The Sobel Filter will give a simple representation of all the elements standing on the image by identifying their silhouettes.

PRESENTED FEATURES

The proposed metrics have already been listed. This section will show the features used in the experiments which are related to each of those metrics.

Before entering into a detailed explanation of the features used, we must explain the way in which they will be obtained. Four auxiliary images are generated from every image. Three of those images are obtained by separating the color channels following the HSV model. The fourth image stems from an attempt to solve the existing problems of the HSV color model for the extreme values of the H and V channels. For instance, a totally black pixel (V = 0) can be represented with any value of S and H. This new image is determined by multiplying pixel by pixel the S and V channels within the range [0, 255]. It will be referred to from now on as CS or Colorfulness (Correia, Machado, Romero, & Carballal, 2013).

Control Features

We have chosen to use a set of basic features related to the statistical variability of the pixels integrating an image. Said features calculate: (i) the mean (ii) and the typical deviation of the pixels with regard to the adjacent pixels in each channel.

Since the Hue channel is circular, the mean and standard deviation are calculated based on the angle values of Hue and its norm. In addition, it is performed the multiplication of the Hue angle by the pixel intensity values of CS, and a new value of the norm is calculated using values from H and CS. Splitting the image in mentioned color channels and applying the metrics to each of the resulting images yields a total of 12 features per image, 7 related with Average and 5 related with Standard Deviation.

Complexity Features

As already explained in the "Hypothesis" section, the use of the JPEG and FRACTAL compression are used as estimates of an image complexity; while the Subject Saliency and the Sobel Filter are used for the identification of the main elements in the scene, as well as all the items appearing in it.

In the case of the compression methods, since they are both lossy compression schemes, there might be a compression error, i.e., the compressed image will not exactly match the original. In our case, three levels of detail for the JPEG and fractal compression metrics are considered: low, medium and high. For each compression level the process is the same. The image is encoded in JPEG or FRACTAL format, and its complexity is estimated as following:

$$Complexity\left(\text{Image}\right) = RMSE\left(\text{Image}, CT\left(\left(\text{Image}\right)\right)\right) \times \frac{File_{Size}\left(CT\left(\text{Image}\right)\right)}{File_{Size}\left(\text{Image}\right)}$$

where RMSE represents the root mean square error and CT is the JPEG or fractal compression transformation.

$$Complexity\left(I\right) = \varepsilon\left(I, I_{\gamma}\right) \times \frac{\theta\left(I_{\gamma}\right)}{\theta\left(I\right)}$$

The quality settings of the JPEG encoding for low, medium, and high level of detail were 20, 40, and 60, respectively. Nonce, a quadtree fractal image compression scheme was used to calculate de PC of the image. More info available at (Romero et al., 2012).

Splitting the image in mentioned color channels and applying the complexity metrics to each of the resulting images gives a total of 32 features.

It must be noted that these 32 features will be calculated based on the original image, having applied the subject saliency and the Sobel Filter again. Therefore, we will achieve a total number of 96 features.

EXPERIMENTS ON AESTHETIC COMPOSITION

The previous section has identified all the features to be used in the experiment shown next. A total of 1961 landscape images of high aesthetic quality in their composition have been compiled for carrying out this experiment, most of them wallpapers in landscape format. All of them have a resolution higher than 1024x1024 pixels. Their visual topics vary a great deal: night, day, mountain, beach, etc. From this initial dataset, a random algorithm was created which will provide sub-images with a width/height ratio equal to the original image (see functioning in Algorithm 1). Said algorithm has been used on every image, thus providing a second set of images of the same sampling size.

A photography expert has identified those images which, because of the random cropping, generated a new image which was better than the original one as regards framing. All these images have been discarded, achieving a final dataset integrated by two sets of 1757 images each.

Figure 1 shows a simple subset of images of both sets. The left side shows images of the original set, while the right side shows the same subset once the algorithm has been applied.

Algorithm 1. Random Image Cropping

```
Per each image

1. A random height is established (between 400 and 1/2 of the height of the
original image).

2. A width is established according to the ratio of the original image

3. Random loc_x and loc_y are created (>0, <original size)

4. If the cropped image does not exceed the original on the right or at the
bottom:

cropping

otherwise

return to 1
```

Figure 1. Images of both sets (images of the original set on the left and the cropped version on the right) (© 2018, A. Carballal. Image may be subject to copyright.)

RESULTS

Both images to be used in this experimental part and the features which will characterize them individually have been presented so far. The present section explains the experiment carried out in order to try to validate the initially proposed hypothesis.

As already explained in the Control Features section, we have a set of 12 basic features related to the statistic variability of the pixels integrating the image (Avg and STD) calculated on the different color channels. This set will be referred to as BASE from now on.

Besides, we have a second set which will be integrated by those 12 features and by another 96 features related to the complexity of the whole image, to the main attention element and to the boundaries of the items integrating that image. This set of 108 features will be referred to as COMPLEX from now on.

The classification model chosen has been the SNNS (Stuttgart Neural Network Simulator). In particular, a backpropagation MLP is used with 3-layer architecture: an input layer with 108 neurons, a single hidden layer of 15 and an output layer with 1 neuron. This configuration has been established based on previous experiments and experiences of the research team in tasks of the same field (Machado, Romero, Nadal, Santos, Correia, & Carballal, 2015).

The network training will finish when a maximum number of 1000 cycles is reached. The initial network weights are determined at random within the range [-0.1, 0.1]. A maximum error tolerance of 0.3 has been used.

The 10-fold Cross-Validation (10-fold CV) model has been used for the generation of the training data sets so that their results are statistically relevant. Each of these runs has a different training and validation set which have been randomly generated. The results shown correspond to the average results obtained in these 10 runs.

Given that the neural network provides a number value within the range of 0 and 1, a dichotomic system has been used for cataloguing the images. Those images which have a network output of less than 0.5, once they have been presented to the system, will be catalogued as having a low aesthetic composition.

According to the data, it may be seen that the image classification when using the BASE set seems to achieve relatively satisfactory results. It should be noted that the problem itself contributes to the achievement of such high results. Let's imagine that there is a landscape photography similar to the one in Figure 2A. Having applied the random cropping, the new image may result as the one seen in Figure 2C. In this case, as is usually the case in this kind of images, the cropped landscapes usually have an extreme pixel variability compared to the original image. That is, the mean and the typical deviation of the pixels integrating the resulting image either increases or decreases considerably. Anyhow, no element of the real content of any of the two images is taken into account for the classification. Similarly, it may also be seen that both the accuracy and the recall for that feature set are clearly outbalanced (particularly in the case of the recall, with a 14% difference).

Table 1. Precision and recall using ANNs

	Precision			Recall		
	ORIGINAL	**CROPPED**	**GLOBAL**	**ORIGINAL**	**CROPPED**	**GLOBAL**
BASE	71.9%	79.2%	74.5%	82.2%	67.9%	75.0%
COMPLEX	82,6%	85.8%	84.2%	86.5%	81.7%	84.1%

Figure 2. Cropping example (© 2018, A. Carballal. Image may be subject to copyright)

A) Original Image   B) Cropping selection   C) Resulting image

As regards the second metrics set, we may observe an increase in accuracy over 9%. It must be noted that a great part of the improvement corresponds to the increase in the capacity to detect cropped images (from 67.9% to 81.7%). Similarly, both the individual recall and accuracy seem to be better offset with the global one.

DISCUSSION

The expert was presented with the number data and the images which the BASE and COMPLEX sets were not capable of identifying correctly, without having any kind of information about the classification system or the metrics used.

According to his criterion, the BASE features tend to classify non-cropped images incorrectly when there are minimal hue or texture differences among the composition elements (Figure 3A). Even in those images where there is some element of brightness, light or where the differentiating element is relatively small with regard to the image (Figure 3B). On the contrary, in the case of cropped images, it tends to classify erroneously those images whose content bears a great symmetry, regardless of their content or originality (Figure 3C), or those where the differentiating element is in the foreground, while the background is out of focus and homogeneous (Figure 3D).

With regard to the COMPLEX features, one of the most frequent mistakes happens in images with framing based on the horizon line (Figure 4A). It seems that the system cannot find any differentiating element in the image, understanding that it is made of two similar parts. In that case, where we are almost faced with two textures, it is possible that it interprets it as a cropped image. It is also classified as a cropped image when the differentiating element is placed on one of the far ends of the image, partially complying with the three thirds framing, but leaving the other half practically empty (Figure 4B).

On the contrary, in the case of those cropped images which are classified as original ones, sometimes the mistake is perfectly justified: cropped image pieces partially comply with the principles of framing; they structure a differentiating element at the centre while their environment goes totally unnoticed as a uniform background (Figure 4C). Color contrasts may also cause confusion; for instance, if we are faced with a horizon or, simply, with areas of a well differentiated color (such as water foam, a specific color in a bouquet of flowers or tree leaves) which is an element in itself. The fact that these occupy a significantly bigger part than the true differentiating elements may lead to error (Figure 4D).

Figure 3. Examples of wrongly classified images using the BASE set (Carballal, 2018)

A)

C)

B)

D)

Figure 4. Examples of wrongly classified images using the COMPLEX set (Carballal, 2018)

A)

C)

B)

D)

The expert concluded that the mistakes generated by the COMPLEX set were not trivial and were sometimes understandable.

ACIC PROTOTYPE

In the previous experiment, we have seen the capacity of the COMPLEX set for classifying images according to their aesthetic composition. A prototype has been developed from that set of metrics with the purpose of determining the composition aesthetics on the images integrating a video. The present section will explain in further detail the functioning of the ACIC.

Design and Implementation

ACIC embeds a light indicator on a video, identifying those frames with a high aesthetic composition (green light) or those with a low aesthetic composition (red light). The prototype is based on the use of different modules, which allow the performance of specific independent tasks in an automated way. The Algorithm 2 and Figure 5 show how the identification process for video frames is carried out.

The breaking down and remaking of the video in the corresponding frames is made under the support of the FFMpeg API. The frames modifications for adding the indicators are made by using, in this instance, the API of ImageMagick. The features extraction is made by means of an automated serial process, following the same extraction method seen in (Romero et al., 2012), but changing the edge detection filter used by the Sobel filter and adding the Saliency Subject.

In our case, since it is a prototype, only 1 out of 10 frames are used, due to the fact that the extraction system is not optimized yet for using parallel processing on every frame.

Testing

A series of tests have been made with videos containing different types of landscapes. In particular, the expert was asked to search for 3 videos considered as having a high aesthetic composition (well framed compositions, stable camera movements and professional preparation), and 3 more with a low aesthetic

Algorithm 2. ACIC Workflow

```
1. The video is broken down into its key frames with a frame rate of 25fps.

2. The first in a group of 10 frames is selected as the representative frame
in the set.

a. Its 108 corresponding features are extracted.

b. These values are presented as inputs to the ANN classifier.

c. If the classifier output value is >=0.5, then the green light is added to
the 10 frames, otherwise, the red light is added.

3. The video is remade from the frames resulting from section 2.
```

Figure 5. ACIC Workflow (Carballal, 2018, used with permission.)

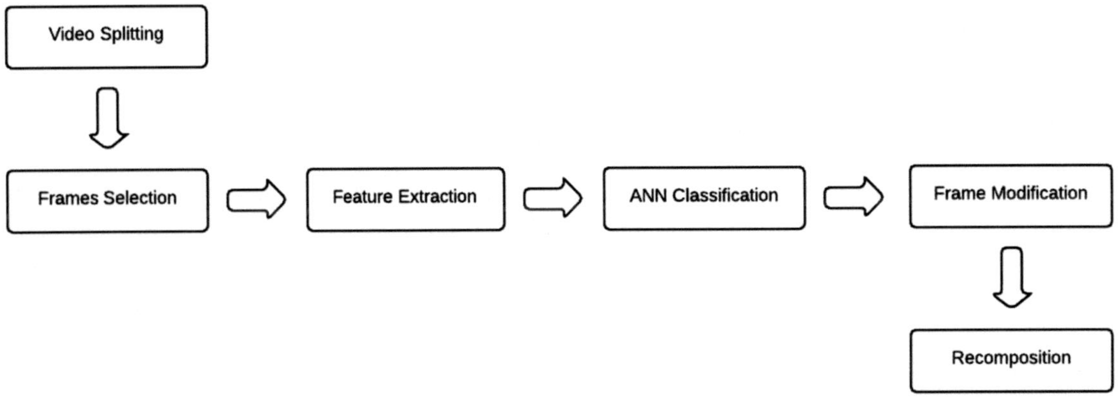

composition (wrong framings, totally out of focus, inconsistent movements, something considered as amateurish). YouTube was the platform chosen for the compilation of the study videos.

Given that these were videos compiled from a multimedia portal whose main feature is the great variety of themes and contents, some modifications had to be made on the videos before presenting them to the ACIC. They were downloaded in 360p format using the H.264 codec. Those initial or final frames containing any kind of subtitles were discarded, given that they could be treated as an integral part of the image, and, probably, the system would determine that the text is the main subject, thus biasing the results achieved by the framing classifier.

Having chosen those videos and applied the ACIC system, we studied the capacity of the system for differentiating high aesthetic composition videos qualified by the expert as professional ones from those with a low composition classified as amateur (indexing), as well as the classification quality of the frames inside a video (quality).

Indexing Performance

The purpose is to analyze if the system can detect a greater number of frames correctly placed in "professional" videos than in "amateur" ones. In order to test this hypothesis, the outputs of the classifier were tested for each of the frames obtained in the sampling process for the six compiled videos. In the case of the 3 videos catalogued as professional by the expert, 74.4% out of the 1576 sampled frames were classified as having a high aesthetic composition. On the contrary, in the case of the 3 videos catalogued as amateur, only 16.8% out of the 1958 sampled frames were classified as having a high aesthetic composition (see Table 2).

Quality Performance

As previously mentioned, the ACIC prototype was used with each one of the chosen videos, and the expert was asked to evaluate its functioning. This section will explain concisely the expert's conclusions for one of the professional videos which is available at http://youtu.be/yJGXlZHtuJY.

Table 2. Accuracy of frames marked as "Professional" for the six compiled videos

Video Examples	Frames Marked as "Professional"	Frames Marked as "Amateur"	Accuracy of Frames Marked as "Professional"
Professional 1	309	46	87.04%
Professional 2	710	221	76.26%
Professional 3	153	137	52.76%
Amateur 1	185	404	31.41%
Amateur 2	123	612	16.73%
Amateur 3	21	613	3.31%

The system seems to interpret the currently most frequently used types of framings, such as the *Horizon's law*, *Vanishing Point* or even the *Rule of Thirds* (Figure 6A), differentiating and assigning a weight to each of the elements in the image. Even in those times when there is a clear intention to comply with the *Rule of Thirds* and this is not achieved, the system will label it as wrong (Figure 6B).

It also interprets *vanishing points* and *central point composition*, although they have a smaller size and scarce contrast against the background, thus positioning itself as a detailed and thorough system which is capable of recognizing elements with an objective visual weight (Figure 7).

At given times, the images possess a well-delimited and highly contrasted area with a very saturated color or an extreme brightness level with regard to the rest of the surrounding environment. In that case, the system seems to determine that the visual weight of the image is exactly located at that point, and so it is correctly classified as out of focus (see Figure 8).

The system is capable of recognizing the selective focus on the foreground. This is achieved by means of focusing on the object at the foreground while leaving the background out of focus. Although the object framing the composition may be placed in an area which is out of focus and scarcely contrasted, the system is capable of acknowledging the image as a correct one (at given times, the images possess a well delimited and highly contrasted area with a very saturated color or an extreme brightness level with regard to the rest of the surrounding environment. In that case, the system seems to determine that the visual weight of the image is exactly located at that point, and so it is correctly classified as out of focus, see Figures 8A and 8B).

Figure 6. Examples of well and badly framed images, according to the system, using the Rule of Thirds as criterion (Carballal, 2018)

A) 00:37   B) 00:10

Figure 7. Example of well framed image according to ACIC related to the Vanishing Point (Carballal, 2018)

Figure 8. Examples where the system seems to work by determining the visual weight (A) and the selective focus on the foreground (B) (Carballal, 2018)

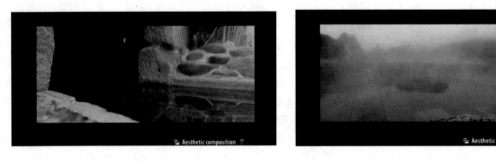

A) 00:26   B) 00:02

Sometimes we find overlaying framings in professional photography compositions. We may expect the system to fail in that case, since it would not be able to judge which of the contrasted elements has the highest weight, although this is not the case. It is capable of classifying an image with more than 3 different types of added framings as correct. For instance, Figure 9 shows a *Horizon's law* framing (blue), a *Rule of Thirds* one (red) and a *Vanishing Point* one (purple).

However, the system is not unerring. When a composition is framed based on a central element occupying an excessively big proportion, then the system makes some mistakes when classifying the framing. This happens when there are elements such as fog, sea foam, smoke, etc. which are overlaying the central element, and generating a contrast against the background. Thus, the system will classify it as a priority object and label it as out of focus (Figure 10A).

Figure 9. Example of image where several types of framings are observed: Horizon's law, Rule of thirds, and Vanishing point. (Carballal, 2018)

When the element with the visual weight in an image, for instance, the man in the photograph following the Rule of Thirds, is about to exit the framing and his position is doubtful, perhaps there is a variation and the system will recognize it as framed most of the time and out of frame at the next second, almost without variation (Figure 10B).

Another problem consists of the fact that it may recognize vegetation as an element with a high visual weight in order to analyse framings. Vegetation is usually unnoticed by the human eye, while the system takes it as a reference for classification. This is the case in Figure 11A, where the system determines the bush branches as a main element and thus, the image as well framed.

Besides, excessively cropped foreground elements are often classified as correct even if they are not, such as in the following case, where the carpet is established as a foreground element (Figure 11B).

CONCLUSION

This paper has presented a set of metrics based on complexity which seem to be useful for judging the aesthetic composition in landscape images as well as a prototype known as ACIC which would allow the final user of a multimedia device whether the image captured could be labelled as having a "high aesthetic composition".

A neural network has been used as a binary classification using the presented features as inputs, achieving accuracy and precision results of more than 84%. The trained network integrates the main axis of the ACIC, which shows by means of a green or red light if the aesthetic composition of the shown image is of high or low quality, respectively.

Figure 10. Examples of false negatives achieved by the ACIC (Carballal, 2018)

A) 00:05   B) 00:38

Figure 11. Examples of false positives achieved by the ACIC (Carballal, 2018)

A) 00:41   B) 01:25

ACIC has been tested on professional and amateur videos and seems to be capable of differentiating them based on the percentage of frames classified as well framed. Moreover, the individual classifications of the frames obtained in the simple videos, in spite of not being perfect, seem to achieve satisfactory results.

Among the most immediate enhancements, we may mention above all the elimination of all those cases identified by the expert where the classifier fails, both in the case of false positives and negatives. For this purpose, we intend to search for another set of metrics which can help the already existing one with that task, and even to find alternatives for the Sobel and Saliency Subjects, so that their detection problems do not have a direct impact on the prototype.

Another problem of use stems from the need to improve the classification times to be used in real time, so that the used images have a bigger sampling size. We intend to modify the classification system so that asynchronous tasks can be performed by means of parallel programming, thus reducing the time of the task of extracting metrics from each image, which currently entails the biggest bottleneck.

ACKNOWLEDGMENT

This work was supported in part by Xunta de Galicia, project XUGA–PGIDIT10TIC105008PR; the Portuguese Foundation for Science and Technology, project PTDC/EIA–EIA/115667/2009, the General Directorate of Culture, Education and University Management of Xunta de Galicia (Ref. GRC2014/049), and the Juan de la Cierva fellowship program by the Spanish Ministry 350 of Economy and Competitiveness (Carlos Fernandez-Lozano, Ref. FJCI-2015-26071).

REFERENCES

Arnheim, R. (1956). *Art and Visual Perception*. London: Faber and Faber.

Correia, J., Machado, P., Romero, J., & Carballal, A. (2013). *Feature Selection and Novelty in Computational Aesthetics. In Evolutionary And Biologicaly Inspired Music, Sound, Art* (pp. 133–144). Vienna, Austria: Springer.

Forsythe, A., Nadal, M., Sheehy, N., Cela-Conde, C., & Sawey, M. (2011). Predicting beauty: Fractal dimension and visual complexity in art. *British Journal of Psychology, 102*(1), 49–70. doi:10.1348/000712610X498958 PMID:21241285

Levin, A. (2006). Blind motion deblurring using image statistics. In *Proceedings of the 19th International Conference on Neural Information Processing Systems* (pp. 841-848). MIT Press.

Liu, L., Chen, R., Wolf, L., & Cohen-Or, D. (2010). Optimizing Photo Composition. *Computer Graphic Forum*, 469-478.

Luo, Y., & Tang, X. (2008). Photo and Video Quality Evaluation: Focusing on the Subject. In *Proceedings of the 10th European Conference on Computer Vision: Part III* (pp. 386-399). Marseille, France: Springer-Verlang. 10.1007/978-3-540-88690-7_29

Machado, P., & Cardoso, A. (1998). Computing Aesthetics. In *Brazilian Symposium of Artificial Ingelligence* (pp. 219-228). Springer.

Machado, P., Romero, J., & Manaris, B. (2007). Experiments in Computational Aesthetics. In J. Romero & P. Machado (Eds.), The Art of Artificial Evolution (pp. 381-415). Springer.

Machado, P., Romero, J., Nadal, M., Santos, A., Correia, J., & Carballal, A. (2015). Computerized measures of visual complexity. *Acta Psychologica, 160*, 43–57. doi:10.1016/j.actpsy.2015.06.005 PMID:26164647

Rigau, J., Freixas, M., & Sbert, M. (2008). Informational Aesthetics Measures. IEEE Computer Graphics and Applications, 28(2), 24-34.

Romero, J., Machado, P., Carballal, A., & Osorio, O. (2011). Aesthetic Classification and Sorting Based on Image Compression. In EvoApplications (pp. 394-403). Torino, Italy: Springer.

Romero, J., Machado, P., Carballal, A., & Santos, A. (2012). Using complexity estimates in aesthetic image classification. *Journal of Mathematics and the Arts*, 6(2-3), 125–136. doi:10.1080/17513472.2012.679514

Ross, B. J., Ralph, W., & Zong, H. (2006). Evolutionary Image Systhesis Using a Model of Aesthetics. In *Proceedings of the IEEE Congress on Evolutionary Computation* (pp. 3832-3839). Vancouver: IEEE Press.

Santella, A., Agrawala, M., DeCarlo, D., Salesin, D., & Cohen, M. (2006). Gaze-based interaction for semi-automatic photo cropping. In *Proceedings of the SIGCHI Conference on Human Factors in Computing Systems* (pp. 771-780). Montreal, Canada: ACM.

Suh, B., Ling, H., Bederson, B. B., & Jacobs, D. W. (2003). Automatic thumbnail cropping and its effectiveness. In *Proceedings of the 16th annual ACM symposion on User interface software and technology* (pp. 95-104). Vancouver, Canada: ACM.

Wang, J., & Cohen, M. F. (2007). Simultaneous Matting and Composition. In *IEEE Conference on Computer Vision and Pattern Recognition*. Minneapolis, MN: IEEE Press.

Zhang, M., Zhang, L., Sun, Y., Feng, L., & Ma, W. (2005). Auto cropping for digital photographs. In *IEEE International Conference on Multimedia and Expo*. Amsterdam: IEEE Press.

KEY TERMS AND DEFINITIONS

Aesthetic Criteria: Standards upon which judgements are made about the artistic merit of a work of art.

Dichotomy: A division of the members of a population, or sample, into two groups.

Lossy Compression: The decompressed data will not be identical to the original uncompressed data.

Subjective Phenomenon: As distinguished from "objective," is a classification for mental phenomena that are not capable of objective validation, as in the case of physical phenomena.

Visual Artifacts: Are anomalies apparent during visual representation as in photography.

Visual Complexity: The level of detail or intricacy contained within an image.

Chapter 10
Approach to Minimize Bias on Aesthetic Image Datasets

Adrian Carballal
University of A Coruña, Spain

Luz Castro
University of A Coruña, Spain

Nereida Rodríguez-Fernández
University of A Coruña, Spain

Iria Santos
University of A Coruña, Spain

Antonino Santos
University of A Coruña, Spain

Juan Romero
University of A Coruña, Spain

ABSTRACT

Over the last few years, numerous studies have been conducted that have sought to address automatic image classification. These approaches have used a variety of experimental sets of images from several photography sites. In this chapter, the authors look at some of the most widely used in the field of computational aesthetics as well as the capacity for generalization that each of them offers. Furthermore, a set of images built up by psychologists is described in order to predict perceptual complexity as assessed by a closed group of persons in a controlled experimental setup. Lastly, a new hybrid method is proposed for the construction of a set of images or a dataset for the assessment and classification of aesthetic criteria. This method brings together the advantages of datasets based on photography websites and those of a dataset where assessment is made under controlled experimental conditions.

DOI: 10.4018/978-1-5225-7371-5.ch010

INTRODUCTION

In the history of humanity we have always used art as a form of expression for our inquisitiveness, thoughts and experiences. However, it is with the birth of IT and Artificial Intelligence that art and aesthetics have come into the sphere of computerized systems.

In recent years computer systems have been developed that are able to classify and rank sets of images similarly to the way humans do. For the purposes of this classification such criteria as aesthetics, originality or theme are followed. To this end, large groups of images are used to contrast information, a determining factor to be able to obtain conclusive and easily comparable results. Most of them are built from the same sources (website, online photography competitions, …). In the pages that follow we will also analyze a set that includes pictures and photographs from a number of books and a set of images from other sources.

We know of no other study to date that has focused on establishing the validity of these datasets or on whether they are able to provide a generalized representation for classification tasks. In this chapter we will therefore study some datasets that have been used in the past in computational experiments dealing with aesthetic quality and we will put forward a new method for the construction of this type of sampling sets.

The classification of images meets its first handicap due to a marked characteristic of human nature. An aesthetic evaluation can be influenced by a great quantity of subjective aspects, which if not actually mistaken, may not be wholly universal. For this reason, images are classified according to criteria merely aesthetic or objective such as shapes, colours and composition which allow us a quantitative evaluation, leaving to one side the content. The features used in both the studies analyzed in the state of the art section and the proposal we put forward can be calculated for each image regardless of its nature and content.

Employing these sample groups simple characteristics will be detailed which will be used to classify the images in function of a series of quantitative criteria. Later, with the results obtained, an individual analysis will be carried out on each dataset separately. We will present a study showing their capacity for generalization about images obtained both from the same and different sources in such a way as to show if it is possible to extrapolate from their results.

This chapter is structured as follows: (i) State of the Art of the datasets used in the automatic image classification studies; (ii) study of the most widely used image sets from photography websites; (iii) experiment to assess the ability to generalize of the datasets from photography websites; (iv) study of a set of data suggested by psychologists; (v) a proposal of a new construction method for sample sets; (vi) discussion of results and conclusions.

STATE OF THE ART

Datta, Joshi, & Wang (2006), Wong & Low (2008), Ke, Tang, & Jing (2006), and Luo & Tang (2009) conducted a number of studies focused on automatic image classification, where the authors resorted to a variety of technical features, including lightness, saturation, rule of thirds etc. in pursuit of the best results. Their research projects have always relied on experiments using a variety of photographs from websites and the ratings provided by the users of such sites.

These datasets have some defects: their assessment system is not subjected to the same control as a psychological test because it is not possible to have all the information about the users rating the images. For instance, Datta, et al. (2006) use a dataset from Photo.net, where users can rate each photograph on the basis of "aesthetics" or "originality" but where users do not have notions to be able to differentiate between both aspects. On the other hand, Ke, et al. (2006) used a dataset taken from DPChallenge. com, another photography website with 16,509 images, although in this case the portal operates on a competition mode and images have a greater variety of ratings. Photography websites are conditioned, as they tend to have a particular bias: their users prefer certain styles over others because of some fad or a sudden surge in popularity of some style. Many participants are professional photographers, but their aesthetic assessment might be over influenced by the images' originality, uniqueness, etc.

Both sets have been used by other researchers to study new methodologies and features. So far no one has studied whether the results of these image banks can be extrapolated or their suitability. Although some features could be used to study a specific set of images, this does not mean that these characteristics are universal or that they should be applied to new photographs. To ensure their validity we need to have a large and representative enough reference group. As part of this research, we put forward a dataset that meets the characteristics required to ensure their validity.

The methodology used in the construction of the datasets studied has a problem, as classifiers are trained and validated using the same source and therefore the same set or sets of images obtained from it. As these sample groups have not been studied previously, universality cannot be ensured. It is for this reason that we believe the use of a variety of sets of images during the learning phase would help assess the coherence and the consistency of results correctly and therefore we suggest that the suitability of the sample groups should be studied using simple classifiers with basic characteristics obtained from images belonging to the datasets provided by Datta, et al. (2006, 2008) and Ke, et al. (2006).

DATASETS CONCERNING AESTHETICS

Once we have established the foundations of the experiments conducted by researchers such as Datta, et al. (2006, 2008) and Ke, et al. (2006) regarding data classification, we go on to discuss in greater detail some of the sets of images that have been more widely used for these tasks using PHOTO.NET (2006) as a source.

Datta, et al. (2006) created a dataset based on the photography website Photo.net, which has over a million images and more than 400,000 users. Each image is rated from 1 to 7 (1 being the worst possible score and 7 the best) for aesthetics and originality. Statistical information on the ratings is given on the website. However, no information is provided regarding those assessing the images. The full dataset consists of 3,581 images rated by at least 2 people and has an average score between 3.55 and 7 as well as an overall average scoring of 5.06 with a statistical deviation of 0.83. The high correlation found between the criteria of originality and aesthetics could be an indicator that users are not able to tell them apart satisfactorily.

This dataset has some problems: the number of images could be insufficient as there is no valid explanation for the sample size and there is a very marked difference between the number of persons who rate each image, the average assessment being sometimes based on as few as two ratings.

Datta, et al. (2006) and other researchers who have used this sampling group (such as Wong et al., 2009) performed a division to obtain two different groups. Images with an average score equal to or greater than 5.8 are branded high quality photographs while those with scores equal to or lower than 4.2 are branded low quality photographs. In the case of the study conducted by Datta, et al. (2006), 832 high quality images and 760 low quality images were analyzed taking into account some intuition-based visual characteristics. The authors hold that it is possible to distinguish between aesthetically pleasing and displeasing images, and they seek to explore the relationship images trigger on people using such features as exposure, white balance, saturation, composition, etc. Using these metrics, Datta, et al. (2006) achieved, using PHOTO.NET (2008) as a source, a 70.12% of successes in the global classification using Support Vector Machines (Vapnik, 1997; Witten & Frank, 2002): 68.08% in the case of High quality images and 72.31% in the case of Low quality images.

A study was also published by Datta, et al. (2008), in which they presented a series of data that could be used for aesthetic classification tasks. Besides, a second dataset was presented from the website consisting of 20,278 images, whose average rating was 12 per person with a standard deviation of 13. Currently, not all these images are available on the website.

By comparing this dataset with the previous one, we can see that this is a more complete statistical analysis as it provides more specific data on the classifications of each image. The total set of images has at least four ratings per image with an average ranging between 2.33 and 6.99, an overall average of 5.15 and an average deviation of 0.58. Despite this, the previously discussed drawback persists as there are images that have been assessed by as few as 4 people while in some other cases images have been rated by hundreds of persons, thus leading to an unbalanced sample.

On the other hand, Wong and Low (2009) show 44 metrics grouped in three categories with global characteristics based on basic techniques (sharpness, contrast, brightness…), photography rules and camera adjustments. They have used a reduced set out of the total images in the original experiment, which is now down to 3,161 images as they were unable to access the whole set of photographs because the site Photo.net has deleted some of them. After classifying them using SVM with a linear kernel and a cross-validation with 5 independent runs 78.2% of the images were classified correctly: 82.9% High Quality images and 75.6% Low Quality images (Source: DPCHALLENGE.COM).

Ke, et al. (2006) built a different image sampling set, which is among the most widely used in aesthetic classification experiments such as for instance those by Luo and Tang (2008). The latter is one of the most remarkable so far, as it has yielded the best results. Its percentage of success was 93% by resorting to such features as lightness, brightness, simplicity, geometrical composition, color harmony, and region extraction. However, the experiment on which it is based only obtained 72% of success using measurements associated with special distribution of the axis, color distribution, hues, and blurring.

For these experiments the photography portal DPChallenge.com was used with a total of 60,000 images, which, unlike in those from Photo.net, were rated by at least one hundred people. However, some data such as average per image or average deviation are not available. In this case ratings go from 1 to 10, where 1 is the lowest score and 10 the highest score.

In order to conduct aesthetic classification experiments, two sets of 6,000 photographs were created by extracting the top and bottom 10% of photos after arranging them in accordance with the average rating. The top set was categorized as high quality and the bottom set as low quality. Subsequently, Ke, et al. (2006) made a subdivision into two new random sets obtaining 4 sets with 3,000 images (two sets of high quality images and two sets of low quality images). A set of each type was used to train the systems proposed while the other was used to validate its capability and efficacy.

Other Published Datasets

Datta, et al. (2008) presented the scientific community with four testing datasets for conducting experiments. All four consisted of sets of photographs taken from the above-mentioned website portals Photo.net and DPChallenge.com. The other websites used are Terragalleria.com and Alipr.com. The dataset from Photo.net consists of 20,278 photographs; some of them cannot be retrieved as they are no longer available on the website. The average number of ratings per image is 12 with a standard deviation of 13. The DPChallenge.com set consists of 16,509 photographs with at least one rating. The mean number of assessments per image is 205 with a deviation of 53.

The third dataset presented by Datta, et al. (2008) is taken from Terragalleria.com and consists of 14,449 images. This portal includes only travel photographs from Quang Tuan Luong, which have been rated by peers like in DPChallenge.com from 1 (worst) y 10 (best). The average number of ratings per image is 22 with an average deviation of 23.

Lastly, Aplipr.com includes 13,010 images – some of them repeated – which are also rated by their users. This website does not include statistical information either.

There is no record that these datasets have been used in the aesthetic classification experiment, but we do know that these datasets have the same deficiencies in terms of control of ratings, sample size and acquired features resulting from the development and assessment of the collections.

Murray, Marchesotti, & Perronnin, 2012) made a dataset using Aesthetic Visual Analysis (AVA). To this end, they introduced a new large-scale database comprising over 250,000 images from a variety of themes with a great number of aesthetic ratings for each image.

CROSS-VALIDATION EXPERIMENT AMONG DIFFERENT DATASETS

Out of all the datasets designed to study this subject, only those from Photo.net and DPChallenge.com have been used experimentally. It is for this reason that we have conducted a simple experiment that will allow us to see if other photographs could be aesthetically classified using the results obtained with those sets of images, regardless of their source.

For this test a binary classifier was used that was fed with a set of basic characteristics (statistical and entropy estimator) with images from Photo.net and DPChallenge.com independently and testing the generation capability of the different systems whether own source or those from other sources. In the case of the DPChallenge.com classifier, the 6,000 images from the Ke, et al. experiment could be used. In the case of Photo.net only 23,700 images could be obtained as some of the ones used in the previous experiments conducted by Datta, et al. are no longer available on the website. Other researchers such as Wong and Low (2009) had already encountered this complication.

In Table 1, we detail the four image groups, which will be used indicating their origin. Those works, which have been shown for the first time, show the number of original images which it has been able to access and finally; we shall also give it a name.

The metrics and the statistics used, as well as the issue concerning entropy, are explained below.

Table 1. Information relative to the dataset used in the experiment part

Source	Publication	#Original Set	#Available Set	Name
Photo.net	Datta, et al. 2006	3,581	3,247	PN06
Photo.net	Datta, et al. 2008	20,278	18,105	PN08
DPChallenge.com	Ke, et al. 2006	6,000	6,000	DPCt
DPChallenge.com	Ke, et al. 2006	6,000	6,000	DPCv

Basic Features Used

Generally, technically related elements such as brightness or saturation are used to achieve the best results in image classification tasks by associating them with aesthetic criteria.

The objective of this study is to test whether the choice of the results of the images is trivial for this type of tests. To this end, we will use two sets of features: one obtained from the average and standard deviation of the value of the pixels in the image and another one by resorting to the values used to estimate the relative entropy of an image on the basis of the difference between the value of the adjoining pixels (Machado, et al. 2011, 2012).

For the first set, two statistical measures have been used for the color of each image: average and standard deviation. These measures consist of two values for each image of the HSV color channel with the exception of the representations for channel H (H and HCS), which have four values for the average (norm and angle) and two for standard deviation. From this set we obtain a total of ten statistical key figures: six for the average deviation and four for the standard deviation. This set of key figures will be called AvgStd.

The second set consists of image entropy estimators (which measure the degree of disorder existing in the system regardless of its nature). Although there are many entropy estimators, for this experiment we have resorted to Zipf's Law (Zipf, 1949), which states that the statistical range of an event is inversely proportional to its size. This law is based on the observation of phenomena generated by self-adaptive organisms and is known as the "principle of least effort". A variation within the law uses the size of the phenomenon instead of its range, thus creating the size-frequency distribution, a formula which will be used in our experiment. In this case we are talking a set of 8 key values which we will call SizeFreq.

Classification Models Used

Typically, classifiers known as Support Vector Machines (SVM) from the family of linear classifiers are used. An SVM represents sampling data that form a decision surface, which are not linearly separated and are converted by a function or a kernel into a space of characteristics of a greater size. Subsequently, the system determines a decision boundary separating the points in the sample into different classes, representing the hyperplane and making it possible to differentiate which data belong to each class.

There is a great deal of applications that make it possible to use these classifiers, among which WEKA (Wakato Environment for Knowledge Analysis) stands out. Datta, et al. (2006), Ke, et al. (2006), Luo & Tang (2008) and Wong & Low (2009) have used this type of classifiers as both default parameters and specific parameters.

EXPERIMENTS CONDUCTED

In this section we carry out two independent studies: (i) the generalization obtained training and validating our classifiers with distinct datasets but obtained from the same source, and (ii) the generalization obtained from using distinct datasets coming from different sources. For this we will use four sets of images belonging to the state of the art seen in previous sections.

We have conducted two experiments with the same values, the same classifiers and the same parameters of learning, only interchanging the data of training and validation. This allows us to draw two sets of conclusions, which will serve to evaluate the generalization capacity obtained with both sets of sample images.

In our case, we use a training procedure named 5-fold cross-validation (Browne, 2000), which consists in dividing the training patterns into 5 sets without any being of the same size. The process of learning is carried out five times in total. In each case one of the five sets is used as a test set and the other four to train. For this reason, all of the patterns are used once for the test and four times for the training (this phase we call *Train*). After, we will present another set of distinct images to each training classifier. After, to each independently trained classifier, we will present a distinct set of images using the previous stage. The reported results in this experiment refer to those of this external validation (this phase we will call *Validation*).

Experiment 1: Distinct Datasets Belonging to the Same Sources

Given that we have two sources, we will start with the dataset belonging to Photo.net, which we previously called PN06 and PN08. In Figure 1 we show the results for the validation obtained for each set of data, (PN06 on the left and PN08 on the right) training in turn with the same set and then with the other. The data obtained show that the set of training images, which are in this case different, does not significantly affect the classification. In the case of the set of features *AvgStd* results plus *SizeFreq*, the difference is always inferior to 2% accuracy. For this reason, we could conclude that the generalization reached is satisfactory.

On the other hand, in Figure 2 are shown the results obtained from those two datasets originating in DPChallenge.com (DPCt and DPCv). Unlike what was observed in the previous case, there exists a clear difference between validating one set and another. On validating the set DPCt, with whichever of the two we obtain similar results. On the contrary, on validating the set DPCv the results are very different in two ways: (i) when training with distinct sets the difference is superior 5% and (ii) the difference validating both sets by themselves is close to 30%. These results could indicate various situations: either DPCv is a subset of images with characteristics clearly differentiable by means of the information obtained by the set DPCt or the images which conform to the set DPCv have some intrinsic bias which permits a clear distinction even with basic features.

If we not only attend to the metrical statistics and entropy, but also the colour channels, we then obtain the results shown in Figure 3. There exists a clear internal difference within set DPCv that becomes more evident in the channels value and saturation. Directly observing the values obtained for those said channels in the samples, we detected that those ranges, when values are moved for the high and low sets, hardly overlapped. This allows us to differentiate with greater ease.

Figure 1. Results obtained training and validating with each set on an individual basis and interchanging those sets in a process of validation with images from photo.net (Carballal, 2018, Used with permission)

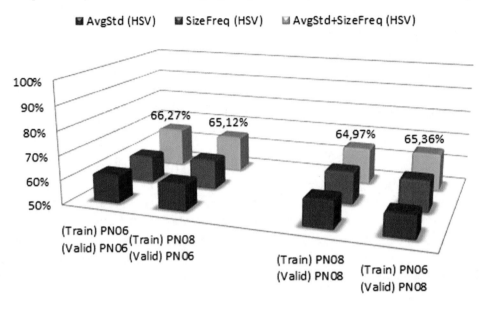

Figure 2. Results obtained training with each set and on an individual basis and interchanging those sets in a process of validation with images from DPChallenge.com (© 2018, A. Carballal, used with permission)

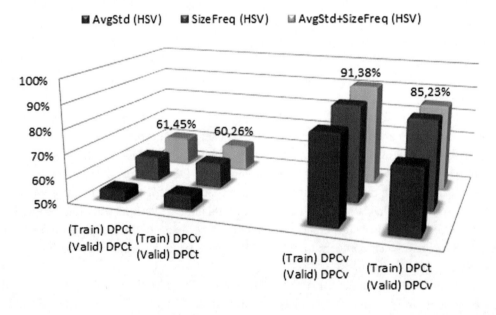

Figure 3. Results obtained according to each colour channel individually and all trained and validated with each one of the presented data sets (© 2018, A. Carballal, used with permission)

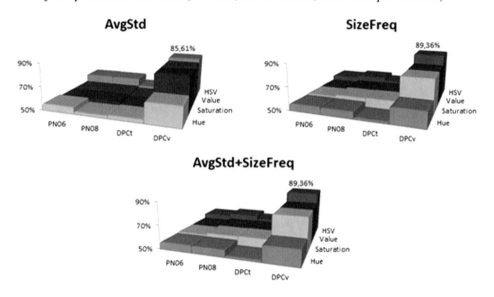

Experiment 2: Distinct Datasets Belonging to Different Sources

Once the capacity for generalization has been studied among the datasets coming from the same source of information, we precede to observe the behaviour of the classifiers previously created when presenting images originating from a different source.

The behaviour of the three sets of metrics is similar (see Figure 4) in the case of developing and validating the two sets of images obtained from Photo.net we observe that both sets offer similar results. If we compare the difference with those extracted from the DPCt set of images, although being superior, it seems to follow the same principles. The rate of accuracy varies within a range of [61.54%, 52.84%] for *AvgStd* [63.17%, 57.02%] for *SizeFreq* and [63.27%, 58.05%] for *AvgStd+SizeFreq*.

The fact that these results generally come close to 50% accuracy is logical seeing as we have to remember we are using simple metrics that only attend to variability of the pixels that conform to an image. We are going to come across the problem again in the set DPCv as we observe in the three cases training and validating with the same set we obtain results much superior in comparison with the rest of the experiments, with an accuracy capacity of 91,38% using *AvgStd+SizeFreq*. Even training with DPCt and validating with DPCv we obtain an accuracy rate of 80.23% also with *AvgStd+SizeFreq*.

We must remember that the best state of art results (training with DPCt and validating with DPCv) have been those by Luo, et al. (2008) with 93% accuracy using characteristics based on clarity, brightness, simplicity, geometrical composition, colour harmony and the plane (identifying the background and foreground).

If we study the performance of the colour channels with these statistical features, the difference of accuracy becomes clear in the case of validation with the DPCv set itself. If we attend specifically to the colour channel saturation we obtain an accuracy rate of 83,85% which is more than a 20% difference in respect to the other combinations (see Figure 5).

Figure 4. Results obtained in all of the "train" and "valid" possible within the four datasets used (© 2018, A. Carballal. Used with permission)

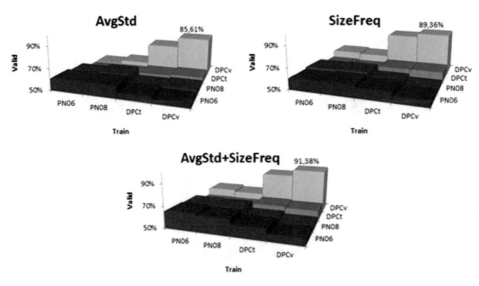

Figure 5. Results obtained accord to each colour channel using the statistical estimation in all possible combinations among the four datasets used (© 2018, A. Carballal. Used with permission)

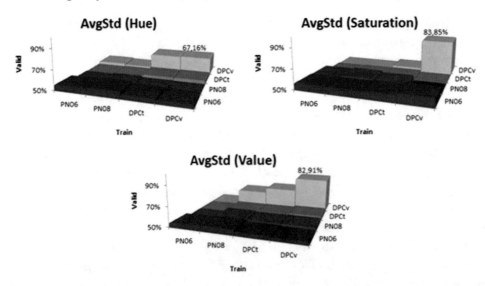

This leads us to think that a great difference exists in the saturation between the images categorised as High and the images categorised as Low in the set DPCv. The opposite is the case in the combinations of the set DCPt with the sets PN06 and PN08, which are similar on the level of metrical statistics, entropy and the distinct colour channels.

DATASET CREATED BY PSYCHOLOGISTS

Forsythe, Nadal, Sheehy, Cela-Conde, & Sawey (2011) created a dataset consisting of over fifteen hundred scanned images which include both abstract and representational images. Some of them are works of art and some are not. The difference between representational and abstract images is the presence or absence of explicit content, respectively. The distinction they make between artistic and non-artistic works is analogous to that which Winston and Cupchik (1992) make between high art and popular art. These authors indicate that while popular art emphasizes the theme, particularly its pleasant aspects, high art covers a wide range of emotions and knowledge in an effort to attain a balance between content and style.

Works of art include reproductions of paintings by renowned artists, which were catalogued and exhibited in museums. Paintings from a variety of styles and movements were selected, particularly Realism, Cubism, Impressionism and Post-Impressionism. This selection was taken from the collection *Movements in Modern Art* from London's Tate Gallery, and extended with European paintings from the 17th and 18th centuries. Non-artistic works consist of photographs taken from the book series *Boring Postcards*, an extract of images from the CD-ROM series *Master Clips Premium Image Collection* (IMSI, San Rafael, CA) used in industrial design for the illustration of books, etc. along with photographs taken by Forsythe, et al. (2011). This category also includes artifacts, landscapes, urban scenes, and other familiar visual stimuli that are not usually considered for museum exhibition.

In order to minimize the influence of external variables, some of the images of the first section were discarded or modified. Only relatively unknown works of art were selected to prevent the impact of familiarity; stimuli containing human figures or motive scenes were removed to prevent the influence of ecological variables and in order to prevent psychological variables the resolution of stimuli was reduced to 150 ppp, and their size to 9 x 12 cm. The color spectrum was also adjusted for all images and the luminance values and harsh shadows were adapted to obtain a global tone range that allowed for a greater detail. The stimuli which contained a distribution of pixels concentrated on the left (dark) and right (bright) ends of the histogram were discarded. Subsequently, the luminance of stimuli was adjusted between 370 and 390 lx and finally the signature was removed in those paintings with signature. Any stimuli which could not be modified on the basis of these specifications were discarded.

The final standardized dataset includes 800 images comprising 5 categories: 262 artistic abstract (AA), 141 non-artistic abstract (AN), 149 artistic representational (RA), 48 non-artistic representational (RN), and 200 photographs of natural scenes and human constructions (NHS). The set was divided into 8 pseudo-randomized sets to balance the stimuli categories in all subsets.

Table 2. Descriptive statistic of the complexity qualification provided by humans to the images from each category; the number of images, the minimum and maximum values, mean and standard deviation are given for each category

Category	n	Min	Max	Avg	Std
Abstract artistic (AA)	262	1,36	4,94	3,75	0,60
Abstract decorative (AN)	141	1,06	3,91	1,79	0,51
Figurative Representational (RA)	149	1,42	4,67	3,45	0,49
Figurative decorative (RN)	48	1,30	4,39	2,74	0,81
Environmental scene photographs (NHS)	200	1,24	4,42	2,79	0,67

In Table 2, we can see that the subset of non-artistic representational images (RN) is significantly less numerous and also the one with a greater standard deviation. The subset of non-artistic abstract images (AN) presents the lowest levels in perceived complexity – with an average of 1.79, well below the average value of the scale (3). On the opposite end, the images of the artistic abstract group (AA) have the highest scores in complexity with an average of 3.74 points.

A group of 240 participants (112 male and 128 female with a mean age of 22.03 and a standard deviation of 3.75) was randomly divided into 8 subsets of 30 people. The images were inserted into PowerPoint with a 710x530 pixel configuration and presented on a PC (Dell Optiplex 760) with a 400cmx225cm screen, aspect ratio 16:9. Each image was shown for 5 seconds and participants had to record their responses in this period of time. Each subset rated the visual complexity of a subset of stimuli on a Likert scale (1-5) where five was the rating for a very complex image and 1 the rating for a very simple image. The average value obtained by each subgroup for each stimulus was the value considered to represent the perception of complexity of that stimulus in the final set. The stimuli of this set were used by Forsythe, et al. (2011), Nadal, et al. (2010), and Machado, Romero, Nadal, Santos, Correia, & Carballal (2015).

PROPOSAL FOR THE DEVELOPMENT OF A NEW DATASET

As an alternative to the sample dataset discussed above we present a new method for the development of a dataset for the aesthetic classification and assessment of images verified with human criterion under controlled experimental conditions. This new method encompasses the advantages of the sets of images studied in this chapter after having ascertained that their generalization capacity is not entirely satisfactory.

The steps to follow are explained next: (i) a great number of images obtained from a photography website are rated by a variety of humans; (ii) those images meeting a number of minimum conditions are selected; (iii) images are arranged in groups on the basis of their assessment; (iv) out of each group a specific set of equal number of images with lower standard deviation are selected; (v) images are assessed by a group of humans under controlled experimental conditions.

First, a set of sample images from the photography portal DPChallenge.com was collected. This portal has been used previously to obtain data for aesthetic classification experiments (Ke, et al., 2006), (Luo & Tang, 2008). The images in this portal are rated by users within a 1-10 range.

In order to obtain the images a brute force process was used whereby the data from all images whose identifier was between 10,000 and 172,000 were downloaded. Only those images in which the ratings data were available were used. Subsequently, those images with over 100 ratings were selected. Thus, we tried that the mean value that we will later assign to each image was as little biased as possible. A file with the assessment data and the images used is available at https://doi.org/10.6084/m9.figshare.6127295.v1

The set of original images consists of 44,047 images. In our case, the scores obtained for each image are available, which makes it possible to study the distribution of the ratings in relation to the whole dataset of images.

All the images in the sample set were rated by at least 100 different persons with approximately 233 ratings per image. The mean score for the images is 5.23 with an average deviation of 0.78. Other descriptive data from the ratings are shown on Table 3.

Figure 6 shows the distribution of votes on the basis of each range showing that apparently they follow a Gaussian model. Figure 7 shows the distribution of the mean scores of the images within the scoring range.

Table 3. Descriptive data of the ratings made by the users of DPChallenge on the whole set of images in the sample

Descriptive data	
Images	44047
Average	5.2305
Std	0.7821
Variance	0.6117
Kurtosis	0.2480
Skew	-0.0182
Min	2.0000
Max	8.3900

Figure 6. Distribution of the number of ratings within the range of allowed scores (© 2018, A. Carballal used with permission)

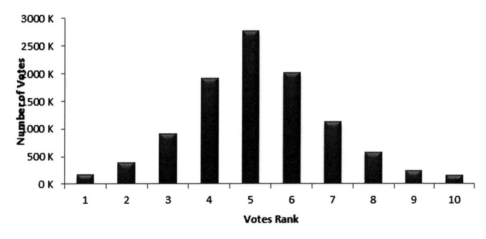

Figure 7. Distribution of the mean ratings of the images within the range of allowed scores (© 2018, A. Carballal used with permission)

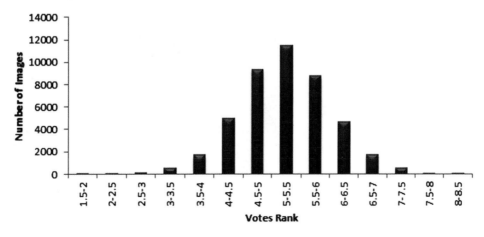

All these data tally with those obtained in 2012 from the photography portal.

Once the selection was completed, the images were distributed into groups on the basis of the average score obtained in DPChallenge.com. The images in our selection were classified into the following scoring ranges [≥1, <2] [≥2, <3] [≥3, <4] [≥4, <5] [≥5, <6] [≥6, <7] [≥7, <8] [≥8, <9] [≥9, <10]. Then, a minimum number of images for all groups was attempted. In our case, the condition was established that every group should have at least 200 images. As generally speaking most images have an intermediate score, the groups at both ends of the range might not attain the minimum number, thus making it necessary to rearrange the sets. It turned out that there were not enough images with average scores lower than 3 or higher than 8 to attain the minimum number of images established. Out of the groups that did meet the conditions as defined the 200 images with the least standard deviation were selected, namely, those having scores with the greatest internal consistency. Consequently, our groups were reduced to 5: i) 200 images with an average score between 3 and 4; ii) 200 images with an average score between 4 and 5; iii) 200 images with an average score between 5 and 6; iv) 200 images with an average score between 6 and 7; v) 200 images with an average score between 7 and 8.

As shown in Figure 8, this process provided a set of images with the same number of elements differently assessed by the users of DPChallenge.com, high coherence of ratings for each image and which might be ultimately representative of the greater set.

Once the sample dataset has been built, the images are scored by a set of humans under controlled experimental conditions. In this case, it might be interesting to use a methodology similar to that used Forsythe et al. (2011) with 30 human assessments per image. However, after analyzing whether 30 ratings per image were actually necessary, it was concluded that 10 ratings were sufficient to achieve results that can be generalized. To this end, 5 subsets were created with randomly selected images out of the 1,000-image set that made up the 5 score-based sets detailed above. Each of these sets will be scored by 10 people (10,000 scores in total). The average and standard deviation of the aesthetic assessment of each image will be calculated. Averages will also be analyzed on the basis of age, gender, and education criteria to see whether there is any tendency associated to these factors.

Figure 8. Distribution of sample groups after the selection (© 2018, A. Carballal, used with permission)

Furthermore, all 1,000 images in the dataset will be analyzed by 10 people in order to create an aesthetic imprint of these persons for future experiments of personalized prediction.

The assessment of these images is currently under way in experiments under controlled conditions.

CONCLUSION

In this chapter we have studied whether the selection of images in the training stage can be performed randomly without this significantly affecting the degree of generalization obtained in aesthetic classification tasks. In order to show its importance, we have studied the image datasets used by other researchers in a variety of experiments.

For the purposes of this study we have created four binary classifiers from the basic characteristics obtained for each of the datasets. Subsequently, we have sought to validate them by using photographs from other datasets, which had not been used during the classifiers' training stage. The results obtained suggest that the systems trained with a specific dataset cannot reach an acceptable level of generalization when associated with the images from a different source.

We have also studied a set of sample images created by psychologists. This method has allowed us to identify the positive nature of the assessment by a specific group of humans under controlled experimental conditions. We consider, however, the deliberate and balanced selection of images that makes up our sample extremely relevant.

To solve the weaknesses found, we have developed a new method for the making of sampling sets. This method brings together the strengths found in the studies we have analyzed: it uses a photography portal as the source of images; it uses the ratings given by the users of the portal to create a coherent and balanced sample and ensures the generality of the results by making assessment experiments using groups of people in a controlled environment.

We are currently developing the aesthetic assessment process for the image dataset in experiments with human groups under controlled conditions. The results we have obtained so far are coherent and have a good internal correlation, which has led us to conclude that the method employed for the construction of the dataset is functional and meets the expectations. At a later stage, we will analyze the full data calculating the average and standard deviation in the aesthetic assessment of every image. We will also look at averages on the basis of age, gender and education criteria to see whether there is any tendency associated to these factors.

ACKNOWLEDGMENT

This research was partially funded by: Xunta de Galicia, research project XUGA-PGIDIT10TIC105008-PR; Spanish Ministry for Science and Technology, research project TIN2008-06562/TIN; Portuguese Foundation for Science and Technology, research project PTDC/EIA-EIA/115667/2009 and the General Directorate of Culture, Education and University Management of Xunta de Galicia (Ref. GRC2014/049).

REFERENCES

Browne, M. W. (2000). Cross-Validation Methods. *Journal of Mathematical Psychology*, *44*(1), 108–132. doi:10.1006/jmps.1999.1279 PMID:10733860

Chang, C.-C., & Lin, C.-J. (2011). LIBSVM: A library for support vector machines, 2(27). *ACM Transactions on Intelligent Systems and Technology*, *2*(3), 1–27. doi:10.1145/1961189.1961199

Datta, R., Joshi, D., & Wang, J. (2006). Studying Aesthetics in Photographic Images Using a Computational Approach. In *European Conference on Computer Vision* (pp. 288-301). Graz, Austria: Springer. 10.1007/11744078_23

Datta, R., Li, J., & Wang, J. (2008). Algorithmic inferencing of aesthetics and emotion in natural images: An exposition. In *15th IEEE International Conference on Image Processing* (pp. 105-108). San Diego, CA: IEEE. 10.1109/ICIP.2008.4711702

Forsythe, A., Nadal, M., Sheehy, N., Cela-Conde, C., & Sawey, M. (2011). Predicting beauty: Fractal dimension and visual complexity in art. *British Journal of Psychology*, *102*(1), 49–70. doi:10.1348/000712610X498958 PMID:21241285

Ke, Y., Tang, X., & Jing, F. (2006). The design of high-level features for photo quality assessment. In *CVPR '06 Proceedings of the 2006 IEEE Computer Society Conference on Computer Vision and Pattern Recognition - Volume 1* (pp. 419-426). New York: IEEE.

Luo, Y., & Tang, X. (2008). Photo and video quality evaluation: Focusing on the subject. In *European Conference on Computer Vision* (pp. 386-399). Marseille, France: Springer. 10.1007/978-3-540-88690-7_29

Machado, P., Romero, J., Nadal, M., Santos, A., Correia, J., & Carballal, A. (2015). Computerized measures of visual complexity. *Acta Psychologica*, *160*, 43–57. doi:10.1016/j.actpsy.2015.06.005 PMID:26164647

Murray, N., Marchesotti, L., & Perronnin, F. (2012). Ava: A large-scale database for aesthetic visual analysis. In *IEEE Computer Society Conference on Computer Vision and Pattern Recognition*. Providence, RI: IEEE. 10.1109/CVPR.2012.6247954

Romero, J., Machado, P., Carballal, A., & Osorio, O. (2011). *Aesthetic Classification and Sorting Based on Image Compression. In EvoApplications* (pp. 394–403). Torino, Italy: Springer.

Romero, J., Machado, P., Carballal, A., & Santos, A. (2012). Using complexity estimates in aesthetic image classification. *Journal of Mathematics and the Arts*, *6*(2-3), 125–136. doi:10.1080/17513472.2012.679514

Vapnik, V. (1997). The Support Vector Method. In *International Conference on Artificial Neural Networks* (pp. 261-271). Lausanne, Switzerland: Springer.

Winston, A., & Cupchik, G. (1992). The evaluation of high art and popular art by naive and experienced viewers. *Visual Arts Research*, *18*, 1–14.

Witten, I., & Frank, E. (2002). Data mining: Practical machine learning tools and techniques with java implementations. *SIGMOD Record*, *31*(1), 76–77. doi:10.1145/507338.507355

Wong, L.-K., & Low, K.-L. (2009). Saliency-enhanced image aesthetics class prediction. In *Proceedings of the 16th International Conference on Image Processing* (pp. 997-1000). Cairo, Egypt: IEEE Press.

Zipf, G. (1949). *Human behavior and the principle of least effort*. Oxford, UK: Addison-Wesley Press.

KEY TERMS AND DEFINITIONS

Cross-Validation: A model validation technique for assessing how the results of a statistical analysis will generalize to an independent data set.

Entropy: Lack of order or predictability; gradual decline into disorder.

Extrapolate: To use existing information to discover what is likely to happen or be.

Generalization: Capability to predict outcome values for previously unseen data.

Information Bias: Referred to as observational bias and misclassification.

Intrinsic Bias: Subconscious stereotypes that affect the way we make decisions.

Visual Perception: The ability to interpret the surrounding environment using vision.

Chapter 11
The Origins of Music and of Tonal Languages

Robert C. Ehle
University of Northern Colorado, USA

ABSTRACT

This chapter offers the author's theory of the origins of music in ancient primates a million years ago, and what music would have sounded like. Origins of nasal and tone languages and the anatomy of larynx is discussed, and then a hypothesis is presented that these creatures would fashioned a tone language. They had absolute pitch that allowed them to recognize other voices, to read each other's emotions from the sounds they made with their voices, and to convey over long distances specific information about strategies, meeting places, etc. Having an acute sense of pitch, they would have sung, essentially using tonal language for aesthetic and subjective purposes. Thus, they would have invented music. Then the physicality of the human (or hominid) voice is discussed and the way an absolute pitch can be acquired, as the musicality still lies in the vocalisms it expresses. The reason for this is that music is actually contained in the way the brain works, and the ear and the voice are parts of this system. The final part discusses the origins of musical emotion as the case for imprinting in the perinatal period.

NASAL AND TONE LANGUAGES AND THEIR RELATION TO MUSIC

Introduction

The great ice age lasted from about 100 thousand years ago until about 11 thousand years ago, when the ice was gone in North America, Northern Europe, and Northern Asia. This was only the latest of ice ages, of course, and it isn't the last. The ice will be back and we are actually living in an interglacial era today called by German earth scientists a Würm glaciation (Whittow, 1984). In my backyard in Colorado are millions of rocks, large and small, that are rounded like footballs, making it obvious that they had been rolled and ground down by giant ice sheets.

During the great ice age, there were primates living in Africa. Their bones have been discovered mainly in the sub Saharan part of the African continent. They have been dated to a million years ago

DOI: 10.4018/978-1-5225-7371-5.ch011

and even earlier. These ancient hominids looked like apes but they had bipedal locomotion, meaning that they could walk on the ground and did not live in trees. They might have walked along the southern shores of Asia, too, but did not travel north because the ice (and the cold) blocked their passage.

The questions I am entertaining are simple ones. How did these ancient beings make sounds? Did they have music? In other words, did they sing, and, if so, what would it have sounded like? I have collected some available evidence from the bones, the rocks, and from modern humans and animals, and have come up with a picture of what might have happened. This evidence comes from anthropology, physiology, psychoacoustics, ethnomusicology, psycholinguistics, and other fields. As we will see, it is just a theory, but there is a lot of evidence supporting the theory of the origins of music in ancient primates about a million years ago.

The Origins of Tone Language and Music

Music is the remnant of an ancient nasal, and tone language in which variations in pitch distinguish different words (Merriam Webster's Dictionary, 2017). A tone language is a language in which the pitch of a syllable carries substantial linguistic meaning. The Wikipedia article on tone languages says that there are over 200 tone languages in the world today and that around 70% of the world's people speak a tone language. Yet tone languages are largely unknown in the United States and Europe. There is still much research to be done in this area.

Tone language was spoken by our hominid ancestors in Africa, who had very high larynxes. A high larynx connects directly to the nose, bypassing the mouth, making it possible for its possessor to drink, breathe, and communicate simultaneously, a very valuable ability when you must drink from crocodile-infested rivers and lakes. A very high larynx makes articulate oral speech and singing impossible, however. They would have had to speak and sing primarily through their noses. This is not as far-fetched as it sounds, as we will see.

The tones of the nasal tone language are in three ranges within the harmonic structure of the larynx. Low tones create perfect tones, and major intervals are happy, contented and powerful. Tones of medium pitch height create minor intervals and are sad or melancholy. High pitches create dissonant intervals and represent fear and terror. Within each range, detail is added by pitch inflections (direction and speed). Imagine communicating by humming and then try to do it. It works.

Absolute pitch (the ability to remember and identify specific pitches) gives the nasal tone language much greater specificity. This is helpful because a nasal language does not have access to the specificity of oral, articulate speech like vowels and consonants.

A universal grammar of nasal speech is genetically transmitted (in the Chomskyian sense) and is available to us today in varying degrees. It is this what makes music the universal language of emotions that is understood by everyone. We acquire the connections between tones and emotions from our mother's voice in our earliest days, even prenatally.

The Structure of Larynx and Survival of Hominids

In Africa it is often said that the most dangerous time in the life of an animal is when it is drinking from rivers or lakes. Going up to the edge of a body of water, the animal is often captured, drowned, and eaten by a crocodile lurking in the mud and reeds at the water's edge. An animal that could drink and breathe simultaneously would be able to reduce its exposure to the danger and thus live longer. An animal that was able to drink deeply very fast would be especially safer. In the same way, an animal that had the ability to communicate with the other members of its troop while drinking would share a benefit with them by informing them of dangers or telling that it is safe to come and drink.

The hominids' ancestors ate fruit high in the trees and got enough water from the fruit they ate to survive through the dry periods, but the land-dwelling hominids have to find water to drink. No longer able to climb through the trees easily, they must go down to the rivers and lakes. Thus they are exposed to the crocodile menace. In an area such as the Okavango Delta in central Africa there will be plenty of pools, streams, and small lakes during the wet season. As the dry season progresses, they dry up, and the animals are forced to find water in the major rivers and largest lakes where the crocodiles proliferate. An animal might have a few seconds to drink and then retreat before a crocodile attacks. Thus the fastest animals will be the ones to survive. Those who can gulp large amounts of water the quickest without choking will be the ones to survive. A very high larynx confers this advantage on its owner. When the larynx is very high, the velum of the soft palate can wrap around the top of the larynx, sealing it off from the oral cavity and making it possible for the animal to drink fast in large gulps while breathing. For an animal in which the larynx began to descend (a common pattern), life would be short and death would come swiftly as the animal was condemned to spend too much time at the watering hole. For this reason, a very high larynx that can seal off the nasal passage from the oral passage would be strongly conserved in animals in sub-Saharan Africa. A high larynx confers an additional advantage on animals in great danger. It allows breathing to be continuous while eating and drinking and thus allows the sense of smell to be continued during these times. Smell being a primary source of information about danger.

Origins of Nasal and Tone Languages and the Anatomy of Larynx

Once the animals had migrated to the Middle East, to Asia or Europe (after the ice had retreated) they would no longer face this scourge and the larynx would normally begin to descend as the neck became longer. While this pattern would apply to any animals capable of migrating, it would apply particularly to hominids who had evolved in southern Africa but were capable of moving around because of their more flexible eating habits and an ability to adapt to cooler climates. Books on the larynx suggest that the larynx does not actually descend, but that hominids began to grow taller and that the skeleton was gradually lengthened. One can see this in the fossils. The apes and early hominids all seem to have very short necks. As the necks of primates lengthened, the larynx would end up lower in the neck, approximately behind the mouth rather than approximately behind the nose where it was before.

Once the neck had lengthened, there was a gap between the nasal passage and the larynx. Both water and air had to travel through this same passage and so the individual faced the problem that it could not breathe and drink at the same time. The air and water had to pass through this same gap. The individual faced the possibility of choking. While not able to benefit from the invention of the Heimlich maneuver, an animal faced the strong chance of choking on its food, as well. Obviously, the long neck and low larynx are not conducive to survival, but they are conducive to singing and speaking articulated languages through the mouth. Studying fossils of hominids with regard to neck length should produce interesting results with regard to the passage from nasal tone language to oral articulated language. I recently traveled to Indonesia where I had the opportunity to examine fossils and a reproduction of Java Man. My impression was that Java Man had a modern neck and thus, presumable, a modern larynx with the possibility of articulated speech.

Thus, we can see that hominids living in sub Saharan Africa would not be able to develop vocal languages because of the persistence of the high larynx. Once they had migrated out of Africa, the process of the gradual lowering of the larynx would have made vocal languages more and more accessible. While in Africa, selective pressures would have only allowed nasal languages. A hominid could communicate with other members of its troop by nasally produced sounds. That is, by nasal languages. The mouth may be engaged to some extent but most of the sound produced by the vocal cords would be emitted through the nose. This denies the access to oral articulations. It is because of a high larynx that most animals have only one sound available to them to make. Even children know, "The dog goes bow wow, the cat goes miaow, the horse says neigh, and the cow goes moo."

The Acquisition of Language and the Acquisition of Musical Skills

Recently has come the suggestion that there might be a strong connection between the acquisition of language and the acquisition of some musical skills and tastes. In particular, Diana Deutsch's (2013) suggestion that perfect, absolute pitch (AP) might be acquired in the language acquisition stage of early life. And so, we must study linguistics as well, especially the early acquisition of language. It appears that the way an infant learns the basic phonemes of its native language holds a key to my search. It is clear that the study must deal with musical emotion for emotional reasons have to have a lot to do with what music is and why we like it. Scholars have a tendency to ignore this and treat music as a mechanical system. Most people will be attracted by music's emotional potential, however.

At this point it is important to get back to music theory in order to study specific musical techniques that might produce specific musical emotions. A big question is the relation between the two. Do musical techniques (for example, borrowed chords from the parallel key) produce specific musical emotions or is the emotion merely learned at some early stage? It has seemed to me that there is a relationship between the harmonic series, specific musical techniques and musical emotion and I have written and lectured on this topic many times. Generally, my conclusion is that we learn phonemic sounds in the perinatal period during what are termed "critical periods" that are genetically timed. During these critical periods, if one is exposed to musical sounds, one acquires a special attachment to those sounds, as if they were to be the basic sounds of one's native language and that must be learned. These sounds carry learned emotions as well.

My main idea is that starting several months before we are born, we create phonemic templates in the brain. This process continues for an undetermined time after birth but there is a difference between pre-birth templates and post-birth templates in the sense that before birth templates are able to have a richer array of mother's emotions attached to them. These templates are employed in the language acquisition stage of life a year or two after birth, but they might be employed in music as well. An example is absolute pitch (AP); others might include partials in the harmonic series, melodies, harmonies and rhythms.

These templates are created under a genetic impulse developed under evolutionary pressure, and thay serve the infant for creating automatic responses to sounds. The acquisition of language is greatly facilitated by these templates in that incoming sounds are filtered automatically, and only templated sounds pass through producing automatic linguistic triggers. Sounds that are not used in the native language or were not present in the perinatal environment are automatically excluded, thereby creating a faster language mechanism. A faster music mechanism, too, may be created as a side effect.

Tone Languages

Did such nasal languages exist? Well, all modern apes and monkeys make a wide variety of grunts, hoots, and howls. It seems reasonable that their close cousins, the early hominids would be able to make those sounds as well. Do they constitute language? I would argue that the apes and monkeys communicate with their sounds. The larger brains of the hominids would allow an increase in the variety of possible communication. In nasal languages this would take place through increasing the variety of available tones. In other words, they would be using and developing tone or tonal languages. Tone languages still exist in the world. Mandarin Chinese is the best known of them, but the Bantu languages in sub-Saharan Africa are tone languages, as are many pre-Columbian Central American languages, and other Asian languages like Cantonese and Vietnamese.

Tone languages are capable of being enriched by absolute pitch (AP). Diana Deutsch (2013) has shown that speakers of tone languages are much more likely to develop AP than speakers of non-tone languages. Possessors of AP have the ability to remember and recognize a variety of pitch levels. They would learn these pitch levels very early in life. Patricia Kuhl (2017) has shown that humans learn the sounds of their native language before their first birthday. If that is a tone language, then they would learn a variety of tones and they would have absolute pitch.

Tone Languages Become the Language of Emotions and It Becomes Music

This would not yet be music; it is language, but it gets the individual working with tone, so that once the individual realizes the expressing possibilities in the tones, he or she would begin to sing (through the nose at first, and then later through the mouth). The individual would have discovered music. Thus we can see that we have a definition of music: music is a vocal/tonal language employed to communicate, at first anything that need to be said, but primarily the emotions, as we shall see.

The reason tone languages are particularly good at expressing emotion has to do with the harmonics of the harmonic series produced by the larynx. I have done spectrum analyses of my voice using iSpectrum on a Macintosh computer, and I can produce more than 50 partials when pronouncing a strong "r" sound.

I have written extensively of this before, especially in the Journal SONUS. Tones at the bottom of the range are easily produced while relaxed. The higher the tones, the greater amount of tension is required to produce them. Also, an individual undergoing stressful situations is naturally inclined to produce higher and higher pitches, corresponding to the stress of the situation. With AP, an individual would learn and remember the tones and the amount of tension they require to produce. The individual would be able to recognize the ranges of the laryngeal resonance where the tones lie and would quickly make the association between the tones and the various harmonics. One can say that the harmonics number 1 through 4 are strong; 5 is happy; 6, 7, and 9 are sad. Above number 9 the tendency is to express terror (as in a scream). In this way a tone language becomes the language of the emotions and it becomes music.

A person can work with this. Speak calmly in the lowest part of your voice range and you will immediately feel the confidence and comfort this induces. Speak emotional words in the high part of your range and you can hear and feel the worry they carry with them. Then force your voice into the highest, most unnatural part of your range and you can hear and feel the terror in your voice.

This process could have begin in Africa in the nasal languages used there and would have developed further after hominids left Africa. The impetus to develop musical tone languages would have been the preservation of the high larynx in Africa and the need to communicate in tones rather than vowels and consonants that would have come later. While still living in Africa, hominids would have used tones as language and also as proto-music. After leaving Africa, the descending larynx would allow the development of vocally articulated language. AP would no longer be necessary in non-tone languages but would be preserved in tone languages. Music and language would diverge.

A few definitions are in order here. The first is the type of music we are discussing. This is not classical music. It is not modern popular music with all its guitars and gear. It is not even folk music because that implies a long span of existence. It is not instrumental music, either. We are discussing the first groups of hominids; their ancestors were apes and they had just emerged from the trees. They were just learning to live on the ground.

These hominids are just beginning to make and use tools. Thus they are not yet able to make musical instruments. No doubt, they take advantage of naturally occurring artifacts for musical purposes: a hollow log becomes a log drum and a hollow limb becomes a didjeridoo-type of instrument (Figure 1). They might learn to blow across a blade of grass. They might discover some of the things they can do with their voices, but most of all, they discover that they can sing. It is singing that I am discussing here. We are talking about vocal music. Speaking a tone language primarily through the nose, naturally leads an individual to discover singing. There would be little difference other than purpose between the two.

Figure 1. The author playing Didjeridoo (2015, © A. Ursyn, used with permission)

Acquiring an Absolute Pitch

Diana Deutsch (2013), in a series of remarkable experiments, has proven that speakers of tone languages are much more likely than speakers of non-tone languages to have absolute pitch. Absolute pitch, today, is often tested by having students identify piano notes without a reference note. Absolute pitch, though, is much older than keyboard instruments and we are discussing that in the ancient era it would have been related to voice ranges. A person with absolute pitch would know the low, medium, and high voice ranges and probably several sub-ranges within these categories. They would know them from identification of their mother's emotions in her voice and would remember them and would be able to replicate them.

A person with AP would hear one pitch as the root pitch and all the other pitches would have a relationship to the root pitch that would imply degrees of tension. The root pitch would have to be learned but could be commonly held and known in any linguistic area. In fact, there have been suggestions that everyone is capable of acquiring absolute pitch at a very early stage, probably the first year of postnatal life, and that if tones are used in the native language system, it will be acquired. On the other hand, if specific tones or pitches are not heard in the mother's voice, the ability to acquire AP will be lost forever, and the ability to hear with AP will also be lost so that the individual will no longer be able to comprehend tone-based speech. That means that tone-based speech will sound uninformative, whereas to a person with AP a wide range of expressive information will be acquired from tone languages.

One of my students, who had been studying Mandarin Chinese, commented that the Chinese have a massive amount of homonyms, which creates a problem; he implied that so many words sound the same. If he had AP though, he would not have thought that this was a problem because different syllables are clarified by tonal levels and trajectories. People who speak a non-tonal language such as English, rarely acquire AP while those who speak a tone language such as Mandarin Chinese usually do acquire AP at an early age, and not for musical but for linguistic purposes.

The Relation of Tone Languages to Music

The hypothesis of this chapter is that tone languages are much closer to music than non-tone languages are and that a primarily nasally spoken tonal language would be so close to singing that singing would naturally evolve from it. The difference would be primarily one of functions. But, as we have seen, a modern non-tone language speaker cannot normally hear the tones in a tone language, and so is unaware that anything is going on. There is a brain function that blocks the hearing of tones in a person who failed to acquire them at an early age. Patricia Kuhl (2017) describes how newborn babies listen to all the sounds around them. It starts around 8 months of age but later babies begin to eliminate infrequently occurring sounds from their experience. This would apply specifically to tones. People who rarely hear tones lose their ability to hear them, while those who hear tones frequently retain their ability to hear them. The two groups cannot comprehend each other's experience.

In the Kuhl's (2017) TED video we learn that an infant learns all the sounds in its environment during the first 10 months of life, paying closest attention those sounds occurring the most often. Thus we can see that if an infant is raised in a musically rich environment during their first year (and probably beginning a few months before birth) they will imprint musical tones or other musical sounds as a part of their native language. They will be creating phonemic templates in their brains for musical tones as if their native language was a tone language. As Diana Deutsch (2013) has pointed out, these tone templates might be transferred to actual musical applications at some later time, probably around age 3, when they might be learned as if they were a part of a second language.

It turns out that emotions can be learned at this time, too. A series of German studies have shown that emotions are encoded in musical tones as amplitudes of the harmonic partials.

The author wrote about this topic for years, recently in a chapter "How We Hear and Experience Music: a Bootstrap Theory of Sensory Perception" (Ehle, 2016). In the title, bootstrap refers to phonemic templates in the brain that facilitate the learning in music or the native language. Obviously, speakers of tone and non-tone languages need to compare their experiences so that they can understand each other. For speakers of English, Mandarin Chinese is the obvious object to study. The auditory system and the vocal system in any animal are complementary systems. As Alfred Tomatis (1991) said, the voice can only produce what the ear can hear. In other words, if you cannot hear a sound you cannot produce it.

I've been studying the human and animal auditory systems, but I realized that I needed to study the human and animal vocal systems. This has taken me in a new direction in the definition of music. What animals and humans produce with their voices depends on what sounds and their functions as language and music have to their animal and human auditory systems. They would not produce it if it failed to produce the desired communication. The radical and interesting thing in all of this is that tone languages and absolute pitch are foreign to our experience in the US and Europe. Because we do not hear them we are almost completely unaware of them, and, of course, we cannot produce them, either, with our voices. Even though we are not responding to piano notes, there is a good chance that we are responding on a coarser scale to human voice ranges. We may be hearing vocal emotion, too.

The point is that once our hominids had acquired even a primitive tone language that was mostly nasally spoken they would naturally be led to use it to sing. The mouth need not be shut; it just would not contribute much. It would be roughly like singing vowels and consonants with a glottal stop.

Evidence Through Examples

What is the evidence such a remarkable series of events actually occurred? After all, languages don't leave fossils. In actuality, the evidence is all around us in our world, today. One just needs to learn to look for it. Such groups as ethnomusicologists, ethnolinguists, and psycholinguists are involved in such work as we will see.

Evidence can be found in our own voices, what we are able to do with them, and what other groups of people in the world are and have been able to do. An interesting group are the Mongolians who, being born to the saddle and spending most of their lives on a pony, have had lots of time to sing and explore what they can do with their voices. All of this is available on Youtube. Anyone interested can hear examples of overtone singing, singing with the false vocal cords, simultaneous whistling and singing, and other amazing vocal feats. Presumably people in the Mongolian area (including the Altais of the Altai mountain area and the Tuvans of the country of Tuva, as well as the people of Inner Mongolia (a part of China), and the large country of Outer Mongolia (the home of Genghis Khan) have these vocal abilities. One can listen to the music of Cambodia and of Indonesia where nasal singing is pursued. Again, Youtube provides many examples. Or, one can listen to Central Asian Maqaam as sung by people such as Monadjat Yulchieva of Uzbekistan. One can also mention Western opera as an example of an extreme use of the human voice.

It's not that any of these types of music are in any way primitive. I just wish to point out the variety of vocal music in the world. I have traveled to Uzbekistan and also to Nepal, Tibet, and China to hear the

Buddhist Monks reciting their chants. There is opera in many Asian countries and regions. It is sophisticated singing. One could recount Mandarin Chinese opera in the Beijing region and in the Guangzho region, Cantonese opera, and Vietnamese opera. There is Japanese Kabuki and Noh theaters.

In the area of vocal languages, the range is no less varied. There is the humming language of the Piraha that can be hummed, whistled, or encoded in music. It can be heard on Youtube. There are a number of whistled languages from around the Mediterranean Sea. There are the click languages of the Bushmen, Zulus, and the Khoisan peoples of Africa. These, too, can be heard on Youtube. The point is that any group of individuals that make tones with their voices are just a short step away from using those tones in a tone language. With the absolute pitch that normally accompanies a tone language they are just another short step away from singing.

Figure 2 presents an old instrument from Thailand, while Figure 3 displays the rGye-gling instrument.

Figure 2. The instrument from Thailand (2015, © A. Ursyn, used with permission)

Figure 3. The rGye-gling instrument (2015, © A. Ursyn, used with permission)

Conclusions About the Origins of Music

Between 200 thousand and more than a million years ago, hominids walked the savannas of Africa. They left their footprints in soft volcanic ash that subsequently hardened so we can find them today. They left small assortments of bones and partial skulls too, that we can find now. The best known of them is 'Lucy' discovered by a paleoanthropologist Donald Johansen in Hadar, Ethiopia on November 24, 1974. We have given these assorted remains names such as Ramapithecus and Australopithecus and we place them on a scale between ape-like and more hominid-like. With small brains, but larger than those of apes and monkeys we can imagine that they were just dimly beginning to comprehend their world and become more than animals. This much we know.

I am hypothesizing that these creatures would have taken the grunts, hoots, and howls made by their monkey and ape cousins, and fashioned from them a tone language such that they had tone names for each other and for the things and places in their world. I am further speculating that they had absolute pitch of a sort that allowed them to recognize each other voices in the dark and to read each other's emotions from the sounds they made with their voices. They had the ability to call to each other over long distances and to convey specific information about strategies, meeting places, etc. over these distances.

I am further speculating that, working with tones as they were, and having an acute sense of pitch, they would have sung, essentially using tonal language for aesthetic and subjective purposes. Thus, they would have invented music.

To summarize, music on earth is well over one million years old. Its original singers were African hominids who looked rather like apes but walked in a bipedal manner on the ground. The music sounded rather like humming with the mouth open, and the words that were sung had no consonants and very few vowels. This early music was sung over a very wide pitch range, with big swoops and dips, and its listeners had absolute pitch so that all the pitch ranges carried specific descriptive and particularly emotional meanings. In its earliest manifestations there were no musical instruments, as its singers did not yet use tools, but their music was exclusively vocal. This use of the voice was highly developed, so that singers could sing quite loudly and communicate with their songs over large distance. The woodlands would ring with their group singing in the evenings rather like the hoots of gibbons or howler monkeys do today. They would be singing about their lives and each other, making plans, and recounting adventures in the way historic humans did in their ballads, so common in our ancient history. They would have their Iliad and Odyssey, their Beowulf and Hobbit, and these would be recounted.

There is nothing like it on earth today, but one might imagine Chinese tones delivered with an Italian manner of delivery. The combination of the flexibility of tonal delivery in Chinese combined with the open mouth style of delivery as in the Italian language can be imagined. It would have been an ideal and very effective singing language, and the singers would have been powerful and very attractive to their fellows.

It is important to note that in the definition of music we must begin with the physicality of the human (or the hominid) voice, and the physical condition it expresses. Instrumental music is an imitation of the voice, and, while it may have capacities that greatly outdistance vocal music, the musicality still lies in the vocalisms it expresses. The reason for this is that music is actually contained in the way the brain works, and the ear and the voice are parts of this system. Figure 4 displays the Chinese Er-hu instrument.

HOW THE HUMAN AUDITORY SYSTEM WORKS

People who think about how the auditory system works might be inclined to think that it works rather like a stethoscope, with little rubber tubes connecting the eardrums to the brain so that the brain can hear the sounds and the music. The eardrums would be like the diaphragm of the stethoscope. This would seem to be the case because we seem to hear everything with so much clarity that it seems almost impossible that sounds are encoded and then decoded in the brain. Yet physiological studies make it absolutely clear that there are no little rubber tubes connecting the ears to the brain. The sounds are encoded by the inner ear in the organ called the cochlea into neural impulses, and it is only these neural impulses that travel over nerve fibres to the brain. In other words, no sounds ever reach the brain.

Fundamental to this concept is the point that no sound ever reaches the brain, only neural codes. The inner ear, the cochlea is a transducer that converts auditory sounds into neural impulses that travel to the brain. The neural impulses carry information about the sounds through a number of encoding processes and these codes can be to a certain extent decoded by the brain. Still, anything that was not encoded in the first place will not be available for decoding. More importantly, though is the idea that neural codes

Figure 4. The Er-hu (China) instrument (2015, © A. Ursyn, used with permission)

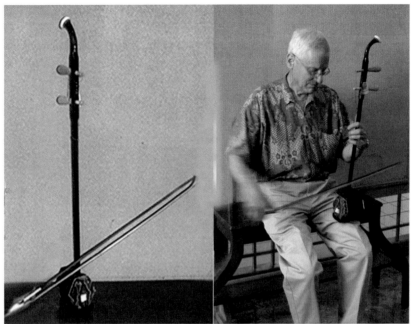

can be templated, probably in the hippocampus, and then transferred to the auditory cortexes. Auditory codes can easily be filtered too, employing templates. Any code that does not match a template will automatically be rejected like a key that does not match a lock.

In this way, the auditory system becomes extremely responsive to the phonemes of its native language while sounds foreign to the native language are automatically and immediately rejected. The phonemes of the native language can be learned individually so that each one instantaneously triggers a linguistic response as it is received. The particularly interesting thing to me, though, is that musical sounds can also be templated if they are heard prominently and repeatedly in the perinatal period.

How Nerve Fibres Transmit Signals

There are about 30,000 nerve fibers in the human auditory nerve (the cochlear nerve) and even more in other mammals, for example, about 50,000 nerve fibers in the cat auditory nerve. This makes the auditory system massively parallel in data terms. The signals traveling on those nerve fibers are pulses, traveling much slower than computer pulses. Some have said that the cochlea in the inner ear acts analogically to a digital converter, which converts music into digital pulses in recording systems. This is only roughly the case because the word "digital" is commonly used to mean digital code, that is code that encodes numbers in digital form. In the computer, analog signals are converted into ones and zeros, in what is called a base-2 number system and then these base-2 numbers are used to perform mathematical and logical operations. For display purposes, the base-2 numbers are converted into base-10 numbers, allowing the computer operators to read them like numbers in a math or accounting book.

There is no evidence that the brain actually uses numbers or digits in its operation and the brain is primarily not digital, at least in the way we use the term. The neural impulses that travel through the nervous system and operate in the brain are binary, however, in the sense that they have two states, so that a nerve is either ON or OFF. In this way, they carry information rather like computer networks although the coding is different.

The nerve cells in the nervous system were discovered by Santiago Ramón y Cajal (1988) in the early 20th century. Before Ramón y Cajal, nerves were thought to be like wires connecting fingers and muscles to the brain. René Descartes drew pictures showing wires in this way and he probably thought of them as mechanical linkages. When the telephone was invented, the idea of wires like telephone cables became even more popular.

Ramón y Cajal noted that a nerve was made up of cells and that every cell had a nucleus and a number of projections that have been called axons and dendrites. The axons are output lines and the dendrites are input lines. A nerve connection from an ear (or a finger) to the brain might pass from one to the next neuron over anywhere from a few to dozens of neurons. The neurons are like little battery cells that have the ability to turn on and off. When they turn on they are depolarized and when they turn off they are polarized.

One of the big breakthroughs in neural science was the discovery of the synapse in the 1950s, at the juncture of two neurons. The discovery of the synapse revolutionized neuroscience by showing that the nerves of the nervous system were not like wires. The cells communicated one to the next by chemical means, the chemicals being neurotransmitters and the synapse being a very narrow gap that was not seen until the electron microscope became available in the early television era.

The result is that signals travel through neurons by means of their becoming depolarized and then between neurons by means of neurotransmitter chemicals being released from the end terminals of axons, traveling across the synapse gap, and being absorbed by one of the dendrites of the next cell in line. That cell then depolarizes and emits neurotransmitters from the end terminals of one of its axons and the process continues. What is not always noticed is that each cell receives inputs from many other cells and emits neurotransmitters over one or more synapses to additional cells, allowing the synapses to operate like logic gates. Logic gates are devices found in a digital computer and they form a basic part of the decision-making ability of computer systems. So, in this way, the nervous system can be said to resemble digital computers.

The issue though is, that binary signals travel through massively parallel neural networks communicating with chemicals. Chemicals from outside the networks can intrude and change the disposition of many cells at the same time. This was the case in the discovery in the 1950s of mood-altering chemicals called antidepressants. These chemicals, taken by mouth over a period of time, will affect a population of nerve cells and alter behavior to such an extent that patients in mental hospitals were able to go home. As long as they continued to take their medications, their behavior was controlled and they could live fairly normal lives. This was a great vindication of the synapse/neurotransmitter theory.

The Human Auditory System

When it comes to auditory signals, though, speed is a factor. The other senses and operations of the nervous system can operate slowly (seconds) or very slowly (days or weeks), but auditory signals frequency falls within the range of 20 to 20,000 Hz (cycles per second) for humans and even higher frequencies in mice and bats among many others. Nerve cells have been shown to have a maximum switching frequency of about 1 thousand Hertz. The volley-coding theory, one of the frequency theories states that many nerve cells must be involved in conveying a single frequency employing a coding scheme (Langner, 2015).

It has been sometimes imagined that enough nerve cells firing in a semi-random way (called stochastic) are able to convey the shapes of auditory waves. When it is remembered that frequencies have a sine-wave (sinusoidal) shape, the output can be reconstructed in the process known as Fourier synthesis. The 18th century French mathematician Joseph Fourier had shown that any arbitrarily complex wave could be broken down into many individual frequencies. In the case of periodic sounds like musical tones, the frequencies are members of a harmonic series. This means that if you know the fundamental frequency, you can predict the higher frequencies, and if you know at least two adjacent higher partials of a harmonic series you can predict the fundamental one.

The human auditory system appears to make use of these facts to predict the likelihood of certain waves that cannot be conveyed intact over the auditory network. In other words, the human auditory system has a series of expectations in place, and it takes whatever information is conveyed over the auditory system through the encoding process and matches it against stored expectations in order to come up with likely sounds. This is the way that the slow nervous system can deal with fast signals.

Where do these expectations come from? It is my opinion that they are created early in life while the nervous system is wiring itself. They are stored in the form of templates that are permanent parts of memory. The creation of new templates begins months before birth and probably continues to puberty, at which time pruning of the neural system takes place removing unused connections and locking in place connections that are used regularly. The earliest template acquisition is subconscious. Later stages are consciously available in memory and people can remember events when they heard exciting new sounds or voices.

Neurotransmitters have been implicated in emotions; it was as shown that large doses of neurotransmitter-producing medications were able to allow mentally ill patients get their emotions under control. Sounds that trigger the release of neurotransmitters have the ability to modulate emotions. You can actually feel this mechanism at work if you pay close attention to your feelings as you listen to sounds and voices. There is a constant up and down fluctuation of various feelings that is mostly subconscious but can be brought into consciousness by paying close attention.

Emotions can lead to liking, wanting, needing, seeking or aversive behavior. Sounds can trigger various emotions, for instance from happiness to sadness. The question for us involved in music is whether some music is inherently happy or sad. Elements such as speed, accent, rhythm, and pitch height, tessitura (the range within which most notes of a vocal part fall) are obvious emotional cues; but beyond that, are emotions inherent in the music, or are they learned? I have argued that they are learned. The human voice produces low harmonics when relaxed, and higher harmonics when in a state of tension. I think this relationship is learned early in life so that the first 5 harmonics in the harmonic series are heard as being happy or contented (they are major intervals, keys, chords) and the higher intervals in the harmonic series come to represent states of emotional tension (simplistically called "sad"). I think that different sets of harmonics have subtly different emotional aspects leading to the subtlety of harmony but that the various emotional aspects if the harmonics of the human voice are learned. These are phonemes and are conveyed by phonemic templates.

Unlike the laryngeal system, the auditory system appears to have been stable across millions of years and many mammalian species. In fact, the auditory systems of cats and chimpanzees are often studied as surrogates for that of humans and, presumably, other primates and ancient hominids.

Harmonic Series

The brain has built-in mechanisms that enable vocal music to work. The first of these is the harmonic series that is heard in the resonances of the voice. The second is interval cycles created from specific intervals in the harmonic series. Everyone can understand an interval cycle made up of octaves because this is the interval distance between men, women, and children.

The interval cycle built of musical intervals fifths can be also well understood. The interval of a fifth is the strongest non-identity interval, and is the strongest interval in music. Five fifths produce the pentatonic scale, seven fifths produce the diatonic scale, and twelve fifths produce the chromatic scale. Of course, most people only use a few fifths in their tunes, but the use of the notes from a few fifths is something that vocalists discover very quickly. Children all over the world sing a tune that goes: G, E, A, G, E, D, D E. Derived from a circle of four fifths: G, D, A, E. It seems that we have these simple tone maps in our brains just from hearing the fifth as a strong overtone.

When a singer sings up the scale: *do, re, mi, fa, sol*, the notes they sing might be compared to the numbers of the harmonics in the harmonic series. *Do* is like 8. *Re* is like 9. *Mi* is like 10. In fact, you get the idea that the harmonic series is where the notes came from in the first place, and that is true. The numbers of the harmonic series are also the divisions of a vibrating body, like our vocal cords. Vibrating as a whole produces 1 or the fundamental. Vibrating in two halves produces 2, the second partial. Vibrating in thirds produces the third partial and so on. If you study overtone singing you can learn to do this and demonstrate the harmonic series with your voice. There are many great instructional videos on Youtube that teach how to do this.

When you get to *fa* and the 11th partial of the harmonic series, this relationship breaks down. *Fa* is not the 11th partial. Neither is *fi* (raised *fa*). *Fa* is the subdominant. A note that comes from the Pythagorean circle of fifths, that is a perfect fifth below *do*. And therein lies a paradox and the essential element in our story.

The 11th partial represents a note that is not found in our music system. It is not on our pianos and it is not available in our music notation, yet we all know it. We learned it, along with all the standard notes from our mother's voice in our earliest days. I claim that we all want to hear and sing the 11th partial, yet we seem to be unable to do so. The 11th partial is "the unreachable dream," to quote from The Man of La Mancha. It has come to represent the ultimate dream, and its pursuit often drives our lives. The interval between the 10th and 11th partials is a microtone. The harmonic singers of central Asia sing this interval. It is the first interval in the Muslim call to prayer. It is the mystery of Spanish music. It is a force that drives jazz. It is found in primitive fiddle playing. It is found in Indian ragas. It is sometimes found in Gregorian Chant. But it is not allowed. We all know down deep that the rational subdominant is the "correct" note, and that we are not allowed to go to the 11th partial. I hope to be able to tell the tale of the 11th partial in a way that will clarify the understanding of music.

In the first place, the human voice is rich in harmonics. I have taken a spectrogram of my voice while singing an "r" sound that brings out the higher partials, and more than fifty partials can be seen. When we speak or sing, we manipulate the amplitude of these partials with our mouths and that is how we get our vowels. The band of partials from 7 through 17 or so is particularly useful for this because they are close enough together that we can manipulate several at the same time. For example, the short *a*, short *e*, and short *i* form what is called the vowel triangle. A is in the back of the mouth, *e* is in the front of the mouth and *i* is at the top. We get these differences by moving the tongue in and out and up and down, thus manipulating the amplitudes of the various partials. When you speak those vowels you will see that your tongue moves in a triangle, hence the name vowel triangle. The 11th partial is right in the middle of those we manipulate, and so we hear it every day. We heard it as infants in our mother's voice and so we know it intimately.

Yet it is not in our musical system and we cannot sing or play it. The powerful subdominant and dominant notes take control. We are left trying to imply it. When a singer or composer finds a way to strongly imply the 11th partial, people like that and come back to listen again. They used to buy LPs and CDs and download songs. If a singer can manipulate her, or less frequently his voice to bring out the 11th partial, people like that. Women are better at this than men because their higher voices put their 11th partials in the middle of their speaking range. Among male voices, tenors do this best, and that is probably the reason for the greater popularity of tenors than baritones. Women learn how to bring out the cluster of partials centered on the 11th partial. This is what gives women a strident sound in their voices. They learn quickly how to use this effect to control their children and to dominate conversations. We have all seen instances where children will freeze in their tracks when they receive a sharp command from their mother.

Human hearing has a loudness advantage between 3000 and 5000 Hz. You can see this on the Fletcher/Munson curves where the threshold of hearing drops below 0 decibels in this range. Since 10 decibels is approximately a two to one loudness advantage, sounds in this range are strongly heard and not easily covered. The harmonics of the human voice cluster in this range, specifically the cluster of partials from the 7th through the 20th or so.

If you think of the harmonic series on C, then C is 8 (it is also 1, 2, 4, 16 and so forth); D is 9; E is 10; G is 12. But 11 is halfway between F and F#. It is neither F nor F#, but under some circumstances it can be represented by F or F#. The point is that the 11th partial is right in the middle of the presence range but is the one partial in the harmonic series that is not well represented by a note in the equal-tempered scale. Hence it is not well represented by the notes available on our common musical instruments or in our notation system.

My general hypothesis is that the 11th partial is well known to people because they learn it from their mother's and others' voices in their earliest days, yet it is not well represented in our music. Therefore people have a deep subconscious craving to hear it and will go to great lengths to try to get a dose of it.

I am speculating that even primitive hominids as long ago as a hundred thousand years to a million or more years ago would have discovered some of these things in their own voices. In so doing they would have discovered the origin of music.

PRENATAL ORIGINS OF MUSICAL EMOTION: THE CASE FOR FETAL IMPRINTING

Background

At the end of the 19th century, Ernst Haeckel (1902) summarized the biogenetic law in a phrase, 'ontology recapitulates phylogeny' and posed that the fetal growth and development goes through stages resembling the stages of animals in evolutionary history. In his 1871 book, *The Descent of Man* Charles Darwin (2004) proposed a view, confirmed later by the evolutionary developmental biology, that early embryonic stages resemble embryonic stages of previous species but not the adult stages of these species. Charles Darwin's theory has been extensively discussed and attacked.

In 1960s Paul McLean (1990) formulated the triune brain model of the vertebrate forebrain evolution and behavior. According to then acclaimed model, the triune brain comprises three sequentially evolved structures. First was the primitive reptilian complex, and then followed the paleomammalian complex including the limbic system consisting of a number of separate components: the thalamus, the hypothalamus, the hippocampus, and the amygdala, among them. Further on, the neomammalian complex (neocortex) was added to the forebrain. The parts of MacLean's triune brain develop sequentially in the human fetus or child; specifically before birth, a human being does not yet have a developed cerebral cortex but is able to learn general sensory and emotional things in their limbic system. The limbic system along with the sense organs is said to have begun to function in the third trimester of gestation and so is available to do this task (Panksepp & Biven, 2012).

There were controversies related to the theories about the prenatal imprinting, mostly at the beginning of this century. Imprinting is primarily determined by basal forebrain structures (including the cerebral hemispheres, the thalamus, and the hypothalamus), to which the hypothalamus is integral (Keverne, 2015). Developmental changes occur in neocortical (concerned with sight and hearing) forebrain. After birth, development of the neocortex lets free the child's behavior from hormonal mechanisms and the dependence on pheromonal cues. Nicolaïdis (2008) examined the role of under- or over-nutrition in the pregnant mother in feeding preferences in her offspring. Merlot, Couret, & Otten (2007) suggested that prenatal and early life events, such as stress experienced by the pregnant mother might cause future disorders of the child's immune system. Richard Parncutt (2011/1989) asserted that a newborn child recognizes its mother's voice. Parncutt (2011) described how a newborn lamb could identify its mother's bleat, which seems to be a trait common in mammals. Paul (2011) provided cases of prenatal imprinting including the imprinting of tones in the mother's voice associated with her native language, and gave documented examples where a newborn child of a French speaking mother shown a preference for tones used by French speakers over German speakers, even though the child did not known French or German. A newborn child's cerebral cortex is undeveloped at that age, so the implication was made that a lower portion of the brain has done the learning.

We typically associate emotion with things or events; we say, "the boy was sad because his toy was lost" or "the girl was sad because her mother left." It is almost as if we cannot imagine disembodied emotion that lacks some object in things or experiences. We do recognize disembodied emotion occasionally as melancholy or joy, but when pressed we will ascribe it to some object such as a rainy day or a sunny sky.

It can be assumed that the centers of emotion in the brain are prepared long before birth, and we do experience disembodied emotions that we get from our mothers. Before birth, we are able to pick up mother's emotions from her voice, her movements, perhaps through hormones and neurotransmitters. In this way we experience the emotions of life vicariously, before we have had a chance to live it. This is a way to get us prepared for the experiences we will eventually have.

These emotions may eventually be employed by artists to portray all the feelings of life, even those the artist has not experienced. This can apply to all aspects of aesthetic expression including such things as the taste of various foods, the sounds of musical passages, the aesthetic attributes of various colors, and even feelings such as related to faith or hope. This is why it is sometimes said that an artist can create a work that allows us to experience all the emotions of life, even those we have never experienced in life. We can experience emotions vicariously, which is seemingly a very mysterious thing. Strange though it may seem, we have these things imprinted from our mother, who had them imprinted from her mother. Thus they are passed on for generations to make up the fabric of culture and life as it is experienced. In this way there is continuity in experiences and feelings passed on from generation to generation.

However, this mechanism can break down in a culture that is a fusion of many cultural traditions. For example, a child can be imprinted with a traditional culture, yet after birth can be faced with one or more other cultures that present new emotional experiences. The child can reach out to these cultures and old cultural models can be lost, at least temporarily. I would say that this particularly describes the American experience with its cultural fusion.

The place where I live, Greeley, Colorado is one of the new places on the planet. Two hundred years ago a Native American nomadic population occupied this region. Some of them disappeared, e.g., prehistoric Pueblo Indians in a Colorado high plateau of Mesa Verde. Since then there was an influx of people from all over the globe. The primary language is English, but the population contains many Hispanics, Native Americans, Europeans, Asians, South Americans, and other people from everywhere. This set of circumstances represents a cultural fusion that characterizes our time and particularly newly settled areas like Greeley, Colorado.

The fascinating question is why there are so many different musical styles in the world, while every person shows a general fondness for the music of their homeland that they heard in their youth. One may assume that the prenatal fetal imprinting takes place before birth, so the unborn child imprints the sounds and emotions, and this becomes the bedrock of one's musical taste later in life.

A Bootstrap Theory of Sensory Perception

When the brain receives acoustic impulses, the meaning of various codes can only be understood with respect to the built-in interpretation systems. Many of these systems are genetically programmed. My theory, which I call a bootstrap system of sensory perception, is that in the perinatal period, which stretches from several months before birth until several months after birth, the subcortical brain records sensory perceptions along with the mother's emotions that accompany them. The emotions are recorded directly from the mother's body (through the action of neurotransmitters, hormones, and physical behavior plus the mother's emotions) before birth and by a close physical connection after birth. These sensations are stored in a subcortical part of the brain and are available throughout the entire lifespan of the individual. It is believed that the stored emotional responses to sensory inputs become a bootstrap, which the individual will use to understand his or her perceptions of the world throughout their entire life. They become a bootstrap by which the world is understood.

We start recording safety and danger messages at least three months before we are born and an undetermined period after birth, but probably no more than a year, and use this mechanism to encode our mother's voice. We also encode our mother's emotions in conjunction with her voice so that we will be able to detect her responses to our actions when we enter the world. The pleasure we receive from music is the pleasure we receive from sounds we heard in our mother's voice. The emotions are built in to our brain and have nothing to do with specific pitches or sounds, but rather they are the patterns (templates) of nerve impulses received. The pre-natal imprinting is important because at that stage our mother's voice and emotions are separate from every one else's and we take advantage of that fact.

Many popular concepts may be explained by the bootstrap theory, such as a convention that the color red is a warm color and the color blue is a cool color. Another example may be the perception of the major keys and chords as happy and the minor keys and chords as sad. The lowest harmonics in the harmonic series are major and higher ones are minor (5, 6, 7, 8, and 9). When the mother's voice is at rest and happy, it stresses the lowest harmonics of the vocal tract; hence happy gets imprinted with major and perfect intervals. But when the mother is sad, she raises her voice stressing the higher harmonics in her vocal tract. Hence sad gets imprinted with minor intervals. People intuitively know all of this and, although it is mostly unconscious, they practice using it during all their lives. Nursery rhymes and baby talk, for example, are designed to exercise this pitch identification system. Food preferences and food (tastes) to be avoided are conveyed to the young child by this means (see Paul's TED video, *What We Learn Before We Are Born*). Fear, hope, and numerous other feelings are conveyed in the same way, being recorded before birth in the subcortical parts of the brain (before the neocortex is mature enough to do anything), and then they are available throughout life as a bootstrap system by which we understand the incoming sensations. We learn to understand the world with reference to our mother's feelings.

In this way we learn our mother's perceptions directly, but we also learn the standards of our culture that are transmitted from generation to generation. Later in life we may maintain transmitted ideals of behavior; we may rebel against them, but we always know what they are because we got and documented them in our subconscious mind before birth. During the prenatal imprinting phase we are in a direct contact with our mothers; after being born, this connection is less direct.

My assertion is that once the cerebral cortex is sufficiently developed (beginning about the second year of life) the human is capable of learning many things including language. Before that, the learning takes place in other structures such as the limbic system, and it is not intellectual, having no logical structure. Items acquired in the prenatal and the early postnatal periods are not characterized by names, pictures, or intellectual constructs such as physical descriptions. They are however characterized by emotions they evoke. The limbic system has been just called by Ramon y Cajal (1988) and other neurohistologists the center of emotion in the brain.

Emotion Induced by Harmonic Series Voicings

The goal of the described project concerning music theory is to identify emotional responses. I want to identify evidence of emotions induced by music. As music theorist, most of the time I have been using my own emotional responses as points of departure. There is no guarantee that others will have the same emotional responses as I do. In fact, a major part of my hypothesis is that they will not. My hypothesis is that the emotional basis for each person's musical preferences lies in the sound imprinting created by the mother's voice that took place in their limbic system before they were born.

Methodology adopted in this project involved collecting the accounts of musical emotion experienced in specific places from specific pieces of music. Physical evidence of such emotions might result from oral reports or from accounts of chills, goose bumps, tears, or other physical responses. In cases where music is written and scores can be obtained, the method was to circle specific notes, chords, and passages in the music that produced these emotions, and then to perform a thorough analysis of these sounds based on music theory and acoustics with a goal of categorizing them in specific ways.

My work on this process over the years has suggested that harmonic series voiced sonorities are particularly powerful. I call these effects the Harmonic Series Voicings. I have written extensively about harmonic series voicings present in the Stravinsky's *The Rite of Spring* and in modern jazz. In cases where no scores are available, the analysis will be performed aurally from the available recordings and descriptions of the general or specific places where these effects have been felt.

Example 1

The first example is taken from Nikolay Andreyevich Rimsky-Korsakov's composition *Scheherazade Op. 35.* A passage that I have identified as having a particular emotional impact is found near the beginning of the first movement after the violinist plays the introduction to the movement. This passage, intended to describe the ocean waves, consists of the famous motto theme played by the trombones accompanied by four chords. These four chords may be analyzed as follows: French sixth on the tonic, half-diminished seventh on the second scale degree and a V chord. The passage is heard as modulating, not just progressing to the dominant chord, and thus the passage is repeated, this time in the dominant key and so on, around the circle of fifths.

Rimsky-Korsakov could have chosen a simpler and more conventional chord progression, such as I, V7/IV. V4/2/V, V. It is clear that he wanted to achieve the tonicization of the dominant chord, in order to create a modulation, and that these more conventional chords would have accomplished this. The question is why he chose using a French sixth chord in place of the V7/IV, and a half-diminished sonority in place of a secondary dominant. The answer to this question goes to the heart of my research.

I would claim that the French sixth and the half-diminished chord are harmonic series voicings. The French sixth chord is found in the harmonic series at harmonics 7, 8, 9 and 11. The half-diminished seventh chord is found in the harmonic series at harmonics 5, 6, 7, and 9. These are higher in the harmonic series than the usually employed sonorities, particularly the major triad (harmonics 4, 5, and 6) and the dominant seventh chord (harmonics 4, 6, 7, and 9). The point is that a person elevates their voice when they are emotionally driven. The elevated voice falls in a higher harmonic series range of the harmonics of the larynx, and thus represents higher emotion. The formula is that higher partials represent elevated emotion.

Example 2

The second example consists of the first five chords at the beginning of the last movement of Pyotr Ilyich Tchaikovsky's *Symphony No. 6, Pathétique, Op. 74.* The first two of these chords are half-diminished seventh chords. The third chord is a minor seventh chord, the fourth is a half-diminished 11th chord, the fifth chord is a 13th chord, and the last is an augmented dominant chord that becomes a dominant triad. All these chords can be found in the fourth and fifth octaves of the harmonic series.

Tchaikovsky is often accused of wearing his heart on his sleeve, displaying his feelings openly and habitually. He actually does so in fact, but what people should ask is, how is it that you can wear your heart on your sleeve in abstract notes. What is it about notes that allow a composer to express his deeply felt emotion? Tension and release? Dissonance and consonance? Of course, but that's not enough for Tchaikovsky's brand of emotionalism; there has to be something more. Prenatal imprinting of mother's emotions is the answer.

Example 3

The third example is *Prelude No. 1* from the book of 24 Preludes by Fryderyk Chopin. Each of the measures of this work consists of an arpeggiated triad plus one or more non-harmonic tones. The first measure for example, contains an arpeggiated C-major triad plus a neighboring tone. The second measure contains an arpeggiated G major triad in first inversion plus a neighboring tone. The third measure is like the first, and the fourth measure contains an arpeggiated C-major triad in first inversion plus an accented passing tone, etc. Some of the no-harmonic tones are appoggiatura, and some are escape tones, but throughout this small piece all of the measures may be analyzed employing traditional 18th -century harmonic analysis techniques. In each case, though, each measure may be alternatively heard implying an extended tertian chord that may be mapped onto the third and fourth octaves of the harmonic series, which may be heard as triggering subconscious emotion. For example, the first measure may be verticalized into a I+6 chord, the second measure into a V6+9 chord and the fourth chord into a I major-seven chord in first inversion and so forth. Every measure may be analyzed in these two ways, but each measure may also be heard in these two ways depending on your aesthetic preference. Triad plus non-harmonic tone or a tall tertial chord, the difference depends on your preference, but your preference depen ds upon your sonic prenatal imprinting. If you have the tall chords imprinted, then you will hear them, but if you have imprinted triads, then Chopin gives you an alternative way to his music. Gustav Mahler does the same thing.

Example 4

The fourth example is the second chord of Franz Liszt's *Hungarian Rhapsody No. 2*. This famous piece is well known, partly because it has been often turned into commercial music in radio, television, and the movies. The second chord, occurring immediately in the first moments of the piece is a half-diminished seventh chord in a place where a simple dominant seventh chord would work well.

This example further highlights my basic methodology. I ask why it is that many famous composers in their most famous compositions substitute some other sonority for I, IV, or V chords or the dominant seventh chord. The answer to this question could simply be a desire for greater variety, and I am sure there is some of this. Still, I like to point out that the substitute sonorities can generally be mapped on to the harmonic series in the upper fourth and fifth octaves, and I think that this is significant. My claim is that we get to know these higher harmonics in the prenatal period of our lives, and that they carry the emotional meaning for us.

Sonorities frequently encountered as substitute sonorities include the half-diminished seventh chord (5, 6, 7, 9), the minor-major seventh chord (6, 7, 9, 11), the augmented seventh chord (7. 9. 11, 13), the French sixth chord (1, 5, 11, 7), the minor seventh chord (5, 6, 15, 9), the so-called dominant 9th chord (1, 5, 3, 7, 9), and so on. The various types of ninth, eleventh, and thirteenth chords most frequently encountered may be so mapped as well.

The so-called ninth chord with sharp 9, flat 5 may be found in the harmonic series at 5, 6, 7, 9, 11 and the thirteenth chord is 1, 3, 5, 7, 9, 11, 13. Beethoven used this chord occasionally, as did other older composers, probably because it is so similar to a first -inversion minor chord (1, 3, 13), when some of the pitches are omitted and the 13th chord is rarely presented with all seven of its pitches sounded (there is a famous example of all 7 pitches sounded in Mahler's Tenth Symphony).

The movie composer John Barry commented about the precious half-diminished seventh chord. I think that the half-diminished chord is the poster child for emotionally heightened chords because it is low enough in the harmonic series that many people would have had a chance to imprint on it in their mother's voice, yet high enough that it can represent heightened emotion. The major triad (1, 5, 3) represents no emotion other than rest or contentment. The dominant seventh chord (1, 5, 3, 7) represents a need for action and the minor chord (6, 7, 9 or 10, 12, 15) represents sadness or melancholy. The reason this is so is that you would have heard those harmonics in your mother's voice, when it was in an elevated pitch state while she was expressing these types of feelings. The association of the major triad with happy feelings and the minor triad with sad feelings goes back to prenatal imprinting from the mother's voice. These sonorities are imprinted in subcortical regions of the brain, and they remain available for life. They are not normally noticed however, and might be thought of as subconscious, although they may be noticed with practice.

CONCLUSION

In my own case, a thirteenth chord produces a strong physical jolt that I observe and then after the fact can comment on. I can say that I just heard a 13th chord because I felt a jolt. On going back and examining the music I just heard, the 13th chord will be found. This will normally be an incompletely voiced thirteenth chord (1, 7, 5, 13 or 1, 3, 7, 5, 13, or occasionally 1, 3, 7, 9, 13). I might encounter 1, 3, 11, 7, 9, 13, as well. Actually all combinations are possible, but most composers delete many of the members of a thirteenth chord simply because of the amount of dissonance that is built up. The closer to the modern era (20th century) the more chord members might be included, until Mahler used all 7 of the chord members in his modernistic 10th Symphony. Note that the 3rd harmonic is the fifth of the chord, and the fifth harmonic is the 3rd of the chord.

The general rule is that the lower in the harmonic series the pitches are found, the greater is the number of listeners who will have imprinted an emotional response to the sonority. Thus higher groupings of more pitches are just dissonances, and no imprinted emotion exists other than horror. Still, a composer needs to express horror occasionally, and a minor second cluster 13, 14, 15, 16, 17, 18, etc. will do it.

It seems to be pretty clear that some people have imprinted on the higher partials of the harmonic series in conjunction with specific emotions, while other people have not. I would guess that nearly everyone imprints on something though, just depending upon one's mother's specific vocalizations. Perhaps it might be non-pitched vocalizations, rhythmic patterns, or melodic configurations. While this chapter focuses on classical music, there might be certain patterns found in popular music of various types that could be imprinted. The evidence is to be found in some people liking and deriving specific feelings from the sounds of different types of sounds, as found in a variety of music.

It seems to be true that everybody likes some sorts of music or sounds that bring back good feelings imprinted from their mother at the time these sounds were being heard. So, can you learn before you are born? Well, we hear of the Mozart Effect, so obviously people think some things are possible. However, there is a big error in the so-called Mozart effect; it is assumption that the music will produce the learning effect alone. This is definitely not the case. It is not an intellectual thing. It is an emotional thing and the key to prenatal learning involves the mother's emotions. For a small animal, amygdala is a source of decision when to run from a danger. The subcortical place in the brain where prenatal learning occurs is the center of emotions in the brain.

There's plenty of general evidence that one can learn before one is born. *de Villers-Sidani, Chang, Bao, & Merzenich (2007)* summarized the findings as follows: "Like many areas in the neocortex, the functional properties of the adult primary auditory cortex (A1) are highly dependent on the sounds encountered early in life." And, "The change is persistent in that it lasts throughout life." If this is correct, then there is a vast amount of music and musical sounds in the world to be explored and documented. There is considerable evidence that this is possible, a lot of it coming from native Mandarin Chinese language speakers. It turns out that Chinese people are much more likely than westerners to have perfect pitch because their language is tone based. The speakers of Chinese use the same pitches over and over again and their infants hear these same pitches repeated constantly. They will learn typical phonemes from their native language, and they will use that learning to improve their language performance later on. A transition of the tones to music will come later.

The conclusion is that emotion is the nature's way of getting us to do something. The emotions we feel when we listen to the music or sounds imprinted in our brains come not exactly from that music or those sounds. The emotion we feel seems to be an evolutionary trick that evolved for the purpose of promoting social cohesion over multiple generations. In my case, it is not the music of Tchaikovsky or Mahler that produces my emotions per se. It is caused by the fact that my mother (and my grandmother before her) liked the late Romantic music, listened to it, played it, and sang it during the critical periods in my earliest development. I have imprinted this music and I now receive emotions from it. For other people who grew up in different times and in different places other types of music and sound patterns will produce emotions. I have learned that I should not allow myself to be fooled.

REFERENCES

Darwin, C. (2004). The Descent of Man. Penguin Classics.

de Villers-Sidani, E., Chang, E. F., Bao, S., & Merzenich, M. M. (2007). Critical period window for spectral tuning defined in the primary auditory cortex (A1) in the rat. *The Journal of Neuroscience*, *27*(1), 1809. doi:10.1523/JNEUROSCI.3227-06.2007 PMID:17202485

Deutsch, D. (Ed.). (2013). *The Psychology of Music* (3rd ed.). Cambridge, MA: Academic Press.

Ehle, R. C. (2016). How We Hear and Experience Music: a Bootstrap Theory of Sensory Perception. In A. Ursyn (Ed.), *Knowledge Visualization and Visual Literacy in Science Education*. Hershey, PA: IGI Global. doi:10.4018/978-1-5225-0480-1.ch008

Keverne, E. B. (2015). Genomic imprinting, action, and interaction of maternal and fetal genomes. *PNAS*, *112*(22), 6834–6840. Retrieved from www.pnas.org/cgi/doi/10.1073/pnas.1411253111

Kuhl, P. (2017). *The Linguistic Genius of Babies*. The TED Video. Retrieved from http://search.myway.com/search/video.jhtml?n=&p2=&pg=video&pn=1&ptb=&qs=&searchfor=infant+learns+sounds+TED+video&si=&ss=sub&st=tab&tpr=sbt&trs=wtt&vidOrd=3&vidId=M-ymanHajN8

Langner, G. (2015). The Neural Code of Pitch and Harmony. Cambridge UK: Cambridge University Press. doi:10.1017/CBO9781139050852

MacLean, P. D. (1990). The Triune Brain in Evolution: Role in Paleocerebral Functions. Springer.

Merlot, E., Couret, D., & Otten, W. (2008). Prenatal stress, fetal imprinting, and immunity. *Brain, Behavior, and Immunity*, *22*(1), 42–51. doi:10.1016/j.bbi.2007.05.007 PMID:17716859

Merriam-Webster's Dictionary. (2017). *Music*. Retrieved from https://www.merriam-webster.com/dictionary/dictionary

Nicolaïdis, S. (2008). Prenatal imprinting of postnatal specific appetites and feeding behavior. *Metabolism: Clinical and Experimental*, *57*(Suppl 2), S22–S26. doi:10.1016/j.metabol.2008.07.004 PMID:18803961

Panksepp, J., & Biven, L. (2012). The Archaeology of Mind: Neuroevolutionary Origins of Human Emotions (Norton Series on Interpersonal Neurobiology). W. W. Norton & Company.

Parncutt, R. (2011). Harmony: A Psychoacoustical Approach. Springer.

Paul, A. M. (2011). What babies learn before they are born. *TED Global 2011*. Retrieved from https://www.ted.com/talks/annie_murphy_paul_what_we_learn_before_we_re_born/transcript?language=en

Ramón y Cajal, S., & DeFelipe, J. (1988). Cajal on the Cerebral Cortex: An Annotated Translation of the Complete Writings. Oxford University Press.

Tomatis, A. A. (1991). The Conscious Ear. Paris: Station Hill Press.

Whittow, J. (1984). *Dictionary of Physical Geography*. London: Penguin.

ADDITIONAL READING

Backus, J. (1977). The Acoustical Foundations of Music, Musical Sound, Its properties, production, behavior, and reproduction, Second Edition. W. W. Norton & Company. ML 3805. B245. A3

Chen, M. Y. (2000). Tone Sandhi. Cambridge University Press. Cambridge, U.K. etc. PL 1213. C 445

Haeckel, E. (1902). The Riddle of the Universe: At the Close of the Nineteenth Century. J. McCabe, translator. Harper & Brothers Publishers; Early Edition edition (1902).

Harrison, D. F. N. (1995). The Anatomy and Physiology of the Mammalian Larynx. The Cambridge University Press: New York. QM 331.H37 doi:10.1017/CBO9780511525766

Heine, B., & Narrog, H. (Eds.). (2010). The Oxford Handbook of Linguistic Analysis. The Oxford University Press: Oxford, UK. P126.Q94 (especially Chapter 19)

Heller, E. J. (2013). Why You Hear What You Hear, An Experimental Approach to Sound, Music and Psychoacoustics. Princeton University Press. QP 461. H 395

Hiranu, M., & Sato, K. (1993). Histological Color Atlas of the Human Larynx. Singular Publishing Group, Inc.: San Diego, CA. QM 331.H57

Howie, J. M. (1976). Acoustical Studies of Mandarin in Vowels and Tones, Cambridge University Press. Cambridge, U.K. PL. 1201 H 68 1976

Jerger, J. (2009). Audiology in the USA. Plural Publishing: San Diego, CA. RF 291. J47

Kasper, G., & Zhang, Y. (Eds.). (1995). Pragmatics of Chinese as Native and Target Language. University of Hawai'i Press. Honolulu, Hawaii PL129. P 73

Langner, G. The Neural Code of Pitch and Harmony. Cambridge University Press. Cambridge UK. 2015. QG 510.5 L 36 doi:10.1017/CBO9781139050852

Nelson, C. A., & Luciana, M. (2001 and 2008). Handbook of Developmental Cognitive Neuroscience. MIT Press: Cambridge, Massachusetts. QP 363.5 H365

Rubin, J. S., Sataloff, R. T., & Korovin, G. (Eds.). (2014). Diagnosis and Treatment of Voice Disorders, Fourth Edition. Plural Publishing: San Diego, CA. RF510. D53

Sanes, D. H., Reh, T. A., & Harris, W. A. (2001). Development of the Nervous System. Academic Press: San Diego. QP 363.5. S 26

Smith, C. G. (1985). Ancestral Voices. Prentice Hall: Englewood Cliffs, N.J. BF 791. S 98

Tomatis, A. A. (1991) The Conscious Ear. Station Hill Press: Barrytown NY. RF 38 T 65. A 313

KEY TERMS AND DEFINITIONS

Acoustic Waves: Longitudinal waves with the same direction of vibration as the direction of their traveling in a medium such as air or water. Linear mixing of acoustic waves results in forming periodicity pitches of the resultant tones.

Chord: A harmonic set of several pitches heard as simultaneously sounding notes.

Fifth Interval: An ordered pair of notes that have an interval of 6 to 8 semitones.

Harmonic Series: A set of pure tones (sinusoidal waves) comprising a fundamental lowest frequency and its exact multiples.

Interval: A musical interval is the difference between two pitches.

Interval Class: Also known as interval distance is the shortest distance in a pitch class space between two unordered pitch classes.

Interval Cycle: A collection of pitch classes created from a sequence of the same interval class.

Pitch: A sound quality describing the highness or lowness of a tone, defined by the rate of vibration that produces it (e.g., of a string or human voice). The musical pitch of a note is the lowest component of a musical sound, a frequency created by vibration the string or the air column.

Pitch Class: A set of all pitches that are a whole number of octaves apart.

Semitone: Also called a half tone is the smallest musical interval usually existing in Western tonal music.

Sonority: A chord where sonority of a sound defines its loudness in comparison to other sounds.

Sound Waves: Sinusoidal waves characterized by their frequency, amplitude, intensity (sound pressure), speed, and direction. Pairs of sound waves may reveal additive and subtractive interference.

Tessitura: The range within which most notes of a vocal part fall.

Tonotopic Organization: The arrangement of spaces in auditory cortex where sounds of different frequency are processed in the brain. Tones close to each other frequency are represented in topologically near regions in the brain.

Tritone: An interval of three whole tones with an augmented fourth. For example, between C and F sharp.

Section 3
Interfaces That Support Learning

Chapter 12
Leveraging Computer Interface to Support Creative Thinking

Robert Z. Zheng
University of Utah, USA

Kevin Greenberg
University of Utah, USA

ABSTRACT

How to design computer interface that facilitates learners' creative thinking can be challenging. This chapter discusses the cognitive processes, the types of divergent thinking, visualization, and brain-functions in relation to human learning. Informed by the research in previous areas, the authors examine the features of computer interface that aligns with brain-functions to support various types of creative thinking. An example is included to demonstrate, at the conceptual level, how computer interface can be leveraged to support learners' creativity, imagination, originality, and expressiveness in learning. Discussions are made with respect to the implication and limitation of the chapter. The chapter concludes with suggestions for future research and studies.

INTRODUCTION

Creative thinking is perhaps one of the most important outcomes in education. It accounts for learners' cognitive abilities in making connections between concepts and information across domains and disciplines, exploring novel approaches in problem solving, and generating solutions pertaining to complex social and environmental issues (Goldschmidt, 2016; Lince, 2016). Research has shown a significant correlation between learners' academic achievement and creative thinking, suggesting that creative thinking can enhance learners' academic performance in terms of deep understanding, multi-level problem solving, and far knowledge transfer within and outside academic domains and disciplines (Birgili, 2015). Substantial efforts have been made in the past to develop learners' creative thinking skills in language acquisition (Sehic, 2017), science education (Widiana & Jampel, 2016), mathematical thinking (Vale, Bragg, Widjaja, Herbert, & Loong, 2017), and so forth. With the advancement of digital technology, new ways of teaching creative thinking skills have been introduced. For example, the Internet is considered to

DOI: 10.4018/978-1-5225-7371-5.ch012

be a viable platform to promote learners' creative thinking skills (DeSchryver, 2017; Lin & Wu, 2016). Recent emerging technologies like Artificial Intelligence (AI), 3D virtual reality, simulation, and video games have found their ways into classrooms and other educational settings to facilitate learners' creative thinking (Lin, Wang, & Kuo, 2017; Moffat, Crombie, & Shabalina, 2017; Neo & Neo, 2013). However, there are challenges associated with digital technologies in teaching creative thinking skills due to (a) a lack of proper knowledge in understanding the complexity of creative thinking processes and (b) an absence of sufficient pedagogical supporting system that facilitates individuals' creative behaviors and activities when engaged in technology-support creative thinking processes. The purpose of this chapter aims to explore the unique cognitive processes associated with creative thinking and examine the pedagogical role of digital technology in supporting creative thinking.

THEORETICAL BACKGROUND

Creative thinking is a cognitive process that often results in novel approaches to learning and production. According to Merrian-Webster Dictionary, *create* means "to produce through imaginative skill" (Merrian-Webster Dictionary, 2018). Within the literature of creative thinking research, the term is defined as originality, expressiveness, and imagination (Goldschmidt, 2016; Lopez-Ortega, 2013; Widiana & Jampel, 2016). There are two aspects of creative thinking, divergent thinking, which is defined as generating many ideas, and convergent thinking that is developing a plausible solution to a problem (Colzato, Ozturk, & Hommel, 2012). The reductionist approach which typically employs convergent thinking in reasoning, researchers in creative thinking advocate divergent thinking as a vehicle to achieve innovation, expressiveness and resourcefulness (Boden, 1998; Lopez-Ortega, 2013; Smith & Kosslyn, 2007).

This chapter focuses on divergent creative thinking, as digit technology can provide a great aid to this aspect of creativity. There are several types of divergent thinking: spontaneous, deliberate, and constructive thinking. Spontaneous divergent thinking refers to the process of on-going idea generation. Deliberate divergent thinking refers to the deliberating process in creative thinking. Finally, constructive divergent thinking is marked by a process in the genesis of knowledge. A discussion of each type of divergent creative thinking follows.

Types of Divergent Thinking

Spontaneous Divergent Thinking

Idea generation is considered a critical part of creative thinking process. Spontaneous Divergent Thinking (SDT) reflects an on-going thinking process in which the individuals generate novel ideas while working on projects. According to Lopez-Ortega (2013), SDT activities are associated with the central and posterior cortical areas of brain which are not guided by conscious planning or preconceived mental paradigms. In other words, SDT is an automatic process that is neither initiated nor operated deliberately. Examples of SDT include spontaneous brain-storming, non-linear idea generation, and free association in solution seeking. There are several cognitive benefits associated with SDT. For example, SDT which takes a goal-free approach reduces learners' cognitive load as they seek solutions to the goal-free problems (Sweller, 1988; Sweller & Chandler, 1991). Other benefits include allowing for expressiveness and imagination, nurturing open-mindedness and multiple perspectives, along with developing innovative perceptions when exploring ideas and concepts.

Deliberate Divergent Thinking

Differing from SDT, deliberate divergent thinking (DDT) is marked by a deliberate process. In DDT activities, the learner is mindful of the expected goal and explores the solution by taking a means-end approach. Research in neuroimaging has shown that DDT is associated with the activation of the pre-frontal cortex of the brain which involves mental planning of future activities, selective attention, categorization and supervision of working memory (Lopez-Ortega, 2013; Smith & Kosslyn, 2007). In other words, DDT is a process of conscious exploration of diverse ideas and concepts through deliberation and elaboration (Boden, 1998; Graeme, 2006). DDT has been widely adopted as an effective strategy in business planning and policy making in government and organizations. Examples of DDT include goal-oriented brain-storming and thinking divergently through causal relationship. The outcomes of the DDT are often seen as more focused and relevant reflecting the process of deliberate thinking.

Constructive Divergent Thinking

Constructive divergent thinking (CDT) mirrors the cognitive process of DDT but relies less on goals and objectives. Rather, it goes beyond the goals and objectives to generate out of the box ideas and concepts garnered by collective wisdom and knowledge. In CDT, learners construct new knowledge by generating and synthesizing diverse ideas and concepts. The difference between DDT and CDT is that the former focuses on finding the solutions relevant to the goals and objectives whereas the latter highlights the importance of knowledge construction. Examples of CDT include working on science projects in schools where students think divergently to generate new knowledge in learning, or teaching students in architectural design by generating ideas and concepts independent from visual references in the real world (Hamza & Hassan, 2016; Thompson, 2017; Sripongwiwat, Bunterm, & Srisawat, 2016; Zakirova & Purik, 2016).

Summary

Creative thinking reflects divergent, imaginative, and innovative thinking processes. The forms of divergent thinking like spontaneous, deliberate, and constructive divergent thinking are often employed to elicit creativity, expressiveness, imagination and originality in learners. However, there are concerns about the pedagogy pertaining to ways of nurturing divergent thinking skills for creative and innovative thinking for learners (Glaveanu, Sierra, & Tanggaard, 2015). In fact, the pedagogy in creative thinking instruction has been in different directions. Some focus on scenario, problem-based practice (Birgili, 2015; Seechaliao, 2017), others emphasize particular learning strategies such as heuristic learning and open-ended, ill-defined questions (Peters & Maatman, 2017; Tandiseru, 2015), still others explore the roles of technology to promote divergent, creative thinking (DeSchryver, 2017; DeSchryver & Yadav, 2015; Moffat et al., 2017). The following sections provide an overview of the current pedagogical practices in creative thinking.

Approaches to Teaching Creative Thinking

As it was mentioned above, the pedagogical practices in creating thinking instruction has been in many directions, each with their own strengths and limitations. A discussion of the strengths and limitations follows.

Scenario and Problem-Based Approach

The scenario and problem-based approach is one of the popular methods favored by teachers, trainers, and other educational practitioners. In scenario and problem-based approach, a problem or scenario is presented that delineates the complexity of relationships, along with the constraints to the relationships. This type of problem is usually authentic and open-ended, providing a problem space for divergent thinking and creative imagination (Oncu, 2016). The advantages of applying this approach to creative thinking include (a) facilitating meaningful connection between learners' prior knowledge and the problem, (b) promoting active learning and application, and (c) developing multiple perspectives toward problem solution(s) (Lindvang & Beck, 2015). Therefore, scenario and problem-based approach fits well with divergent thinking training, particularly deliberate and constructive divergent thinking in which the learners are mindful of the means-end relationship in the problem. As such, it is limited in training spontaneous divergent thinking, which is connected with the central and posterior cortical areas of brain and therefore not to be guided by conscious planning or preconceived mental paradigms (Lopez-Ortega, 2013).

Learning Strategies

It is not uncommon to find that the training of creative thinking in the past several decades has been heavily focused on specific learning strategies. This is because there is often an observable relationship between the direct outcomes of creative thinking and the strategies used, such as cognitive prompts, heuristic learning, and open-ended, ill-structured questions. For example, Tandiseru (2015) implemented a heuristic learning model to enhance students' creative thinking skills. It was found that students who received the heuristic learning model training scored higher on Creative Thinking Skills (CTSs) test and performed better in mathematical problem solving than these who did not. Peters and Maatman (2017) took a different approach by providing an open-ended, ill-structured problems at the beginning of the learning session and then let the students navigate through the session by independently and freely exploring the issues without considering the means-end relationship. That is, the learner had the opportunity to explore and generate as many novel ideas and concepts as they wanted. Based on the ideas and concepts generated the learner then decided the next possible route for exploration and analyses. The advantage of this approach is the learner is free to imagine and think about new ideas and concepts without running the risk of overloading his/her working memory. In this process the ideas and concepts are fluid and may change depending on the next generated ideas and concepts. Evidently, the divergent process is spontaneous, fluid, and non-linear. The limitation is that it is time-consuming and that the learner may run into impasses during the spontaneous brain-storming process.

Instructional Technology

One of the promising areas in creative thinking training is digital technology (e.g., multimedia, virtual reality, simulation, gaming, etc.) which has been to facilitate novel imagination and expression, as well as promoting originality and creativity in idea and concept generation. Moffat et al. (2017) explored the role of video games in promoting students' creative thinking. The study tested the hypothesis that different sorts of video games may have different effects on the types of creativity. Torrance Tests of Creative Thinking (TTCT) was used to measure students' creative thinking. The results confirmed their hypothesis revealing that the games had different effects on creative thinking, with flexibility - one of the indicators of creativity - showing the largest variances. Aihara and Hori (1998) asserted that computers may play a fundamental role in promoting human creative thinking. They found that features like enabling information accessibility and connecting to previous thoughts, arguments, and issues in computers contributed to learners' creative thinking. They developed a system called *En Passant 2* in which the learner was able to retrieve research notes about arguments and suggestions on issues through computerized indices and attributors. They found that the system supported the four important stages in creative thinking: preparation, incubation, illumination, and verification.

Summary

Creative thinking is a multifaceted construct, so the approaches to teaching creative thinking are wide-ranging. In this chapter we focus primarily on three approaches that represent the main stream practice in creative thinking instruction. These approaches allow at various degrees for innovative and creative mental activities. While each approach is unique in its way to tap into expressiveness, imagination, and creativity, digital technology has overall shown promises in bringing the learner's potential to full play. Evidence has shown that digital technology has the capability of helping people to look at things from different angles and perspectives (Helmick, 1984; Lubart, 2005; Statham, 2014). Zheng (2007) pointed out that the cognitive function of digital technology plays a crucial role in influencing our perceptions and way of thinking. For the purpose of this chapter, we examine the functional role of visual representation by showing its cognitive functionality in learning.

Cognitive Functionality of Visualization

The concepts of visualization and perceptions are related (Blake & Sekuler, 2006). It is believed that the way how the visuals are presented can influence humans' perception and processing of information (Haroz, 2013). Haroz noticed the relationship between the design of visuals and the individual's visual perception and attention. According to Blake and Sekuler, four types of visualization can critically affect the learner's choice of perception and information process. They include constructive, contextual, interpretative, and synthetic visualizations.

Constructive Visualization

It is believed that the user's ability to construct meaning is determined by the visual elements that create "the constructive nature of visual perception" (Blake & Sekuler, 2006, p. 111). In other words, the visual interface should allow the brain to go beyond the optical information provided by the eye and generate plausible interpretations. Research in cognitive visualization has shown that learners are more likely to engage in constructive and creative thinking when the visual representation provides mental space for imagination (Hyerle, 1996; Zheng, Dahl, & Flygare, 2008). Figure 1 Panel A presents an example of constructive visualization. The picture consists of five circles with one portion cut from the center of each circle. The circles are placed in certain positions forming a mental space for imagination and constructive thinking. The learner draws from his/her experience to predict the missing figure. Constructive visualization is conducive to deliberate and constructive divergent thinking. In this case the learner forms a hypothesis about the missing figure and then deliberates on the information given (i.e., five circles) to construct an answer to the problem by drawing on his/her prior knowledge and experience.

Contextual Visualization

The concept of contextual visualization in visual learning refers to a visual context in which isolated objectives and images become meaningfully connected. In their discussion on contextual visualization Blake and Sekuler (2006) point out that the brain does not concentrate on individual features in isolation, instead it exploits relationships among features as contextual clues about how those features ought to be knitted together. For example, Figure 1 Panel B has two separate images. The top image contains a fragmented geometry figure showing two connected triangles. By looking at the top image the learner may not fully understand the purpose of the triangles until he/she sees the hexagon figure below and understands the triangles are actually part of the hexagon. Blake and Sekuler thus argue that meaningful perception occurs when the part is perceived as relevant to a whole object. It is believed that contextual

Figure 1. Types of visual representation (© 2018, R. Zheng, used with permission)

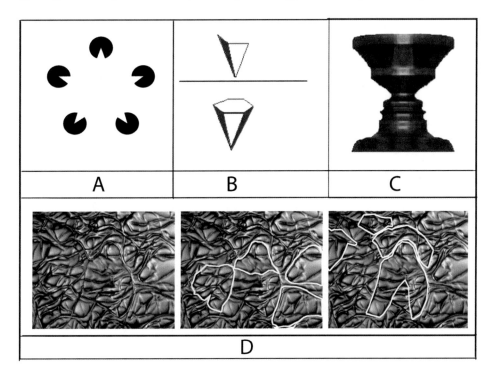

visualization provides the necessary condition for deliberate divergent thinking where the learner tries to resolve the tension between the isolated and the whole image through mental association.

Interpretative Visualization

Like other types of visualization, interpretative visualization captures the changes of human perceptions through alternative viewpoints. This type of visualization has been used to facilitate multiple perspectives in creative thinking (Seels & Dunn, 1989). The notion of interpretative interface originates from the concept of the relativity of human perception. Human perception can fluctuate between alternatives when an ambiguous interface is presented. For example, Figure 1 Panel C is a picture that is subject to multiple interpretations: at one moment the figure appears to be a chess trophy against a white background; at another moment, without warning, it turns into a pair of white faces looking at each other against a mahogany background. Interpretative visualization can serve as a cognitive tool for incubating ideas and concepts where the learner takes multiple perspectives to make assumptions about the things he/she perceives. From a pedagogical perspective interpretative visualization provides the necessary mental space for imagination and novel idea generation.

Synthetic Visualization

Synthetic visualization provides a platform for learners to synthesize bits of information that are initially considered indecipherable. Research suggests that the learner's ability to synthesize is critical to creative thinking (Doering & Henrickson, 2015; DeSchryver, 2017). Figure 1 Panel D presents a collection of pictures. The first picture contains a blotch of random lines and shapes before synthesizing. To make sense of this picture, your visual system must synthesize the line and contour information gathered from a large portion of the picture, and try to figure out which pieces go together. The second picture demonstrates the first attempt of synthesizing process depicting subdued faces of animals and a human being as perceived by the learner. The third picture shows the next attempt by the learner who identifies new images of human face and figure through visual reorganization. This process may continue as the learner reorganizes the lines and shapes to conjecture new images and figures, a process that is invigorated by an unfettered space for mental imagination and creative thinking. The human ability to visually synthesize clues from a seemingly random collection of splotches, proves that visual perception depends on more than just the pattern of light striking the retina. Perception, rather than being a mindless process of measuring how much light enters the eye, is an intelligent activity of a finely tuned brain (Blake & Sekuler, 2006). Understanding human ability to visually synthesize information is significant for educators, graphic designers, and software engineers who are interested in developing interface and activities that nurture learners' creativity, imagination, and expressiveness.

Summary

Visualization reflects the fundamental activities of our brain in which we try to make sense of the world around us. In this chapter we discussed four types of visualization with each representing a unique cognitive process related to learning and divergent thinking. For example, constructive visualization provides the necessary mental space for imagination and constructive thinking and facilitates deliberate and constructive divergent thinking; contextual visualization aids deliberate divergent thinking through association; interpretative visualization enables the learner to engage in multiple perspectives and is conducive to idea origination and imagination; finally, synthetic visualization makes it possible for the learner to engage in creative thinking like spontaneous divergent thinking through information reorganization and synthesis. Understanding the cognitive functionality and the utility of above visualization has significant pedagogical implications in terms of designing meaningful and user friendly computer interfaces to support creative thinking in learning.

Research on Cognitive Function

Of interest to researchers and educators is how the brain functions in ways that support certain type of thinking process. It is believed that different parts of the brain are responsible for different kinds of cognitive processes (Herrmann, 1990; Saputra & Sabana, 2016). Kantak, Stinear, Buch, and Cohen (2012) discovered that premotor cortex is related to individual's motor control and learning. Herrmann (1990) proposed that human performance and information processing are related to and controlled by particular areas in brain. He described four areas of brain, which he named four quadrants that related to emotional, cognitive and behavioral outcomes of individual performance. According to Herrmann, the left side of the brain is related to logical and organizational thinking, whereas the right side of the brain has to do with holistic thinking and interpersonal relationship. However, both hemispheres are involved in most cognitive processes, but one hemisphere tends to have more activation than the other depending on the process (Kolb & Whishaw, 2009).

Left-Cerebral Area

It is believed that the left-cerebral area provides the neural foundation for verbal perception, differentiation and identification, and activates the linguistic labelling of visual and auditory information (Flor-Henry, 1983). It plays the critical role in logical, analytical thinking and engages in fact-based and quantitative cognitive processes. In light of its role in learning, the left-cerebral area is often identified as part of brain that supports critical thinking and problem solving.

Right-Cerebral Area

Differing from its left counterpart, the right-cerebral area is marked by holistic and intuitive thinking. It is an area that relates to individual visuospatial ability which has to do with creativity and arts. This area is also believed to be responsible for cognitive processes such as synthesizing and integrating information (Herrmann, 1990). From a learning viewpoint, the right-cerebral area functions primarily to support visual learning and creative thinking.

Left-Limbic Area

The limbic system is generally associated with motivation, emotion, learning, and memory. The limbic system is a complex system that includes (a) the basal ganglia which consist of a set of subcortical structures that direct intentional movements and (b) hypothalamus and cingulate cortex which involve hormone regulation and aspects of emotion. Herrmann (1990) believes the left-limbic area supports cognitive

Figure 2. Areas of brain and related cognitive and affective processes. (© 2018, R. Zheng, used with permission)

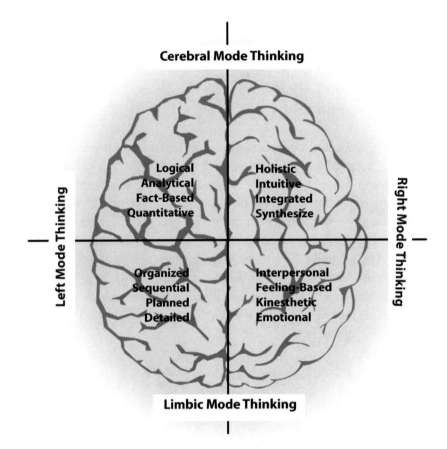

processes such as organized, sequential, planned, and detail-oriented activities. Since the limbic system includes hypothalamus and cingulate cortex, it also regulates emotional aspects. Regarding its function in learning, the left-limbic area plays the dual roles of supporting (1) detail-oriented procedural knowledge acquisition, task organization and planning, and (2) affective aspects in learning such as motivation.

Right-Limbic Area

This is the area in the brain that is responsible for emotionally and socially related processes. Specifically, it supports interpersonal, emotional, and feeling-based activities. It is also responsible for controlling the kinesthetic movement which is considered a psycho-motor coordination between the brain and body. As it was mentioned previously, the limbic system involves hypothalamus and cingulate cortex, the right-limbic area which is part of limbic system functions primarily to regulate the emotions, feelings, and other affective aspects. Regarding its role in learning, the right-limbic area is identified as a place where emotionally related expression and motivation are processed.

Summary

Research indicates that the areas of brain function differently in terms of cognitive and affective processes. The left-cerebral area is related to logical, analytical, fact-based, and quantitative processes whereas the right-cerebral area is related to holistic and intuitive thinking marked by holistic, intuitive, integrated, and synthesizing processes. The left-limbic area supports organized, sequential, planned, and detail-oriented processes. Finally, the right-limbic area is responsible for processing interpersonal, feeling-based, kinesthetic, and emotional activities. The research on human brain suggests that human activities including cognitive and affective are controlled by and processed in specific parts of the brain which also suggests that the design of learning including the design of computer interface should be aligned with the brain functions to optimize the information process for learners (Shahin, 2008; Zheng et al., 2008).

DESIGNING PEDAGOGICALLY SOUND COMPUTER INTERFACE FOR CREATIVE THINKING

Recent advances in technology have generated substantial interest in developing brain-function compatible computer interfaces to meet the needs of different users ranging from people with special needs to individuals seeking ways to engage in critical and creative thinking (Donoghue, 2002; Wolpaw et al., 2000). Shahin (2008) argues that the design of computer interface should consider the function of brain and that the computer system should be designed in a way "that is capable of creative and innovative 'thinking' (or processing)" (p. 549). Zheng et al. (2008) also proposed that the design of visuals in computer learning should put brain functions in perspective. In a study Zheng et al. (2008) noticed a perceptual-conceptual relationship pertaining to human-computer interface processing. The authors assert that the learner's initial process of the computer interface usually focuses on aesthetic aspects – a process related to the right-limbic area of the brain (e.g., motivation, engagement, etc.). However, the initial interaction may wax and wane unless it is supported by the sense-making process in which the learner proceeds to conceptualize the concepts through analyses, syntheses and evaluation – a process related to left-cerebral area of the brain. Zheng et al.'s study unveiled the relationship between computer interface and brain function but focused primarily on critical thinking. Based on Zheng et al.'s finding, the current chapter further examines the relationship between computer interfaces and creative thinking by considering brain function, cognitive visualization, divergent thinking, and pedagogical aspects in creative thinking.

Developing Brain Compatible Computer Interface for Creative Thinking

Creative thinking involves "observation, imaging, abstraction, pattern recognition, pattern formation, analogizing, body thinking, empathizing, dimensional thinking, modeling, playing, transforming, and synthesizing" (DeSchryver & Yadav, 2015, p. 413). These skills mirror at various degrees the brain function associated with learning. Skills that are related to higher level thinking processes like abstraction, dimensional thinking, and so forth can be mentally challenging and thus require some form of cognitive scaffolding which, according to Tillman, An, and Boren (2015), can be accomplished through the design of brain-function compatible computer interface. DeSchryver and Yadav (2015) points out that creativity and technology are mutually beneficial and that "technology can enhance creativity, but technology can also require creativity" (p. 412) which suggests a computer interface with support for creativity is likely to promote learners' creative thinking. Likewise, thinking innovatively about the design of computer interface can enhance the functions of technology that enable the learner to think creatively.

One of the challenges in developing brain-function compatible computer interface is to identify the features that foster a wide range of creative thinking skills and stimulate multiple areas of the brain. In the following sections, we present an example with computer interface features that support the cognitive and creative thinking in alignment with brain functions.

Leveraging Computer Interface to Support Creative Thinking: An Example

The example involves training students' creative thinking skills. To ensure that the students master the skills in creative thinking, the design of the training takes multiple factors into consideration including pedagogical, visual, and cognitive aspects. Pedagogically, the training incorporates the scenario and problem-based approach. As Oncu (2016) points out, the scenario and problem-based approach provides a problem space for creative imagination. Visually, scenario and problem relevant materials are provided to stimulate perceptual engagement. Cognitively, tools that facilitate divergent and elaborative thinking are included to support the cognitive process in learning.

Background

A team of geologists are conducting a survey in a mountain area. They come to a lake where there is no bridge. They decide to build the bridge themselves by following the suspense bridge style with ropes hung from a post and a pine tree which are on each side of the lake (Figure 3). They have the height of the post which will be erected on their side of the lake. They however need to figure out the height of the pine tree on the other side of the lake as well as the distance between the post and the pine tree. The team is required to come up with creative way to find out the height of the pine tree and the distance between the post and the pine tree.

Computer Interface for Creative Thinking

Based on Zheng et al.'s (2008) perceptual-conceptual framework, computer graphics are used to engage learners in learning, a step that attempts to stimulate the limbic system of the brain which controls emotion and feelings. Two features, i.e., cognitive support tools for divergent thinking and cognitive processes, are integrated to enhance creative thinking (Figure 4). The divergent thinking tools are developed to support students' creative thinking. The tools include constructive, contextual, interpretative, and synthetic visualizations. As discussed early, these tools support at different levels creative thinking processes in light of cerebral and limbic functions. The cognitive support tools include voice command, selection, brain-storm, try-it, cognitive prompts/hints, and search. The tools feature the elaborative and deliberate thinking processes and at the same time they facilitate the creative thinking process such as thinking from multiple perspectives.

Figure 3. The problem scenario (© 2018, R. Zheng, used with permission)

Figure 4. Support tools for creative thinking (© 2018, R. Zheng, used with permission)

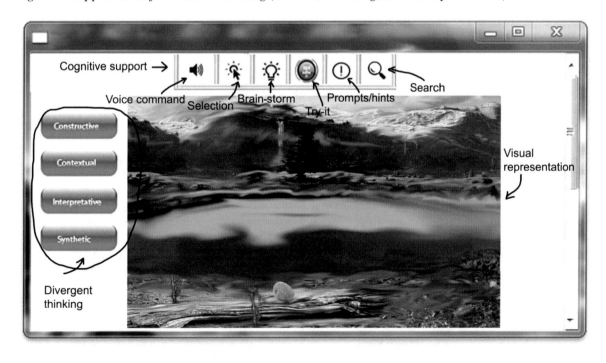

Support for Divergent Thinking

In this example two divergent thinking strategies are employed to assist learners to think creatively. The first is constructive visualization with a purpose of prompting learners to think divergently about the ways to find the solutions. The second is contextual visualization that nurtures creative association through contextual clues.

Constructive Visualization

Constructive visualization enables the learner to think constructively about the solutions (Table 4). As the learner clicks the constructive button, yellow dots appear in the pictures (Figure 5a). These yellow dots provide the mental space for creative imagination and association as he/she explores the solutions. The expectation is that the learner will discover two triangles (see Figure 5b), one being a vertical triangle and the other a horizontal triangle. With the horizontal triangle, the learner is expected to make it a right triangle with other two angles set at 30 and 60 degrees. Then he/she will apply the Pythagorean Theorem to find the perpendicular edge which is the distance between the pine tree and the post. The vertical triangle will be used to find the height of the pine tree with a different method which is discussed in the next section.

Contextual Visualization

To facilitate divergent creative thinking, which in this example requires the learner to use different methods to solve the problem, the contextual visualization is used (Figure 6). By clicking on contextual button, the learner will see two similar triangles, one is a smaller one with white color and the other is a larger one with grey shade. They both share the same angle and parts of the edge of the vertical right triangle. By providing the contextual visualization, the learner will understand the role of small white

Figure 5. Constructive visualization for creative thinking in problem solving (© 2018, R. Zheng, used with permission)

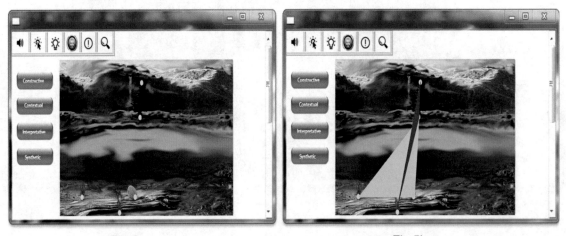

Fig 5a   Fig 5b

right triangle in the context of the larger one. More importantly, the contextual visualization is expected to stimulate the association and helps him/her see that both triangles are actually the same except the difference in sizes. This observation is to help activate the learner's prior knowledge about the ratio in two similar triangles. That is, instead of using the Pythagorean Theorem, the learner can use the ratio method to find out the height of the pine tree.

Cognitive Support

The cognitive support tools are integrated in the computer interface to facilitate the creative thinking process. In this example, several cognitive support tools are integrated in the computer interface to support creative thinking. Let us take a look at the brain-storm tool, which can help with interpretative visualization. Suppose the learner still feels challenged in finding out the solution even after using the constructive and contextual visualization tools. He/she then clicks the brain-storm tool hoping this may open the door to more creative ideas. Figure 7 shows multiple approaches to the solutions. That is, the learner can use ratio, equilateral, and obtuse methods to find the solutions. Evidently, the tool provides more options to the solutions and meantime enables him/her to think the solutions from multiple perspectives.

Discussion

Developing brain-function compatible computer interface can be challenging. It requires a good understanding of human learning, the cognitive processes, the brain functions, and the functions of visual and cognitive tools. In this chapter we present an example that addresses critical issues in computer interface design in relation to creative thinking. The computer interface includes three sets of tools: graphic, cognitive support, and visualization tools. The tools at various stages support the learner's creative and divergent thinking. The constructive and contextual visualization tools promote constructive

Figure 6. Contextual visualization for creative thinking in problem solving (© 2018, R. Zheng, used with permission)

Figure 7. Cognitive support for creative thinking (© 2018, R. Zheng, used with permission)

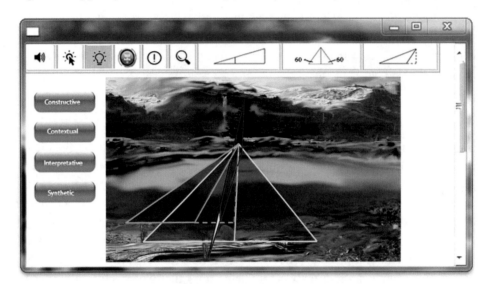

and deliberate divergent thinking. The computer graphic (i.e., the picture for scenario scene) provides visual stimuli for comprehension and exploration. The cognitive tool facilitates the learner's novel thinking and idea generation by exposing him/her to multiple perspectives using the brain-storm option in this example. Overall, the computer interface is designed to align with the functions of the brain as outlined in the framework by Herrmann (1990). The contextual visualization and many of the cognitive tools like brain-storm support the left-cerebral function of the brain such as logical, analytical thinking and fact-based and quantitative processes. The real-world pictures provide a sense of authenticity and engagement, a feature in the computer interface that supports the right cerebral and limbic processes of the brain. In short, the example illuminates the design concepts of a brain-function compatible computer interface that supports creative and divergent thinking in learning. In contrast to the traditional design of computer interface which is primarily utility based, the new concepts proposed in this chapter focus on the cognitive functionality of the computer interface aiming at enhancing the learner's abilities in creativity, originality, imagination and expressiveness.

CONCLUSION

As it was mentioned at the beginning of the chapter, the goal of this chapter is to explore the unique cognitive processes associated with creative thinking and examine the pedagogical role of digital technology in support of creative thinking. To meet this goal, we conducted an extensive literature review to understand the relations between types of divergent thinking and the pedagogy in creative thinking instruction, and the different visualizations and their cognitive functioning, as well as the cognitive and affective functions with respect to brain areas. Informed by the literature and research in brain function, creative thinking, visualization, and creative teaching pedagogy, we presented an example with the purpose of showing, at a conceptual level, how the features of a computer interface design may improve learners' creative thinking and cognitive process of information. The example is limited in demonstrating its support of creative thinking process in that it focuses primarily on well-structured problem solving and deliberate divergent thinking. It fails to illustrate how other types of divergent thinking like spontaneous divergent thinking which is important to the domains of arts and writing, can be nurtured and facilitated with the features of computer interface. Evidently, further research is needed to understand the features of computer interface to support creative thinking. More features, in addition to these introduced in this chapter, need to explore ways to benefit the process of creative thinking and imagination. Creative thinking is considered one of the essential competencies for 21st century learners (National Research Council, 2012). This line of research will certainly contribute to our understanding of how the computer interface may aid creative thinking.

FUTURE RESEARCH

The concepts and ideas including the example proposed in this chapter are still at the conceptual level. More empirical research is needed to test out the concepts to fully understand the impact of the features of the computer interface in terms of their impact on learners' creative thinking, cognitive processes, and their abilities to discover and generate new ideas and concepts. While the example in the current chapter includes some cognitive features in support of creative thinking, they are by no means the exhaustive list. More studies should be conducted to explore other features that may be incorporated in the computer interface design. Finally, studies that examine the relations between the features of computer interface and the brain functions are warranted to further our understanding of how the computer interface, with its cognitive and affective features, may optimize the brain functioning in terms of cognitive learning and creative, divergent thinking.

REFERENCES

Aihara, K., & Hori, K. (1998). Enhancing creativity through reorganizing mental space concealed in a research notes stack. *Knowledge-Based Systems*, *11*(7-8), 469–478. doi:10.1016/S0950-7051(98)00080-X

Birgili, B. (2015). Creative and critical thinking skills in problem-based learning environments. *Journal of Gifted Education and Creativity*, *2*(2), 71–80. doi:10.18200/JGEDC.2015214253

Blake, R., & Sekuler, R. (2006). *Perception* (5th ed.). Boston: McGraw Hill.

Boden, M. A. (1998). Creativity and artificial intelligence. *Artificial Intelligence*, *103*(1-2), 347–356. doi:10.1016/S0004-3702(98)00055-1

Colzato, L. S., Ozturk, A., & Hommel, B. (2012). Meditate to create: The impact of focused-attention and open-monitoring training on convergent and divergent thinking. *Frontiers in Psychology*, *3*. PMID:22529832

DeSchryver, M. (2017). Using the web as a higher order thinking partner: Case study of an advanced learner creatively synthesizing knowledge on the web. *Journal of Educational Computing Research*, *55*(2), 240–271. doi:10.1177/0735633116667356

DeSchryver, M. D., & Yadav, A. (2015). Creative and computational thinking in the context of new literacies: Working with teachers to scaffold complex technology-mediated approaches to teaching and learning. *Journal of Technology and Teacher Education, 23*(3), 411–431.

Doering, A., & Henrickson, J. (2015). Fostering creativity through inquiry and adventure in informal learning environment design. *Journal of Technology and Teacher Education, 23*(3), 387–410.

Donoghue, J. P. (2002). Connecting cortex to machines: Recent advances in brain interfaces. *Nature Neuroscience, 5*(Supp), 1085–1088. doi:10.1038/nn947 PMID:12403992

Flor-Henry, P. (1983). *Cerebral basis of psychopathology.* Boston, MA: John Wright.

Glaveanu, V. P., Sierra, Z., & Tanggaard, L. (2015). Widening our understanding of creative pedagogy: A north-south dialogue. *Education 3-13, 43*(4), 360-370.

Goldschmidt, G. (2016). Linkographic evidence for concurrent divergent and convergent thinking in creative design. *Creativity Research Journal, 28*(2), 115–122. doi:10.1080/10400419.2016.1162497

Graeme, R. (2006). The transformational creativity hypothesis. *New Generation Computing, 24*(3), 241–266. doi:10.1007/BF03037334

Hamza, T. S., & Hassan, D. K. (2016). Consequential creativity: Student competency and lateral thinking incorporation in architectural education. *International Journal of Technology and Design Education, 26*(4), 587–612. doi:10.100710798-015-9321-4

Haroz, S. (2013). *Perception and attention for visualization* (Doctoral dissertation). University of California at Davis, Davis, CA.

Helmick, R. (1984). Enhancing creativity in art and design through stochastically generated computer graphics. *Art Education, 37*(4), 36–39. doi:10.2307/3192746

Herrmann, N. (1990). *The creative brain.* Lake Lure, NC: Brain Books.

Hyerle, D. (1996). *Visual tools for constructing knowledge (ERIC Document Reproduction Service No. ED399257).* Alexandria, VA: Association for Supervision and Curriculum Development.

Kantak, S. S., Stinear, J. W., Buch, E. R., & Cohen, L. G. (2012). Rewiring the brain: Potential role of the premotor cortex in motor control, learning, and recovery of function following brain injury. *Neurorehabilitation and Neural Repair, 26*(3), 282–292. doi:10.1177/1545968311420845 PMID:21926382

Kolb, B., & Whishaw, I. Q. (2009). *Fundamentals of human neuropsychology.* Macmillan.

Lin, C.-S., & Wu, R. Y.-W. (2016). Effects of web-based creative thinking teaching on students' creativity and learning outcome. *EURASIA Journal of Mathematics, Science & Technology Education, 12*(6), 1675–1684.

Lin, M. T.-Y., Wang, J.-S., & Kuo, H.-M. (2017). A study on the effect of virtual reality 3d exploratory education on students' creativity and leadership. *EURASIA Journal of Mathematics, Science & Technology Education, 13*(7), 3151–3161.

Lince, R. (2016). Creative thinking ability to increase student mathematical of junior high school by applying models numbered heads together. *Journal of Education and Practice*, *7*(6), 206–212.

Lindvang, C., & Beck, B. (2015). Problem based learning as a shared musical journey--Group dynamics, communication and creativity. *Journal of Problem Based Learning in Higher Education*, *3*(1), 1–19.

Lopez-Ortega, O. (2013). Computer-assisted creativity: Emulation of cognitive processes on a multi-agent system. *Expert Systems with Applications*, *40*(9), 3459–3470. doi:10.1016/j.eswa.2012.12.054

Lubart, R. (2005). How can computers be partners in the creative process: Classification and commentary on the special issue. *International Journal of Human-Computer Studies*, *63*(4-5), 365–369. doi:10.1016/j.ijhcs.2005.04.002

Merrian-Webster Dictionary. (2018). Retrieved from https://www.merriam-webster.com/dictionary/create

Moffat, D. C., Crombie, W., & Shabalina, O. (2017). Some video games can increase the player's creativity. *International Journal of Game-Based Learning*, *7*(2), 35–46. doi:10.4018/IJGBL.2017040103

National Research Council. (2012). *Education for life and work: Developing transferable knowledge and skills in the 21st century*. Washington, DC: National Academies Press.

Neo, M., & Neo, T.-K. (2013). Exploring students' creativity and design skills through a multimedia project: A constructivist approach in a Malaysian classroom. *Journal of Design and Technology Education*, *18*(3), 48–59.

Oncu, E. C. (2016). Improved creative thinkers in a class: A model of activity based tasks for improving university students' creative thinking abilities. *Educational Research Review*, *11*(8), 517–522. doi:10.5897/ERR2015.2262

Peters, R. A., & Maatman, J. (2017). Long-term trends accentuate the import of creative and critical thinking skills developed by design thinking and ill-defined questions. *Teaching Public Administration*, *35*(2), 190–208. doi:10.1177/0144739416680850

Saputra, Y. H., & Sabana, S. (2016). Building creativity training: Drawing with left hand to stimulate left brain in children age 5-7 years old. *Journal of Education and Practice*, *7*(2), 1–8.

Seechaliao, T. (2017). Instructional strategies to support creativity and innovation in education. *Journal of Education and Learning*, *6*(4), 201–208. doi:10.5539/jel.v6n4p201

Seels, B., & Dunn, J. (1989). A visual literacy walk: Using a natural learning environment. *TechTrends*, *34*(6), 26–29. doi:10.1007/BF02761242

Sehic, S. (2017). The Effect of English Language Learning on Creative Thinking Skills: A Mixed Methods Case Study. *English Language Teaching*, *10*(3), 82–94. doi:10.5539/elt.v10n3p82

Shahin, T. M. (2008). Computerizing conceptual design without hindering creativity. *Computer-Aided Design and Applications*, *5*(1-4), 548–556. doi:10.3722/cadaps.2008.548-556

Smith, E. E., & Kosslyn, S. M. (2007). *Cognitive psychology: Mind and brain* (1st ed.). Upper Saddle River, NJ: Prentice Hall.

Sripongwiwat, S., Bunterm, T., & Srisawat, N. (2016, December). The constructionism and neurocognitive-based teaching model for promoting science learning outcomes and creative thinking. *Asia-Pacific Forum on Science Learning and Teaching, 17*(2), Article 9.

Statham, M. (2014). Change the way your pupils learn by practicing creative thinking and visualization. *Primary Science, 134*, 13–16.

Sweller, J. (1988). Cognitive load during problem solving: Effects on learning. *Cognitive Science, 12*(2), 257–285. doi:10.120715516709cog1202_4

Sweller, J., & Chandler, P. (1991). Evidence of cognitive load theory. *Cognition and Instruction, 8*(4), 351–362. doi:10.12071532690xci0804_5

Tandiseru, S. R. (2015). The effectiveness of local culture-based mathematical heuristic-KR learning towards enhancing student's creative thinking skill. *Journal of Education and Practice, 6*(12), 74–81.

Thompson, T. (2017). Teaching Creativity through Inquiry Science. *Gifted Child Today, 40*(1), 29–42. doi:10.1177/1076217516675863

Tillman, D. A., An, S. A., & Boren, R. L. (2015). Assessment of creativity in arts and STEM integrated pedagogy by pre-service elementary teachers. *Journal of Technology and Teacher Education, 23*(3), 301–327.

Vale, C., Bragg, L. A., Widjaja, W., Herbert, S., & Loong, E. Y.-K. (2017). Children's mathematical reasoning: Opportunities for developing understanding and creative thinking. *Australian Primary Mathematics Classroom, 22*(1), 3–8.

Widiana, I. W., & Jampel, I. N. (2016). Improving students' creative thinking and achievement through the implementation of multiple intelligence approach with mind mapping. *International Journal of Evaluation and Research in Education, 5*(3), 246–254. doi:10.11591/ijere.v5i3.4546

Wolpaw, J. R., Birbaumer, N., Heetderks, W. J., McFarland, W. J., Peckham, P. H., Schalk, G., ... Vaughan, T. M. (2000). Brain-computer interface technology: A review of the first international meeting. *IEEE Transactions on Rehabilitation Engineering, 8*(2), 164–173. doi:10.1109/TRE.2000.847807 PMID:10896178

Zakirova, V. G., & Purik, E. E. (2016). Creative Environment Formation in Design Professional Training. *International Journal of Environmental and Science Education, 11*(9), 2323–2332.

Zheng, R. (2007). Cognitive functionality of multimedia in problem solving. In T. Kidd & H. Song (Eds.), *Handbook of Research on Instructional Systems and Technology* (pp. 230–246). Hershey, PA: Information Science Reference/IGI Global Publishing. doi:10.4018/978-1-59904-865-9.ch017

Zheng, R., Dahl, L., & Flygare, J. (2008). Cognitive perspective on human-computer interface design. In M. Syed & N. Syed (Eds.), *Handbook of Research on Modern Systems Analysis and Design Technologies and Applications* (pp. 320–341). Hershey, PA: Information Science Reference/IGI Global Publishing. doi:10.4018/978-1-59904-887-1.ch020

KEY TERMS AND DEFINITIONS

Constructive Divergent Thinking: This type of divergent thinking is marked by a process in the genesis of knowledge. It is originated from the constructivist educational philosophy that advocates social interaction in learning by taking into account the background and culture of the learner throughout the learning process.

Contextual Visualization: Contextual visualization refers to a visual context in which isolated objectives and images become meaningfully connected. It facilitates deliberate divergent thinking in learning where the learner relates meaningfully the isolated image to the whole image through mental association.

Convergent Thinking: The convergent thinking follows a procedure where a set of logical steps are employed to arrive at one particular solution, often defined as a "correct" solution. It is in contrast to divergent thinking which is characterized by a spontaneous, free-flowing, and "non-linear" manner.

Deliberate Divergent Thinking: It generally refers to the deliberating process in creative thinking. In deliberate divergent thinking ideas are generated in an emergent cognitive fashion guarded by a reflective process. Many possible solutions are explored in a short amount of time, and unexpected connections are drawn. After the process of divergent thinking has been completed, the convergent thinking process is often used to organize and structure the ideas and information.

Spontaneous Divergent Thinking: A term refers to the process of on-going idea generation. Spontaneous divergent thinking occurs in a spontaneous, free-flowing, "non-linear" manner. The emphasis is on developing learners' ability to explore many possible solutions through knowledge association, multiple perspectives, and dimensional thinking.

Synthetic Visualization: Synthetic visualization is one of the visual strategies to help learners synthesize information that are initially indecipherable. This type of visuals usually contains a blotch of random lines and shapes which require the learner to mentally figure out the images, shapes and patterns through synthesizing. Its purpose is to develop human ability to visually synthesize clues from a seemingly random collection of splotches that eventually nurture learners' creativity, imagination, and expressiveness.

Chapter 13
Cognitive Learning Through Knowledge Visualization, Art, and the Geometry of Nature

Jean Constant
Independent Researcher, USA

ABSTRACT

Scientific modeling applied to the study of a mineral structure at the unit level provides a fertile ground from which to extract significant representations. 3D graphics visualization is equal part mathematics, geometry, and design. The geometric structure of 52 minerals was investigated in a specific modeling program to find if meaningful visualization pertaining to the field of art can be extracted from a mathematical and scientific resource. Working with the lines, spheres, and polygons that define crystal at the nanoscale provided the author with an exceptional environment from which to extract coherent visualizations sustainable in the art environment. The results were tested in various interactive platforms and opened a larger debate on cross-pollination between science, humanities, and the arts. Additionally, the experiment provided new ground of investigation for unexpected connections between mathematics, earth sciences, and local cultures.

INTRODUCTION

There is no branch of mathematics, however abstract, which may not some day be applied to phenomena of the real world. - Nikolai Lobachevsky. (G. E. Martin, The Foundations of Geometry, Springer, 1998, p. 225.)

Euclidian and non-Euclidian geometry, algebraic geometry, all share a common thread, defining or describing the space of our physical universe. Geometry, a significant branch of Mathematics, is for many a very abstract world, yet its expression has been with us since antiquity. It can be found in all cultures worldwide and is anchored on a sound observation of nature and the environment.

DOI: 10.4018/978-1-5225-7371-5.ch013

While doing a research on mathematics and visual communication, I stumbled upon that sentence from famous mathematician Nikolai Lobachevsky (1792–1856). I often went back to it when I was getting lost in the abstract reasoning of a world I understood very little as an untrained scientist. Mathematics is a science studying theoretical concepts. Yet, it is the source of many improvements in our daily life as well as the engine of future discoveries. It is also, unfortunately, the source of many frustrations for many, unfamiliar with the abstract world mathematics explores and investigates. Mathematicians are aware of this problem, knowing that, ultimately, the mathematical discourse needs to be grounded in the physical reality we live in, to both validate the researchers' reasoning and be comprehended by all benefiting from this unique effort. Can meaningful art communicate in non-mathematical terms the beauty and significance of this language and participate in a constructive manner in the communication effort of the many mathematicians involved in expending the borders of universal knowledge?

Throughout history, artists have often been fascinated by the mathematical sciences and in particular by the beauty of pure geometry. From antiquity to the Renaissance and today, the art world got inspired and expressed in many forms mathematical concerns of the time, from Albrecht Durer in *"Treatise on Mensuration"* (1538) (Swetz & Katz, 2011), or closer to us, Man Ray in *"Shakespearean Equations"* (Grossman, 2015), to mention but a few. Today, our virtual environment and the multiplication of scientific visualization programs help mathematicians and scientists share with the public the exceptional beauty of the universe they explore. Indeed, a large part of the material coming out of highly specialized research labs is abundantly distributed in scientific and non-scientific venues and on public platforms not necessarily specialized in the promotion of science itself. Today, it is not uncommon to find high qualities images of a sophisticated scientific nature such as the fascinating mathematical imagery on Kleinian group limit sets by Jos Leys (2018) relayed in unexpected but influential public venues such as YouTube or Facebook. A substantial number of mathematically inspired works available in these virtual galleries deal mostly with the exploration of geometrical forms and other topological concerns made available through recent technological development in computer visualization and image-processing techniques. A subject I studied recently, testing and implementing mathematical imagery on 12 distinct mathematical visualization programs (Constant, 2016). Lobachevski's citation was very present in my mind at that time, as often I needed to reconnect the abstract beauty of an ever-expanding hyperbole or a 4th-dimensional design to some more tangible reality. It gave me the impetus to follow on this experiment, explore the mathematical world anew. However, instead of studying pure geometric forms for their intrinsic elegance, I set as a goal to bring geometry back in its true context, the definition of the existing world, and try to obtain an outcome I could enjoy, share with others, and be of benefit to all.

A few years ago, I worked on a project based on the structure, and properties of crystals (Constant, 2013). This rewarding project seemed to have a suitable potential to direct this new project, explore geometry in the physical world, develop mathematically coherent visualizations and likewise, be attractive on the perceptual level. Crystals are identified after a very precise set of mathematical and topological rules developed in the mid-1800s, after the work of J. Hessel (1830), who determined that their morphological forms combine to give exactly 32 kinds of crystal symmetry in Euclidean space. Could a study of the geometry of minerals meet Lobachevsky's expectation, bring together such distinct scientific fields asabstract geometry and geoscience, deliver a meaningful statement and be a gateway for larger humanistic and artistic enrichment?

METHODOLOGY

Symmetry is the common thread that brings close together mathematics, abstract geometry, and geoscience. Minerals are identified and classified in part according to their symmetry. From a broader perspective, the study of symmetry is a substantial component of most knowledge-based activities. Symmetry theory identifies its properties and characteristics after the structure of the physical world. Symmetries of objects fascinated ancient Greeks who believed that their properties would be mirrored in the structure of nature itself. In Euclid's Elements, symmetry is synonymous with commensurable (Keno, 2005).

Johannes Kepler formulated the laws on the motion of planets after an extensive observation of symmetry in nature. Theoretical physicist David Gross (1996) pointed that Newton's laws of mechanics embodied symmetry principles, primarily the principle of equivalence of inertial frames, or Galilean invariance. The concept of symmetry is also central to the study of geometry. In mathematics, symmetry deals with the property of a system that can be applied to a structure. British geometers H. Coxeter & Greitzer (1970, p. 80) defined it as the mapping of a space into another or into itself, so that the distance between any two points in the original space is equivalent to the distance between their reflection in the second space.

Mathematicians and geometers have mapped the principles by which symmetry is specifically defined with descriptors such as reflection, rotation, point symmetries, as well as non-isometric symmetries, scale symmetries, and fractals. Symmetry has been defined in Euclidean geometry as well as other branches of mathematics studying invariance. The recurring commonality between the various mathematical fields investigating symmetry is the axis, or line of symmetry, without which symmetry could not happen.

Minerals are identified after the symmetrical characteristic of their crystal structure. Accordingly, crystals are classified after 7 well-defined systems of 32 crystal classes. A unique three-dimensional geometry defines each crystal family in 219 distinct space group types, 230 if chiral copies are considered as distinct. In mathematics, physics, and chemistry, a space group is the symmetry group of a configuration in space. It follows the classification method used by Russian scientist Evgraf Stepanovich Fedorov (1891) and Hungarian mathematician George Polya (1924) to identify 17 groups of symmetries in two dimensions, later called wallpaper groups, and 230 symmetries in three dimensions.

Art is form and content. In art, visualization can be approached from two separate perspectives: fully intuitive and spontaneous, or deliberate and constructed to meet the requirement of a more reasoned and intellectual approach. The rational and persuasive merit of symmetry in science and art helped me choose the latter approach to be consistent with this undertaking and bring together notions of mathematics, applied sciences, and art. My larger objective was to draw a representative group of visualizations extracted from existing geometry. Minerals, as defined by crystallographers, and according to their unique geometry, were a tempting ground from which to start such experiments. However, more than 3,800 distinct minerals have been recorded thus far and the list is expanding annually of an additional fifty or sixty new entries. More modestly, I made the decision to focus on only 52 minerals, which could represent the expression of a larger common trait defining the mineral universe. Since I was going to carry this project over a year's time, it had the non-trivial advantage of according me seven days to explore thoroughly each mineral's specific geometry. Accordingly, I adjusted my selection to the Hermann-Mauguin (Hermann, 1928; Mauguin, 1931) 32 point groups' notation grid (Figure 1).

Figure 1. Hermann–Mauguin notation in the three-dimensional crystallographic point groups (© 2012, Perditax. Free media repository. Wikimedia Commons. Used with permission)

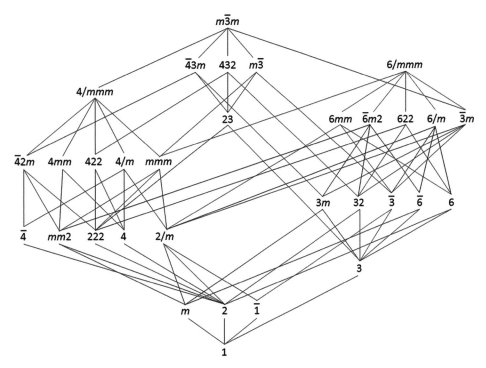

This notation includes all the translational symmetry elements as well as the direction of the symmetry axes. It is also called the international notation, and has become a standard adopted by crystallographers all around the world since 1935. The grid is organized around seven distinct families of three-dimensional geometry: cubic, hexagonal, trigonal, tetragonal, orthorhombic, monoclinic, and triclinic. Choosing this system of classification would alleviate the risk of selecting randomly from a 3,800 items' list, ensure that within each category, I would have sufficient space to determine which particular mineral could help me best articulate my hypothesis, and that each mineral I selected would have a distinct identity that both ties it to the larger geometry group and singularizes its expression according to other factors such as a particular symmetry or a unique structure. This decision had also the merit of keeping mathematics and geoscience together in one visualization project. As Professor Hestenes (2002) pointed out, "Geometric algebra greatly facilitates representation, analysis and application of the groups to molecular modeling and crystallography."

The VESTA Program

After some thorough research, I found a framework that could meet my expectations, handle my computing time requirements, and solve my background material issue. To meet the objective I set forth in the project, I knew I probably would have to change from purely mathematical visualization software to more a appropriate scientific visualization program designed to meet applied sciences expectations, particularly in geoscience, geochemistry, and geology. After testing various programs, I selected the VESTA software to evaluate my proposition.

VESTA is a 3D visualization program used to study structural models, volumetric data, and crystal morphologies. It gives the user the possibility to investigate an unlimited number of objects such as atoms, bonds, polyhedra, and polygons on isosurfaces, and visualize interatomic distances and bond angles. Scientist and researcher Mr. Koichi Momma (2017) of the Japanese National Museum of Nature and Science in Ikabari maintains and update the software regularly. The architecture, structure, and clarity of the software met my expectation as an untrained geoscientist and guaranteed I could extract from the models' meaningful geometry shapes. It also provided me with an opportunity to learn in real time some significant features of this discipline, alter and reconfigure crystal profiles to create new models I could convert into enhanced visualizations.

The RRUFF Library

Nevertheless, a decisive component of the experiment required that, rather than create new geometry in the program VESTA and leave it at that, it would be more profitable to extract existing crystal geometry forms from the program, and later rearrange them in a graphics editor, more suited to the enhanced image-making process. The VESTA program is designed for crystallography analysis based on a specific language and file format. Crystallographers archive and exchange data using a format called CIF (Crystallographic Information File) defined in 1991 by the International Union of Crystallography.

A CIF file is a standard text file that consists of data names and data items constructed hierarchically so as to form self-descriptive data categories. The sorted list of data names, together with their precise definitions, constitutes a CIF Dictionary that covers the fundamental and most commonly used data items relevant to crystal structure analysis. Additional dictionaries compile tags identifying separate data items and the attributes of the associated data. They are used for independent applications within crystallography, such as structures, powder diffraction; electron density; symmetry data and other relevant information (Hermann, 1928).

Following an exhaustive research on various mineral databases, I determined that the library of the Geoscience Department at the University. of Arizona would meet my expectation. The RRUFF library host an extended set of high-quality spectral data from well-known minerals and provides to mineralogists, geoscientists, gemologists an integrated database for the identification of minerals (Lafuente, Downs, Yang, & Stone, 2015). After contacting and getting the support of both JNMNS's K. Momma and RRUFF director R. Down, I set to define the graphics parameters by which I would conduct this experiment and select the material to work from.

Materials and Methods

I established a relatively standard procedure used by a graphics designer to extract and recompose visual information throughout the entire experiment. Hence, I will use the following example to detail the steps I used to complete each visualization throughout the project.

That week, I was investigating a mineral called Zoisite. Among others, I had imported from the RRUFF library a file studying a variant of that family of crystals called Tanzanite (Alvaro, Angel, & Camara, 2012). This mineral was discovered fairly recently, in 1967 in Northern Tanzania, near Mount Kilimanjaro. It has an attractive blue to blue-violet color. It's a variety of Zoisite composed of three elements: silicon (SI), a dark gray with a slight bluish cast iridescent element; aluminum (AI), a gray-white, metallic luster element; and carbon (C) a gray-to-black, opaque, nonmetallic element. Tanzanite belongs to the orthorhombic crystal system. It is di-pyramidal and its space group or symmetry is of order Pnma (Tanzanite. Hudson Institute of Mineralogy).

In three-dimensional Crystal geometry, the orthorhombic system distinguishes itself by three axes, which meet at 90 degrees to each other. However, all the axes are of various lengths (*Tanzanite*, Hudson Institute of Mineralogy). These space groups are all characterized by the presence of twofold rotation or two-one screw axes parallel to each unit cell's direction. The Tanzanite belongs to the Pnma group and is centrosymmetric, with 8 points of inversion per unit cell (Orthorhombic-crystal-system. Earth Sciences Museum, University of Waterloo, Ontario, CND). The CIF description file that Alvaro, Angel and Camara (2012) made available on the RRUFF electronic library converted into a splendid model in the Vesta program. It displayed a cohesive, well-balanced structure, and a very dynamic symmetry.

The program VESTA allows to alter the model configuration, change the crystal properties, its boundaries and orientation. or the unit cell structure and volumetric data. The Tanzanite crystal I imported was composed of 176 bonds, 32 polyhedra, 124 atoms, and of course, a Pnma symmetry, as it is a defining element of this family of minerals (Orthorhombic Space Groups. School of Crystallography, Birkbeck College, University of London). This front view iteration of the Tanzanite CIF profile shows some of the most distinct characteristics of the crystal (Figure 2).

I found some promising features in the symmetry of the wireframe, the solidness of its structure and the positioning of the silicon atoms. I exported in my 2D graphics editor several separate views as independent layers to rearrange and combine as a final statement.

Figure 2. Tanzanite unit cell profile: a) bonds, b) polyhedra, c) atoms. (© 2018, J, Constant, used with permission)

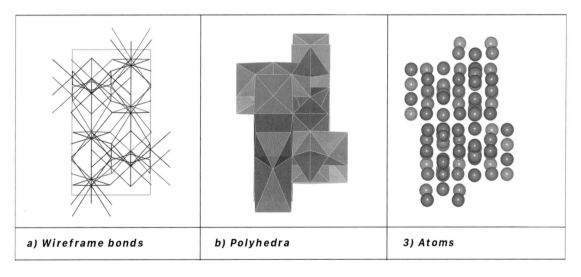

| a) **Wireframe bonds** | b) **Polyhedra** | 3) **Atoms** |

2D Conversion

Space

I intended to share the final product and make it accessible on flat screens, print, or canvas to encourage the audience feedback and interaction. Transferring a 3 D model to a flat two-dimensional surface requires a reassessment of the geometry by which the shapes are defined and a new calculation of the lines angles, depending on the effect sought after.

The orthographic method, commonly used in engineering, produces objects that communicate dimensions unambiguously, as each line of one-unit length appears to have the same length everywhere on the drawing. It wasn't suitable for my purpose

The perspective method instead, contains information on size and distance whereas, in the orthographic view, all objects appear at the same scale. Perspective drawing, made famous in the Western culture during the Renaissance by architects Brunelleschi and Alberti (Wright, 1984) has been used extensively in architecture and two-dimensional art from Monet, Sergeant, and even Russian suprematist K. Malevich (Rynne, 2006).

Most computer modeling software favor the isometric approach to prepare designs for display on a flat surface. In isometric projection, the angles between the projection of the axes are equal. The isometric axes can be placed in any desired location and in a way that the object will be in the position that best describes it. However, the angle between the projections of axes must always be 120° (Pantone, 2018a).

I tasked the program VESTA to calculate the model angles according to a flat 2D representation of a 3D projection where distances measured along an isometric axis are correct and to scale, exported the results as single TIFF layers and started to work on the visual and perceptual aspect of the project.

Shapes

Initially, I started the transformation from a scientific model into a visual statement by working on a grayscale monochrome image. Hue, Chroma, and Brightness define color. Color variation can be infinite. Computer screens today easily display color depths in thousands or millions of simultaneous colors. The well-known Pantone matching system has a system of 1,867 spot colors to use in printing [Pantone, 2018b]. Color interferes significantly with the creative process and the decision-making modus operandi.

Using a monochrome palette has been a common art studio practice known already in the early middle ages. Its goal is to reduce the painting to its simplest form so that the artmaking process prioritizes the purely physical elements of a shape or a collection of various shapes on a canvas. Separating Light from Hue and Chroma for surfaces allows for what programmers and coders refer to as a binary decision process while the polychromatic process or senary process requires a much more complex method of evaluation. Da Vinci (Zöllner, 2000), Goya (Ward, 2008)., or later Picasso (Giménez, 2012) eventually explored at length the dynamic and depth of this technique to create meaningful visual statements. I resized and positioned the shapes until I found a robust and persuasive positioning.

Color

I went back to the Vesta modeling program and imported the color profile of each element I had selected to start adding color to my 2D visualization. In chemistry, colors are attributed according to the chemical profile of the elements composing the crystal structure.

CPK coloring, named after its initial designers: Corey, Pauling, and Koltun, is intended to distinguishing atoms and their individual chemical elements in molecular models (Corey & Pauling, 1953). This scheme is based on a system developed by Robert and Linus Pauling at Caltech in the late 1940s and early 1950s (*Changing Colors and Display Formats.* Center for Biomolecular Modeling, 2018) and has been later made more performing in the computer environment with the addition of two scripts, Jmol and RasMol (Molecular Graphics Visualization Tool, *RasMol and OpenRasMol*, 2009) two free, open source molecule viewers that define color in the RGB and hexadecimal format.

As we recall, the three elements that define a Tanzanite are silicon, aluminum, and carbon. Accordingly, the model displayed an arrangement of blue (SI), red (O), and grey-blue (CA) atoms and the lattices of the polyhedral structure acting as a transparent film, which reflected the color of the central atom.

I first concentrated on the dynamic of the symmetry of the atoms anchored around the few strong blue colored silicon atom (SI) and added some texture to the red aluminum ones (O) to decrease the intensity of the bright primary. Still, for reference and also to reinforce the design's dynamic, I positioned a single, fully formed red sphere out of the structure, on the upper left side of the composition. The symmetry pattern and lines of the binding had a striking stain glass window look that I preserved and enhanced by converting its shape into a metallic or lead-like frame, as most such windows are distinguished by. It also inspired me to move the polyhedral structure behind it and blur its original definition to add an extra perceptual element to the composition.

Last, prompted by the element of transparency and reflection inherent propriety of most minerals, I added between the polyhedra and the binding pattern a gradient strip yellow to purple enhance the dynamic of the window-like effect. I composed my center theme as two half panels, a design stratagem that subconsciously invites the eye to question and compare the two sets of tiling and reconcile the symmetry progression. Likewise, it makes the narrative visually more engaging. I added the background last as an abstract framework that would reunite the separate part into a single unified statement. It stands as both a reminder of the geometrical aspect of the content and a signal of order, repetition, and stability. I test printed the image several times to ensure the light, shadow, and color balance effect I was capturing on a backlit screen would reproduce correctly on a printed surface.

RESULTS

The results went beyond my expectation. From a designer's perspective, the geometry of the shapes retained key information on the identity of the crystal, its atoms' structure, and its unique Pnma symmetry signature, while the careful coloring captured the essence of the mineral, its glow, warm tones and indistinct strikes of deep blue and red overtone one can recognize in nature (Figure 3).

Public feedback was the last but essential element of the project to validate my hypothesis. Over-forty positive responses I collected from the various websites I posted this particular image on confirmed my first impression.

Figure 3. Jean Constant, Merelani window; graphical interpretation of a Tanzanite crystal's geometry (© 2017, J. Constant, used with permission)

Statistics

No real or accurate metric can determine whether visualization qualifies as an artwork or not. However, popularity, as imperfect as it might be, is one of the criteria that constitute the definition of an artwork inasmuch that it communicates a statement, and the statement is understood and appreciated by the viewer.

The length of the project precluded I restricted testing to the academic world or a group of students for such an extended period. Instead, I decided to release publically each artwork on a daily basis, as soon as I had completed it. I created a generic website on the platform WordPress to post and track my progress (Constant, 2017).

Additionally, to reach a larger audience, I posted each week on various other sites the first visualization of the mineral I was going to review for that week. I segmented my field of intervention into three distinct categories and according to the specific profile of each platform: one knowledgeable in mathematics and applied science on a Facebook private group, one knowledgeable in visual imagery on Instagram and on a gallery site, one general audience who would be the random element in my testing on Twitter and my own Facebook timeline.

Testing, when not done in a lab or a controlled environment, needs to allow for some level of flexibility in defining expectations and intended results. Moreover, I could not select the audience with which I was going to interact. However, the platform I selected were each built around specific and distinct groups of users and followers. I surmised it would benefit the scope of my survey.

I modeled my statistic framework after the University of Pennsylvania Statistics Department's guidelines and an approach called Hypothesis testing (PennState Eberly College of Science, (2017), The Pennsylvania State University). This form of testing can be traced back to mathematician P. S. La-place in the 1800s. It's based on the P-value or the Critical value approach. The critical value approach involves determining "likely" or "unlikely", and by assessing whether the observed test statistic is more noticeable than would be expected if the null hypothesis were true. Most interactive platforms have a basic statistical apparatus that allows users to monitor the number of visits, regular followers, and potential comments that could operate as tentative metrics for this survey. I established a simple system of evaluation by which null would be no response, up to 10 positive responses would be average, 10 to 20 – good, 20 and above – excellent. The survey ran January to December 2017. I collected a substantial amount of information that not only responded to my expectations but also brought to light additional positive aspects of this experiment.

Figure 4. The WordPress statistic report, January– December 2017 (© 2017, J. Constant, used with permission)

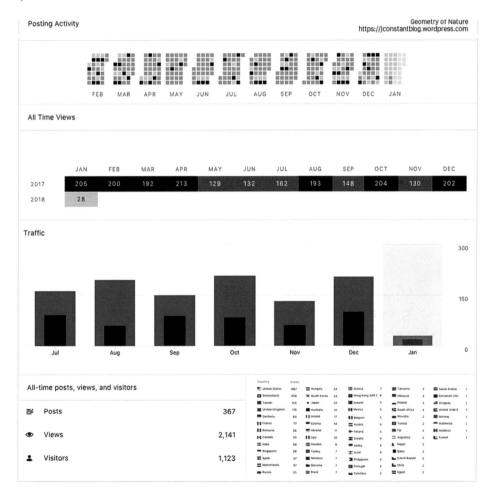

2,141 individuals visited the generic WordPress site (Figure 4). It went well beyond my expectations, considering I made no effort to advertise or promote it. 23 individuals registered as "followers", meaning they were informed in real time of my daily updates. Similarly, 48 followers registered on Instagram. I had an average of 100 visitors per months on each platform. Throughout the year, I only received one negative comment from an individual who liked the image but was dismayed by the complexity of the message. All other commentaries were positive, one-third relating to technical points and processes and two-thirds purely subjective and perceptual. Interestingly while most of the responses originated from the US (667), the sites collected a substantial amount of visitors from Europe (582), Asia (327) and various other countries in South America and worldwide.

Each post contained an image and a short text highlighting relevant facts about the particular crystal inspiring the work, its original location, the salient part of its geometry and the source file I started from. That so many that may or may not have been familiar with the English language came to visit the site regularly and check the visualizations was an unanticipated but welcome information reinforcing the narrative that sustained this project.

Going into the details of the results would be beyond the scope of this article, but the large picture demonstrates in no uncertain terms that the work was of interest to many, independently of their cultural and educational background, and attracted comments validating part of what constitutes an objective definition of an artwork: the positive reception of a visual message based on objective scientific data.

DISCUSSION AND CONCLUSION

I was unable to assess if similar projects had been conducted for such an extended period and including such a large quantity of material. It is undeniable, as the various reports and statistics returned from the sites I posted the images demonstrate that the project provided a positive response to my initial question bring together distinct scientific fields as abstract geometry and geoscience, deliver a meaningful statement and be a gateway for larger humanistic and artistic enrichment.

The digital graphics environment today has reached such an extended level of complexity that numerous studies are conducted every day in scientific, engineering or design, and they modulate their research according to specifics of their discipline. However, further collaboration and cross-pollination between fields of expertise may bring richer and more compelling results.

My main handicap in this research was the limited resources I had, both technically and in relation to time. Practically, I could only allocate a maximum of two hours a day to the completion of each artwork. Sometimes it served me well. In the design environment, one needs to know when to stop. Sometimes I felt some images could have used additional attention. I eventually succeeded in completing most, if I could find additional time-resource throughout the day. Through it all, it is a testimony to the quality of the software and resource I used that I could concentrate on the visual challenge before me, rather than having to address complex scientific or technical issues that would have distracted me from my primary task.

Lobachevsky vision of mathematics inspired me to implement this project. It helped me discover the amazingly diverse geometry of the mineral world and share it with a supportive audience. In technical terms, this work may not have a deep significance for the mathematical or geoscience universe, but as I found later, it contributes in tangible terms to the concern of other disciplines such as neuroscience and the comprehending of perception, philosophy, as a reflection on the nature of reality, and how can art have a more direct participation in the public conversation.

Surprisingly, I often found an unanticipated but uncanny relationship between specific minerals' geometry and local cultures. Noteworthy or not, similarities such as this sustained the research direction of ethno-mathematician Dr. Paulus Gerdes, and in broader terms, relates to his extensive work on geometry and cultural traditions in Southern Africa Gerdes, 1998, 1999). Further studies may be required to validate such intriguing proposition, (Figure 5) but mutual collaboration combining the efforts of experts in the field of science, geoscience and art historians would not only preserve the integrity of such research but lead to new conversation and possibly unforeseen conclusion.

I also found, through several commentaries sent to me that the project had an educational component inasmuch that many, not initially drawn to obscure and challenging disciplines were discovering in a less rigorous manifestation of the scientific world, elements of motivation that were encouraging them to investigate further the many aspects of science and the richness of its expression.

History is replete with examples of scientists being inspired by art under its many forms, visually and other. To name a few, Simon Lake, known as the father of the modern submarine apparently had been captivated by the idea of undersea travel and exploration ever since he read Jules Verne's Twenty Thousand Leagues Under the Sea in 1870, or Igor Sikorsky, the inventor of the modern helicopter, was inspired by another of Verne book, Clipper of the Clouds, which he had read as a young boy.

The conclusive outcome of this project is an invitation for others to continue and expand such close and fruitful collaboration, enhance the quality of each other's finding and possibly inspire more to join this captivating journey of discovery.

Figure 5. (a) 10-07 Rutile #7. Geometry of a rutile crystal from the Gauteng area, South Africa Traditional African pattern; (b). 08-27 Kornerupine #1. Geometry of a kornerupine, first discovered in Greenland in the late 1800s; Kalaallit beaded collar from the early 1900s, West Greenland (© 2018, J. Constant, used with permission)

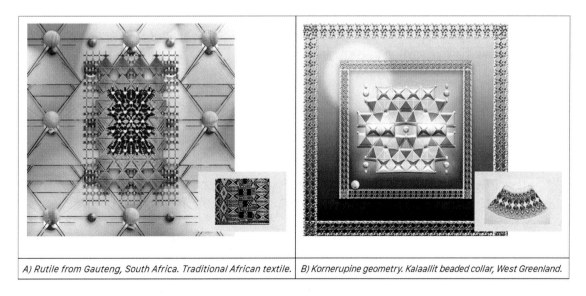

| A) Rutile from Gauteng, South Africa. Traditional African textile. | B) Kornerupine geometry. Kalaallit beaded collar, West Greenland. |

ACKNOWLEDGMENT

This work could not have been done without the invaluable help, advice, and support of the following: R. Downs and the UofA Geoscience department library, Hubert Heldner, Albertine Gentoux, Noreen Masaki, Koichi Momma and the VESTA team, the many engineers and programmers of WorldPress, FaceBook, and Twitter who make communication so pervasive, and the many followers and participants to this experiment I won't name here but thank warmly for their continuing interest and support.

REFERENCES

Alvaro, M., Angel, R. J., & Camara, F. (2012). High-pressure behavior of zoisite. *The American Mineralogist, 97*(7), 1165–1176. doi:10.2138/am.2012.4014

Constant, J. (2013). Symmetry in Mathematics, Physics and Art. *Journal of Symmetry: Culture and Science, 24*(1-4), 57-68.

Constant, J. (2016). *The 12-30 Project*. BLb publishers. Retrieved from https://jcdigitaljournal.wordpress.com/

Constant, J. (2018). *Geometry of Nature*. Retrieved from https://jconstantblog.wordpress.com/

Corey, R., & Pauling, L. (1953). Molecular Models of Amino Acids, Peptides, and Proteins. *The Review of Scientific Instruments, 24*(8), 621–627. doi:10.1063/1.1770803

Coxeter, H. S. M., & Greitzer, S. L. (1970). *Geometry Revisited*. Washington, DC: Math. Assoc. Amer.

Fedorov, E. (1891). Symmetry in the plane. *Proceedings of the Imperial St. Petersburg Mineralogical Society*.

Gerdes, P. (1998). *Women, Art and Geometry in Southern Africa*. Lawrenceville, NJ: Africa World Press.

Gerdes, P. (1999). *Geometry from Africa. In Mathematical and Educational Explorations*. Washington, DC: The Mathematical Association of America.

Giménez, C. (2012). *Picasso Black and White*. Prestel.

Gross, D. (1996). The role of symmetry in fundamental physics. *Proceedings of the NSA, 93*(25). 10.1073/pnas.93.25.14256

Grossman, W. (2015). *Man Ray: Human Equations*. Hatje Cantz.

Hall, S., Allen, F. H., & Brown, I. (1991). The Crystallographic Information File (CIF): A New Standard Archive File for Crystallography. *Acta Crystallographica. Section A, Foundations of Crystallography, 47*(6), 655–685. doi:10.1107/S010876739101067X

Hermann, C. (1928). Zur systematischen Strukturtheorie. *Zeitschrift fur Kristallographie, 68*, 257–287.

Hessel, J. F. C. (1830). *Krystallometrie oder Krystallonomie und Krystallographie* (Vol. 5). Gehler's Physikalisches Wörterbuch.

Hestenes, D. (2002). *Point Groups and Space Groups in Geometric Algebra*. Tempe, AZ: Department of Physics and Astronomy Arizona State University. doi:10.1007/978-1-4612-0089-5_1

Keno, L. (2005). Reflection on the concept of symmetry. *European Review, 13*(S2).

Lafuente, B., Downs, R. T., Yang, H., & Stone, N. (2015). The power of databases: the RRUFF project. In T. Armbruster & R. M. Danisi (Eds.), *Highlights in Mineralogical Crystallography* (pp. 1–30). Berlin: De Gruyter. doi:10.1515/9783110417104-003

Leys, J. (2018). *Mathematical Imagery*. Retrieved from http://www.josleys.com/

Malevich, K. (1913). *Samovar*. The Museum of Modern Art.

Mauguin, Ch. (1931). Sur le symbolisme des groupes de repetition ou de symetrie des assemblages cristallins. *Zeitschrift fur Kristallographie, 76*, 542–558.

Momma, K. (2017). *The VESTA program*. Japanese National Museum of Nature and Science.

Pantone. (2018a). *Pantone Numbering system*. Pantone Color Institute.

Pantone. (2018b). *Pantone matching system*. Author.

Pólya, G. (1924). Über die Analogie der Kristallsymmetrie in der Ebene. *Zeitschrift fur Kristallographie*.

Rynne, A. (2006). *Axonometric Projection*. University of Limerick, Department of Manufacturing and Operations Engineering.

Swetz, F. J., & Katz, V. J. (2011, January). Mathematical Treasures - Albrecht Durer's Treatise on Mensuration. *Convergence*.

Ward, G. W. R. (Ed.). (2008). *The Grove Encyclopedia of Materials and Techniques in Art*. Oxford University Press.

Wright, D. R. E. (1984). Alberti's De Pictura: Its Literary Structure and Purpose. *Journal of the Warburg and Courtauld Institutes, 47*, 52–71. doi:10.2307/751438

KEY TERMS AND DEFINITIONS

Chiral: Chiral is a term applied to molecular systems whose asymmetry results in the existence of a pair of non-superimposable mirror-image shapes. First used by W. H. Thompson in 1884, this term is associated with the breaking of symmetry.

Chroma: Hue, value, and chroma define a color. Chroma is the perceived degree of visual difference from a neutral grey of the same lightness. It is calculated by the brightness and luminance of the pigment.

Crystal: A crystal is a solid material where the component atoms are arranged in a definite stable pattern. Its surface regularity reflects its internal symmetry regardless of its size.

Geometry: Geometry is a branch of mathematics that focuses on the properties and relation of points, line and surfaces to computes areas and volumes. Remarkably, plane elliptic or hyperbolic geometry builds models with no parallels to a given line through a given point. Lobachevsky reached the conclusion that in the geometry of a spherical surface on which antipodal points are identified, all lines expand as circles.

Geoscience: Geoscience is a wide concept that relates to many fields of science studying the physical components of the environment such as geology or geochemistry and the study of the atmosphere, hydrosphere, and biosphere.

Mathematics: Mathematics can tentatively be defined as the science of structure and order relying on repeatable proof. It has evolved from elemental practices of counting to the study of form, quantity, space and the investigation of more abstract concepts including game theory, statistic, optimization, and non-Euclidian, hyperbolic geometry.

Mineral: A mineral is as a naturally occurring homogeneous solid with a definite chemical composition and a highly ordered atomic arrangement. All have an inorganic substance and a regular internal structure. Over 5,000 unique mineral species have already been recorded following that strict identification template.

Symmetry: In mathematics, symmetry is the mapping of an object onto itself that preserves its initial structure. In physics, the concept that the properties of particles such as atoms and molecules remain unchanged when subjected to a variety of symmetry transformations. In crystallography, symmetry reflects on the fundamental property of the orderly arrangements of atoms found in crystalline solids.

Topology: Topology is the study of mathematical spaces and geometric configurations that stem from their shape independently from their deformation. Arguably, many mention Leonard Euler's "Seven Bridges of Konigsberg Problem" as among the first topological theorems.

Wallpaper: In mathematics, a wallpaper group relates to the symmetrical repetition of a pattern and refers to any of the17 possible plane symmetry groups. The groups are commonly represented by Hermann-Mauguin-like symbols, named after the scientists who first identified and classified all the possible wallpaper group arrangements on a two-dimensional surface.

Chapter 14
Augmented Reality in Informal Learning Environments:
A Music History Exhibition

José Duarte Cardoso Gomes
Universidade do Algarve, Portugal

Mauro Jorge Guerreiro Figueiredo
Universidade do Algarve, Portugal

Lúcia da Graça Cruz Domingues Amante
Universidade Aberta, Portugal

Cristina Maria Cardoso Gomes
Universidade do Algarve, Portugal

ABSTRACT

Augmented reality (AR) allows computer-generated imagery information overlays onto a live real-world environment in real time. Technological advances in mobile computing devices (MCD) such as smartphones and tablets (internet access, built-in cameras and GPS) made a greater number of AR applications available. This chapter presents the Augmented Reality Musical Gallery (ARMG) exhibition, enhanced by AR. ARMG, focused on twentieth century music history, and aimed at the students from the 2nd Cycle of basic education in Portuguese public schools. In this chapter, the authors introduce AR technology and address topics like constructivism, art education, student motivation, and informal learning environments. They conclude by presenting the first two parts of the ongoing research conducted among a sample group of students contemplating the experiment in an educational context.

DOI: 10.4018/978-1-5225-7371-5.ch014

INTRODUCTION

New and innovative technologies continue to modify every aspect of home, life and work: the way we communicate, learn, and socialize. Computer technologies are changing the ways we think and make sense of our world (Collins & Halverson, 2009).

While educators may legitimately debate strategies and methods of education, all agree that participation in the world of the 21st century will demand technology competence. Technology is essential in teaching, communications, mathematics and science, and it is no less important in the arts. Technology is an important tool that can improve the educational system, but the challenge of integrating technology into the delivery of educational content remains. Digital technologies, in all areas, can enhance student achievement by addressing introductory and advanced skills, assessment of student progress and student motivation (Assey, 1999).

Presently, Information Technology (IT) has become a ubiquitous component of undergraduate education. The use of computers and mobile computing devices (MCD) in educational context are commonplace in terms of usefulness and acceptance over the past few years – technology has found its place inside and outside the classroom for academic purposes (Sandler, 2010). These MCDs have increased processing power and usability, and are accessible on a large scale, which has significantly contributed to their ease of use and at implementing innovative educational processes in numerous educational institutions and universities (Figueiredo, Gomes, Gomes, & Lopes, 2014).

Augmented Reality (AR) is a technology that combines real-world objects and digital information in real-time. AR, according to Azuma (1997), is a system that features three main characteristics: First, it combines the real and the virtual world; second, allows interaction, and third, it incorporates the possibility of visualizing three-dimensional (3D) digital objects. Early AR experiments date back to the late 1960's and to Ivan Sutherland's work. At present, AR is widely available through mobile computing devices such as smartphones and tablets. According to the 2012 Horizon Report, AR was identified as "an emerging technology with high relevance for teaching and learning and predicted to have a large adoption by 2015 (NMC Horizon Report: 2012 higher education edition, 2012).

Constructivist pedagogical approaches are inherent in most performance-based music courses. Students can apply new knowledge and receive synchronous feedback from teachers. However, knowledge-based courses such as music appreciation, theory, and music history have historically relied on direct instruction and the lecture-model. Technology offers new opportunities to bring constructivist pedagogy to knowledge-based music courses, adding the possibility of autonomous exploration of interactive multimedia content (Keast, 2009) into the teaching-learning process in music history.

This paper introduces the concept and development of the Augmented Reality Musical Gallery (ARMG), focusing an audience of 2nd Cycle of basic education students at Portuguese public schools. ARMG is an interactive exhibition that aims to provide a constructivist pedagogical approach to the music history teaching-learning process and to promote AR technology as a means to deliver educational multimedia content to young students in an informal learning environment. The ultimate exhibition goals are to enhance student motivation towards music history learning and to improve their educational outcomes in music classes.

This paper's organization is the following: Section II introduces how AR technology is used for educational purposes and its major affordances. Section III introduces the concept of the constructivist pedagogic model and the topics of art, motivation and informal learning environments. Section IV describes the concept and development of the ARMG. Section V presents the first and the second part of the ongoing research conducted among students, focusing their experience with the exhibition. The study hereby presented surveys the current usage of mobile computing devices by the target-audience and user perception concerning the usability of the AR prototypes. Section VI presents conclusions and further work possibilities.

AUGMENTED REALITY

The first AR prototypes appeared in the late 1960's as a result from Ivan Sutherland´s and his students work in the Harvard and Utah Universities. AR is a variation of the Virtual Environments, also known as Virtual Worlds or Virtual Reality (VR).

Augmented Reality (AR) is a technology that allows computer-generated virtual imagery information to be overlaid onto a live direct or indirect real-world environment in real-time. AR differs from virtual reality (VR) in that VR user experience a computer-generated virtual environment, whereas in AR, the environment is real, but extended with information and imagery from the system (Lee, 2012). AR is also defined as a technique that allows interacting and visualizing virtual graphics on top of the real-world view (Jaramillo, Quiroz, Cartagena, Vivares, & Branch, 2010). Milgram's continuum (Milgram & Kishino, 1994) proposes that AR is a mixed reality environment, with one part belonging to the real-world, and other purely virtual. However, the real environment predominates (Figure 1).

This mixed-reality environment presents large possibilities for human-computer interaction (HCI) and it has been used in different areas, namely medicine, architecture, education, training, military, astronomy, chemistry, biology, mathematics, geometry, amongst many others.

AR can contain various functions, namely, interaction or display. A good example of this can be a museum, where the visitor uses a given application to scan a bar code on the base of a statue and the application shows a picture of the statue with a fully interactive description (Ward, 2012). In comparison to virtual reality, aimed to immerse the user in a synthetic environment, AR supplements the user perception of the real world by adding computer-generated content registered to real-world locations. A significant part of the AR environment consists of real-world objects, for which it is not necessary to create detailed 3-D models, while offering a high level of reality (Wojciechowski & Cellary, 2013).

The field of learning and training, both in academic and corporate settings, has seen in the last few decades a growing interest by researchers focusing on the potential of AR to enhance the learning and training efficiency of students and employees. Concerning the educational uses of AR in school contexts, AR has not been much adopted into academic settings due to the insufficient funding by the government and lack of awareness regarding the needs for AR in academic settings (Lee, 2012) and this is particularly true in Portugal regarding the academic environment of basic education.

Figure 1. José Duarte Cardoso Gomes, Simplified representation of a "virtuality continuum" (© 2018, J. D. C. Gomes, used with permission)

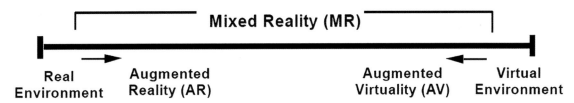

Augmented Reality has been subject to a vast number of studies in the educational field focusing areas as:

- Science (Kerawalla, Luckin, Seljeflot, & Woolard, 2006; Veloso, 2011; Wojciechowski & Cellary, 2013; Wu, Lee, Chang, & Liang, 2013)
- Geometry (Figueiredo, 2007), mathematics (Figueiredo, Amado, Bidarra, & Carreira, 2015; Noval, 2013; Salinas, González-Mendívil, Quintero, Ríos, Ramírez, & Morales, 2013; Sommerauer & Müller, 2014)
- Electromagnetism/electricity (Ibanez, Di-Serio, Villaran-Molina, & Delgado-Kloos, 2015; Ibáñez, Di Serio, Villarán, & Kloos, 2014), and
- Music (Corrêa, Lima, Melo, & Santos, 2012; Zorzal, Buccioli, & Kirner, 2005).

Although AR technology is not new, its potential in education is only commencing to be explored; some examples are stated below:

- Woods et al., 2004 (in Pérez-López & Contero, 2013), enumerated benefits driven by AR technology, such as improvement of the interpretation of spatial, temporal and contextual content.
- Freitas and Campos, 2008 (in Pérez-López & Contero, 2013) have confirmed that AR enhances student learning.
- Seo, Kim and Kim, 2006 (in Pérez-López & Contero, 2013) state that a number of authors have suggested that AR technology improves kinesthetic learning because students interact directly with the educational material, associating the content with body movements and sensations.
- Lin, Hsieh, Wang, Sie, and Chang. 2011 (in Pérez-López & Contero, 2013) used AR and a touch-screen to enhance the educational resources about fish conservation in Taiwan and their results were focused on system usability.
- Ibáñez, Delgado, Leony, García, and Maroto, 2011 (in Pérez-López & Contero, 2013), developed a multi-user AR platform for learning Spanish as a second language. Results showed that AR has a positive effect on student motivation and improves the language learning process.
- Connolly, Stansfield, and Hainey, 2011 (in Pérez-López & Contero, 2013) developed an AR game for learning English to study how motivation could be improved through collaborative methods.

Overall, all of the above research studies evaluated system usability and student's results in order to show improvement in learning processes (Pérez-López & Contero, 2013).

Other studies reported a number of AR affordances for education, such as ways to:

- Commute between the real and virtual world (Billinghurst, 2002)
- Develop specific learning applications (Zorzal et al., 2005)
- Support formal and informal learning (Cruz-Cunh, Reis, Peres, Varajão, Bessa, Magalhães, ... & Barreira,, 2010)
- Develop hybrid learning environments, by combining physical and virtual objects (Dunleavy, Dede, & Mitchell, 2009)
- Transform printed materials into sources of multimedia information (Kesim & Ozarslan, 2012) and
- Act as a novel form to interact and manipulate learning resources (Wu et al., 2013).

THE ARMG: A CONSTRUCTIVIST APPROACH

Constructivism is an ideological movement based on the paradigm of progressive knowledge, and read as a construct in constant development that never can be finite. Supports the idea that individuals are born with a set of neurophysiological predispositions to the logical-deductive reasoning that need work over a lifetime to be able to develop. Constructivism is a system that allows the reinterpretation of reality, depicted by Jean Piaget's cognitive ontogenetic development process, regarding the socialization of the child, either by individuality as by personality. In this perspective, the interactions between the subject and the environment continuously originate new levels of knowledge. In education, constructivism drifts from Jean Piaget's genetic theory and from ideas born at the school of Geneva, anchoring in meaningful learning concepts, in previous organizers and assimilation theories (Ausubel, 2012).

Piaget was particularly interested in the origin and evolution of intelligence from individual cognitive construction. In this perspective, knowledge is acquired through the action of the subject of learning. The author posits that the child establishes early relations of interaction with the environment and will build knowledge based on experience; the process occurs in a phased manner with the steps or stages well demarcated, with an origin and a development. The first phase of this process encompass, from the age of 6-7 years the mental representation of movements and images, giving way to elementary logic structures and formal logic, until it reaches the adult thought.

Piaget recognized that education could not succeed without recognizing, using and extending the "authentic" activity with which a child is "endowed." Piaget was an early adopter of the constructivist pedagogy, and in this view of learning, the meaning that is constructed by an individual is dependent on the situation itself, the individual's purposes and active construction of meaning. Constructivism also recognizes that prior experiences and knowledge influence perception and interpretation (Jain, Tedman, & Tedman, 2007).

The theory of constructivism stems from the field of cognitive science, particularly of the works of Jean Piaget, Lev Vygotsky, Jerome Bruner, Howard Gardner, and Nelson Goodman, and describes the construction of knowledge through learning as a process of active meaning construction in relation to the environment in which the learning takes place (Nunes & McPherson, 2007). The most important feature of constructivism resides in focusing activities and environments, rather than learning objects. The constructivist approach effectively motivates students, allowing active learning processes, based on exploration and interaction. This means that students build their own knowledge (Tomei, 2009).

ARMG aims to deliver a constructivist-learning environment by providing students an experience where the following characteristics are present and valued, namely:

- The role of previous knowledge;
- The role of context and concrete learning experience;
- The interactive and cooperative character of learning;
- The importance of the concept change that must occur to deliver effective learning;
- The new roles assumed by teachers and students; the importance on the reflection of the students over the undertaken process: It's this reflection that will empower the competence to "learn to learn" (Lebrun, 2002).

Gardner's Multiple Intelligence Theory (MIT) arises from the dissatisfaction of the inequities of traditional intelligence tests in the early 1980's. Gardner pointed eight aptitudes that define the human mental range: linguistic intelligence, interpersonal intelligence, intrapersonal intelligence, logical-mathematical intelligence, musical intelligence and a body-kinesthetic intelligence that met a series of criteria he called "signs". Later, in the mid 1990s, Gardner included a new type of human aptitude, the naturalist intelligence (Eberle, 2011).

MIT provided a new platform for conceptualizing how students learn and understand content. However, few teachers use instructional strategies designed to employ multiple intelligence-based format. The most frequent teaching pedagogy is framed in expository, direct instruction. Additional research on the value of arts for influencing learning and teaching is currently being reported in the professional literature. The work of Gazzaniga (2008) suggests that the arts provide benefits for improving motivation, attention and cognition. Among his findings, there is preliminary evidence that the exploration in the arts impact brain functioning by influencing the development of sequencing, manipulation of semantic information, and motor learning skills (Pool, Dittrich, & Pool, 2011).

Artists often describe their ability to create art as if the information and knowledge about their particular art exists in a multidimensional environment. Digital space is also multidimensional, and as artists do, those with the ability to understand and interact with digital information are able to arrange, manipulate and display it according to their perceptions. In this sense, these people possess another intelligence – an intelligence made up of the components of other intelligences, just as musical or spatial intelligence is described by Gardner to exist (Adams, 2004).

In the digital age, the integration of social learning and social media technologies lead to the concept of the connectivity theory. Learning is no longer an internal, individualistic activity, learners gather information from connecting to others. The teacher role in not just to define, generate or assign content, but it is to help students build learning paths with existing and new knowledge resources (Chen & Bryar, 2012).

Motivation and engagement can be regarded as the driving forces behind learning. According to OECD successful learning depends not just on good instruction and the ability to storage knowledge, but also on how students approach the process of learning. The report "Learners for Life – Student Approaches to Learning, provides evidence that students with strong motivation towards learning, perform much better at school (OECD, 2003). Some simple learning can occur without motivation, but most of learning is motivated. Motivated students engage in classes, perform search activities and relate new knowledge with previous experiences. Motivated students persevere on solving problems and won't quit. Essentially, motivation engages students in activities that promote learning (Schunk, 2012).

Motivation may be intrinsic or extrinsic. In the first case, the motivation originates as an internal process. The latter, originates to external processes and influences. Motivation plays a key role in learning and in musical performance It is generally accepted, that motivation has a weight percentage of approximately 20% in school performance; the remaining 80% would be distributed by intelligence, socio-economic status, ability, etc., of the students. However, in the case of musical learning, this percentage is even higher, some studies pointing out even for a share of influence in the order of 38%. In this area, it appears that the motivation is the driving force which may lead a student to participate in learning activities and acquire knowledge and skills that constitute the core of music (Eggen & Schellenberg, 2010).

ARMG aims to enhance and strengthen student motivation for learning through the use of AR by adding realism-based practices. "AR has the potential to further engage and motivate learners in discovering resources and applying them to the real world from a variety of diverse perspectives that have never been implemented in the real world" (Lee, 2012, p. 32). Motivation is directly linked to learning achievements, and AR applications, which are interactive and visually attractive seem more appealing and motivating than traditional tools (Pérez-López & Contero, 2013).

Music and other forms of art are known to develop discipline, higher order of thinking skills, creativity and to engage students in a variety of different learning styles. Technology applied to arts education can be thought as an applied science (anything that uses science to achieve a desired result) and can act as the extension of student capabilities and as a way to expand their ability to learn (Assey, 1999).

The use of technology can accelerate the learning of the arts, and this is also true in the music history field (as in many others), where the comprehension of a given aesthetic period characteristics requires students to listen the musical works of that period, to read about composer biographies and works, and to analyze musical instruments, imagery, paintings or photography, depicting historical backgrounds and environments. Different types of media are essential to comprehend the evolution of music in time and how it relates and influences different cultures. Presently, Music Education Portuguese students use mostly traditional textbooks and printed materials to support the learning process. AR can deliver digital multimedia content (audio, video, image, 3-D models) overlapping real-world educational resources (books, textbooks, posters, images, and so on), improving the quality of these educational resources both in formal or informal environments.

In Portugal, currently, Musical Education is part of the Arts and Expressions Curriculum defined by the Ministry of Science and Education and educational goals are clearly defined concerning students from the 1st, 2nd and 3rd Cycles of basic education. However, in the 1st Cycle, Music Education is only available as complementary activity, and the History of Music it is not relevant to younger students. In the 2nd cycle, Music Education it is part of the curriculum, but weekly class hours are insufficient to convey the extensive program to the 5th and 6th grades. The 3rd Cycle Music Education has gradually become an optional educational area, as the official entities tend to neglect and undervalue the importance of music education in public schools. The use of IT in music education is addressed in the official program, mostly as a mean to create music. This approach, dating back to 2001, is clearly outdated. In this context, AR can contribute to improve this gap, by delivering rich-media music related educational content in formal or informal learning environments and by exploring the native young student's motivation towards technology (Harris & Rea, 2009; Prensky, 2001) and technological devices.

ARMG proposes an innovative educational approach by delivering digital interactive educational music history related content supported by AR technology in an informal learning environment aiming to:

- Offer a constructivist educational approach in the field of music history by using student previous knowledge;
- Provide alternative strategies to the teaching-learning process by using informal learning environments;
- Promote a new technology-based learning experience;
- Promote the use and development of multiple intelligence skills;
- Promote the motivation to learn and improve educational outcomes;
- Explore the potential of the ubiquitous MCD, as smartphones and tablets, to deliver interactive educational content;
- Explore the potential of AR technology in educational context.
- Promote collaboration and connection to others.

THE ARMG: CONCEPT

The ARMG exhibition aimed to promote music history learning and motivate students to autonomous learning in a constructivist-based approach, by using mobile computing devices, such as smartphones and tablets to access multimedia content through AR technology. The exhibition consists of sixteen A3 size posters featuring imagery and text information, namely the composer image and biography, and the musical instruments images and main characteristics.

In order to enhance the information available on the exhibition posters, allowing students to deepen their knowledge on the given subject, additional digital content and interaction was delivered through AR technology, namely video, sound, 3-D musical instrument models, diagrams, and quiz games. For research purposes, only eight posters had AR content, which was identified to users by the Aurasma logo (Figure 2).

The posters where placed on vertical panels at the school's library exhibit area, allowing individual and group exploration (Figure 3).

The exhibition was organized according to the following sequence: The first two posters included information about AR technology and instructions concerning the proper configuration of student mobile computing devices. The remaining posters presented educational content focusing the twentieth century music history. Poster sequence, real-world/digital content and interactivity are depicted in Table 1.

ARMG was held in the school's library and featured an introductory session attended by all classes from the fifth and sixth grades. These sessions focused the gallery educational contents, research objectives, the AR technology and the configuration of student mobile computing devices. Students received a brochure concerning major aspects of the exhibition and a book marker featuring AR content. Students were also briefed on the main poster areas, namely the poster information structure and the identification of the images designed to trigger the AR digital content. Figure 4-A depicts the brochure, Figure 4-B the book marker, Figure 4-C the trigger image, and Figure 4-D the textual information.

Figure 2. José Duarte Cardoso Gomes, Information of augmented reality content to users (Aurasma logo) (© 2018, J. D. C. Gomes, used with permission)

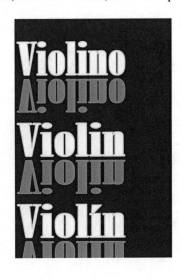

Figure 3. José Duarte Cardoso Gomes, Augmented Reality Musical Gallery (ARMG) exhibition (© 2018, J. D. C. Gomes, used with permission)

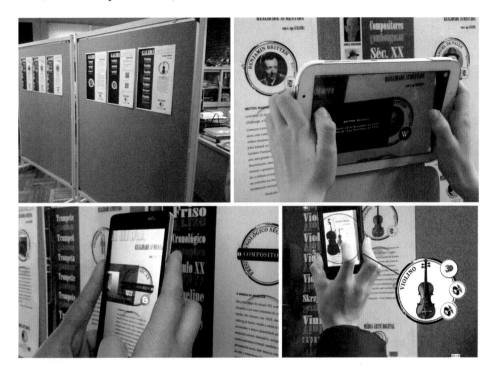

Students explored the gallery using their own mobile computing devices, or by requesting the library pre-configured tablet.

To develop and implement the AR content displayed in the gallery we have used the AR engine Aurasma, the online tool Aurasma Studio 2.0 and the Aurasma app, available for Android and iOS platforms. These tools are free and are easy to use, both relevant issues in educational context. Digital multimedia content, namely video, sound excerpts, diagrams and 3-D models, were produced by using open-source and free programs. Interactive quiz games were developed with Educaplay and delivered in HTML5 format. Music history content was adapted from the CD-ROM Musicalis, published by Porto Editora in 2005.

The gallery was on exhibition on January 2015, in the school's library.

THE ARMG: RESEARCH

General Objectives and Research Questions

Since the ARMG exhibition relies on AR technology and therefore on mobile computing devices, it is considered of relevance to know the current type of usage students make of these portable artifacts. Ease of use and ease of learning, are key pedagogical usability features required in educational medias (Hersh & Leporini, 2013), so it's deemed as important to survey students reactions to the augmented reality experiences concerning usability issues. Finally, it's relevant to perceive how this informal activity impacts learning outcomes. Seeking to answer to these concerns, were posed three research questions, namely:

Table 1. Augmented Reality Musical Gallery (ARMG) real world and digital content

Exhibit Printed Poster (A3) Theme	Educational Printed Content	Educational Digital Content Supported by AR	Interactivity Supported by AR and Touch
Poster 1 – Introduction to the AR technology	Text is presenting AR technology.	3-D animation intended to demonstrate AR capabilities.	No interactivity available.
Poster 2- Information	Text and images (QRcodes) explaining how to install and configure the app Aurasma.	Hyperlinks to Aurasma installation tutorial and to the aura channel. The hyperlinks were presented by QRcodes.	No interactivity available.
Poster 3 - Violin	Text and violin image.	Three dimensional (3-D) model of the violin, a diagram featuring the instrument principal components, three audio excerpts, and a quiz game.	Interaction available (touch buttons).
Poster 4 - Cello	Text and cello image.	Not available	Not available
Poster 5 – Upright piano	Text and upright piano image.	A 3-D model of an upright piano and three audio excerpts, piano diagram, hyperlinks to piano playing technique videos and a quiz game.	Interaction available (touch buttons).
Poster 6 - Oboe	Text and oboe image	Not available	Not available
Poster 7 - Trumpet	Text and trumpet image.	A 3-D model of a trumpet, three audio excerpts, trumpet diagram, hyperlinks to trumpet playing technique and a quiz game.	Interaction available (touch buttons).
Poster 8 - Trombone	Text and trombone image.	Not available.	Not available.
Poster 9 – Twentieth century composers timeline	Text and image.	The video presents the most important composers of the twentieth century, featuring subtitles and audio narration, the author biography and works, audio excerpts and a quiz game.	Interaction available (touch buttons).
Poster 10 – Arnold Schoenberg (1874-1951)	Text and image.	Not available.	Not available.
Poster 11 – Carl Orff (1895-1982)	Text and image.	Video on the author's biography featuring subtitles, audio narration, musical excerpts and a quiz game.	Interaction available (touch buttons).
Poster 12 – George Gershwin (1898-1937)	Text and image.	Not available.	Not available.
Poster 13 – Manuel de Falla (1876-1946)	Text and image.	Video on the author's biography featuring subtitles, audio narration, musical excerpts and a quiz game.	Interaction available (touch buttons).
Poster 14 – Igor Stravinsky (1882-1971)	Text and image.	Not available.	Not available.
Poster 15 – Maurice Ravel (1875-1937)	Text and image.	Video on the author's biography featuring subtitles, audio narration, musical excerpts and a quiz game.	Interaction available (touch buttons).
Poster 16 – Benjamin Britten (1913-1976)	Text and image.	Not available.	Not available.

Figure 4. José Duarte Cardoso Gomes, Augmented Reality Musical Gallery (ARMG) printed resources (© 2018, J. D. C. Gomes, used with permission)

1. What is the current usage of mobile computing devices, such as smartphones and tablets, made by 2nd Cycle basic education students?
2. How students react to the AR experience in terms of usability?
3. Which are the contributions from this AR based exhibition concerning the learning outcomes to music education?

Research questions were answered using mixed research methods involving qualitative and quantitative approaches and by implementing questionnaire and direct observation techniques. Data concerning question one was collected by questionnaire and direct observation; for question two was used an adapted version of the System Usability Scale (SUS) proposed by Brooke (1996), and, finally, data concerning question three was collected by an experimental design involving pre/post-tests, experimental and control groups (Kumar, 2011).

This chapter presents only the results concerning research question one and two. Results concerning question three and will be presented as future work.

Question One

Research Instruments

The questionnaire concerning research question one focused the following parameters:

- Demographic data: Age, gender and school grade;

- Access to MCD (smartphone/tablet or hybrid);
- Availability of the MCD to students and principal usage locations;
- Type of MCD most frequently used, ownership and characteristics;
- Activities conducted in MCD and time spent in each;
- Frequency of use for school related tasks;
- Frequency of use for non-school related tasks.

The direct observation grid surveyed the following parameters:

- Usability parameters concerning the ease of use and ease of learning of the augmented AR experiences;
- How students interacted with the exhibition and;
- How students interacted with each other.

Goals

The ARMG exhibition relies on AR technology. AR content developed for this interactive exhibition is accessed using MCD, namely smartphones and tablets running Android or iOS platforms. Thus, perceive how students access and use these devices is key to enable further learning experiences/environments based on AR technology. Data gathered from direct observation on the ease of use, ease of learning and user interaction with the exhibit may contribute to improve the exhibition in further development iterations.

Participants

Participants were randomly selected (using the "RAND()" function in Microsoft Excel) from the 2nd Cycle classes universe, namely, one class from the fifth grade and one class from the sixth grade, which were deemed representative of the target audience.

Procedures

All participants were previously briefed on how to use the AR exhibit, and prompted to bring their personal mobile devices and headphones to the exhibition. They received a leaflet with the research goals, a summary description of the exhibition, and the hyperlink to an online questionnaire hosted by Google Forms. The questionnaires were filled in the subsequent week from visiting the exhibition. The questionnaire used closed questions, range questions, multiple choice questions, multiple selection questions and ranking questions. The direct observation grid was filled by the logger during the exhibition period. Data treatment and related graphics were created in Microsoft Excel.

Results

Questionnaire Group One: Demographic Data

Concerning the student age, results show that 24.0% is ten years old, 46.0% is eleven years old, 28.0% is twelve years old, and 2.0% is fourteen years old. Results concerning gender reveal that 41.0% are female and 59.0% are male. Finally, results regarding school grade reveal that 43.0% belong to the fifth grade and 57.0% belong to the sixth grade (Table 2).

Questionnaire Group Two: Access to Mobile Computing Devices

Results concerning question 2.1: Have you access to a mobile computing device (smartphone/tablet/ hybrid)? show that 100% of the participants has access to at least one of these devices. Results regarding question 2.2: Is the mobile device always with you? reveal that 67.4% of students have the mobile devices always with them, while 32.6% don't. Finally, question 2.3: Places where you can access and use a mobile device, show that 87.5% of the participants access and uses mobile devices at home, 43.8% at school, and 25.0% in other places such as the cafe or the family car (Figure 5).

Questionnaire Group Three: Most Frequently Used Mobile Computing Device, Ownership and Specifications

Results regarding question 3.1: Which are the mobile computing devices you use more frequently, at home, school or elsewhere? reveal that 76.1% of the participants use more frequently the smartphone,

Table 2. Student gender, age and class

Gender		Age					School Level	
Male	Female	9	10	11	12	14	Fifth grade	Sixth grade
27 (58.7%)	19 (41.3%)	0 (0%)	11 (23.9%)	21 (45.7%)	13 (28.3%)	1 (2.2%)	20 (43.5%)	26 (56.5%)

Figure 5. José Duarte Cardoso Gomes, Access level and places where participants use mobile devices (© 2018, J. D. C. Gomes, used with permission)

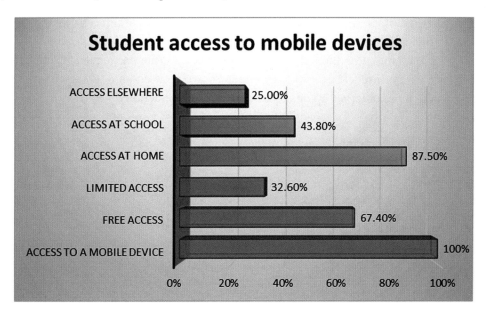

63.0% tablets, and 10.9% hybrid devices. Question 3.2: Identify the mobile computing device (or devices) you own, and if so, identify their principal characteristics, revealed that 84.8% of students own a smartphone, 73.9% own a tablet, and that 8.7% own a hybrid device. Question 3.2.1: Identify your smartphone main characteristics, shows that 17.1% of these devices have screens bigger than five inches, and 82.9% have screens equal or smaller than five inches. Of these, 87.8% are using Android OS, and 4.9% use iOS. Question 3.2.2: Identify your tablet main characteristics, 41.0% of students stated they own tablets with screens bigger than 10 inches, 41.0% tablets with screens between 8 and 10 inches, and 10.3% stated they have tablets with screens smaller than 8 inches. Concerning tablets operating systems, 61.5% of the participants are using Android OS, and 35.9% use iOS (Table 3).

Question Four: Activities Conducted on Mobile Computing Devices and Time Spent in Each

Results concerning question 4.1: List all the activities you conduct using your mobile device, reveals that 93.5% of the participants use the mobile device for gaming, 87.0% for listening music or watching videos over the internet, 76.1% for communications, 76.1% for internet browsing, 56.5% for messaging, 52.2% for Facebook or other social networks, and 37.0% for homework and study. Results regarding question 4.2: Time spent in your favorite activity, show that 37.0% of students spend more time listening to music or watching videos over the internet, 30.4% gaming, 8.7% communicating, and 6.5% in Facebook, internet browsing, or sending and receiving email. Homework and study (2.2%) is the less time-consuming activity undertaken by students (Figure 6).

Question Five: MCD Usage Frequency of School and Non-School Related Activities

Results regarding question 5.1: How frequently do you use your mobile computing device to study or study related activities? reveal that 32.6% of the participants use the mobile device rarely or never for study related activities, 23.9% use 2 to 3 times a month, 21.7% weekly and 21.7% daily. Concerning question 5.2: How frequently do you use your mobile computing device for non-school related activities? results show that 4.3% of students use it rarely or never, 4.3% 2 to 3 times a month, 21.7% weekly, and 69.6% daily (Figure 7).

Direct observation focused on three items. Item one surveyed the participant reactions concerning the AR experience ease of use and ease of learning; item two focused on how they interacted with the AR content and item three observed spontaneous participant interactions.

Table 3. Most frequently used mobile device, ownership, operative system and screen size

| | Device Frequency of Use | Device Ownership | Device screen size | | | | | Android OS Based | iOS Based |
			> 5 Inches	<= 5 Inches	<= 7 Inches	8 or 9 Inches	> 10 Inches		
Smartphone	35 (76.1%)	39 (84.8%)	7 (17.1%)	34 (82.9%)	--	--	--	36 (87.8%)	2 (4.9%)
Tablet	29 (63.0%)	34 (73.9%)	--	--	4 (10.3%)	16 (41.0%)	16 (41.0%)	24 (61.5%)	14 (35.9%)
Hybrid	5 (10.9%)	4 (8.7%)	--	--	--	--	--	--	--

Figure 6. José Duarte Cardoso Gomes, Activities conducted on mobile devices and time spent (© 2018, J. D. C. Gomes, used with permission)

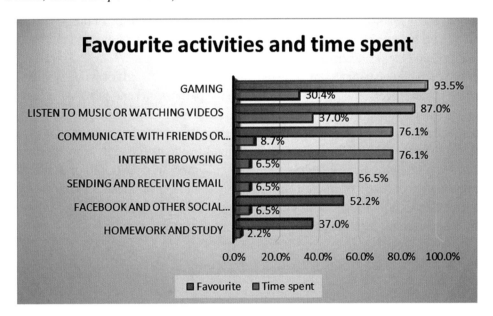

Figure 7. José Duarte Cardoso Gomes, Mobile device use for school and non-school related activities (© 2018, J. D. C. Gomes, used with permission)

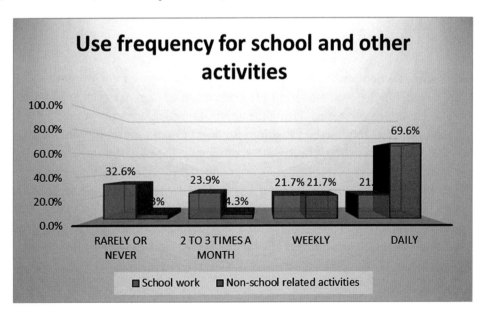

Concerning item one – All participants easily and successfully used the app Aurasma to visualize the augmentations. The only noticeable usability problem refers to the slow internet connection provided by the wireless network available in the school's library, leading to slow loading of the AR content. On item two – Interaction with the exhibition -, direct observation record analysis revealed that the participants tended to flock around the posters marked with the AR logo.

This was a predictable behavior arising from the student curiosity towards the novelty of the experience. Non-interactive posters received far less attention from the participants and general audience. Observation concerning the interaction with each other revealed that the more technology savvy students were happy to help colleagues in either properly configure their devices or interacting with the educational content. Game quiz promoted an immediate competition to achieve the high scores, since user names and scores were stored in the Educaplay platform. Other visitors to the exhibition, students and teachers mostly, revealed high levels of interest in AR, posed a number of questions concerning AR major affordances, and declared their interest in the technology as a support to formal and informal learning activities in the near future, regarding their fields of expertise.

Question Two

The usability study aims to answer research question "2 - How students react to the AR experience in terms of usability?" The study is an exploratory user-centered test, and was designed to discover how users respond to the AR prototypes.

Research Instruments

System Usability Scale (SUS)

User-centered testing is accomplished by identifying representative users, relevant tasks, and developing a procedure to observe the problems users are experiencing when using an application to perform certain tasks. These tests are conducted during the application development cycle and use formative or summative evaluations. The formative evaluations are used to obtain usability information about the design of the prototype with regard to effectiveness, efficiency and satisfaction. Summative evaluations are used for the same purpose, considering the final version of the software development (Scholtz, 2004).

According to Brooke (1996), the usability of any tool or system should be analyzed in the context of use, and in its suitability to that context. In the concrete case of information systems, this usability perspective reflects in the ISO 9241-11 standard and the European Community project "Measuring Usability of Systems in Context." According to the ISO 9241-11 standard the usability parameters should address issues related to:

- **Effectiveness:** The ability of users to complete tasks using the system, and the quality derived from those tasks.
- **Efficiency:** The level of resources spent on the execution of tasks.
- **Satisfaction:** The subjective reactions of users to the system.

The need to obtain answers to these questions led to the development of the System Usability Scale (SUS), a simple scale based on ten items, which aims to provide a global view of subjective perceptions regarding usability. Each item uses a statement evaluated on a five or seven-point Likert scale, where one item is "Strongly Disagree" and five is "Strongly Agree."

The SUS scale is usually used immediately after the participant has used the system to be evaluated. In this instrument, all items must be marked. In case of doubt, the participant should mark the neutral option at the center of the scale.

The SUS returns a simple number representing a composite measure of the general usability of the system being studied. The scores of each item have no meaning in themselves. To calculate the SUS score it is necessary to add the values of each item. The contribution of each item varies between 0 and 4. For items 1, 3, 5, 7, and 9 the contribution to the score is the position of the scale minus 1. For items 2, 4, 6 and 8 the contribution is 5 minus the position marked on the scale. Finally, multiply the sum of the scores by 2.5 to obtain the SUS score (Brooke, 1996).

Despite the wide use of SUS, there is little guidance on the process of interpreting scores. According to Bangor, Kortum, & Miller (2009), the concept of applying letter graduation to the usability of a system presents an easy to understand reference point. According to this classification system, the scores are ordered as follows:

- **A - Scores Above 90:** Exceptional product/ system.
- **B - Scores Between 80 and 90:** Good product/ system.
- **C - Scores Between 70 and 79:** Acceptable product/ system.
- **Scores Below 70:** Product/ system with usability issues.

The analysis of the answers to the questions posed in the SUS illustrates the perceptions of the participants regarding each parameter. The relationship between the parameters and the SUS issues is presented in Table 4.

Goals

The usability study aims to collect and analyze information on the impact of the design of the interface for a set of parameters, namely:

Table 4. System Usability Scale, relation between evaluated parameters and questions

Parameters	Question
Satisfaction	1
Ease of use	2, 4, 8
Ease of learning	3, 7, 10
Functionality/ interface consistency	5, 6
Trust/ confidence	9

- Satisfaction.
- Ease of use.
- Ease of learning.
- Functionality/ consistency of the interface.
- Trust/ confidence.

The test aims to know specific aspects of the prototypes that can be redefined in the preparation of an intermediate/ final version, ensuring that these comply with usability/usability standards.

Participants

Participants were selected among the pupils of the school according to their profile, namely students of the 5th or 6th grades attending the discipline of Music Education in the 2nd Cycle of Basic Education. No prerequisites where established concerning the level of digital literacy. The selection of the sample group of participants obeyed a set of criteria: A group of the 5th grade and a group of the 6th grade were randomly selected, in the universe of the school classes. In these classes, also using a random process, five students from the 5th grade and 5 students from the 6th grade were chosen, making a total of ten participants.

Results

The statistical data treatment shows that the average SUS score for the prototypes is 93,7%, so it scores as a class A system. Further analysis on collected data allowed additional reflections on parameters like satisfaction, ease of use, ease of learning, functionality, interface consistency and trust.

- **Satisfaction Parameter Relates to Question 1:** I think that I would like to use this type AR exhibition frequently.
- **Ease of Use Parameter Is Perceived in Question 2:** I found the AR exhibit prototypes unnecessarily complex, question 4: I think I need a specialist to use the AR exhibit prototypes, and question 8 - I found that the AR exhibit prototypes are very sluggish and difficult to use.
- **Ease of Learning Relates to Data Collected Through Questions - Question 3:** I thought the AR exhibit prototypes were very easy to use, question 7: I would imagine that most people would learn to use these AR prototypes, and question 10: I needed to learn a lot of things before I could get going with the AR experiences in the exhibition.
- **Functionality/Consistency Perception Is Perceived in Questions 5:** I found the various functions in this virtual world were well integrated, and question 6: I thought there was too much inconsistency in the AR experiences depicted in the exhibition.
- **Trust Indicators Are Related to Question 9:** I felt very confident using the AR experiences of the exhibition.

Table 5 synthesizes data collected through the SUS instrument.

The analysis of the data shows that 100% of the students involved in this study show complete agreement in the sense they would like to use this type of AR application frequently. Regarding the ease of use (questions 2, 4 and 8) there is strong evidence that the application is easy to use. Therefore, there

Table 5. Data collected through the System Usability Scale questionnaire

	Q1	Q2	Q3	Q4	Q5	Q6	Q7	Q8	Q9	Q10
1. Completely disagree	0 (0%)	80 (0%)	0 (0%)	2 (20%)	0 (0%)	8 (80%)	2 (20%)	8 (80%)	0 (0%)	8 (80%)
2. Disagree	0 (0%)	20 (20%)	0 (0%)	6 (60%)	0 (0%)	1 (10%)	0 (0%)	2 (20%)	0 (0%)	2 (20%)
3. Neutral	0 (0%)	0 (0%)	0 (0%)	2 (20%)	0 (0%)	1 (10%)	0 (0%)	0 (0%)	0 (0%)	0 (0%)
4. Agree	0 (0%)	0 (0%)	2 (20%)	0 (0%)	2 (20%)	0 (0%)	6 (60%)	0 (0%)	0 (0%)	0 (0%)
5. Completely agree	10 (100%)	0 (0%)	8 (80%)	0 (0%)	8 (80%)	0 (0%)	2 (20%)	0 (%)	10 (100%)	0 (0%)

is a clear convergence between ease of use and the desire to use. In this scenario, one should consider the degree of ease of learning to use (questions 3, 7 and 10), and the results show that students feel that they can easily use the application without the help of the teacher/ specialist. Therefore, Augmented Reality exhibition prototypes are, perceived by users as desirable, cognitively economic and ergonomic, requiring no major learning effort and easily apprehended by all.

As far as application functionality is concerned, 80% of the participants fully agree "that the application features are well integrated. In addition to functionality, it is important to understand the graphical and screen-consistency, where the results show 80% full agreement that "the screens are clear and consistent (similar)", which demonstrates internal graphical coherence of the application prototypes, which also promotes cognitive economy and ease of use.

CONCLUSION

In this chapter the authors described the concept and deployment of an interactive exhibition supported by AR – Augmented Reality Musical Gallery (ARMG). The exhibition focuses on the twentieth century music history, and it is aimed at an audience of students from the 2nd Cycle of public basic education in Portugal. ARMG proposes a constructivist pedagogical approach, set in an informal learning environment, applied to a traditional lecture-based course Music History. This approach promotes the combination of autonomous exploration, informal learning environment, and interactive multimedia educational resources delivered by AR. The constructivist approach intends to enhance student motivation, leading to active learning processes based on exploration and interaction.

This chapter introduced AR current usage and affordances to educational contexts. At present, this technology is effectively being used in several educational areas, from science to geometry, mathematics and music, amongst many others. AR technology can support and contribute to improve the teaching-learning processes, by affording attractive ways to learn and by increasing motivation. AR, by combining real-world elements and computer-generated content is usually perceived as a mixed-reality environment, where the real-world element is prevalent. This characteristic is key to enhance traditional educational environments where most of the educational resources are based on traditional printed materials, such as textbooks. However, how to deliver educational contents with AR technology remains a challenge to be addressed by educators, researchers, developers and education officials.

This chapter suggests that constructivist pedagogical approaches and informal learning environments can enhance student motivation and engagement toward learning. Also suggests that art education is known to develop discipline, higher order of thinking skills, creativity and the ability to engage students in a variety of different learning techniques. That learning and motivation are connected – motivated students actively seek new knowledge showing engagement towards learning – and, finally, that AR technology has the potential to engage and motivate students in a variety of new pedagogical approaches and perspectives.

Finally, the authors presented the first and second part of an undergoing study concerning this experience, conducted among a sample group of students from the fifth and sixth grade of a northern Portuguese public school. The study surveyed what is the present usage level of MCD among 2nd Cycle basic education students and their perceptions concerning usability parameters of the AR prototypes used in the exhibition.

Results concerning demographic data revealed that the majority of participants has eleven years old, an average expected in these school levels. Gender results show a majority of male students (58.7%). The class from the sixth grade had more students than the class from the fifth grade. However, these results are common in fifth and sixth grade typical classes, so the sample can be considered representative of the target population. The results also suggest that students have wide access (100%) to MCD, namely smartphones and tablets. These devices are mostly used in informal contexts (home and other places than school), a fact that can be explained by school limitations to its use in formal classroom settings. The most used MCD is the smartphone (76.1%), followed by tablets (63.0%). Only 10.9% of the participants have access to a hybrid device. Most of these devices are personal property of the participants and accessible on a permanent basis. Regarding these device characteristics, results show that the majority of the smartphones is an Android based (87.8% versus iOS with 10.9%) having screen sizes up to five inches (82.9%). Tablets are also mostly Android based (61.5%) but the percentage of iOS based devices are higher comparatively to smartphones with 35.9%. Tablet screen size is mostly between eight and nine inches (41.0%) versus smaller sizes (10.3%). The activities performed in these devices, according to the results, are mostly gaming (93.5%) and listening to music or watching videos over the internet (87.0%). These activities are also the most time consuming according the participants statements. Results on frequency usage, show that most MCD users rarely or never use it for school related activities (32.0%).

These results suggest that these devices are mostly used for non-school related tasks, such a leisure and communications, and undervalued as educational supporting tools. However, the wide access and characteristics of these devices suggest the existence of logistic conditions to implement AR based innovative educational approaches in educational settings.

Concerning the ease of use, and the ease to learn, direct observation revealed that the AR experiences are easy to use. However, the internet connection speed posed a usability challenge by imposing slower access to the multimedia content. Observation concerning the participant interactions revealed that the augmented exhibit items aroused curiosity and interest. The informal learning environment contributed to the establishment of a cooperative behavior among participants.

The usability study sought to know the reactions of the students to the AR prototypes presented in the exhibition, focusing on parameters of satisfaction, ease of use, ease of learning, functionality / consistency of the interface and trust. The score obtained in the System Usability Scale (Brooke, 1996) was 93.7 for the RA experiments, which defines it as Class A system (Bangor et al., 2009) in terms of usability, satisfying the pedagogical usability requirements of the exhibition prototypes. The perceptions regarding parameters such as satisfaction and confidence were extremely positive (100%).

Thus, it is evident that there are no critical factors inhibiting the promotion of the use of RA in informal teaching-learning contexts. It is therefore necessary to increase the initiatives that lead to the production of content with AR and its naturalization in the context of informal learning activities.

In summary, the results of the present study suggest that the combination of informal learning environments, AR and mobile devices can effectively be used in teaching-learning contexts, whether in formal or informal settings. It is also observed that the interventions/ prototypes meet all pedagogical usability requirements and were perceived by users as easy to use and learn, constituting themselves as resources that they would like to use in the future as a support for learning.

These early results suggest that ARMG, supported by AR and the accessibility/ ubiquity of the MCD, the constructivist approach and the informal learning environment, reinforced by the natural interest of younger generations towards technology, can improve student motivation and engagement towards learning activities in informal learning environments.

Future work will contemplate research question three, providing data on ARMG effects concerning music education learning outcomes.

REFERENCES

Adams, N. B. (2004). Digital Intelligence Fostered by Technology. *Journal of Technology Studies*, *30*(2), 93–97. doi:10.21061/jots.v30i2.a.5

Assey, J. (1999). The Future of Technology in K-12 Arts Education. *Forum on Technology in Education: Envisioning the Future. Proceedings*, 15.

Ausubel, D. P. (2012). *The acquisition and retention of knowledge: A cognitive view*. Springer Science & Business Media.

Azuma, R. T. (1997). A Survey of Augmented Reality. *Presence (Cambridge, Mass.)*, *6*(4), 355–385. doi:10.1162/pres.1997.6.4.355

Bangor, A., Kortum, P., & Miller, J. (2009). Determining What Individual SUS Scores Mean: Adding an Adjective Rating Scale. *JUS Journal of Usability Studies*, *4*(3), 114–123.

Billinghurst, M. (2002). Augmented reality in education. *New Horizons for Learning, 12*.

Brooke, J. (1996). SUS: a quick and dirty usability scale. In P. W. Jordan, B. Thomas, I. L. McClelland, & B. Weerdmeester (Eds.), *Usability Evaluation In Industry*. London: CRC Press.

Chen, B., & Bryar, T. (2012). Investigating Instructional Strategies for Using Social Media in Formal and Informal Learning. *International Review of Research in Open and Distance Learning*, *13*(1), 87–104. doi:10.19173/irrodl.v13i1.1027

Collins, A., & Halverson, R. R. (2009). *Rethinking education in the age of technology: The digital revolution and schooling in America* (M. C. Linn, Ed.). New York: Teachers College Press.

Corrêa, A. G. D., Lima, M., Melo, D. G. de, & Santos, I. I. dos. (2012). Desenvolvimento de um Livro Interativo em Realidade Aumentada para Ensino e Aprendizagem Musical. *CINTED-UFGRS Novas Tecnologias Na Educação, 10*(3).

Cruz-Cunha, M. M., Reis, M., Peres, E., Varajão, J., Bessa, M., Magalhães, L., ... Barreira, J. (2010). Realidade Aumentada e Ubiquidade na Educação. *IEEE-RITA*, *5*(4), 167–174.

Dunleavy, M., Dede, C., & Mitchell, R. (2009). Affordances and limitations of immersive participatory augmented reality simulations for teaching and learning. *Journal of Science Education and Technology*, *18*(1), 7–22. doi:10.100710956-008-9119-1

Eberle, S. G. (2011). Playing with the Multiple Intelligences: How Play Helps Them Grow. *American Journal of Play*, *4*(1), 19–51.

Eggen, P., & Schellenberg, S. (2010). Human Memory and the New Science of Learning. In M. S. Khine & I. M. Saleh (Eds.), New Science of Learning Cognition, Computers and Collaboration in Education. New York: Springer Science+Business Media, LLC. doi:10.1007/978-1-4419-5716-0_5

Figueiredo, A. S. L. (2007). *Realidade Virtual no Ensino e na Aprendizagem de Geometria Descritiva* (Master's Thesis). Instituto Superior de Tecnologia e Gestão do Instituto Politécnico da Guarda. Retrieved from https://repositorio-aberto.up.pt/handle/10216/11043

Figueiredo, M., Amado, N., Bidarra, J., & Carreira, S. (2015). *A realidade aumentada na aprendizagem da matemática no ensino secundário*. Retrieved from http://hdl.handle.net/10400.2/4566

Figueiredo, M., Gomes, J., Gomes, C., & Lopes, J. (2014). Augmented Reality tools and techniques for developing interactive materials for mobile-learning. *Journal Recent Advances Educational Technologies and Methodologies*, *395*(7), 63–72.

Gazzaniga, M. (2008). Arts and cognition: Findings hint at relationships. *Learning, Arts, and the Brain: The Dana Consortium Report on Arts and Cognition*, 93–104.

Harris, A. L., & Rea, A. (2009). Web 2.0 and virtual world technologies: A growing impact on IS education. *Journal of Information Systems Education*, *20*(2), 137.

Hersh, M. A., & Leporini, B. (2013). An Overview of Accessibility and Usability of Educational Games. In C. Gonzalez (Ed.), *Student Usability in Educational Software and Games*. Hershey, PA: Information Science Reference (an imprint of IGI Global). doi:10.4018/978-1-4666-1987-6.ch001

Ibáñez, M. B., Di Serio, Á., Villarán, D., & Kloos, C. D. (2014). Experimenting with electromagnetism using augmented reality: Impact on flow student experience and educational effectiveness. *Computers & Education*, *71*(0), 1–13. doi:10.1016/j.compedu.2013.09.004

Ibanez, M. B., Di-Serio, A., Villaran-Molina, D., & Delgado-Kloos, C. (2015). Augmented Reality-Based Simulators as Discovery Learning Tools: An Empirical Study. *Education. IEEE Transactions on*, *58*(3), 208–213. doi:10.1109/TE.2014.2379712

Jain, L. C., Tedman, R. A., & Tedman, D. K. (2007). *Evolution of Teaching and Learning Paradigms in Intelligent Environment*. New York: Springer. doi:10.1007/978-3-540-71974-8

Jaramillo, G. E., Quiroz, J. E., Cartagena, C. A., Vivares, C. A., & Branch, J. W. (2010). Mobile Augmented Reality Applications in Daily Environments. Revista EIA - Escuela de Ingenieria de Antioquia, Medellín (Colombia), (14), 125–134.

Keast, D. A. (2009). A Constructivist Application for Online Learning in Music. *Research and Issues in Music Education, 7*(1).

Kerawalla, L., Luckin, R., Seljeflot, S., & Woolard, A. (2006). "Making it real": Exploring the potential of augmented reality for teaching primary school science. *Virtual Reality (Waltham Cross), 10*(3–4), 163–174. doi:10.100710055-006-0036-4

Kesim, M., & Ozarslan, Y. (2012). Augmented Reality in Education: Current Technologies and the Potential for Education. *Procedia: Social and Behavioral Sciences, 47*(0), 297–302. doi:10.1016/j.sbspro.2012.06.654

Kumar, R. (2011). *Research Methodology a step-by-step guide for beginners* (3rd ed.). London: SAGE Publications Lda.

Lebrun, M. (2002). *Teorias e Métodos Pedagógicos para Ensinar e Aprender*. Lisboa: Instituto Piaget.

Lee, K. (2012). The Future of Learning and Training in Augmented Reality. *InSight: A Journal of Schorlaly Teaching, 7*, 31–42.

Milgram, P., & Kishino, F. (1994). A taxonomy of mixed reality visual displays. *IEICE Transactions on Information and Systems, 77*(12), 1321–1329.

NMC Horizon Report. (2012). *2012 higher education edition*. Retrieved May 2, 2015, from http://redarchive.nmc.org/publications/horizon-report-2012-higher-ed-edition

Noval, M. D. M. (2013). *Realidade Aumentada no ensino da Matemática: um caso de estudo* (Master's Thesis). Universidade de Aveiro. Retrieved from http://repositorio.utad.pt//handle/10348/3029

Nunes, M. B., & McPherson, M. (2007). Why Designers cannot be Agnostic about Pedagogy: The Influence of Constructivist Thinking in Design of e-learning for HE. In L. C. Jain, D. K. Tedman, & R. A. Tedman (Eds.), *Evolution of Teaching and Learning Paradigms in Intelligent Environment* (p. 309). Berlin: Springer-Verlag. doi:10.1007/978-3-540-71974-8_2

OECD. (2003). *Learners for Life: Student Approaches to Learning*. OECD Publishing.

Pérez-López, D., & Contero, M. (2013). Delivering educational multimedia contents through an augmented reality application: A case study on its impact on knowledge acquisition and retention. *TOJET: The Turkish Online Journal of Educational Technology, 12*(4), 19–28.

Pool, J., Dittrich, C., & Pool, K. (2011). Arts Integration in Teacher Preparation: Teaching the Teachers. *Journal for Learning through the Arts, 7*(1).

Prensky, M. (2001). Digital Natives, Digital Immigrants Part 1. *On the Horizon*.

Salinas, P., González-Mendívil, E., Quintero, E., Ríos, H., Ramírez, H., & Morales, S. (2013). The development of a didactic prototype for the learning of Mathematics through Augmented Reality. *Procedia Computer Science, 25*, 62–70. doi:10.1016/j.procs.2013.11.008

Sandler, M. E. (2010). *Teaching and Learning with Technology: IT as a Value-Added Component of Academic Life*. Annual Meeting of the American Educational Research Association, Denver, CO.

Scholtz, J. (2004). *Usability evaluation*. National Institute of Standards and Technology.

Schunk, D. H. (2012). *Learning Theories* (6th ed.). Boston, MA: Pearson.

Sommerauer, P., & Müller, O. (2014). Augmented reality in informal learning environments: A field experiment in a mathematics exhibition. *Computers & Education*, 79(0), 59–68. doi:10.1016/j.compedu.2014.07.013

Tomei, L. (2009). *Information Communication Technologies for Enhanced Education and Learning: Advanced Applications and Developments*. New York: Information Science Reference (an imprint of IGI Global). doi:10.4018/978-1-60566-150-6

Veloso, N. F. O. (2011). *Realidade Aumentada no Ensino: Prototipagem com um Manual Escolar* (Master's Thesis). Universidade de Aveiro. Retrieved from http://ria.ua.pt/handle/10773/7503

Ward, T. (2012). *Augmented Reality using Appcelerator Titanium Starter*. Birmingham, UK: Packt Publishing Ltd.

Wojciechowski, R., & Cellary, W. (2013). Evaluation of learners' attitude toward learning in ARIES augmented reality environments. *Computers and Education*, 570–585.

Wu, H.-K., Lee, S. W.-Y., Chang, H.-Y., & Liang, J.-C. (2013). Current status, opportunities and challenges of augmented reality in education. *Computers & Education*, 62(0), 41–49. doi:10.1016/j.compedu.2012.10.024

Zorzal, E. R., Buccioli, A. A. B., & Kirner, C. (2005). *O Uso da Realidade Aumentada no Aprendizado Musical*. Workshop de Aplicações de Realidade Virtual, Minas Gerais. Retrieved from http://www.lbd.dcc.ufmg.br/colecoes/warv/2005/0012.pdf

KEY TERMS AND DEFINITIONS

Affordances: The concept, initially proposed by J. Gibson, relates to the functional properties of an object, which allows it to be used in a certain environment. Affordances can be positive or negative characteristics that occur between subjects and objects. In education, the term relates to educational interventions and to students learning characteristics.

Augmented Reality: A technology that allows real-time overlapping of digital content to real-world objects or environments. At present, is widely available to designers, by using Web 2.0 tools requiring no programming skills, and to users by using mobile computing devices such as smartphones or tablets.

Constructivism: Psychological and philosophical perspective based on hypothesis and research by Piaget and Vygotsky contending that individuals work or construct significant parts of what they understand and learn, by mediating on their personal experiences and previous knowledge.

Informal Learning Environments: Relates to the direction of who controls and defines the learning objectives and goals. In a formal learning environment, the teacher sets the goal and objectives. On informal learning environments, the learner has a high degree of freedom in setting his learning goals and objectives.

Mobile Computing Devices: Handheld computers that can be easily carried around by users. Currently, the most usual and widespread mobile devices are smartphones, tablets, and e-readers.

Motivation: Internal (intrinsic) or external (extrinsic) factors that stimulate people toward achieving a certain goal. Motivated actions may encompass the choice of tasks, effort, persistence, and achievement.

Usability: Measure that relates to a product's potential to accomplish the goals of a user. In ICT, it's often used regarding software applications or web sites, but the concept is also used for any product designed to accomplish a determined task.

Chapter 15
Building Virtual Driving Environments From Computer–Made Projects

Carlos José Campos
Polytechnic of Porto, Portugal

Hugo Filipe Pinto
Polytechnic of Porto, Portugal

João Miguel Leitão
Polytechnic of Porto, Portugal

João Paulo Pereira
Polytechnic of Porto, Portugal

António Fernando Coelho
University of Porto, Portugal

Carlos Manuel Rodrigues
University of Porto, Portugal

ABSTRACT

The virtual environments used in scientific driving simulation experiments require extensive 3D models of road landscapes, correctly modeled and similar to those found in the real world. The modeling task of these environments, addressing the terrain definition and the specific characteristics required by the target applications, may result in a complex and time-consuming process. This chapter presents a procedural method to model large terrain definitions and adjust the roadside landscape to produce well-constructed road environments. The proposed procedural method allows merging an externally modeled road into a terrain definition, providing an integrated generation of driving environments. The road and terrain models are optimized to interactive visualization in real time, by applying most state-of-art techniques like the level of detail selection and spatial hierarchization. The proposed method allows modeling large road environments, with the realism and quality required to perform experimental studies in driving simulators.

DOI: 10.4018/978-1-5225-7371-5.ch015

INTRODUCTION

Procedural modeling of realistic driving environments is a rich research area that is usually addressed to the generation of 3D models, not only for entertainment but also for scientific applications, such as driving simulation. Driving simulators are usually considered as a very important scientific tool to conduct immersive experimental studies in different areas, like psychology, ergonomics, and roadways engineering. Experimental work in driving simulators requires a terrain and a road network definitions, both realistically modeled and prepared to real time visualization. The two models must match perfectly with each other, imposing that they be created together or within strongly interconnected tasks (Campos, Leitão, & Coelho, 2015a).

The large extensions of the environments and the detailed requirements imposed for each experimental work makes the manual design by specialists impracticable. Depending on the specific requirements of each experimental work, the use of previous created terrains or the use of models acquired from dedicated repositories may not be suitable and cannot provide the detail needed to generate the desired driving models according to the road network provided. Also, the use of data sources of real terrains, doesn't allow the freedom to impose particular terrain relief scenarios, such as ridge line at a specific point of the landscape, or even modify the mountains distribution in the specific terrain area. Large terrain definition, correctly modeled, corresponding to specific terrain areas, can be procedurally generated, significantly decreasing the preparation time of complete road environments that meet all the required specifications of each experimental work.

This paper presents an approach to generate driving environments, integrating several independent processes that can be applied sequentially to produce complete driving environments. The proposed integrated method to produce complete driving environments tries to mimic the three working phases that occur in the real world construction of road environments. First, the nature creates a terrain. Then, knowing the available terrain, civil engineers design a road that follows and fits the selected areas of the terrain. At last, when physically implementing the road, several adjustments are performed to the terrain, not only under the constructed road but also on its sides.

This paper is organized as follows: next section presents the state of art in the generation of virtual road environments, focusing the relevant related work. Following that, in section *Virtual Road Environments*, the proposed method is described and each included module is explained in detail. Then the results obtained with the implemented prototype are presented in the *Results* section. Finally, last section presents conclusions and some guidelines for future work.

STATE OF ART

To generate virtual road environments, that fit the realism imposed for scientific driving simulation applications, a terrain model definition is required, where the road network can be implemented (Campos, Leitão, & Coelho, 2014; Campos, Leitão, Pereira, Ribas, & Coelho, 2015b; Campos, Leitão, & Coelho, 2015c). To generate terrain model definitions, typically known as digital elevation maps (DEM), several approaches have been suggested and developed. Although most known methods are suitable to generate terrains that can be used in several simulation applications, most of them do not allow the correct adjustment of the terrain required after imposing an externally designed road.

DEMs can be defined as a two-dimensional grid where each cell contains an elevation value and are the most used representation of terrains. Among the classical techniques for generating elevation maps are techniques based on subdivision and techniques based on noise generators (Miller, 1986; Fournier, Fussell, & Carpenter, 1982; Musgrave, Kolb, & Mace, 1989). The result is a mountainous terrain with a natural appearance.

An example of a noise generator's use is the Perlin's noise (Perlin, 1985), which was developed with the aim of creating realistic terrain elevations. To control the generation process the definition of some initial variables is required, not very intuitive and the models generated shown excessive homogeneity, especially on large terrain. In order to solve the problem of positioning features on a terrain, Stachniak and Stuerzlinger (2005) proposed a method where constraints on the terrain creation process are specified by masks (sketch images).

Schneider Boldte, T., & Westermann (2006) present an interactive interface editor (WYSIWYG), where the user can paint base functions represented by gray-scale sketches. These sketches can replace the Perlin's noise in the generation process of terrains.

The solution proposed by Belhadj & Audibert (2005) combines a classic technique of subdivision algorithm, a *triangular edge*, with the definition of ridge lines and river tracings, producing an elevation map with a satisfactory realism. The lines that represent the ridge lines are created using a couple of ridge particles that are randomly placed on the elevation map and are subjected to lateral impacts in order to describe a *Fractional Brownian* motion (Fournier, Fussell & Carpenter, 1982). Based on this resulting temporary terrain, river particles are randomly placed in the mountain ranges and, by physical simulating the action of the gravity force they describe a river course. The *midpoint displacement's inverse* (MDI) algorithm is used to calculate the altitudes.

A technique developed by Zhou & Zhou (2007) starts from a real elevation map and a sketch with lines representing characteristics of the terrain, like ridge lines and valleys, to generate a new terrain definition. The algorithm smoothly combines characteristics extracted from the example of the elevation map and the sketch of feature lines in a new definition of elevation map.

Doran and Parberry (2010) present a method where software agents are used to generate certain characteristics of a terrain: coastlines, beaches, mountains, and rivers. In order to improve the controllability of the terrain creation process, parameters have been introduced that allow influencing the behavior of the software agents, allowing the control to be carried out by users without technical knowledge.

Génevaux, Galin, Guérin, Peytavie, & Benes (2013) present a framework that allows the creation of terrains through concepts based on hydrology. The generation process is based on two sketches that contain parameters provided by the user. The first sketch indicates the type of main rivers and their trajectories and the second sketch indicates the mountainous areas and the plains zones. During the generation process, information related to the process operations and the characteristics of terrain is stored.

Techniques based on natural effects, such as erosion, may also be used to improve the realism of the generated models (Cordonnier, Galin, Gain, Benes, Guérin, Peytavie, & Cani, 2017). Simulation of erosion allows significant improvements in the realism of elevation maps. These techniques are commonly divided into two types: thermal erosion and hydraulic erosion (Musgrave, Klob & Mace, 1989; Benes & Forsbach 2002). Thermal erosion simulates the sedimentation of particles at points of lower altitude resulting from the release of rocks at higher altitudes. Hydraulic erosion simulates the sedimentation of transported particles in rainwater (precipitation). When applied in elevation maps, the realism of the result obtained is expressively improved (Benes & Forsbach 2001).

VIRTUAL ROAD ENVIRONMENTS

Driving simulation requires visual models of road environments, usually composed by roads and terrain landscape combined in a symbiotic environment. In order to avoid the mutual dependence between modeling tasks of the terrain and the road, and to achieve a functional independence between them, it's proposed a division of the terrain generation into two processes: the Terrain generation and the terrain adjust. The following figure presents the proposed architecture of the integrated modeling method, applying two main modules that are closed related to these phases. The complete road environment generator can then be structured as presented in Figure 1.

The *Terrain Generator* module is responsible for procedural generation of terrain definitions. To allow a fully controllable generation of terrain definitions, the models preparer can be able to interact with the generation process, by imposing specific requirements to terrain elevation (e.g. location of specific ridge lines). This feature is crucial in the generation of specific road environments for immersive driving simulation.

Besides generating the models of the road paths, is necessary to edit the surrounding terrain model of each road, to produce environments that meet the required visual quality. The *Road Adjust* module is responsible for edit the roadside landscape according to the road network definition, to provide a complete well-constructed environment.

Terrain Generation

The terrain model can be obtained from the definition of the terrain relief, represented by an elevation map. The elevation map can be acquired from real earth surfaces, it can be created by designers or procedural generation methods. Algorithms that represent natural evolution of the terrain surface can be applied in order to obtain improved realistic models (Pinto, 2017).

The method adopted to generate terrain models was inspired on the proposal presented by Smelik, Tutenel, de Kraker, & Bidarra, 2008), where the process workflow is organized in different layers, in charge for the different characteristics of the terrain (Smelik, Tutenel, de Kraker, & Bidarra, 2011; Pinto, 2017). These characteristics can be: relief, rivers, oceans and lakes, vegetation, road networks and urban environment. In this work, the initial terrain generation is only focused on the natural layers such as the relief, water areas and vegetation. In this way, the terrain generation can be carried out autonomously, without dependencies from human defined elements. This restriction also matches the natural sequence of processes that happens in the real world, the terrain is always created before the road design takes place.

Figure 1. Overview of process workflow (© 2018, C. J. Campos, used with permission)

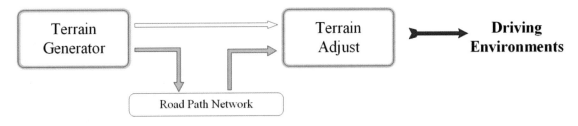

In order to define the relief, a digital elevation map (DEM) is used. This map is a two-dimensional grid where each cell has an altitude value and is the most commonly used representations for describing a terrain relief.

The implemented technique for the generation of elevation maps, was inspired on the one presented by Belhadj & Audibert (2005). In that work, a technique for creating a terrain definition with ridge lines was proposed, using a *triangular edge* subdivision algorithm combining with a *midpoint displacement's inverse* (MDI) algorithm. The MDI algorithm, inversely calculates the elevation points that supposedly origin the ridge line, allowing a believable relief continuity in the terrain near the mountains.

In the current work, the *triangular edge* algorithm was replaced by the *diamond square algorithm* (Olsen, 2004) that is also a subdivision algorithm and is expected to produce more realistic landscapes. To allow feeding the generation pipeline with an initial definition of relief lines, was added a ridge mountain algorithm, which can also be replaced by an interactive sketch editor. Additionally, before the end of the terrain generation process, was added an erosion algorithm to produce environments that meet the required visual quality. This approach results in an integrated pipeline combining the four selected algorithms: erosion, the *triangular edge*, the MDI, and the ridge mountain algorithm, as presented in Figure 2.

The implemented method requires, as input parameters, the number (d_g) of cells in the grid map and the length (d_c) of the side cell in meters. The dimension (g) of the elevation map to be generated (in m²) is mathematically calculated (1).

$$g = d_g * d_c^2 \qquad (1)$$

A maximum allowable elevation value (meters) is also specified in order to limit the ridge line elevation of the mountains. The procedure for modeling elevation maps is initiated by the generation of ridge lines. These ridge lines are created using a couple of ridge particles, which are randomly placed on the altitude map, with opposite directions. Then, these particles are subjected to lateral impacts in order to describe a *Fractional Brownian* motion (Fournier et al., 1982). The orientation of the particles are modified according to the lateral impacts. The movement of the particles over the elevation map will describe the ridge line, as illustrated in Figure 3.

The initial elevation value (a) of the particles are decreased along its displacement (c), according to a *Gauss* function, centered in the initial position (b) of each particle (2).

Figure 2. Terrain generation (© 2018, C. J. Campos, used with permission)

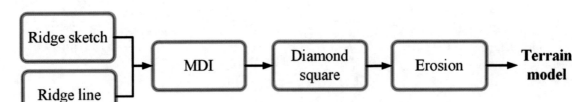

Figure 3. Ridge line generation (© 2018, H. F. Pinto, used with permission)

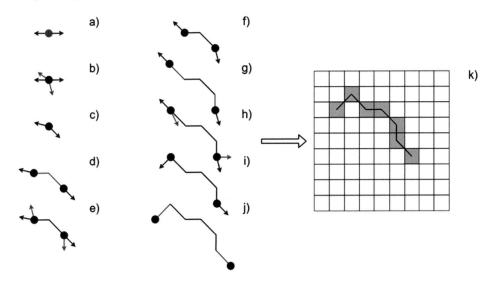

$$f(x) = a.e - \frac{\left(x - b\right)^2}{2c^2}$$
(2)

The process stops when the particles reach the end of the grid, collide with other particle trajectory, or reach zero elevation value.

The ridge line algorithm can be replaced by a sketch drawn by the user. A dedicated sketch editor was developed to allow the draw and erase of ridged lines.

After the generation of ridge lines and before the execution of the subdivision algorithm, it is necessary to obtain the elevation values of the grid cells (green), which would give rise to the already calculated cells of the ridge lines (red), as illustrated in Figure 4.

This approach allows solving the problem of the continuity of the elevations of the ridge lines with the elevations obtained from the method of subdivision. To obtain these elevations, the *midpoint displacement's inverse* (MDI) algorithm is used. The elevation values of the grid cells are obtained considering the distance between the ridge cell (red) and the grid cell (green) being analyzed (*Gauss* function).

This algorithm does not receive any input parameterization, however, like the algorithm for the generation of ridge lines, the *Gauss* function is also used.

Once the problem of the continuity of the ridge line elevations is solved, the *diamond square* algorithm is executed, obtaining the remaining elevations values of the elevation map (Miller, 1986).

The parameterization of this algorithm can be done using a rough terrain sketch made by the user. The sketch editor developed was configured with a base color that defines the intermediate roughness, and using five different colors, which allow changing the roughness in five levels.

The subdivision algorithms generates rough elevation maps with abrupt elevation variations that contrast with the eroded profile of real terrains due to the influence of physical phenomena that affect geological formations, such as rain, snow, ice formation, thaw, wind and temperature variations. These effects influence the formation and movement of sediments that alter the landscape and, on a larger scale, soften the elevation variations.

Figure 4. Cells elevation MDI calculation (© 2018, H. F. Pinto, used with permission)

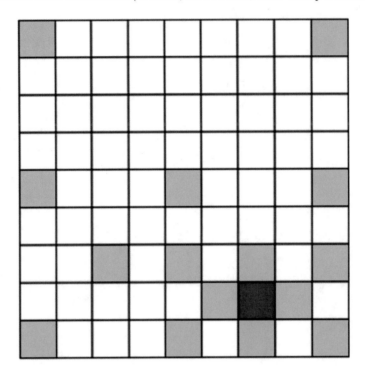

For this reason, erosion has been used with regard to the generation of elevation maps, and there are some approaches that start from erosion as a method to modeling realistic elevation maps.

To improve the realism of the elevation map generated, two erosion simulation algorithms were added, thermal erosion and hydraulic erosion. The approach on which this erosion implementation is based, starts by a previous generated elevation map, moving the elevation according to the simulation of thermal and hydraulic erosion (Musgrave et al., 1989; Benes & Forsbach 2002). These algorithms can be controlled for its intensity by the modification of some known constants and parameterized with the number of iterations. The use of erosion effects softens the elevation map keeping the singular characteristics of the terrain, as can be seen in Figure 5.

Thermal erosion simulates deposition of material on the mountain slope base. This material results from the erosion and consequent deposition of sediments that slide down the slope. Erosion is caused by temperature differences resulting from rain, sun, frost and thaw that expand and contract the rocks, creating cracks and breaking them.

The implementation of this algorithm is inspired by the procedures described by Olsen (2004). As described above, this erosion algorithm can be controlled for its intensity, indicating the number of iterations that are performed on the elevation map.

Hydraulic erosion simulates the movement of sediments by the action of water. Part of the soil is diluted in water, which flows along the terrain to areas of lower elevation, depositing the sediments. The dilution and deposition of sediments depends on the saturation level of the water. As the sediments are diluted, the water saturates. Due to evaporation, the saturation level of the water also increases until reaching the saturation limit and causes the deposition of excess sediments. The implemented thermal erosion algorithm, was also based on the procedure described by Olsen (2004).

Figure 5. Elevation map with erosion effect (© 2018, H. F. Pinto, used with permission)

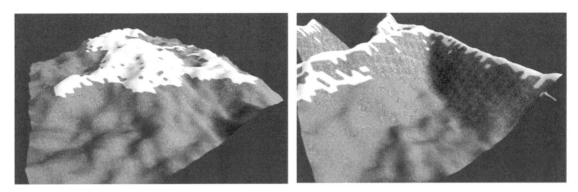

The number of interactions of the erosion algorithm allows controlling the intensity of the changes made in the elevation map. As happened in the thermal erosion algorithm, the erosion can also be controlled through sketches to influence the constants involved in the calculations, simulating respectively the rainfall, soil type and temperature of different regions of the elevation map.

Terrain Adjust

The construction of roadways in the real world implies earthworks in the terrain where the road is implemented. These works modify the terrain relief not only behind the implemented road but also in its neighborhood.

In the same way, when a new road model is added to a terrain model, several adjustments must be performed to produce a perfect match between the terrain and the road models. Without these adjustments, the road environment won't be correctly represented and won't reproduce virtual realistic models, similar to those found in real world. In the proposed method, this adjustment is carried out by the Terrain Adjust module that receives as input the original model of the terrain and any designed road network. This module adjusts the definition of the terrain to produce the final well-constructed visual model.

An efficient method for adapting the altimetry of the terrain, consists in checking for each point of the terrain, if its altitude is influenced by the roads layout. One way to optimize this calculation process for all points is to use a spatial hierarchy of the terrain model, which makes possible to eliminate distant terrain areas that are not affected by the road network.

A slope is the terrain surface which is located along the road and can be originated from an excavation or an embankment on the terrain during construction of a road. Generally, the cut slope and embankment slopes have a maximum declivity of 1 to 1.5 (Vertical/Horizontal) so that the stability of the ground is guaranteed (EP, 1994). Even though of this default parameterizations, the user can specify different values or functions for the cut and embankment slopes.

For each point of the terrain, the minimum distance to the road is calculated and, according to this distance, the necessity to change the z coordinate of the point of terrain is evaluated. When the distance from the terrain point (P_0), to the road centerline (D_p), is less than to the road surface width (D_v), the point is vertically shifted to the new position P_f, laying on the road surface, as illustrated in Figure 6.

This is implemented by adjusting the z coordinate of P_0 to a new z value (P_f), using equation (3). Here, alpha (α) is the road lateral inclination or roll angle.

Figure 6. Cut and embankment slope (© 2018, C. J. Campos, used with permission)

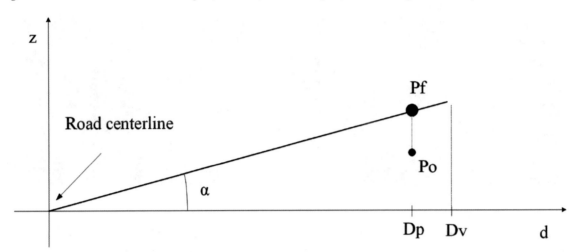

$$Z_{point} = Z_{centerline} + D_p * \tan(\alpha) \tag{3}$$

The z coordinate of the point of the terrain is not changed if it is positioned between the definitions of slopes, as illustrated in Figure 7, for the point P_3.

In Figure 7, two situations are shown where the terrain elevation is modified. If the point being evaluated is located above the calculated cut plan, then its z coordinate is adjusted to the cut slope plan, as happens to point P_1 in the figure. This point it is shifted down to P'_1 point using equation (4), resulting in a cut slope definition. Here, beta is the cut slope inclination angle.

$$Z_{cut} = Z_{centerline} + D_v * \tan(\alpha) + \tan(\beta) * (D_p - D_v) \tag{4}$$

Figure 7. Cut and embankment slope (© 2018, C. J. Campos, used with permission)

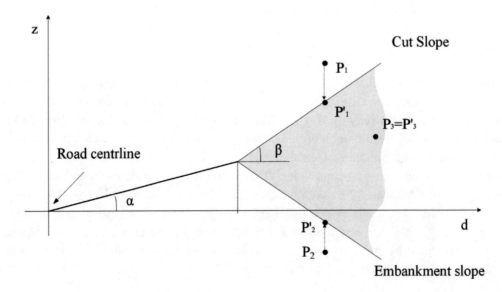

If the point of the terrain is located below the calculated value embankment slope plan, its z coordinate is updated so that the point becomes located in the embankment slope. In the figure, the point P_2 is shifted up to P'_2 point, resulting in an embankment slope (5).

$$Z_{embankment} = Z_{centerline} + D_v * \tan(\alpha) - \tan(\beta) * (D_p - D_v) \qquad (5)$$

In order to optimize this process, the terrain points that are relatively far are not processed. In a natural terrain the green color is predominant, corresponding to local vegetation. It is common to see a change in the color of the terrain when an intervention is carried out with earth works. Typically, in a road area under construction, the color can change from the green of the natural vegetation to the brown corresponding to the earth works. In the edition of the terrain, the modelling information of the edited areas is registered, so that it is possible to render these areas with a different color (typically brown), as shown in Figure 8.

RESULTS

Along this paper, some results were already presented to allow understanding each of the implemented modules. In this section, some examples of resulting driving environments are shown, before and after the roadside landscape edition.

The elevation maps examples presented in this section were generated using grids of cells of 100 meters of length, and a maximum elevation of 2000 meters was defined.

Elevation maps were generated from ridge line defined by of sketches. The number of ridge lines as a significant impact on the relief of the automatically terrain generated. For a high number of ridge lines it is observed that the elevation map appears to have an upper average elevation value (Pinto, 2017). It is due to the proximity of the several ridge lines, not allowing that the elevations can have a high variation, since the mountain feet are relatively near of the ridge lines.

Figure 8. Cut (a) and embankment (b) slope (© 2018, C. J. Campos, used with permission)

(a) (b)

Several sketches were tested and different outputs were obtained. Figure 9 presents an example of a star and circle sketch based for the ridge line.

The erosion effects methods applied (thermal and hydraulic erosion) to the terrain models obtained, produced a more realistic mountain models, and also observed in the Figure 9b and Figure 9c.

After the imposition of the road model, the terrain model was modified, in order to implement the corrective adjustments. This terrain correction was performed by simulating earthworks, resulting in cut and embankments slopes, as shown in Figure 10.

The images of driving environments presented in this chapter, were obtained from the driving simulator *DriS* (Driving Simulator, Engineering Faculty of Porto University). New models of realistic road environments are scheduled to be procedural generated in a near future, and will be applied in driving simulator experiments.

CONCLUSION AND FUTURE WORK

Realistic driving simulation experiments require the preparation of three-dimensional road environments that must be correctly designed and with characteristics similar to those found in the real world. Some experiments also require that these driving environments can be recognized as the road networks from a specific country or region.

The method presented in this paper allows the procedural generation of large terrains and the imposition of roads, meeting the detailed standards of specification. To match the terrain with the road network definition, the adjustment of the roadside landscape is performed, reproducing the earth works, also required in the real world. The cut and embankment slope definitions are implemented with default

Figure 9. Ridge line sketch based with erosion effect (© 2018, H. F. Pinto, used with permission)

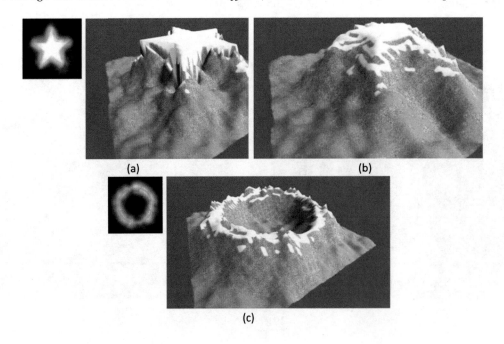

Figure 10. Road environments with cut (a, b) and embankment slopes (c) (© 2018, C. J. Campos, used with permission)

(a)   (b)

functions that meets the standards used in real road design. Additionally, the user can edit and define different functions for the each new type of slope.

The proposed method starts by the definition of the mountain ridge line. This definition can be produced randomly or can be made by user deigned sketch, meeting any specific requirements imposed.

The erosion methods implemented, thermal and hydraulic, allow obtaining realistic mountain shapes, by moving down the soil particles through the mountain hill.

The produced driving environments have all the required characteristics to conduct scientific work in several fields such as psychology, ergonomics and road engineering. The resulting models allow the placement of actors and the implementation of traffic events.

With this implementation, the entire environment can be automatically obtained in an integrated way, dramatically reducing the cost and work involved in the modeling tasks. The generated models are optimized for visual simulation in real time and suitable for integration in driving simulators. As mentioned before, the images of road environments presented in section *Results*, were generated in the *DriS* driving simulator using environments produced by the proposed method.

ACKNOWLEDGMENT

This work had the special contribution of supervisors of the traffic analysis laboratory, where the driving Simulator *DriS* is implemented, Prof. José Pedro Tavares of Civil Engineering Department of FEUP, and Prof. Ângelo Manuel Jacob of Civil Engineering Department of ISEP.

REFERENCES

Belhadj, F., & Audibert, P. (2005, November). Modeling landscapes with ridges and rivers: bottom up approach. In *Proceedings of the 3rd International Conference on Computer Graphics and Interactive Techniques in Australasia and South East Asia* (pp. 447-450). ACM. 10.1145/1101389.1101479

Benes, B., & Forsbach, R. (2001). Layered data representation for visual simulation of terrain erosion. In *Computer Graphics, Spring Conference 2001* (pp. 80-86). IEEE. 10.1109/SCCG.2001.945341

Benes, B., & Forsbach, R. (2002). Visual simulation of hydraulic erosion. *Wscg'2002*, Vols I and II, *Conference Proceedings* (pp. 79-86).

Campos, C., Leitão, M., & Coelho, A. (2014, November). Geração Procedimental de Traçados Rodoviários para Simulação de Condução. In *21º Encontro Português de Computação Gráfica* (pp. 89-96). Instituto Politécnico de Leiria.

Campos, C., Leitão, M., & Coelho, A. (2015a, March). Integrated Modeling of Road Environments for Driving Simulation. In *10th International Conference on Computer Graphics Theory and Applications (Grapp)* (pp. 70-80). Berlin: Academic Press.

Campos, C., Leitão, M., & Coelho, A. (2015c, July). Procedural Generation of Road Paths for Driving Simulation. *International Journal of Creative Interfaces and Computer Graphics*, *6*(2), 37–55. doi:10.4018/IJCICG.2015070103

Campos, C., Leitão, M., Pereira, J., Ribas, A., & Coelho, A. (2015b, June). Procedural generation of topologic road networks for driving simulation. In *Information Systems and Technologies* (CISTI), *10th Iberian Conference* (pp. 1-6). IEEE. 10.1109/CISTI.2015.7170557

Cordonnier, G., Galin, E., Gain, J., Benes, B., Guérin, E., Peytavie, A., & Cani, M. P. (2017). Authoring landscapes by combining ecosystem and terrain erosion simulation. *ACM Transactions on Graphics*, *36*(4), 134. doi:10.1145/3072959.3073667

Doran, J., & Parberry, I. (2010). Controlled procedural terrain generation using software agents. *IEEE Transactions on Computational Intelligence and AI in Games*, *2*(2), 111–119. doi:10.1109/TCIAIG.2010.2049020

EP – Estradas de Portugal. (1994). *Book of Road path Standards*. Junta Autónoma das Estradas.

Fournier, A., Fussell, D., & Carpenter, L. (1982). Computer rendering of stochastic models. *Communications of the ACM*, *25*(6), 371–384. doi:10.1145/358523.358553

Génevaux, J. D., Galin, É., Guérin, E., Peytavie, A., & Benes, B. (2013). Terrain generation using procedural models based on hydrology. *ACM Transactions on Graphics*, *32*(4), 143. doi:10.1145/2461912.2461996

Miller, G. S. (1986, August). The definition and rendering of terrain maps. *Computer Graphics*, *20*(4), 39–48. doi:10.1145/15886.15890

Musgrave, F. K., Kolb, C. E., & Mace, R. S. (1989, July). The synthesis and rendering of eroded fractal terrains. *Computer Graphics*, *23*(3), 41–50. doi:10.1145/74334.74337

Olsen, J. (2004). *Realtime procedural terrain generation*. Department of Mathematics And Computer Science.

Perlin, K. (1985). An image synthesizer. *Computer Graphics*, *19*(3), 287–296. doi:10.1145/325165.325247

Pinto, H. (2017, October). *Framework Para a Modelação Procedimental Integrada de Terrenos Completos* (MSc Thesis). Instituto Superior de Engenharia do Porto.

Schneider, J., Boldte, T., & Westermann, R. (2006, November). Real-time editing, synthesis, and rendering of infinite landscapes on GPUs. Proc. of Vision, modeling, and visualization, 145.

Smelik, R. M., Tutenel, T., de Kraker, K. J., & Bidarra, R. (2008, May). A proposal for a procedural terrain modelling framework. *Proceedings of the 14th Eurographics Symposium on Virtual Environments,* 39-42.

Smelik, R. M., Tutenel, T., de Kraker, K. J., & Bidarra, R. (2011). A declarative approach to procedural modeling of virtual worlds. *Computers & Graphics, 35*(2), 352-363.

Stachniak, S., & Stuerzlinger, W. (2005). An algorithm for automated fractal terrain deformation. *Computer Graphics and Artificial Intelligence, 1,* 64–76.

Zhou, B., & Zhou, S. P. (2007). Motion planning for group movement simulation in dynamic environments. *International Journal of Modelling and Simulation, 27*(4), 379–385. doi:10.1080/02286203.2007.11442440

ADDITIONAL READING

Campos, C., Leitão, M., & Rodrigues, C. (2007, October). Modelação de Ambientes Rodoviários de Grandes Dimensões, *15.º Encontro Português de Computação Gráfica,* (pp. 19-28), Taguspark, Lisbon.

Chen, G., Esch, G., Wonka, P., Müller, P., & Zhang, E. (2008). Interactive procedural street modeling. *ACM Transactions on Graphics, 27*(3), 103. doi:10.1145/1360612.1360702

Coelho, A., Bessa, M., Sousa, A. A., & Ferreira, F. N. (2007, December). Expeditious Modelling of Virtual Urban Environments with Geospatial L-systems. *Computer Graphics Forum, 26*(4), 769–782.

Galin, E., Peytavie, A., Guérin, E., & Beneš, B. (2011, September). Authoring hierarchical road networks. *Computer Graphics Forum, 30*(7), 2021–2030. doi:10.1111/j.1467-8659.2011.02055.x

Galin, E., Peytavie, A., Maréchal, N., & Guérin, E. (2010, May). Procedural generation of roads. *Computer Graphics Forum, 29*(2), 429–438. doi:10.1111/j.1467-8659.2009.01612.x

Génevaux, J. D., Galin, É., Guérin, E., Peytavie, A., & Benes, B. (2013). Terrain generation using procedural models based on hydrology. *ACM Transactions on Graphics, 32*(4), 143. doi:10.1145/2461912.2461996

Smelik, R. M., Tutenel, T., Bidarra, R., & Benes, B. (2014, September). A survey on procedural modelling for virtual worlds. *Computer Graphics Forum, 33*(6), 31–50. doi:10.1111/cgf.12276

Thomas, G., & Donikian, S. (2000, September). Modelling virtual cities dedicated to behavioural animation. *Computer Graphics Forum, 19*(3), 71–80. doi:10.1111/1467-8659.00399

KEY TERMS AND DEFINITIONS

3D Model: A software representation of a three-dimensional element, mainly concerning the object geometry but can also address many other properties.

Driving Environment: A real or virtual world used to conduct driving tasks, including a road network, road side elements, landscapes and other vehicles or participants.

Embankment and Cut Slope: Terrain hills located on the side of the road that can be natural or artificial made during the road construction.

Procedural Modeling: A technique used in computer graphics to automate the creation of 3D models from sets of rules or algorithms.

Road Network: A set of intersecting roads and their interconnections allowing the selection of several different travel paths between the start and end points.

Scientific Driving Simulation: A fully parametrizable and controllable simulation of a car driving task, aimed to conduct scientific studies about vehicle performance, road design or driver behavior.

Sketch: A rough drawing or specification usually made to predict and assisting production of a final product.

Terrain Erosion: The evolutive process of changing the shape of terrain due to wind, water, or other natural agents.

Compilation of References

27 ways to tell a story in VR. (2018). Retrieved from http://alookintolater.blogspot.com/2018/05/27-ways-to-tell-story-in-vr.html

Adams, N. B. (2004). Digital Intelligence Fostered by Technology. *Journal of Technology Studies*, *30*(2), 93–97. doi:10.21061/jots.v30i2.a.5

Adobe Education White Paper. (2011). *Adobe Systems Incorporated*. Retrieved from https://www.adobe.com/content/dam/Adobe/en/education/pdfs/strategies-for-digital-communication-skills-across-disciplines-june-2011.pdf

Aihara, K., & Hori, K. (1998). Enhancing creativity through reorganizing mental space concealed ina research notes stack. *Knowledge-Based Systems*, *11*(7-8), 469–478. doi:10.1016/S0950-7051(98)00080-X

Alexander, B., & Levine, A. (2008). *Web 2.0 Storytelling: Emergence of a New Genre*. Retrieved from http://www.educause.edu/EDUCAUSE+Review/EDUCAUSEReviewMagazineVolume43/Web20StorytellingEmergenceofaN/163262

Alexander, B. (2011). *The New Digital Storytelling: Creating Narratives with New Media*. Praeger.

al-Rifaie, M. M., Cropley, A., Cropley, D., & Bishop, M. (2016). On evil and computational creativity. *ResearchGate*. Retrieved from https://www.researchgate.net/publication/297751482_On_evil_and_computational_creativity

Alvaro, M., Angel, R. J., & Camara, F. (2012). High-pressure behavior of zoisite. *The American Mineralogist*, *97*(7), 1165–1176. doi:10.2138/am.2012.4014

American Psychiatric Association (APA). (2013). *DSM-V*. Washington, DC: American Psychiatric Publishing, Inc.

Arendt, H. (1998). *The human condition*. Chicago: University of Chicago Press. doi:10.7208/chicago/9780226924571.001.0001

Arnheim, R. (1990). Language and the Early Cinema. *Leonardo, Digital Image-Digital Cinema Supplemental Issue, 3-4*.

Arnheim, R. (1956). *Art and Visual Perception*. London: Faber and Faber.

Arnheim, R. (1988). *The power of the center - A study of composition in the visual arts*. Berkeley: University of California Press.

Assey, J. (1999). The Future of Technology in K-12 Arts Education. *Forum on Technology in Education: Envisioning the Future. Proceedings*, 15.

Ausubel, D. P. (2012). *The acquisition and retention of knowledge: A cognitive view*. Springer Science & Business Media.

Azuma, R. T. (1997). A Survey of Augmented Reality. *Presence (Cambridge, Mass.)*, *6*(4), 355–385. doi:10.1162/pres.1997.6.4.355

Backus, J. G. (1969). The Acoustical Foundations of Music – Musical Sound: a Lucid Account of its Properties, Production, Behavior, and Reproduction. W. W. Norton.

Baker, F. W. (2013). Teaching media literacy with technology. *Learning and Leading with Technology, 40*(7), 32.

Baltazar, A. P. (2009). *Cyberarchitecture: the virtualisation of architecture beyond representation towards interactivity* (Unpublished doctoral dissertation). The Bartlett School of Architecture, University College London.

Baltazar, A. P. (2012). Beyond representation: possible uses of new media in architecture. In *V!RUS 8*: RE:PRE:SENTAR. São Carlos: Nomads. Retrieved from http://www.nomads.usp.br/virus/virus08/?sec=4&item=1&lang=en

Baltazar, A. P. (2017). Architecture as interface: a constructive method for spatial articulation in architectural education. In *Architectural Research Addressing Societal Challenges*. London: Taylor & Francis. Retrieved from http://www.mom.arq.ufmg.br/mom/arq_interface/3a_aula/2016_06_16_eaae_baltazar.pdf

Baltazar, A. P., Cabral Filho, J. S., Melgaço, L. M. S., Almeida, M. A., & Arruda, G. F. (2012). Towards socially engaging and transformative urban interactive interfaces. *Proceedings of Artech 2012 – 6th International Conference on Digital Arts*, 279–285.

Baltazar, A. P., Arruda, G. F., Cabral Filho, J. S., Melgaço, L. M. S., & Almeida, M. A. (2014). Beyond the visual in urban interactive interfaces: Dialogue and social transformation. *International Journal of Creative Interfaces and Computer Graphics, 5*(2), 1–15. doi:10.4018/ijcicg.2014070101

Baltazar, A. P., & Cabral Filho, J. S. (2010). Magic beyond ignorance: virtualising the black box. In H. Roscoe, P. Moran, & T. Mucelli (Eds.), *FAD—Festival de Arte Digital 2010* (pp. 19–23). Belo Horizonte: Instituto Cidades Criativas.

Bangor, A., Kortum, P., & Miller, J. (2009). Determining What Individual SUS Scores Mean: Adding an Adjective Rating Scale. *JUS Journal of Usability Studies, 4*(3), 114–123.

Baus, O., & Bouchard, S. (2014). Moving from Virtual Reality Exposure-Based Therapy to Augmented Reality Exposure-Based Therapy: A Review. *Frontiers in Human Neuroscience, 8*, 1–15. doi:10.3389/fnhum.2014.00112 PMID:24624073

Beidel, D. C., & Turner, S. M. (2007). *Shy Children, Phobic Adults: Nature and Treatment of Social Anxiety Disorder* (2nd ed.). Washington, DC: APA.

Belhadj, F., & Audibert, P. (2005, November). Modeling landscapes with ridges and rivers: bottom up approach. In *Proceedings of the 3rd International Conference on Computer Graphics and Interactive Techniques in Australasia and South East Asia* (pp. 447-450). ACM. 10.1145/1101389.1101479

Bendazzi, G. (1999). *Cartoons: One hundred Years of Cinema Animation (Reprint Edition)*. Indiana University Press.

Benes, B., & Forsbach, R. (2001). Layered data representation for visual simulation of terrain erosion. In *Computer Graphics, Spring Conference 2001* (pp. 80-86). IEEE. 10.1109/SCCG.2001.945341

Benes, B., & Forsbach, R. (2002). Visual simulation of hydraulic erosion. *Wscg'2002*, Vols I and II, *Conference Proceedings* (pp. 79-86).

Benjamin, W. (1985). A Obra de Arte na Era da sua Reprodução técnica. In E. Geada (Ed.), *Org.). Estéticas do Cinema*. Lisboa: Publicações Dom Quixote.

Billinghurst, M. (2002). Augmented reality in education. *New Horizons for Learning, 12*.

Birgili, B. (2015). Creative and critical thinking skills in problem-based learning environments. *Journal of Gifted Education and Creativity, 2*(2), 71–80. doi:10.18200/JGEDC.2015214253

Blake, R., & Sekuler, R. (2006). *Perception* (5th ed.). Boston: McGraw Hill.

Bloop Animation Studios. 2017). *How to Make an Animatic (Making an Animated Movie)*. Retrieved from https://www.bloopanimation.com/animatic/

Boden, M. A. (2018). Artificial Intelligence: A Very Short Introduction. Oxford University Press.

Boden, M. A. (1998). Creativity and artificial intelligence. *Artificial Intelligence, 103*(1-2), 347–356. doi:10.1016/S0004-3702(98)00055-1

Boden, M. A. (2016). Skills and the Appreciation of Computer Art. In *Computational Creativity, Measurement and Evaluation, Connection Science*. Taylor & Francis. doi:10.1080/09540091.2015.1130023

BoereeC. G. (2002). *Early Medicine and Physiology*. Retrieved from http://webspace.ship.edu/cgboer/neurophysio.html

Borges, J. L. (2000). *Ficções*. Lisboa: Visão.

Borovoy, R. (2011). Junkyard Jumbotron, *MIT Center for Civic Media*. Retrieved December 27, 2017 from http://civic.mit.edu/blog/csik/junkyard-jumbotron

Bradley, M. M., & Lang, P. J. (1994). Measuring Emotion: The Self-Assessment Manikin and the Semantic Differential. Journal of Behavior Therapy and Experimental Psychiatry, *25*(1), 49–59. doi:10.1016/0005-7916(94)90063-9 PMID:7962581

Bread and Puppet Theater. (2017). Retrieved from http://breadandpuppet.org/

Bregman, A. S. (1990). *Auditory scene analysis*. Cambridge, MA: MIT Press.

Brooke, J. (1996). SUS: a quick and dirty usability scale. In P. W. Jordan, B. Thomas, I. L. McClelland, & B. Weerdmeester (Eds.), *Usability Evaluation In Industry*. London: CRC Press.

Broudy, H. S. (1991). *The Role of Imagery in Learning (Occasional Paper 1)*. Getty Center for Education in the Arts.

Browne, M. W. (2000). Cross-Validation Methods. *Journal of Mathematical Psychology, 44*(1), 108–132. doi:10.1006/jmps.1999.1279 PMID:10733860

Buhamad, A. (2016). *Visual Approach and Design: the Appropriate Characteristics of Instructional Photos as a Tool to Support Elementary Setting in Kuwait*. Doctoral Dissertations, Paper 323. Retrieved April 25, 2017, from http://digscholarship.unco.edu/dissertations/

Buzan, T. (1976). *Use both sides of your brain*. New York: E. P. Dutton & Co.

Calvino, I. (2002). *Se numa noite de Inverno um viajante*. Lisboa: Editorial Teorema.

Campos, C., Leitão, M., & Coelho, A. (2014, November). Geração Procedimental de Traçados Rodoviários para Simulação de Condução. In *21º Encontro Português de Computação Gráfica* (pp. 89-96). Instituto Politécnico de Leiria.

Campos, C., Leitão, M., & Coelho, A. (2015a, March). Integrated Modeling of Road Environments for Driving Simulation. In *10th International Conference on Computer Graphics Theory and Applications (Grapp)* (pp. 70-80). Berlin: Academic Press.

Campos, C., Leitão, M., Pereira, J., Ribas, A., & Coelho, A. (2015b, June). Procedural generation of topologic road networks for driving simulation. In *Information Systems and Technologies* (CISTI), *10th Iberian Conference* (pp. 1-6). IEEE. 10.1109/CISTI.2015.7170557

Campos, C., Leitão, M., & Coelho, A. (2015c, July). Procedural Generation of Road Paths for Driving Simulation. *International Journal of Creative Interfaces and Computer Graphics, 6*(2), 37–55. doi:10.4018/IJCICG.2015070103

Caputo, A. C., Ellison, H., & Steranko, J. (2011). *Visual Storytelling*. Watson-Guptill/Random House.

Chang, C.-C., & Lin, C.-J. (2011). LIBSVM: A library for support vector machines, 2(27). *ACM Transactions on Intelligent Systems and Technology, 2*(3), 1–27. doi:10.1145/1961189.1961199

Chen, B., & Bryar, T. (2012). Investigating Instructional Strategies for Using Social Media in Formal and Informal Learning. *International Review of Research in Open and Distance Learning, 13*(1), 87–104. doi:10.19173/irrodl.v13i1.1027

Christopher, N. (2008). The Bestiary. Dial Press Trade (Reprint ed.).

Chung, D. N. (2012). *Language Arts*. Western Washington University. Retrieved from http://faculty.wwu.edu/auer/Resources/Hayakawa-Abstraction-Ladder.pdf

Cláudio, A. P., Carmo, M. B., Gaspar, A., & Teixeira, R. (2015a). Using Expressive and Talkative Virtual Characters in Social Anxiety Disorder Treatment. In *Proc. GRAPP 2015, 10th International Conference on Computer Graphics Theory and Applications* (pp 348-355). SciTePress.

Cláudio, A. P., Carmo, M. B., Pinheiro, T., & Esteves, F. (2013). A Virtual Reality Solution to Handle Social Anxiety. *International Journal of Creative Interfaces and Computer Graphics, 4*(2), 57–72. doi:10.4018/ijcicg.2013070104

Cláudio, A. P., Carmo, M. B., Pinto, V., Cavaco, A., & Guerreiro, M. P. (2015b). Virtual Humans for Training and Assessment of Self-medication Consultation Skills in Pharmacy Students. In *Proc. IEEE ICCSE 2015- 10th International Conference on Computer Science & Education*, Cambridge, UK (pp 175-180). 10.1109/ICCSE.2015.7250238

Cláudio, A. P., Gaspar, A., Lopes, E., & Carmo, M. B. (2014). Virtual Characters with Affective Facial Behavior. In *Proc. GRAPP 2014, 9th International Conference on Computer Graphics Theory and Applications* (pp 348-355). SciTePress.

Collins, A., & Halverson, R. R. (2009). *Rethinking education in the age of technology: The digital revolution and schooling in America* (M. C. Linn, Ed.). New York: Teachers College Press.

Colonna, F. (1999). *Hypnerotomachia Poliphili: the strife of love in a dream*. London: Thames and Hudson.

Colzato, L. S., Ozturk, A., & Hommel, B. (2012). Meditate to create: The impact of focused-attention and open-monitoring training on convergent and divergent thinking. *Frontiers in Psychology, 3*. PMID:22529832

Constant, J. (2013). Symmetry in Mathematics, Physics and Art. *Journal of Symmetry: Culture and Science, 24*(1-4), 57-68.

Constant, J. (2016). *The 12-30 Project*. BLb publishers. Retrieved from https://jcdigitaljournal.wordpress.com/

Constant, J. (2018). *Geometry of Nature*. Retrieved from https://jconstantblog.wordpress.com/

Cordonnier, G., Galin, E., Gain, J., Benes, B., Guérin, E., Peytavie, A., & Cani, M. P. (2017). Authoring landscapes by combining ecosystem and terrain erosion simulation. *ACM Transactions on Graphics, 36*(4), 134. doi:10.1145/3072959.3073667

Corey, R., & Pauling, L. (1953). Molecular Models of Amino Acids, Peptides, and Proteins. *The Review of Scientific Instruments, 24*(8), 621–627. doi:10.1063/1.1770803

Corrêa, A. G. D., Lima, M., Melo, D. G. de, & Santos, I. I. dos. (2012). Desenvolvimento de um Livro Interativo em Realidade Aumentada para Ensino e Aprendizagem Musical. *CINTED-UFGRS Novas Tecnologias Na Educação, 10*(3).

Correia, J., Machado, P., Romero, J., & Carballal, A. (2013). *Feature Selection and Novelty in Computational Aesthetics. In Evolutionary And Biologicaly Inspired Music, Sound, Art* (pp. 133–144). Vienna, Austria: Springer.

Coxeter, H. S. M., & Greitzer, S. L. (1970). *Geometry Revisited.* Washington, DC: Math. Assoc. Amer.

Create your storyboard in Microsoft Word. (2017). Retrieved from http://digitalstorytelling.coe.uh.edu/pdfs/How-to-Create-Storyboard.pdf

Cruz, T. (2013). *CulturalNature Arga#2.* Retrieved March 30, 2018, from https://www.behance.net/gallery/10404419/CulturalNature-Arga2

Cruz-Cunha, M. M., Reis, M., Peres, E., Varajão, J., Bessa, M., Magalhães, L., ... Barreira, J. (2010). Realidade Aumentada e Ubiquidade na Educação. *IEEE-RITA,* 5(4), 167–174.

Darwin, C. (2004). The Descent of Man. Penguin Classics.

Datta, R., Joshi, D., & Wang, J. (2006). Studying Aesthetics in Photographic Images Using a Computational Approach. In *European Conference on Computer Vision* (pp. 288-301). Graz, Austria: Springer. 10.1007/11744078_23

Datta, R., Li, J., & Wang, J. (2008). Algorithmic inferencing of aesthetics and emotion in natural images: An exposition. In *15th IEEE International Conference on Image Processing* (pp. 105-108). San Diego, CA: IEEE. 10.1109/ICIP.2008.4711702

Davies, M. (2011). Concept mapping, mind mapping and argument mapping: What are the differences and do they matter? *Higher Education,* 62(3), 279–301. doi:10.100710734-010-9387-6

de Villers-Sidani, E., Chang, E. F., Bao, S., & Merzenich, M. M. (2007). Critical period window for spectral tuning defined in the primary auditory cortex (A1) in the rat. *The Journal of Neuroscience,* 27(1), 1809. doi:10.1523/JNEUROSCI.3227-06.2007 PMID:17202485

Deleuze, G. (1985). *A Imagem-Movimento.* São Paulo: Brasiliense.

Deleuze, G. (1990). *A Imagem-Tempo.* São Paulo: Brasiliense.

Dertien, E., Dijkstra, J., Mader, A., & Reidsma, D. (2012). Making a toy educative using electronics. In A. Nijholt, T. Romao, & D. Reidsma (Eds.), Advances in Computer Entertainment, LNCS (Vol. 7624, pp. 477–480), Springer. doi:10.1007/978-3-642-34292-9_39

DeSchryver, M. (2017). Using the web as a higher order thinking partner: Case study of an advanced learner creatively synthesizing knowledge on the web. *Journal of Educational Computing Research,* 55(2), 240–271. doi:10.1177/0735633116667356

DeSchryver, M. D., & Yadav, A. (2015). Creative and computational thinking in the context of new literacies: Working with teachers to scaffold complex technology-mediated approaches to teaching and learning. *Journal of Technology and Teacher Education,* 23(3), 411–431.

Deutsch, D. (2013). *The Psychology of Music* (3rd ed.). Elsevier Inc.

DIGINFO TV. (2012). Pinch interface connects the displays of multiple devices simultaneously. Retrieved December 27, 2017 from https://www.youtube.com/watch?v=jRGLkj-PsCc

Doering, A., & Henrickson, J. (2015). Fostering creativity through inquiry and adventure in informal learning environment design. *Journal of Technology and Teacher Education,* 23(3), 387–410.

Donoghue, J. P. (2002). Connecting cortex to machines: Recent advances in brain interfaces. *Nature Neuroscience,* 5(Supp), 1085–1088. doi:10.1038/nn947 PMID:12403992

Doran, J., & Parberry, I. (2010). Controlled procedural terrain generation using software agents. *IEEE Transactions on Computational Intelligence and AI in Games,* 2(2), 111–119. doi:10.1109/TCIAIG.2010.2049020

Douilliez, C., Yzerbyt, V., Gilboa-Schechtman, E., & Philippot, P. (2012). Social anxiety biases the evaluation of facial displays: Evidence from single face and multi-facial stimuli. *Cognition and Emotion*, *26*(6), 1107–1115. doi:10.1080/0 2699931.2011.632494 PMID:22122070

Download a storyboard template as PDF. (2018). Retrieved from http://digitalstorytelling.coe.uh.edu/storyboard-templates/PDF-storyboard.pdf

Dubberly, H., Haque, U., & Pangaro, P. (2009). What is interaction? Are there different types? *Interactions Magazine*, *16*(1). Retrieved from http://www.dubberly.com/articles/what-is-interaction.html

Dunleavy, M., Dede, C., & Mitchell, R. (2009). Affordances and limitations of immersive participatory augmented reality simulations for teaching and learning. *Journal of Science Education and Technology*, *18*(1), 7–22. doi:10.100710956-008-9119-1

Eberle, S. G. (2011). Playing with the Multiple Intelligences: How Play Helps Them Grow. *American Journal of Play*, *4*(1), 19–51.

Eco, U. (1989). *The Open Work* (A. Cancogni, Trans.). Cambridge, MA: Harvard University Press.

Educational Uses of Digital Storytelling. (2017). Retrieved from (http://digitalstorytelling.coe.uh.edu/page.cfm?id=23&cid=23&sublinkid=37

Eggen, P., & Schellenberg, S. (2010). Human Memory and the New Science of Learning. In M. S. Khine & I. M. Saleh (Eds.), New Science of Learning Cognition, Computers and Collaboration in Education. New York: Springer Science+Business Media, LLC. doi:10.1007/978-1-4419-5716-0_5

Ehle, R. C. (2016). How We Hear and Experience Music: a Bootstrap Theory of Sensory Perception. In A. Ursyn (Ed.), *Knowledge Visualization and Visual Literacy in Science Education*. Hershey, PA: IGI Global. doi:10.4018/978-1-5225-0480-1.ch008

Eibl-Eibesfeldt, I. (1989). *Human Ethology*. NY: Aldine de Gruyter.

Ekman, P., Friesen, W. V., & Hager, J. C. (2002). *Facial action coding system*. Salt Lake City, UT: Research Nexus.

Elkins, J., & DeLuc, R. (2008). *Landscape Theory*. New York: Routledge.

Encyclopedia Britannica. (2018). *Combination tone*. Retrieved from http://www.britannica.com/science/combination-tone

EP – Estradas de Portugal. (1994). *Book of Road path Standards*. Junta Autónoma das Estradas.

Essley, R., Rief, L., & Rocci, A. l. (2017). Visual Tools for Differentiating Reading & Writing Instruction. Strategies to Help Students Make Abstract Ideas Concrete & Accessible. *Scholastic*.

Esteves, F., Isberg, N., Cláudio, A. P., Carmo, B., & Gaspar, A. (2016). Psychophysiological responses to a virtual reality scenario for the treatment of social anxiety. *International Journal of Psychophysiology*, *108*, 138. doi:10.1016/j.ijpsycho.2016.07.403

Falchuk, B., Zernicki, T., & Koziuk, M. (2012). Towards Streamed Services for Co-located Collaborative Groups. In *Proceedings of the 8th IEEE International Conference on Collaborative Computing: Networking, Applications and Worksharing*, IEEE Computer Society. 10.4108/icst.collaboratecom.2012.250426

Farlex. (2012). *Otoacoustic emission*. Farlex Partner Medical Dictionary.

Fedorov, E. (1891). Symmetry in the plane. *Proceedings of the Imperial St. Petersburg Mineralogical Society*.

Ferro, S. (2006). *Arquitetura e trabalho livre*. Belo Horizonte: Cosac Naify.

Figueiredo, A. S. L. (2007). *Realidade Virtual no Ensino e na Aprendizagem de Geometria Descritiva* (Master's Thesis). Instituto Superior de Tecnologia e Gestão do Instituto Politécnico da Guarda. Retrieved from https://repositorio-aberto. up.pt/handle/10216/11043

Figueiredo, M., Amado, N., Bidarra, J., & Carreira, S. (2015). *A realidade aumentada na aprendizagem da matemática no ensino secundário.* Retrieved from http://hdl.handle.net/10400.2/4566

Figueiredo, M., Gomes, J., Gomes, C., & Lopes, J. (2014). Augmented Reality tools and techniques for developing interactive materials for mobile-learning. *Journal Recent Advances Educational Technologies and Methodologies, 395*(7), 63–72.

Flor-Henry, P. (1983). *Cerebral basis of psychopathology.* Boston, MA: John Wright.

Flusser, V. (1999a). Design: obstacle for/to the removal of obstacles. In V. Flusser (Ed.), *The shape of things: a philosophy of design* (pp. 58–61). London: Reaktion.

Flusser, V. (2000). *Towards a Philosophy of Photography.* London: Reaktion Books.

Flusser, V. (2011). *Into the Universe of Technical Images.* University of Minnesota Press. doi:10.5749/minnesota/9780816670208.001.0001

Forsythe, A., Nadal, M., Sheehy, N., Cela-Conde, C., & Sawey, M. (2011). Predicting beauty: Fractal dimension and visual complexity in art. *British Journal of Psychology, 102*(1), 49–70. doi:10.1348/000712610X498958 PMID:21241285

Fournier, A., Fussell, D., & Carpenter, L. (1982). Computer rendering of stochastic models. *Communications of the ACM, 25*(6), 371–384. doi:10.1145/358523.358553

Fowkes, R., & Fowkes, M. (2010). *Unframed Landscapes: Nature in Contemporary Art.* Retrieved March 30, 2018, from http://www.neme.org/texts/unframed-landscapes

Gaggioli, A., Mantovani, F., Castelnuovo, G., Wiederhold, B., & Riva, G. (2003). Avatars in clinical psychology: a framework for the clinical use of virtual humans. *Cyberpsychology & Behavior: The Impact of the Internet, Multimedia and Virtual Reality on Behavior and Society, 6*(2), 117–125. doi:10.1089/109493103321640301

Galanter, P. (2003). *What is Generative Art?* New York: New York University.

Gaspar, A., & Esteves, F. (2012). Preschoolers faces in spontaneous emotional contexts – how well do they match adult facial expression prototypes? *International Journal of Behavioral Development, 36*(5), 348–357. doi:10.1177/0165025412441762

Gaspar, A., Esteves, F., & Arriaga, P. (2014). On prototypical facial expressions vs variation in facial behavior: lessons learned on the "visibility" of emotions from measuring facial actions in humans and apes. In M. Pina & N. Gontier (Eds.), *The Evolution of Social Communication in Primates: A Multidisciplinary Approach, Interdisciplinary Evolution Research* (pp. 101–145). New York: Springer. doi:10.1007/978-3-319-02669-5_6

Gazzaniga, M. (2008). Arts and cognition: Findings hint at relationships. *Learning, Arts, and the Brain: The Dana Consortium Report on Arts and Cognition*, 93–104.

Génevaux, J. D., Galin, É., Guérin, E., Peytavie, A., & Benes, B. (2013). Terrain generation using procedural models based on hydrology. *ACM Transactions on Graphics, 32*(4), 143. doi:10.1145/2461912.2461996

Gerdes, P. (1998). *Women, Art and Geometry in Southern Africa.* Lawrenceville, NJ: Africa World Press.

Gerdes, P. (1999). *Geometry from Africa. In Mathematical and Educational Explorations.* Washington, DC: The Mathematical Association of America.

Ghani, D. A. (2011, January-June). Visualization Elements of Shadow Play Technique Movement and Study of Computer Graphic Imagery (CGI) in Wayang Kulit Kelantan. *International Journal of Art, Culture and Design Technologies, 1*(1), 50–57. doi:10.4018/ijacdt.2011010105

Giannetti, C. (2006). *Estética Digital: Sintopia da arte, a ciência e a tecnologia*. Belo Horizonte: C/Arte.

Giménez, C. (2012). *Picasso Black and White*. Prestel.

Glantz, K., Durlach, N. I., Barnett, R. C., & Aviles, W. A. (1996). Virtual Reality (VR) For Psychotherapy: From the Physical to the social Environment 1. *Psychotherapy, 33*(3), 464–473. doi:10.1037/0033-3204.33.3.464

Glattke, T. J., & Kujawa, S. G. (1991). Otoacoustic Emissions. *American Journal of Audiology, 1*(1), 29–40. doi:10.1044/1059-0889.0101.29 PMID:26659426

Glaveanu, V. P., Sierra, Z., & Tanggaard, L. (2015). Widening our understanding of creative pedagogy: A north-south dialogue. *Education 3-13, 43*(4), 360-370.

Goldschmidt, G. (2016). Linkographic evidence for concurrent divergent and convergent thinking in creative design. *Creativity Research Journal, 28*(2), 115–122. doi:10.1080/10400419.2016.1162497

Graeme, R. (2006). The transformational creativity hypothesis. *New Generation Computing, 24*(3), 241–266. doi:10.1007/BF03037334

Graham, J. (Producer), Bejan, Bob (Director). (1992). *I'm your Man*. [Motion picture]. New York: ChoicePoint Films.

Graham, S. (2004). *The Cybercities Reader*. New York: Routledge.

Greenaway, P. (2003). *Tulse Luper Suitcases*. Delux Productions.

Greenaway, P. (2007). O cinema está morto, vida longa ao cinema. *Caderno SESC Videobrasil, 3*, 3.

Grillon, H. (2009). Simulating interactions with virtual characters for the treatment of social phobia. Doctoral dissertation, EPFL.

Gross, D. (1996). The role of symmetry in fundamental physics. *Proceedings of the NSA, 93*(25). 10.1073/pnas.93.25.14256

Grossman, W. (2015). *Man Ray: Human Equations*. Hatje Cantz.

Gutiérrez-Maldonado, J., Ferrer-García, M., Dakanalis, A., & Riva, G. (2017). Virtual Reality: Applications to Eating Disorders. In W. Stewart & A. H. Robinson (Eds.), *The Oxford HandBook of Eating Disorders* (2nd ed.). Online Publication. doi:10.1093/oxfordhb/9780190620998.013.26

Häkkilä, J. R., Posti, M., Schneegass, S., Alt, F., Gultekin, K., & Schmidt, A. (2014, April). Let me catch this!: experiencing interactive 3D cinema through collecting content with a mobile phone. In *Proceedings of the SIGCHI Conference on Human Factors in Computing Systems* (pp. 1011-1020). ACM.

Halliday, M. (1978). *Language as social semiotic: the social interpretation of language and meaning*. University Park Press.

Hall, S., Allen, F. H., & Brown, I. (1991). The Crystallographic Information File (CIF): A New Standard Archive File for Crystallography. *Acta Crystallographica. Section A, Foundations of Crystallography, 47*(6), 655–685. doi:10.1107/S010876739101067X

Halpers, O. (2014). *Beautiful Data: A History of Vision and Reason since 1945 (Experimental Futures)*. Duke University Press Books.

Hames, P. (Ed.). (2007). *The Cinema of Jan Švankmajer: Dark Alchemy (Directors' Cuts)* (2nd ed.). Wallflower Press.

Hamza, T. S., & Hassan, D. K. (2016). Consequential creativity: Student competency and lateral thinking incorporation in architectural education. *International Journal of Technology and Design Education, 26*(4), 587–612. doi:10.100710798-015-9321-4

Haque, U. (2016-2018). *Umbrellium Group, VoiceOver.* Retrieved from <http://umbrellium.co.uk/initiatives/voiceover/>

Haque, U. (2017). VoiceOver: Citizen Empowerment Through Cultural Infrastructure. *Architectural Design, 87*(1), 86–91. doi:10.1002/ad.2136

Haroz, S. (2013). *Perception and attention for visualization* (Doctoral dissertation). University of California at Davis, Davis, CA.

Harris, A. L., & Rea, A. (2009). Web 2.0 and virtual world technologies: A growing impact on IS education. *Journal of Information Systems Education, 20*(2), 137.

Haworth, M. B., Baljko, M., & Faloutsos, P. (2012). PhoVR: a virtual reality system to treat phobias. In *Proceedings of the 11th ACM SIGGRAPH International Conference on Virtual-Reality Continuum and its Applications in Industry* (pp. 171-174). 10.1145/2407516.2407560

Hayakawa, S. I., & Hayakawa, A. R. (1991). Language in Thought and Action (5th ed.). Harvest Original. (originally printed in 1941)

Heller, E. J. (2012). *Why You Hear What You Hear: An Experiential Approach to Sound, Music, and Psychoacoustics.* Princeton University Press.

Helmick, R. (1984). Enhancing creativity in art and design through stochastically generated computer graphics. *Art Education, 37*(4), 36–39. doi:10.2307/3192746

Hensel, J. (2010). Once Upon a Time. *Meeting Professionals International.* Retrieved from http://www.mpiweb.org/Magazine/Archive/US/February2010/OnceUponATime

Herbelin, B. (2005). Virtual reality exposure therapy for social phobia [Doctoral dissertation]. EPFL.

Hermann, C. (1928). Zur systematische Strukturtheorie. *Zeitschrift fur Kristallographie, 68,* 257–287.

Herrmann, N. (1990). *The creative brain.* Lake Lure, NC: Brain Books.

Hersh, M. A., & Leporini, B. (2013). An Overview of Accessibility and Usability of Educational Games. In C. Gonzalez (Ed.), *Student Usability in Educational Software and Games.* Hershey, PA: Information Science Reference (an imprint of IGI Global). doi:10.4018/978-1-4666-1987-6.ch001

Hessel, J. F. C. (1830). *Krystallometrie oder Krystallonomie und Krystallographie* (Vol. 5). Gehler's Physikalisches Wörterbuch.

Hestenes, D. (2002). *Point Groups and Space Groups in Geometric Algebra.* Tempe, AZ: Department of Physics and Astronomy Arizona State University. doi:10.1007/978-1-4612-0089-5_1

Hinckley, K. (2003). Synchronous gestures for multiple persons and computers. In *Proceedings of the 16th Annual ACM Symposium on User Interface Software and Technology (UIST 2003)* (pp. 149–158). ACM, New York. 10.1145/964696.964713

Hinckley, K., Ramos, G., Guimbretiere, F., Baudisch, P., & Smith, M. (2004). Stitching: pen gestures that span multiple displays. In *Proceedings of the Working Conference on Advanced Visual Interfaces (AVI 2004)* (pp. 23–31). New York: ACM. 10.1145/989863.989866

Hirsh, A. T., Callander, S. B., & Robinson, M. E. (2011). Patient demographic characteristics and facial expressions influence nurses' assessment of mood in the context of pain: A virtual human and lens model investigation. *International Journal of Nursing Studies*, 48(11), 1330–1338. doi:10.1016/j.ijnurstu.2011.05.002 PMID:21596378

Hodapp, C. L. (2010). *Deciphering the Lost Symbol*. Ulysses Press. (originally printed in 1873)

Hodge, R., & Kress, G. (1988). *Social Semiotics*. Cambridge, UK: Polity Press.

Holm, G. (2008). Photography as a performance. *Forum Qualitative Social Research*, 9(2), 38. Retrieved from http://www.qualitative-research.net/index.php/fqs/article/viewArticle/394/856

Huizinga, J. (1992). *Homo ludens: o jogo como elemento da cultura*. São Paulo: Perspectiva.

Hyerle, D. (1996). *Visual tools for constructing knowledge (ERIC Document Reproduction Service No. ED399257)*. Alexandria, VA: Association for Supervision and Curriculum Development.

Ibáñez, M. B., Di Serio, Á., Villarán, D., & Kloos, C. D. (2014). Experimenting with electromagnetism using augmented reality: Impact on flow student experience and educational effectiveness. *Computers & Education*, 71(0), 1–13. doi:10.1016/j.compedu.2013.09.004

Ibanez, M. B., Di-Serio, A., Villaran-Molina, D., & Delgado-Kloos, C. (2015). Augmented Reality-Based Simulators as Discovery Learning Tools: An Empirical Study. *Education. IEEE Transactions on*, 58(3), 208–213. doi:10.1109/TE.2014.2379712

Igoe, T. (2007). *Making things talk: practical methods for connecting physical objects*. Beijing: O'Reilly.

Intelity. (2011). The Intelity 64 iPad Wall. Retrieved December 27, 2017 from https://vimeo.com/

Jackson, S. (1981/2018). *Killer: The Game of Assassination*. Retrieved from http://www.sjgames.com/killer/

Jain, L. C., Tedman, R. A., & Tedman, D. K. (2007). *Evolution of Teaching and Learning Paradigms in Intelligent Environment*. New York: Springer. doi:10.1007/978-3-540-71974-8

James, L. K., Lin, C.-Y., Steed, A., Swapp, D., & Slater, M. (2003). Social anxiety in virtual environments: Results of a pilot study. *Cyberpsychology & Behavior*, 6(3), 237–243. doi:10.1089/109493103322011515 PMID:12855078

Jaramillo, G. E., Quiroz, J. E., Cartagena, C. A., Vivares, C. A., & Branch, J. W. (2010). Mobile Augmented Reality Applications in Daily Environments. Revista EIA - Escuela de Ingenieria de Antioquia, Medellín (Colombia), (14), 125–134.

Jarrett, C. (2009). Get a second life. *The Psychologist*, 22(6), 490–493.

Jarrett, C. (2013). Avatar therapy. *The Psychologist*, 26(7), 478.

Jenkins, H. (2011). Transmedia 202: Further Reflections. *The Official Weblog of Henry Jenkins*. Retrieved from http://henryjenkins.org/blog/2011/08/defining_transmedia_further_re.html

Johnson, S. (2006). *Stephen Johnson on Digital Photography*. O'Reilly.

Johnston, J. (2012). Universal Mind, The iPad Table. Retrieved December 27, 2017 from https://medium.com/universal-mind/the-ipad-table-66129e030b8c

Johnstone, A. H., & Selepeng, D. (2001). A language problem revisited. *Chemistry Education: Research and Practice in Europe*, 2(1), 19–29.

Juster, N. (2000). The Dot and the Line: A Romance in Lower Mathematics (1st ed.). Chronicle Books. (originally printed in 1963)

Kantak, S. S., Stinear, J. W., Buch, E. R., & Cohen, L. G. (2012). Rewiring the brain: Potential role of the premotor cortex in motor control, learning, and recovery of function following brain injury. *Neurorehabilitation and Neural Repair*, *26*(3), 282–292. doi:10.1177/1545968311420845 PMID:21926382

Ke, Y., Tang, X., & Jing, F. (2006). The design of high-level features for photo quality assessment. In *CVPR '06 Proceedings of the 2006 IEEE Computer Society Conference on Computer Vision and Pattern Recognition - Volume 1* (pp. 419-426). New York: IEEE.

Keast, D. A. (2009). A Constructivist Application for Online Learning in Music. *Research and Issues in Music Education*, *7*(1).

Keno, L. (2005). Reflection on the concept of symmetry. *European Review*, *13*(S2).

Kerawalla, L., Luckin, R., Seljeflot, S., & Woolard, A. (2006). "Making it real": Exploring the potential of augmented reality for teaching primary school science. *Virtual Reality (Waltham Cross)*, *10*(3–4), 163–174. doi:10.100710055-006-0036-4

Kesim, M., & Ozarslan, Y. (2012). Augmented Reality in Education: Current Technologies and the Potential for Education. *Procedia: Social and Behavioral Sciences*, *47*(0), 297–302. doi:10.1016/j.sbspro.2012.06.654

Keverne, E. B. (2015). Genomic imprinting, action, and interaction of maternal and fetal genomes. *PNAS*, *112*(22), 6834–6840. Retrieved from www.pnas.org/cgi/doi/10.1073/pnas.1411253111

King, A. E. (2010). *The Landscape in Art: Nature in the crosshairs of an age-old debate.* Retrieved March 30, 2018, from http://www.artesmagazine.com/?p=4744

Klinger, E., Légeron, P., Roy, S., Chemin, I., Lauer, F., & Nugues, P. (2004). Virtual reality exposure in the treatment of social phobia. [PubMed]. *Studies in Health Technology and Informatics*, *99*, 91.

Knödel, S., Hachet, M., & Guitton, P. (2009). Interactive Generation and Modification of Cutaway Illustrations for Polygonal Models. In *Proceedings of the 10th International Symposium on Smart Graphics* (pp. 140-151). Berlin: Springer-Verlag. 10.1007/978-3-642-02115-2_12

Kolb, B., & Whishaw, I. Q. (2009). *Fundamentals of human neuropsychology.* Macmillan.

Korzybski, A. (1995). *Science and Sanity: An Introduction to Non-Aristotelian Systems and General Semantics* (5th ed.). Brooklyn, NY: Institute of General Semantics. (Original work published 1933)

Kress, G., & Leeuwen, T. (2001). *Multimodal Discourse: the Modes and Media of Contemporary Communication.* London: Arnold.

Kuhl, P. (2017). *The Linguistic Genius of Babies.* The TED Video. Retrieved from http://search.myway.com/search/video.jhtml?n=&p2=&pg=video&pn=1&ptb=&qs=&searchfor=infant+learns+sounds+TED+video&si=&ss=sub&st=tab&tpr=sbt&trs=wtt&vidOrd=3&vidId=M-ymanHajN8

Kumar, R. (2011). *Research Methodology a step-by-step guide for beginners* (3rd ed.). London: SAGE Publications Lda.

Lafuente, B., Downs, R. T., Yang, H., & Stone, N. (2015). The power of databases: the RRUFF project. In T. Armbruster & R. M. Danisi (Eds.), *Highlights in Mineralogical Crystallography* (pp. 1–30). Berlin: De Gruyter. doi:10.1515/9783110417104-003

Lane, H. C., Hays, M. J., Core, M. G., & Auerbach, D. (2013). Learning intercultural communication skills with virtual humans: Feedback and fidelity. *Journal of Educational Psychology*, *105*(4), 1026–1035. doi:10.1037/a0031506

Langner, G. (2015). The Neural Code of Pitch and Harmony. Cambridge UK: Cambridge University Press. doi:10.1017/CBO9781139050852

LaViola, J. J. Jr. (2000). A discussion of cybersickness in virtual environments. *ACM SIGCHI Bulletin, 32*(1), 47–56. doi:10.1145/333329.333344

Lebrun, M. (2002). *Teorias e Métodos Pedagógicos para Ensinar e Aprender*. Lisboa: Instituto Piaget.

Lee, K. (2012). The Future of Learning and Training in Augmented Reality. *InSight: A Journal of Schorlaly Teaching, 7*, 31–42.

Leeuwen, T. (2005). *Introducing Social Semiotics*. New York: Routledge.

Lefebvre, H. (1991). *The production of space*. London: Blackwell.

Leiderstam, M. (2006). *See and Seen: seeing landscape through artistic practice*. Lund University.

Leopold, C., & Leutner, D. (2012). Science text comprehension: Drawing, main idea selection, and summarizing as learning strategies. *Learning and Instruction, 22*(1), 16–26. doi:10.1016/j.learninstruc.2011.05.005

Levin, A. (2006). Blind motion deblurring using image statistics. In *Proceedings of the 19th International Conference on Neural Information Processing Systems* (pp. 841-848). MIT Press.

Lévy, P. (1995). *O que é o Virtual?* São Paulo: Editora 34.

Lewis, D., & Larsen, M. J. (1927). The Cancellation, Reinforcement, and Measurement of Subjective Tones. *Proceedings of N.A.S., 23*(7), 415–421. doi:10.1073/pnas.23.7.415 PMID:16588176

Leys, J. (2018). *Mathematical Imagery*. Retrieved from http://www.josleys.com/

Li, K., Chen, H., Chen, Y., Clark, D. W., Cook, P., Damianakis, S., ... Zheng, J. (2000). Building and Using a Scalable Display Wall System. *IEEE Computer Graphics and Applications, 20*(4), 29–37. doi:10.1109/38.851747

Li, M., & Kobbelt, L. (2012). Dynamic tiling display: Building an interactive display surface using multiple mobile devices. In *Proceedings of the 11th International Conference on Mobile and Ubiquitous Multimedia* (pp. 24:1–24:4). New York, NY: ACM. 10.1145/2406367.2406397

Lin, C.-S., & Wu, R. Y.-W. (2016). Effects of web-based creative thinking teaching on students' creativity and learning outcome. *EURASIA Journal of Mathematics, Science & Technology Education, 12*(6), 1675–1684.

Lince, R. (2016). Creative thinking ability to increase student mathematical of junior high school by applying models numbered heads together. *Journal of Education and Practice, 7*(6), 206–212.

Lindvang, C., & Beck, B. (2015). Problem based learning as a shared musical journey--Group dynamics, communication and creativity. *Journal of Problem Based Learning in Higher Education, 3*(1), 1–19.

Lin, M. T.-Y., Wang, J.-S., & Kuo, H.-M. (2017). A study on the effect of virtual reality 3d exploratory education on students' creativity and leadership. *EURASIA Journal of Mathematics, Science & Technology Education, 13*(7), 3151–3161.

Liu, L., Chen, R., Wolf, L., & Cohen-Or, D. (2010). Optimizing Photo Composition. *Computer Graphic Forum*, 469-478.

Lopez-Ortega, O. (2013). Computer-assisted creativity: Emulation of cognitive processes on a multi-agent system. *Expert Systems with Applications, 40*(9), 3459–3470. doi:10.1016/j.eswa.2012.12.054

Lorch, B. (2002). *Landscape*. Retrieved March 30, 2018, from http://lucian.uchicago.edu/blogs/mediatheory/keywords/landscape/

Lorenz, K. (1937). The Companion in the Bird'. *The Auk, 54*(3), 245–273. doi:10.2307/4078077

Lozano-Hemmer, R. (2010). *Summer equation, Relational Architecture 16*. Retrieved December 03, 2013 from http://www.lozano-hemmer.com/solar_equation.php

Lubart, R. (2005). How can computers be partners in the creative process: Classification and commentary on the special issue. *International Journal of Human-Computer Studies*, *63*(4-5), 365–369. doi:10.1016/j.ijhcs.2005.04.002

Lunenfeld, P. (2005). Os mitos do cinema interativo. In *O chip e o caleidoscópio: reflexões sobre as novas mídias*. São Paulo: SENAC.

Luo, Y., & Tang, X. (2008). Photo and Video Quality Evaluation: Focusing on the Subject. In *Proceedings of the 10ᵗʰ European Conference on Computer Vision: Part III* (pp. 386-399). Marseille, France: Springer-Verlang. 10.1007/978-3-540-88690-7_29

Machado, P., Romero, J., & Manaris, B. (2007). Experiments in Computational Aesthetics. In J. Romero & P. Machado (Eds.), The Art of Artificial Evolution (pp. 381-415). Springer.

Machado, P., & Cardoso, A. (1998). Computing Aesthetics. In *Brazilian Symposium of Artificial Ingelligence* (pp. 219-228). Springer.

Machado, P., Romero, J., Nadal, M., Santos, A., Correia, J., & Carballal, A. (2015). Computerized measures of visual complexity. *Acta Psychologica*, *160*, 43–57. doi:10.1016/j.actpsy.2015.06.005 PMID:26164647

MacLean, P. D. (1990). The Triune Brain in Evolution: Role in Paleocerebral Functions. Springer.

Maheu, M. M., Pulier, M. L., McMenamin, J. P., & Posen, L. (2012). Future of telepsychology, telehealth, and various technologies in psychological research and practice. *Professional Psychology, Research and Practice*, *43*(6), 613–621. doi:10.1037/a0029458

Malevich, K. (1913). *Samovar*. The Museum of Modern Art.

Manovich, L. (2002). *The Language of New Media*. MIT Press.

Manovich, L. (2010). *Software take command*. Olivares Edition.

Manovich, L. (2011). *The language of new media*. The MIT Press.

Mathews, M. M., & Moore, F. R. (1970). GROOVE – a program to compose, store, and edit functions of time. *Communications of the ACM*, *13*(12), 715–721. doi:10.1145/362814.362817

Mauguin, Ch. (1931). Sur le symbolisme des groupes de repetition ou de symetrie des assemblages cristallins. *Zeitschrift fur Kristallographie*, *76*, 542–558.

McCloud, S. (2006). *Making Comics: Storytelling Secrets of Comics, Manga and Graphic Novels*. William Morrow Paperbacks.

McKenzie, B., Mims, N., & Ozkan, B. (2010). Identifying the characteristics of photo bloggers: An exploratory study. In D. Gibson, & B. Dodge (Eds.), *Proceedings of Society for Information Technology and Teacher Education International Conference 2010* (pp. 1539-1545). Chesapeake, VA: Association for the Advancement of Computing in Education (AACE).

Merlot, E., Couret, D., & Otten, W. (2008). Prenatal stress, fetal imprinting, and immunity. *Brain, Behavior, and Immunity*, *22*(1), 42–51. doi:10.1016/j.bbi.2007.05.007 PMID:17716859

Merriam-Webster's Dictionary. (2017). *Music*. Retrieved from https://www.merriam-webster.com/dictionary/dictionary

Merrian-Webster Dictionary. (2018). Retrieved from https://www.merriam-webster.com/dictionary/create

Merrill, D., Kalanithi, J., & Maes, P. (2007). Siftables: towards sensor network user interfaces. In *Proceedings of the First International Conference on Tangible and Embedded Interaction (TEI 2007)* (pp. 75–78). New York: ACM. 10.1145/1226969.1226984

Milgram, P., & Kishino, F. (1994). A taxonomy of mixed reality visual displays. *IEICE Transactions on Information and Systems, 77*(12), 1321–1329.

Miller, G. S. (1986, August). The definition and rendering of terrain maps. *Computer Graphics, 20*(4), 39–48. doi:10.1145/15886.15890

Mitchell, W. J. T. (1994). Imperial Landscape. In W. J. T. Mitchell (Ed.), *Landscape and Power*. University of Chicago Press.

Moffat, D. C., Crombie, W., & Shabalina, O. (2017). Some video games can increase the player's creativity. *International Journal of Game-Based Learning, 7*(2), 35–46. doi:10.4018/IJGBL.2017040103

Momma, K. (2017). *The VESTA program*. Japanese National Museum of Nature and Science.

Moreno, R., & Mayer, R. E. (1999). Cognitive principles of multimedia learning: The role of modality and contiguity. *Journal of Educational Psychology, 91*(2), 358–368. doi:10.1037/0022-0663.91.2.358

Murray, J. (1997). *The Future of Narrative in Cybersapce*. New York: The Free Press.

Murray, N., Marchesotti, L., & Perronnin, F. (2012). Ava: A large-scale database for aesthetic visual analysis. In *IEEE Computer Society Conference on Computer Vision and Pattern Recognition*. Providence, RI: IEEE. 10.1109/CVPR.2012.6247954

Musgrave, F. K., Kolb, C. E., & Mace, R. S. (1989, July). The synthesis and rendering of eroded fractal terrains. *Computer Graphics, 23*(3), 41–50. doi:10.1145/74334.74337

National Education Association (NEA). (1920). *Reorganization of science in secondary schools: A report of the commission on the reorganization of secondary education (U.S. Bureau of Education, Bulletin No. 26)*. Washington, DC: U.S. Government Printing Office.

National Research Council of the National Academies. (2008). *Inspired by Biology: From molecules to materials to machines*. Washington, D.C.: The National Academies Press.

National Research Council. (2012). *Education for life and work: Developing transferable knowledge and skills in the 21st century*. Washington, DC: National Academies Press.

Neo, M., & Neo, T.-K. (2013). Exploring students' creativity and design skills through a multimedia project: A constructivist approach in a Malaysian classroom. *Journal of Design and Technology Education, 18*(3), 48–59.

Nicolaïdis, S. (2008). Prenatal imprinting of postnatal specific appetites and feeding behavior. *Metabolism: Clinical and Experimental, 57*(Suppl 2), S22–S26. doi:10.1016/j.metabol.2008.07.004 PMID:18803961

Ni, T., Schmidt, G. S., Staadt, O. G., Livingston, M. A., Ball, R., & May, R. (2006). A Survey of Large High-Resolution Display Technologies, Techniques, and Applications. In *Proceedings of the IEEE Conference on Virtual Reality (VR 2006)* (pp. 223–236). Washington, DC: IEEE Computer Society.

NMC Horizon Report. (2012). *2012 higher education edition*. Retrieved May 2, 2015, from http://redarchive.nmc.org/publications/horizon-report-2012-higher-ed-edition

North, M. M., North, S. M., & Coble, J. R. (1998). Virtual reality therapy: An effective treatment for the fear of public speaking. *The International Journal of Virtual Reality, 3*, 1–6.

North, M., North, S., & Coble, J. (1997). Virtual reality therapy for fear of flying. *The American Journal of Psychiatry, 154*(1), 130–142. doi:10.1176/ajp.154.1.130b PMID:8988975

Noval, M. D. M. (2013). *Realidade Aumentada no ensino da Matemática: um caso de estudo* (Master's Thesis). Universidade de Aveiro. Retrieved from http://repositorio.utad.pt//handle/10348/3029

Nunes, M. B., & McPherson, M. (2007). Why Designers cannot be Agnostic about Pedagogy: The Influence of Constructivist Thinking in Design of e-learning for HE. In L. C. Jain, D. K. Tedman, & R. A. Tedman (Eds.), *Evolution of Teaching and Learning Paradigms in Intelligent Environment* (p. 309). Berlin: Springer-Verlag. doi:10.1007/978-3-540-71974-8_2

OECD. (2003). *Learners for Life: Student Approaches to Learning.* OECD Publishing.

Ohler, J. (2012a). *Digital Storytelling Storyboard Templates.* Retrieved from http://www.jasonohler.com/pdfs/digital-StorytellingStoryBoard-adv.pdf

Ohta, T., & Tanaka, J. (2012). Pinch: An Interface that Relates Applications on Multiple Touch-Screen by 'Pinching' Gesture. In *Proceedings of the 2012 International Conference on Advances in Computer Entertainment Technology (ACE 2012)* (pp. 320–335). New York: ACM. 10.1007/978-3-642-34292-9_23

Ohta, T. (2008). Dynamically reconfigurable multi-display environment for CG contents. In *Proceedings of the 2008 International Conference on Advances in Computer Entertainment Technology (ACE 2008)* (p. 416). New York: ACM. 10.1145/1501750.1501866

Ohta, T., & Tanaka, J. (2010). Automatic configuration of display ordering for multi-display environments. In *Proceedings of the 2010 International Conference on Advances in Computer Entertainment Technology (ACE 2010)* (pp. 24–27). New York: ACM. 10.1145/1971630.1971638

Ohta, T., & Tanaka, J. (2015). *MovieTile: Interactively Adjustable Free Shape Multi-Display of Mobile Devices. In SIGGRAPH ASIA 2015 Mobile Graphics and Interactive Applications.* New York: ACM. doi:10.1145/2818427.2818436

Olsen, J. (2004). *Realtime procedural terrain generation.* Department of Mathematics And Computer Science.

Oncu, E. C. (2016). Improved creative thinkers in a class: A model of activity based tasks for improving university students' creative thinking abilities. *Educational Research Review, 11*(8), 517–522. doi:10.5897/ERR2015.2262

Oosterhuis, K. (2002). Lecture at the Building Centre. London: Academic Press.

Ostashewski, N., & Reid, D. (2012). Digital Storytelling on the iPad: apps, activities, and processes for successful 21st century story creations. In T. Amiel & B. Wilson (Eds.), *Proceedings of EdMedia: World Conference on Educational Media and Technology 2012* (pp. 1823-1827). Association for the Advancement of Computing in Education (AACE).

Paivio, A. (1990). Mental Representations: A Dual Coding Approach. Oxford University Press. (originally printed in 1986)

Paivio, A. (1970). On the functional significance of imagery. *Psychological Bulletin, 73*(6), 385–392. doi:10.1037/h0029180

Paivio, A. (1971). *Imagery and verbal processes.* New York: Holt, Rinehart, and Winston.

Paivio, A. (1991). Dual Coding Theory: Retrospect and current status. *Canadian Journal of Psychology, 45*(3), 255–287. doi:10.1037/h0084295

Panksepp, J., & Biven, L. (2012). The Archaeology of Mind: Neuroevolutionary Origins of Human Emotions (Norton Series on Interpersonal Neurobiology). W. W. Norton & Company.

Pantaleo, S. (2015). Language, literacy, and visual texts. *English in Education, 49*(2), 113–129. doi:10.1111/eie.12053

Pantone. (2018a). *Pantone Numbering system.* Pantone Color Institute.

Pantone. (2018b). *Pantone matching system*. Author.

Park, I., & Hannafin, M. (1993). Empirically based guidelines for the design of interactive multimedia. *Educational Technology Research and Development, 41*(3), 65–85. doi:10.1007/BF02297358

Park, J. (2004). The value of images in science instruction. In R. Ferdig, C. Crawford, R. Carlsen, N. Davis, J. Price, R. Weber, & D. Willis (Eds.), *Proceedings of Society for Information Technology and Teacher Education International Conference 2004* (pp. 4591-4594). Chesapeake, VA: Association for the Advancement of Computing in Education (AACE).

Parncutt, R. (2011). Harmony: A Psychoacoustical Approach. Springer.

Paul, A. M. (2011). What babies learn before they are born. *TED Global 2011*. Retrieved from https://www.ted.com/talks/annie_murphy_paul_what_we_learn_before_we_re_born/transcript?language=en

Paul, C. (2003). *Digital Art*. London: Thames & Hudson Ltd.

Pérez-Gómez, A. (1994, July). The space of architecture: meaning as presence and representation. In S. Holl, J. Pallasmaa, & A. Pérez-Gómez (Eds.), Questions of perception: phenomenology of architecture, a+u, Architecture and Urbanism special issue (pp. 7–25). Tokyo: Academic Press.

Pérez-Gómez, A., & Pelletier, L. (1997). *Architectural representation and the perspective hinge*. Cambridge, MA: MIT Press.

Pérez-López, D., & Contero, M. (2013). Delivering educational multimedia contents through an augmented reality application: A case study on its impact on knowledge acquisition and retention. *TOJET: The Turkish Online Journal of Educational Technology, 12*(4), 19–28.

Perlin, K. (1985). An image synthesizer. *Computer Graphics, 19*(3), 287–296. doi:10.1145/325165.325247

Perrault, C. (2012). *The Fairy Tales Of Charles Perrault*. CreateSpace Independent Publishing Platform.

Pertaub, D. P., Slater, M. & Barker, C. (2001). An experiment on fear of public speaking in virtual reality. In *Studies in health tech. and informatics* (pp. 372-378).

Pertaub, D. P., Slater, M., & Barker, C. (2002). An experiment on public speaking anxiety in response to three different types of virtual audience. *Presence, 11*(1), 68–78. doi:10.1162/105474602317343668

Peters, R. A., & Maatman, J. (2017). Long-term trends accentuate the import of creative and critical thinking skills developed by design thinking and ill-defined questions. *Teaching Public Administration, 35*(2), 190–208. doi:10.1177/0144739416680850

Pierce, J. R. (1990). *Telstar, A History*. SMEC Vintage Electrics.

Pinto, H. (2017, October). *Framework Para a Modelação Procedimental Integrada de Terrenos Completos* (MSc Thesis). Instituto Superior de Engenharia do Porto.

Plato. (2014). The Republic (B. Jowett, Trans.). Simon & Brown.

Pólya, G. (1924). Über die Analogie der Kristallsymmetrie in der Ebene. *Zeitschrift fur Kristallographie*.

Pool, J., Dittrich, C., & Pool, K. (2011). Arts Integration in Teacher Preparation: Teaching the Teachers. *Journal for Learning through the Arts, 7*(1).

Prensky, M. (2001). Digital Natives, Digital Immigrants Part 1. *On the Horizon*.

Price, C. (n.d.). *The Square Book*. Academy Press.

Processing. (2018). Retrieved from https://processing.org/ https://processing.org/download

Puppet Forms in India. (2012). Centre for Cultural Resources and Training. Retrieved from http://ccrtindia.gov.in/puppetforms.htm

Rädle, R., Jetter, H. C., Marquardt, N., Reiterer, H., & Rogers, Y. (2014). Huddlelamp: Spatially-aware mobile displays for ad-hoc around-the-table collaboration. In *Proceedings of the Ninth ACM International Conference on Interactive Tabletops and Surfaces (ITS '14)* (pp. 45-54). New York, NY: ACM. 10.1145/2669485.2669500

Rädle, R., Jetter, H.-C., Schreiner, M., Lu, Z., Reiterer, H., & Rogers, Y. (2015). Spatially-aware or spatially-agnostic? Elicitation and Evaluation of User-Defined Cross-Device Interactions. In *Proceedings of the 33rd Annual ACM Conference on Human Factors in Computing Systems (CHI '15)* (pp. 3913–3922). New York, NY: ACM.

Rall, H. (2009). Tradigital Mythmaking: Singapore Animation for the 21st Century. Singapore: Dominie Press.

Ramón y Cajal, S., & DeFelipe, J. (1988). Cajal on the Cerebral Cortex: An Annotated Translation of the Complete Writings. Oxford University Press.

Read, J. (2011). *From Alchemy to Chemistry*. Dover Publications. (Original work published 1957)

Reia-Baptista, V. (2006). New Environments of Media Exposure - Internet and Narrative Structures: From Media Education to Media Pedagogy and Media Literacy. In U. Carlsson & C. von Feilitzen (Eds.), *The Service of Young People? Studies and Reflections on Media in the Digital Age.*

Rekimoto, J., Ullmer, B., & Oba, H. (2001). DataTiles: a modular platform for mixed physical and graphical interactions. In *Proceedings of the SIGCHI Conference on Human Factors in Computing Systems (CHI 2001)* (pp. 269–276). New York: ACM. 10.1145/365024.365115

Ribeiro, R. W. (2007). *Paisagem Cultural e Património*. Rio de Janeiro: IPHAN.

Ricou, J., & Pollock, J. A. (2012). The Tree, the Spiral and the Web of Life: A Visual Exploration of Biological Evolution for Public Murals. *Leonardo, 45*(1), 18-25.

Rigau, J., Freixas, M., & Sbert, M. (2008). Informational Aesthetics Measures. IEEE Computer Graphics and Applications, 28(2), 24-34.

Roam, D. (2013). *The Back of the Napkin: Solving Problems and Selling Ideas with Pictures (Expanded ed.)*. Portfolio Penguin.

Romero, J., Machado, P., Carballal, A., & Osorio, O. (2011). Aesthetic Classification and Sorting Based on Image Compression. In EvoApplications (pp. 394-403). Torino, Italy: Springer.

Romero, J., Machado, P., Carballal, A., & Osorio, O. (2011). *Aesthetic Classification and Sorting Based on Image Compression. In EvoApplications* (pp. 394–403). Torino, Italy: Springer.

Romero, J., Machado, P., Carballal, A., & Santos, A. (2012). Using complexity estimates in aesthetic image classification. *Journal of Mathematics and the Arts, 6*(2-3), 125–136. doi:10.1080/17513472.2012.679514

Ross, B. J., Ralph, W., & Zong, H. (2006). Evolutionary Image Systhesis Using a Model of Aesthetics. In *Proceedings of the IEEE Congress on Evolutionary Computation* (pp. 3832-3839). Vancouver: IEEE Press.

Rothbaum, B., Hodges, L., & Kooper, R., & Opdyke, D. (1995). Effectiveness of computer-generated (virtual reality) graded exposure in the treatment of acrophobia. *The American Journal of Psychiatry, 152*(4), 626–628. doi:10.1176/ajp.152.4.626 PMID:7694917

Rothbaum, B., Hodges, L., Watson, B., Kessler, G. D., & Opdyke, D. (1996). Virtual reality exposure therapy in the treatment of fear of flying: A case report. *Behaviour Research and Therapy*, *34*(5-6), 477–481. doi:10.1016/0005-7967(96)00007-1 PMID:8687369

Runco, M. A., & Jaeger, G. J. (2012). The standard definition of creativity. *Creativity Research Journal*, *24*(1), 92–96. doi:10.1080/10400419.2012.650092

Russell, J. (2017). Toward a Broader perspective on Facial Expression.Moving on from basic Emotion Theory. In J. M. Fernández-Dols & J. A. Russell (Eds.), *The Science of facial Expression* (pp. 93–105). Oxford University Press. doi:10.1093/acprof:oso/9780190613501.001.0001

Russell, J. A., & Fernandez-Dols, J. M. (1997). What does a facial expression mean? In J. Russell & J. M. Fernández-Dols (Eds.), *The psychology of facial expression* (pp. 3–30). New York, NY: Cambridge University Press. doi:10.1017/CBO9780511659911.003

Ryan, S. E. (2014). *Garments of Paradise: Wearable Discourse in the Digital Age*. The MIT Press.

Rynne, A. (2006). *Axonometric Projection*. University of Limerick, Department of Manufacturing and Operations Engineering.

Salinas, P., González-Mendívil, E., Quintero, E., Ríos, H., Ramírez, H., & Morales, S. (2013). The development of a didactic prototype for the learning of Mathematics through Augmented Reality. *Procedia Computer Science*, *25*, 62–70. doi:10.1016/j.procs.2013.11.008

Sandler, M. E. (2010). *Teaching and Learning with Technology: IT as a Value-Added Component of Academic Life*. Annual Meeting of the American Educational Research Association, Denver, CO.

Santella, A., Agrawala, M., DeCarlo, D., Salesin, D., & Cohen, M. (2006). Gaze-based interaction for semi-automatic photo cropping. In *Proceedings of the SIGCHI Conference on Human Factors in Computing Systems* (pp. 771-780). Montreal, Canada: ACM.

Saputra, Y. H., & Sabana, S. (2016). Building creativity training: Drawing with left hand to stimulate left brain in children age 5-7 years old. *Journal of Education and Practice*, *7*(2), 1–8.

Schneider, J., Boldte, T., & Westermann, R. (2006, November). Real-time editing, synthesis, and rendering of infinite landscapes on GPUs. Proc. of Vision, modeling, and visualization, 145.

Schnupp, J., Nelken, I., & King, A. (2011). *Auditory Neuroscience*. MIT Press.

Scholtz, J. (2004). *Usability evaluation*. National Institute of Standards and Technology.

Schouten, J. F. (1940). The residue and the mechanism of hearing. *Proceedings of the Koninklijke Akademie van Wetenschap*, *43*, 991–999.

Schouten, J. F., Ritsma, R. J., & Cardozo, B. L. (1962). Pitch of the residue. *The Journal of the Acoustical Society of America*, *34*(9B), 1418–1424. doi:10.1121/1.1918360

Schunk, D. H. (2012). *Learning Theories* (6th ed.). Boston, MA: Pearson.

Seechaliao, T. (2017). Instructional strategies to support creativity and innovation in education. *Journal of Education and Learning*, *6*(4), 201–208. doi:10.5539/jel.v6n4p201

Seels, B., & Dunn, J. (1989). A visual literacy walk: Using a natural learning environment. *TechTrends*, *34*(6), 26–29. doi:10.1007/BF02761242

Sehic, S. (2017). The Effect of English Language Learning on Creative Thinking Skills: A Mixed Methods Case Study. *English Language Teaching*, *10*(3), 82–94. doi:10.5539/elt.v10n3p82

Şenyer, E. (2017). *Traditional Turkish Puppet Shadow Play Karagößz Hacivat*. Retrieved from http://www.karagoz.net/english/shadowplay.htm

Shahin, T. M. (2008). Computerizing conceptual design without hindering creativity. *Computer-Aided Design and Applications*, *5*(1-4), 548–556. doi:10.3722/cadaps.2008.548-556

Shama, S. (2004). *Landscape and Memory*. Harper Perennial.

Shershow, S. C. (1995). Puppets and Popular Culture by Scott Cutler Shershow. Cornell University Press. ASIN: B01FJ0UM1W. (originally printed in 1894)

Shiban, Y., Diemer, J., Müller, J., Brütting-Schick, J., Pauli, P., & Mühlberger, A. (2017). Diaphragmatic breathing during virtual reality exposure therapy for aviophobia: Functional coping strategy or avoidance behavior? A pilot study. *BMC Psychiatry*, *17*(1), 1–10. doi:10.118612888-016-1181-2 PMID:28100203

Siler, T. (2012). The ArtScience Program for Realizing Human Potential. *Leonardo*, *44*(5), 417–424. doi:10.1162/LEON_a_00242

Silva, B. (2013). The Forking Paths: a experiência temporal na narrativa fílmica. Ibercom 2013, Santiago de Compostela.

Silva, B. M., & Costa, S. (2014). Rede de Cultura e Arte Digital: O projeto Recardi. *INUAF Studia, 16*(9).

Silva, B., Rodrigues, J., Alves, R., Madeira, M., Ferrer, J., Casta, S., & Martins, R. (2014). Fátima Revisited: An Interactive Installation. *SGEM Proceedings*.

Silva, B. (2014a). The Forking Paths: An Interactive Cinema Experience. *International Journal of Creative Interfaces and Computer Graphics*.

Silva, B. M. (2014b). *Haze em Avanca: apresentação pública do primeiro filme interativo da trilogia The Forking Paths*. Avanca: Avanca Cinema.

Silva, B., António, R., & Rodrigues, J. (2015). Dialectical Polyptych: an interactive movie. *Third International Conference on Advances in Computing, Communication and Information Technology*.

Silva, B., & Dominguez, M. (2014). Between the Sacred and the Profane in the S. João d'Arga's Festivities: A Digital Art Installation. *International Journal of Creative Interfaces and Computer Graphics*, *5*(1), 1–20. doi:10.4018/ijcicg.2014010101

Simmel, G. (2009). *A Filosofia da Paisagem*. Covilhã: LusoSofia.

Slater, M., Antley, A., Davison, A., Swapp, D., Guger, C., Barker, C., ... Sanchez-Vives, M. V. (2006). A virtual reprise of the Stanley Milgram obedience experiments. *PLoS One*, *1*(1), e39. doi:10.1371/journal.pone.0000039 PMID:17183667

Slater, M., Pertaub, D. P., & Steed, A. (1999). Public speaking in virtual reality: Facing an audience of avatars. IEEE Computer Graphics and Applications, *19*(2), 6–9.

Smelik, R. M., Tutenel, T., de Kraker, K. J., & Bidarra, R. (2008, May). A proposal for a procedural terrain modelling framework. *Proceedings of the 14th Eurographics Symposium on Virtual Environments, 39-42.*

Smelik, R. M., Tutenel, T., de Kraker, K. J., & Bidarra, R. (2011). A declarative approach to procedural modeling of virtual worlds. *Computers & Graphics, 35*(2), 352-363.

Smith, E. E., & Kosslyn, S. M. (2007). *Cognitive psychology: Mind and brain* (1st ed.). Upper Saddle River, NJ: Prentice Hall.

Sommerauer, P., & Müller, O. (2014). Augmented reality in informal learning environments: A field experiment in a mathematics exhibition. *Computers & Education, 79*(0), 59–68. doi:10.1016/j.compedu.2014.07.013

Soto-Andrade, J., Jaramillo, S., Gutierrez, C., & Letelier, J.-C. (2015). *Ouroboros avatars: A mathematical exploration of Self-reference and Metabolic Closure*. MIT Press.

Sripongwiwat, S., Bunterm, T., & Srisawat, N. (2016, December). The constructionism and neurocognitive-based teaching model for promoting science learning outcomes and creative thinking. *Asia-Pacific Forum on Science Learning and Teaching, 17*(2), Article 9.

Stachniak, S., & Stuerzlinger, W. (2005). An algorithm for automated fractal terrain deformation. *Computer Graphics and Artificial Intelligence, 1*, 64–76.

StarewiczW. (1999). Retrieved from https://www.awn.com/heaven_and_hell/STARE/stare1.htm

Statham, M. (2014). Change the way your pupils learn by practicing creative thinking and visualization. *Primary Science, 134*, 13–16.

Stein, M. B., & Kean, Y. M. (2000). Disability and Quality of Life in Social Phobia: Epidemiologic Findings. *The American Journal of Psychiatry, 157*(10), 1606–1613. doi:10.1176/appi.ajp.157.10.1606 PMID:11007714

Sterling, C. H. (2009). Encyclopedia of Journalism. SAGE Publications, Inc. doi:10.4135/9781412972048

Stevens, S. S., & Warshofsky, F. (1981). *Sound and Hearing* (Revised Edition). Time Life Education.

Storyboard. (2017). Retrieved from http://www.wikihow.com/Create-a-Storyboard

Storyboarding. (2016). UC Berkeley, Advance Media Institute. Retrieved March 26, 2017, from https://multimedia.journalism.berkeley.edu/tutorials/starttofinish-storyboarding/#sf_form_salesforce_w2l_lead_7_sidebar

Storycenter. (2018). Retrieved from https://www.storycenter.org/

Stralen, M., Baltazar, A. P., Melgaço, L., & Arruda, G. (2012). Congonhas Media Cascade – Ituita: a permanent urban interactive interface for citizenship. In *Proceedings of eCAADe 2012*. Praga: Cumincad. Retrieved from http://www.mom.arq.ufmg.br/mom/arq_interface/3a_aula/stralen_baltazar_ecaade.pdf

Suh, B., Ling, H., Bederson, B. B., & Jacobs, D. W. (2003). Automatic thumbnail cropping and its effectiveness. In *Proceedings of the 16th annual ACM symposon on User interface software and technology* (pp. 95-104). Vancouver, Canada: ACM.

Sweller, J. (1988). Cognitive load during problem solving: Effects on learning. *Cognitive Science, 12*(2), 257–285. doi:10.120715516709cog1202_4

Sweller, J., & Chandler, P. (1991). Evidence of cognitive load theory. *Cognition and Instruction, 8*(4), 351–362. doi:10.12071532690xci0804_5

Swetz, F. J., & Katz, V. J. (2011, January). Mathematical Treasures - Albrecht Durer's Treatise on Mensuration. *Convergence*.

Sylla, C., Gonçalves, S., Branco, P., & Coutinho, C. (2012). t-words: Playing with sounds and creating narratives. In A. Nijholt, T. Romao, & D. Reidsma (Eds.), Advances in Computer Entertainment: LNCS (Vol. 7624, pp. 565–568). Springer.

Tandiseru, S. R. (2015). The effectiveness of local culture-based mathematical heuristic-KR learning towards enhancing student's creative thinking skill. *Journal of Education and Practice, 6*(12), 74–81.

Tandoor, P., Prante, T., Müller-Tomfelde, C., Streitz, N., & Steinmetz, R. (2001). Connectables: dynamic coupling of displays for the flexible creation of shared workspaces. In *Proceedings of the 14th Annual ACM Symposium on User Interface Software and Technology (UIST 2001)* (pp. 11-20). New York: ACM.

Tavares, M., Cruz, T., & Paulino, F. (2014). CulturalNature Arga#2. *International Journal of Creative Interfaces and Computer Graphics*, *5*(1), 21–31. doi:10.4018/ijcicg.2014010102

Terhardt, E. (1974). Pitch, consonance, and harmony. *The Journal of the Acoustical Society of America*, *55*(5), 1061–1069. doi:10.1121/1.1914648 PMID:4833699

Thompson, T. (2017). Teaching Creativity through Inquiry Science. *Gifted Child Today*, *40*(1), 29–42. doi:10.1177/1076217516675863

Tillman, D. A., An, S. A., & Boren, R. L. (2015). Assessment of creativity in arts and STEM integrated pedagogy by pre-service elementary teachers. *Journal of Technology and Teacher Education*, *23*(3), 301–327.

Tippett, C. D. (2016). What recent research on diagrams suggests about learning *with* rather than learning *from* visual representations in science. *International Journal of Science Education*, *38*(5), 725–746. doi:10.1080/09500693.2016.1158435

Tokyo University of Technology, School of Media Science. (2012). Pinch: an interface for connecting multiple smartphone screens. In *Digital Content Expo 2012*. Retrieved December 31, 2017, from http://www.dcexpo.jp/archives/2012/en/program/exhibition/detail.html#IT201210

Tomatis, A. A. (1991). The Conscious Ear. Paris: Station Hill Press.

Tomei, L. (2009). *Information Communication Technologies for Enhanced Education and Learning: Advanced Applications and Developments*. New York: Information Science Reference (an imprint of IGI Global). doi:10.4018/978-1-60566-150-6

Torrance, E. P. (1979). *The Search for Satori and Creativity* (1st ed.). Creative Education Foundation.

Vale, C., Bragg, L. A., Widjaja, W., Herbert, S., & Loong, E. Y.-K. (2017). Children's mathematical reasoning: Opportunities for developing understanding and creative thinking. *Australian Primary Mathematics Classroom*, *22*(1), 3–8.

Vapnik, V. (1997). The Support Vector Method. In *International Conference on Artificial Neural Networks* (pp. 261-271). Lausanne, Switzerland: Springer.

Veloso, N. F. O. (2011). *Realidade Aumentada no Ensino: Prototipagem com um Manual Escolar* (Master's Thesis). Universidade de Aveiro. Retrieved from http://ria.ua.pt/handle/10773/7503

Video. (2013). *Video: An Insider Look at Storyboarding with the Coen Brothers' Storyboard Artist*. Retrieved March 27, 2017, from http://nofilmschool.com/2013/08/storyboarding-with-coen-brothers-storyboard-artist

Wang, J., & Cohen, M. F. (2007). Simultaneous Matting and Composition. In *IEEE Conference on Computer Vision and Pattern Recognition*. Minneapolis, MN: IEEE Press.

Ward, M. O., Grinstein, G., & Keim, D. (2015). Interactive Data Visualization: Foundations, Techniques, and Applications (2nd ed.). A. K. Peters/CRC Press.

Ward, G. W. R. (Ed.). (2008). *The Grove Encyclopedia of Materials and Techniques in Art*. Oxford University Press.

Ward, T. (2012). *Augmented Reality using Appcelerator Titanium Starter*. Birmingham, UK: Packt Publishing Ltd.

welovead, (2013). Pinch Pinup. Retrieved December 31, 2017 from http://www.welovead.com/en/works/details/aaeElowx

Whittow, J. (1984). *Dictionary of Physical Geography*. London: Penguin.

Widiana, I. W., & Jampel, I. N. (2016). Improving students' creative thinking and achievement through the implementation of multiple intelligence approach with mind mapping. *International Journal of Evaluation and Research in Education*, *5*(3), 246–254. doi:10.11591/ijere.v5i3.4546

Wiles, A. M. (2016). Figure analysis: A teaching technique to promote visual literacy and active Learning. *Biochemistry and Molecular Biology Education*, *44*(4), 336–344. doi:10.1002/bmb.20953 PMID:26891952

Wilson, K., Copeland-Solas, E., & Guthrie-Dixon, N. (2016). A Preliminary Study on the use of Mind Mapping as a Visual Learning Strategy in General Education Science classes for Arabic speakers in the United Arab Emirates. *The Journal of Scholarship of Teaching and Learning*, *16*(1), 31–52. doi:10.14434/josotl.v16i1.19181

Winston, A., & Cupchik, G. (1992). The evaluation of high art and popular art by naive and experienced viewers. *Visual Arts Research*, *18*, 1–14.

Wirth, K. R. (2008). *Learning About Thinking and Thinking About Learning: Metacognitive Knowledge and Skills for Intentional Learners*. Retrieved April 25, 2017, from http://serc.carleton.edu/NAGTWorkshops/metacognition/workshop08/participants/wirth.html

Wirth, K. R., & Perkins, D. (2008). *Learning to learn*. Retrieved April 25, 2017, from https://www.macalester.edu/academics/geology/wirth/learning.pdf

Witten, I., & Frank, E. (2002). Data mining: Practical machine learning tools and techniques with java implementations. *SIGMOD Record*, *31*(1), 76–77. doi:10.1145/507338.507355

Wohlrab, S., Fink, B., Kappeler, P. M., & Brewer, G. (2009). Differences in Personality Attributions Toward Tattooed and Nontattooed Virtual Human Characters. *Journal of Individual Differences*, *30*(1), 1–5. doi:10.1027/1614-0001.30.1.1

Wojciechowski, R., & Cellary, W. (2013). Evaluation of learners' attitude toward learning in ARIES augmented reality environments. *Computers and Education*, 570–585.

Wolpaw, J. R., Birbaumer, N., Heetderks, W. J., McFarland, W. J., Peckham, P. H., Schalk, G., ... Vaughan, T. M. (2000). Brain-computer interface technology: A review of the first international meeting. *IEEE Transactions on Rehabilitation Engineering*, *8*(2), 164–173. doi:10.1109/TRE.2000.847807 PMID:10896178

Wong, L.-K., & Low, K.-L. (2009). Saliency-enhanced image aesthetics class prediction. In *Proceedings of the 16th International Conference on Image Processing* (pp. 997-1000). Cairo, Egypt: IEEE Press.

Wortwein, T., Morency, L.-P., & Scherer, S. (2015). Automatic Assessment and Analysis of Public Speaking Anxiety: A Virtual Audience Case Study. In *Proc of IEEE Affective Computing and Intelligent Interaction* (pp. 187-193). 10.1109/ACII.2015.7344570

Wright, D. R. E. (1984). Alberti's De Pictura: Its Literary Structure and Purpose. *Journal of the Warburg and Courtauld Institutes*, *47*, 52–71. doi:10.2307/751438

Wu, W. C., & Yang, Y. T. C. (2009). Using a Multimedia Storytelling to Improve Students' Learning Performance. In G. Siemens & C. Fulford (Eds.), *Proceedings of EdMedia: World Conference on Educational Media and Technology 2009* (pp. 3159-3166). Association for the Advancement of Computing in Education (AACE).

Wu, H.-K., Lee, S. W.-Y., Chang, H.-Y., & Liang, J.-C. (2013). Current status, opportunities and challenges of augmented reality in education. *Computers & Education*, *62*(0), 41–49. doi:10.1016/j.compedu.2012.10.024

Zakirova, V. G., & Purik, E. E. (2016). Creative Environment Formation in Design Professional Training. *International Journal of Environmental and Science Education*, *11*(9), 2323–2332.

Zeng, X., Mehdi, Q. H., & Gough, N. E. (2003). Shape the Story: Story Visualization Techniques. *Proceedings of the 7th International Conference on Information Visualization*, 144-149. 10.1109/IV.2003.1217971

Zhang, M., Zhang, L., Sun, Y., Feng, L., & Ma, W. (2005). Auto cropping for digital photographs. In *IEEE International Conference on Multimedia and Expo*. Amsterdam: IEEE Press.

Zheng, R. (2007). Cognitive functionality of multimedia in problem solving. In T. Kidd & H. Song (Eds.), *Handbook of Research on Instructional Systems and Technology* (pp. 230–246). Hershey, PA: Information Science Reference/IGI Global Publishing. doi:10.4018/978-1-59904-865-9.ch017

Zheng, R., Dahl, L., & Flygare, J. (2008). Cognitive perspective on human-computer interface design. In M. Syed & N. Syed (Eds.), *Handbook of Research on Modern Systems Analysis and Design Technologies and Applications* (pp. 320–341). Hershey, PA: Information Science Reference/IGI Global Publishing. doi:10.4018/978-1-59904-887-1.ch020

Zhou, B., & Zhou, S. P. (2007). Motion planning for group movement simulation in dynamic environments. *International Journal of Modelling and Simulation*, 27(4), 379–385. doi:10.1080/02286203.2007.11442440

Zipf, G. (1949). *Human behavior and the principle of least effort*. Oxford, UK: Addison-Wesley Press.

Zorzal, E. R., Buccioli, A. A. B., & Kirner, C. (2005). *O Uso da Realidade Aumentada no Aprendizado Musical*. Workshop de Aplicações de Realidade Virtual, Minas Gerais. Retrieved from http://www.lbd.dcc.ufmg.br/colecoes/warv/2005/0012.pdf

About the Contributors

Anna Ursyn, PhD, is a professor and Computer Graphics/Digital Media Area Head at the University of Northern Colorado. She combines programming with software and printmaking media, to unify computer generated and painted 2D, 3D, and time-based. Ursyn had over 40 single juried and invitational art shows, over 200 fine art exhibitions, including musea, such as NTT Tokyo and Louvre, Paris. Her articles and artwork are in books and journals. Research and pedagogy interests include integrated instruction in art, science, and computer art graphics. Since 1987 a chair of the Symposium and Digital Art Gallery D-ART iV, 1997-now, and a liaison, Organizing and Program Committee member of International IEEE Conferences on Information Visualization (iV) and CGIV London, UK. Anna has published six books with IGI-Global and book chapters. Her work was selected to be sent to the Moon by NASA as a part of the MoonArc Project by Carnegie Melon University.

* * *

Marcela Alves de Almeida is an architect and Senior Lecturer at the School of Architecture and Urbanism and also a Senior Lecturer at the Interdisciplinary Postgraduate Program in Arts, Urbanities and Sustainability (PIPAUS) at the Federal University of São João del-Rei, Brazil. She received a Master's degree in Architecture from Federal University of Rio de Janeiro, Brazil (2008) and a doctorate degree in Architecture and Urbanism from Federal University of Minas Gerais, Brazil (2014). In 2010 and 2011 she was a postgraduate researcher at LAGEAR, UFMG. Her fields of interest are contemporary architecture, digital technology, design thinking, digital interfaces, responsive environments, arts, contemporary culture, interdisciplinarity and sustainability.

Lúcia da Graça Cruz Domingues Amante has a degree in Educational Psychology at the Higher Institute of Applied Psychology (ISPA - Lisbon); a postgraduate degree in Multimedia Educational Communication and, since 2004, a Ph.D. in Education from the Universidade Aberta of Portugal (UAb). She is member of the Department of Education and Distance Learning of UAb; she coordinated the Graduate Education Program in 2007-2011. She has integrated teacher training programs, directing seminars on educational use of digital technologies in schools and on models of learning assessment. Currently coordinates the Master in Educational Communication and Digital Media. She develops her research activities at the Distance Education Laboratory, Universidade Aberta. Her research interests focus on research in distance education, particularly in the pedagogy of online education, including digital assessment, and in educational psychology connected with the use of digital technologies, (namely social networks) in schools and in informal learning contexts. She joined the research team of assess.he project

(E-learning evaluation in Higher Education - Project funded by the Portuguese Foundation for Science and Technology). She joined the team in Universidade Aberta's Pedagogical Model for Distance Education. Now, she coordinates at UAb the team responsible for developing the research project: Digital Nodes – Literacies, Identity and participation.

Guilherme Ferreira de Arruda is a Brazilian trained architect, MArch and PhD candidate at the School of Architecture of Universidade Federal de Minas Gerais (UFMG), Brazil. He is currently Assistant Lecturer in Architecture and Urbanism at Universidade Federal de Ouro Preto, Brazil, and researcher at LAGEAR (Graphics Laboratory for Architectural Experience, UFMG). As an undergraduate his research was directed towards spectacular audio-visual; in his Masters it gained a political focus associating technology and space for the resumption of the public sphere; and in his PhD he is investigating participatory methods in a non-technocratic perspective emphasising dialogue and plurality. His main research subjects are physical-digital interfaces, public sphere, communication and socio-spatial complexities.

Ana Paula Baltazar is a Brazilian trained architect, MArch, and PhD at the Bartlett School of Architecture, UCL (UK). She is Associate Professor teaching at both graduate and undergraduate programmes at the School of Architecture at Universidade Federal de Minas Gerais, Brazil, where she also co-leads the research groups LAGEAR (Graphics Laboratory for Architectural Experience) and MOM (Living in Other Ways). Since 2014 she holds a CNPq Research Productivity Scholarship. Her research focuses on the use of interfaces (physical, digital and hybrid) to increase the possibilities of autonomy and emancipation of users in the production of space. She has several papers and book chapters published and was awarded four research prizes, two design prizes and a prize for best book chapter.

Carlos José Campos is professor at Department of Electrical Engineering, School of Engineering of Porto Polytechnic (ISEP/IPP). He concluded a PhD thesis in 2015, in a Doctoral Program in Informatics Engineering (ProDEI). Engineering Faculty of Porto University in the area of Computer Graphics. Completed his Master's Degree in Electrical Engineering, Decision Systems and Control, in Technical Higher Institute (IST) in 2006. Graduated from School of Engineering of Porto Polytechnic in Electrical Engineering and Computer. Participated in several research projects in computer graphics area, which resulted in several publications in conference proceedings and journals. His research interests are focused in the areas of Computer Graphics, Interaction, and Environments of Virtual Simulation.

Adrian Carballal holds a BSc and a PhD in Computer Science from the University of A Coruña (Spain), where he is currently working as a post-doctoral research associate and Assistant Professor at the Computer Science Department. He has authored over 20 articles and edited 3 journals. He also participated as a researcher in 6 funded research proposals. His main research interests include Image Processing, Computer Graphics, Aesthetics and Artificial Intelligence.

Maria Beatriz Carmo is graduated in Mathematics from the Faculty of Sciences of the University of Lisbon (FCUL), Portugal. She holds a PhD in Informatics from the same University. She is assistant professor at the Department of Informatics of-FCUL and an integrated member of the group Agent and Systems Modelling (MAS) of the Biosystems & Integrative Sciences Institute (BioISI). Her research interests are in the areas of Visualization, Computer Graphics, Augmented Reality, Virtual Environments and Digital Heritage. She lectures graduation and master courses in these areas. She has been a principal investigator and member of research project teams where she developed work on the Visualization, Augmented Reality and Virtual Reality work packages.

Luz Castro holds a BSc in Computer Science from the University of A Coruña (Spain), where she has been working as an Assistant Professor in the Faculty of Communication Sciences since 2008. She is also working as a researcher in Artificial Neural Networks and Adaptive Systems – Medical Imaging and Radiological Diagnosis (RNASA-IMEDIR) group. She is currently a PhD Student at the Computer Science Department at University of A Coruña. Her main research area of interest is related to evolutionary computation applied to creativity.

Ana Paula Cláudio holds a degree in Applied Mathematics and a PhD in Informatics from the University of Lisbon. She is a teacher at the Informatics Department of the Faculty of Sciences of the University of Lisbon (FCUL) and currently the coordinator of the undergraduate course in Information Technology (IT) of this department. She is a researcher in the BioISI- Biosystems & Integrative Sciences Institute (BioISI), integrating the MAS (Agents and Systems Modelling) group. Her main research interests cover the general are of Computer Graphics, Virtual and Augmented Reality, Serious Games and Digital Heritage. In particular, in the area of Virtual Reality, she has collaborations with psychologists, distance learning educators and communication experts in the health areas, with the purpose of conceiving training and educational solutions. More recently, she is involved in an interdisciplinary project to promote self-care habits for the older ones.

António Fernando Coelho is Assistant Professor at the Department of Informatics Engineering of the Faculty of Engineering of the University of Porto where he teaches in the areas of Computer Graphics, Programming and Digital Games and is the director of the Doctoral Program in Digital Media at the University of Porto. He is also a senior researcher at INESC TEC, coordinating the Computer Graphics and Virtual Environments area of the Information Systems and Computer Graphics Center.

Jean Constant is past professor of Visual Communication, lecturer and researcher in mathematical visualization projects and a reviewer for the American Mathematical Society. This paper is part of a larger, 52 weeks, one mineral a week, project assignment he recently completed testing a modeling software of the Japanese National Science Museum with material from the University of Arizona, RRUFF library archives. He won - best use of mathematics in an artwork - award in the 2015 Mathematics and Art conference at the Baltimore University, MD. Past and present affiliations include the Bridges Mathematics and Art organization, the Imaginary.org educational program of the MFO (Oberwolfach Research Institute for Mathematics), the D-Art, Information Visualization Society, and the European Mathematics and Art Society.

Tiago Filipe Neves Cruz is a Communication Designer, Illustrator, digital-media artist and teaches at University Institute of Maia – ISMAI, Portugal. He studied Scenography, Costumes, and Props at ACE (Porto, Portugal) and worked with directors like António Capelo, Rogério de Carvalho, Paulo Castro and Alan Richardson. In 2006, he graduated in "Multimedia Communication Technologies", in ISMAI (Maia, Portugal), with a thesis in the area of Interaction Design and Visual Semiotics called "IxD@ web – Interaction Design: Form, Function and Behaviour on the web." In 2012 he finished his master program in "Multimedia in the Digital Era: Strategies, Industries and Messages", in ISMAI, focusing on the investigation in the area of Visual Culture, Visual Communication and Visual Semiotics, with a master thesis entitled "From the Private register to the Public Sphere: The Graphic Diary as a means of expression and Visual Communication." In the present year, he finished a PhD on Digital Media-Art, at Portuguese Open University and Algarve's University, context in which he has been developing artistic installations related with the Landscape concept. Along with teaching, he collaborates in research projects with CIAC (Research Center for Arts and Communication), CITEI (Research Center for Technologies and Intermedia Studies) and maintains his activity as a Communication Designer and Illustrator.

Robert C. Ehle, Emeritus Professor of Music Theory and Composition, Electronic Music and Acoustics taught classes in music theory, composition and electronic music at the University of Northern Colorado, continues to serve on dissertation committees as an advisor to honors students. In Who's Who in American Music Ehle is listed as a composer of electronic music. He received a Bachelor of Music degree from Eastman School of Music in Rochester, New York, in 1961; a Master of Music in 1965; and his Ph.D. from the University of North Texas in Denton, Texas in 1970. Among his compositions are: A Sound Piece, A Space Symphony, The City is Beautiful, and A Whole Earth Symphony. He received the Dallas Symphony Rockefeller Foundation Award in 1966. Ehle received a 2008-09 ASCAPLUS Award in the concert music division from the American Society of Composers, Authors, and Publishers.

Carlos Fernández-Lozano is a Juan de la Cierva postdoctoral fellow in Bioinformatics at the Institute of Biomedical Research of A Coruña (Instituto de Investigación Biomédica de A Coruña - INIBIC) and a Lecturer at the Computer Science Department, at the University of A Coruña. PhD in Computer Science and MSc in Intelligent Systems from the University of A Coruña. Main research interests include Feature Selection, Kernel-based Techniques, Image Processing and Complex Biological Systems.

Mauro Jorge Guerreiro Figueiredo has a PhD in computer science from the University of Salford, Manchester, in 2005. He was teacher at University of Coimbra from 1989 until 1996. Since 1996 he is at the Algarve University where he is adjunct professor. His research interests are in the use of information technologies for education, e-learning, b-learning, games and augmented reality. His PhD students are currently working with ebooks and augmented reality tools for e-learning. He is author of more then sixty international journal and conferences articles, book chapters and books and he collaborated and participated in different National projects. He is the international coordinator of the Erasmus+ project MILAGE: Interactive Mathematics by implementing a Blended-Learning model with Augmented Reality and Game books. He has several papers best awards and a school project in augmented reality nationally recognized. He already organized several international conferences. Most of the research is conducted at Univ. Algarve, at CIMA (Center of Marine and Environmental Research) and CIAC (Center for the Arts and Communication Research).

José dos Santos Cabral Filho is an architect and Professor at the School of Architecture at the Federal University of Minas Gerais (Brazil). He received a Master's and a PhD degrees from Sheffield University (UK) and has been a visiting scholar at the School of Architecture at McGill University (Montreal / Canada), NTNU (Trondheim / Norway) and the Royal College of Art (London / UK). Since 1997 he has been in charge of LAGEAR (Graphics Laboratory for Architectural Experience, UFMG) where his research focuses on the liberating potential of ICT, seeking a far-reaching adoption of play into digital design, taking game as framework for the co-existence of determinism and non determinism. His main interests include the philosophy of Vilém Flusser, second-order Cybernetics, as well as architectural performances and electronic music.

Augusta Gaspar is a Psychologist, a Professor of Psychology, and a researcher of the evolution and ontogenetic development of emotion, with a focus on its nonverbal expression and physiological correlates. She is a cross-disciplinary scholar, holding a PhD in Biological Anthropology, and an M.Sc. in Ethology in addition to the BA and MSc. In Psychology. She currently serves as Director of the undergraduate program in Psychology at the Catholic University of Portugal in Lisbon and as member of the Board of the Catolica Research Centre for Psychological, Family and Social Well-being (CRC-W). She has an extensive publication record on emotional expression, empathy and ethics, and collaborative work with other research centres: Centro de Investigação e Intervenção Social of ISCTE-IUL, Centre for the Phylosophy of Sciences of the University of Lisbon's Faculty of Sciences, and she is a visiting Professor at ISCTE-IUL in Lisbon and at MidSweden University in Sweden.

Cristina Maria Cardoso Gomes is Professor of Music Education and started to exercise in 1992. As an initial training, she has the Piano Degree from Porto Conservatory of Music. Held the professional stage at the University of Aveiro, has a degree in Teaching of Music and Art History and Protection of Heritage; has graduate degrees in School Administration, Information and Communication Technology and in Promotion of Reading and School Libraries. Master's degree in Information Technology - Multimedia Communication and PhD in Digital Media-Art.

José Duarte Cardoso Gomes currently coordinates Arouca's Basic School where he teaches ICT and music. He holds a PhD in Digital Media-Art, Master Degree in Promotion of Reading and School Libraries, Master Degree in Information and Communication Technologies - Multimedia Communication, Bachelor Degree in History, Bachelor Degree in Music and a post-graduation in School Administration. He is an associate researcher at the Center for Research in Arts and Communication (CIAC) at the University of Algarve, where he collaborates regularly, contributing to national and international publications. Since 2017 has been a member of the Scientific Committee of the Iberian Conference on Information Systems and Technologies. He is a registered researcher at the FCT and accredited trainer by the Scientific-Pedagogical Council of Continuing Education. His research interests focus on the development, implementation and study of educational digital artifacts, especially in the areas of Augmented/Virtual Reality and the dynamics of innovative educational approaches supported by digital technologies.

Kevin Greenberg is a doctoral student at the University of Utah. His research pertains to learning and cognition, with the focus of cognitive load theory, reasoning, interactive multimedia, attention, and STEM education. More specifically, he has researched what factors contribute to reducing cognitive load, along with how students learn about the physics of climate change. He is interested in examining the aspects of learning and cognition that most benefit education, when it comes to STEM and health-related topics. He has presented at the Utah Conference for undergraduate research and was awarded the University of Utah Outstanding Honors Thesis award.

João Miguel Leitão is a Coordinating Professor of Computer Architecture and Telecommunications at the Polytechnic of Porto and a senior researcher at INESC TEC. He received his doctorate in Electrical and Computer Engineering from the University of Porto in 2000. He also owns a Master degree and a Licentiate from the University of Porto and a Bachelor from the Polytechnic of Porto. During his 25 years research experience, he authored more than 30 scientific publications and participated in more than 20 research projects. His current research interests include Computer Graphics, Visual Simulations, and Virtual Reality.

Penousal Machado is an Assistant Professor at the Department of Informatics Engineering of FCTUC and Scientific Director of the Computational Design and Visualization Lab. of the Centre for Informatics and Systems of the University of Coimbra. His research interests include nature-inspired computation, artificial intelligence, computational creativity, computational art and design. He is the author of more than 100 refereed journal and conference papers in these areas. He is also the recipient of several scientific awards. His work was featured in the Wired UK magazine and included in the "Talk to me" exhibition of the Museum of Modern Art, NY (MoMA).

Lorena Melgaço is an architect and urban planner (BSc. Hon, 2008) with a MPhil in Architecture (Universidade Federal de Minas Gerais – UFMG, Brazil, 2011) and a MSc. in International Cooperation and Urban development (Technische Universität Darmstadt and Université Pierre Mendès France, 2011). She was an undergraduate and postgraduate researcher at LAGEAR, UFMG, from 2005 till 2014 and she is currently a research fellow at University of Birmingham, UK. Her fields of interest include temporary uses of space; 'bottom-bottom spatial practices'; the understanding of forms of local agency and the micropolitics of the connected (albeit marginalised) rurban; the interrelation between space, communities and technology in urban and rural spaces; and South-South and South-North dialogues in and the decolonisation of planning Education and practice.

Takashi Ohta is an Associate Professor of Media Science at Tokyo University of Technology, Tokyo, Japan. He earned B.S. and M.S. in Computational Physics from Keio University, Tokyo Japan, and received Ph.D. from Tokyo University, Tokyo, Japan. Before coming to academia, he worked as a researcher at Tokyo Research Laboratory of IBM Japan, and also at the Center for Promotion of Computational Science and Engineering, Japan Atomic Energy Research Institute. The researches done during these periods include physically-based CG modelling, parallel computation, and grid computing. His current research interests are in dynamic reconfigurable multi-display system, user experience design, user interaction design, interactive digital signage, ambient computing, IoT, ubiquitous computing, and dynamic relation of multiple devices.

Fernando Faria Paulino, PhD in Anthropology (Visual Anthropology), Professor at University Institute of Maia, Dept. of Communication Sciences and Information Technologies (in the areas of visual communication, visual semiotics, documentary video, photography and hypermedia), researcher at CITEI – Research Center for Technologies and Intermedia Studies and researcher at CIAC – Research Centre for Arts and Communication / University of Algarve. He is the Head Coordinator of the undergraduate degree of Multimedia Communication, University Institute of Maia, Coordinator of CLM Multimedia Lab Center ISMAI, and Coordinator of the CCCom Communication Sciences Center, Multiplatform Audiovisual Studio ISMAI. Research interests: anthropology, visual anthropology and anthropology of visual communication; methodology, technology and epistemology of images and audiovisual culture; visual semiotics and visual culture; digital media, documentary film and documentary photography; interactive documentary, idocs and web-docs; anthropology, cultural heritage, culture and tourism development. Author of several scientific articles, documentary filmmaker, as well as hypermedia products author, essentially based on anthropological content nature. Visiting professor of several international universities and jury member of international film festivals.

João Paulo Pereira earned his BSc, MSc and PhD in Electrical and Computer Engineering from the Faculty of Engineering of the University of Porto (FEUP). He is currently teaching at the Computer Science Department of the School of Engineering, Polytechnic of Porto (ISEP-IPP). His main areas of interest are Computer Graphics and Human-Computer Interaction.

Hugo Filipe Pinto is a Software Engineer at Airmenu lda. He completed his Master Degree in Computer Science Engineering in 2017 at the School of Engineering of Porto Polytechnic (ISEP/IPP) in the area of Graphical Systems and Multimedia. Having written a dissertation on the design of a procedural modeling framework to generate complete terrain models. He completed his Degree in Computer Science Engineering in 2009 at the same School. During his professional experience, he has worked in the design and development of multiple projects, ranging from web platforms to analysis tools for holter exams and cardiac rehabilitation. His research interests are focused on the areas of Computer Graphics and Procedural Modeling.

Vítor Reia-Batista was responsible for the creation of the Communication Sciences course at the University of Algarve. He is the coordinator of the Literacy and Communication Research Group at CIAC. He is currently a member of the Cultural and Technical Library Council at the University of Algarve. He has a PhD in Communication in Education specializing in Media Pedagogy and Film Languages, from the University of Algarve. He has a Master's Degree in Cultural Communication from Lund University in Sweden, a qualification recognized as equivalent to the Master's Degree in Social Communication by Universidade Nova de Lisboa, and he also has an undergraduate degree in Comparative Literature, Drama-Theater-Cinema, from Lund University, a qualification recognized by Universidade Nova de Lisboa. He was the Director of the Communication Sciences Course – ESEC (1995/2000 – 2003/2008) and the Department of Communication, Arts and Design (2009-2011).

Carlos Manuel Rodrigues is Associate Professor at the Department of Civil Engineering of the Faculty of Engineering of the University of Porto and is member of the Executive Board Policies with Complementary Functions. Carlos Rodrigues completed his PhD thesis in 1996 at the Faculty of Engineering of the University of Porto in the area of Transport Engineering. He is also a senior researcher at CITTA - Research Centre for Territory, Transports and Environment and his research interests are focused in the areas of Highways Design, Road Safety and Traffic Management.

Nereida Rodriguez-Fernández is a fourth-year student of Audiovisual Communication in University of A Coruña. Scholarship holder in research about image classifiers according to aesthetic criteria by the Spanish Ministry of Education, Culture and Sports and member of the research group of Artificial Neuronal Networks and Adaptive Systems (RNASA), University of A Coruña. Graduated in professional music degree in the trombone specialty by the Professional Music Conservatory of A Coruña.

Juan Romero received the B.S. degree in Computer Science from A Coruña University (Spain) in 1996 and the Ph.D. degree in Computer Science from A Coruña University in 2002. He is associate professor at University of A Coruña. He edited a "Natural Computing" Springer book, published 6 papers in international ISI journals and chaired 5 events published as Springer LNCS. He directed and participated in 10 European and Spanish research projects and research contracts with firms such Microsoft Spain.

António Rui graduated in Computer Science in 1995. He got his M.Sc. in Multimedia Communication in 2012, and a Ph.D. in Media Digital Art in 2017 from University of Algarve and University Aberta, Portugal. He is member of CIAC (Art and Communication Research Center, Portugal). Currently, he develops research in the field of interactive film narratives.

Antonino Santos received the BSc degree in Computer Science from the University of A Coruña (Spain) in 1992 and the Ph.D. degree in Computer Science from University of A Coruña in 1998. At present, he is a professor at the University of A Coruña (Spain). Since 1991, he has worked with several research groups in Artificial Neural Networks, Genetic Algorithms and Internet servers and services. Dr. Santos has authored and edited more than 30 articles, 7 books, and participated as a researcher in 16 funded research proposals concerning Artificial Intelligence, Adaptive Systems and Internet Security.

Iria Santos is a Senior Technician in Audiovisual Image, Graduate in Audiovisual Communication and member of the research group of Artificial Neuronal Networks and Adaptive Systems (RNASA), University of A Coruña, investigates in computer creativity and image classifiers according to aesthetic criteria.

Bruno Miguel dos Santos Mendes da Silva graduated in Cinema and Video in 1995 from School of Arts of Oporto (ESAP), got his post-graduation in Arts Management in 1998 from Macao Institute of European Studies (IEEM). He got his PhD in Literature/Comparative Literature/Literature and Cinema in 2008 from University of the Algarve (UALG), Portugal, and his Post PhD in Interactive Cinema in 2016 also from UAlg. He is an Adjunct Professor at School of Education and Communication (ESEC), also in the UALG, where he lectures Audiovisual Communication since 2000. He is at present the President of the Pedagogical Council. He is the Vice-coordinator of the Research Centre for Arts and Communication (CIAC). He was a TV Producer and Director from 1995 to 2000 at Teledifusão de Macau (TDM), and has been invited to several International Art and Film Festivals such as Fresh (Thailand), Dokanema (Mozambique), Loop (Spain), Festival de la imagen (Colombia), Ecologias Digitales (Colombia). He participated in 11 financed scientific projects and he is author of several Books, Chapters of books and scientific publications. He won a scientific prize Ceratonia in 2008.

Mirian Nogueira Tavares is an Associate Professor at the University of Algarve. With an academic background in Communication Sciences, Semiotics and Cultural Studies (she has earned a PhD in Contemporary Communication and Culture from the Federal University of Bahia), she has developed her research and theoretical work in the fields of Cinema, Literature and other Arts, as well as in the areas of film and arts aesthetics. As a Professor at the University of Algarve, she took part in the development of the Degree in Visual Arts, the Master's and PhD Degrees in Communication, Culture and Arts, and the PhD programs in Digital Media-Art. She is currently the Coordinator of CIAC – Centre for Research in Arts and Communication, and Vice-coordinator of the PhD in Digital Media-Art.

Renato Teixeira has a bachelor and master degree in Computer Sciences from the Faculty of Sciences of the University of Lisbon. Under his master thesis, he had worked on a virtual reality application to assist therapeutic treatment for the public fear disorders. Afterwards, he has been working as a software developer in several companies from different dimensions, industries and countries. He is currently living in Eindhoven working for the largest supplier of integrated circuits machine producers.

Robert Z. Zheng is an associate professor of instructional design and educational technology in the Department of Educational Psychology at the University of Utah, USA. His research area includes multimedia and cognition, instructional design and development, web-based learning, and educational gamification. He has published over 60 refereed journal papers and book chapters. He is the editor and co-editor of ten books published by Routledge, Nova Science, and IGI Global. He was the founding editor of the *International Journal of Cyber Behavior, Psychology and Learning* (2008-2012).

Index

3D Model 320
3D printing 65, 82

A

Absolute Pitch 123, 126, 220-221, 223-224, 226-230
Acoustic Waves 118, 124, 126, 128, 244
Aesthetic Criteria 186, 202-203, 208
Aesthetics 151, 170, 185, 188, 195, 203-205
Affordances 282, 284, 296, 299, 304
Algorithmic Manipulation 169, 184
Animatic 80, 89, 108
Arbitrary Arranged Multi-Display 25
Art Education 281, 300
Audio-visual installation 167
Auditory System 120-121, 124, 227, 230-233
Augmented Reality 83, 85, 99, 154, 281-284, 288-289, 291, 299, 304
Avatar 28, 40, 76, 80, 108, 153

B

Bootstrap Theory 227, 237

C

CANI 131, 136, 141-144, 308
Chiral 268, 279
Chord 112, 118-120, 125, 239-241, 244
Chroma 272, 279
Cinema 142, 150-153, 155-156, 159, 161-163, 165
Cognitive-Behavioural Therapy (CBT) 28, 47
Complexity 31, 117, 141, 185-186, 188-190, 192, 199, 202-203, 214, 247, 249, 276
Computational Aesthetics 203
computer graphics 52, 84, 86-88, 92, 94, 97, 256, 320
Constructive Divergent Thinking 247-249, 251-252, 265
Constructivism 281, 285, 304

Content Design 2, 13
Context 30, 43, 47, 63, 122, 125-126, 129, 131, 135-136, 139, 141, 146, 148, 162, 170, 172-174, 184, 187-188, 251, 259, 265, 267, 281-282, 287, 289, 296, 301
Contextual Visualization 251-252, 258-260, 265
Convergent Thinking 247, 265
Creating a Character 53
creative thinking 246-253, 255-261, 265
Cross-Validation 192, 206-207, 209, 219
Crystal 80, 266-268, 270-271, 273-274, 276-277, 279
Crystallography 269-271, 280
Cultural Models 237

D

Deliberate Divergent Thinking 247-248, 252, 260-261, 265
Dialectics of Spectacle and Experience 131, 133-134, 136, 145, 147
Dialogue 52, 96, 129-131, 133-136, 138, 141-143, 145, 147, 153, 158
Dichotomy 202
Digital Art 162
digital technology 130-131, 133-134, 136, 145, 148, 153, 246-247, 250, 260
Driving Environment 320
Driving Environments 306-307, 315-317
Driving Simulation 306-307, 309, 316, 320

E

Embankment and Cut Slope 320
Enformed 170, 172, 184
Engagement 22, 129-130, 132-134, 137-139, 141, 146, 148, 255-256, 260, 286, 300-301
Entropy 207-209, 212, 219
Evaluation 20-21, 29-30, 42, 186, 204, 255, 272, 275
Event Propagation 18, 25

Experience 2-4, 19, 22, 38, 49-50, 56-57, 74, 89, 99-100, 110-111, 115, 119, 122-126, 129-136, 138, 141, 145, 147-148, 155, 159, 165, 173-174, 177, 226-227, 236-237, 251, 283, 285, 294, 296, 300
Experimentation 151, 159, 163-164
Extrapolate 204, 219

F

Facial Action Units 43
Facial Expression 27, 40
Fear of Public Speaking 30, 40, 43, 47
Fetish of Digital Technology 131, 133, 145, 148
Fiberoptics 68, 80
Fifth Interval 244

G

Generalization 203-204, 209, 211, 214, 217, 219
Generative Art 184
Geometry 60, 251, 266-274, 276-277, 280, 283, 299, 320
Geoscience 267-270, 276-278, 280
Glitch Sound 180, 184
Graphics 3, 12, 20, 52, 54, 80-88, 92, 94-95, 97-99, 109, 129-130, 139-140, 256, 266, 270-271, 273, 276, 283, 292, 320

H

Harmonic Series 113, 121, 223-224, 233-235, 237-241, 244
Hominids 221-225, 227, 229-230, 233, 235
Horse Steps 102, 108

I

Icon 54, 80-81, 108-109
Illustration 88, 98, 213
Informal Learning Environments 281-282, 287, 300-301, 304
Information Bias 219
Installation 7, 132-133, 138-139, 167-173, 175-176, 181-182, 184
Interaction 2-7, 11, 15, 18, 21, 23, 27, 29, 33, 49-50, 53, 84-85, 99, 129-132, 134-135, 137-139, 141-143, 145-148, 152-155, 160-161, 165, 170, 173, 176-177, 180-182, 255, 265, 272, 282-283, 285, 288, 292, 296, 299
Interactive Multi-Display 25
Interactive Pairing 3, 25

Interactivity 3, 5-6, 25, 49, 83, 152-156, 170, 288
Interface 1-8, 11-13, 15, 19, 21-23, 30-36, 42, 50, 60, 84, 115, 129-131, 133-143, 145-146, 148, 170, 246, 250, 252, 255-256, 259-261, 297-298, 300, 308
Interfaces 2, 11-12, 22, 49, 71, 77, 82-83, 88, 104, 110-111, 115, 129-132, 134-135, 145-146, 148, 253, 255
Interval 128, 234, 244
Interval Class 244
Interval Cycle 234, 244
Intrinsic Bias 209, 219
Ituita 131, 136, 139-141, 146

L

Lagear 129-131, 134-140, 143-146
Landscape 59, 91, 167-168, 170-177, 180-182, 184, 186, 190, 192, 199, 306-307, 309, 311, 315-316
Language Acquisition 223, 246
Learning 28, 47, 49, 54, 59, 64, 68, 71, 76-77, 83, 86, 98-102, 110-111, 115-116, 121-123, 205, 209, 225, 227, 236, 238, 241-242, 246-256, 259-261, 265-266, 281-289, 292, 294, 296, 298-301, 304
Liquid Crystal 80
Logic of the Visual 131-133, 138-139, 148
Long Distance Voodoo 131, 136-137, 139
Lossy Compression 189, 202

M

Mathematics 53, 60-61, 64, 266-269, 274, 276, 280, 282-283, 299
Mineral 266, 268-270, 273-274, 276, 280
Mobile Computing Devices 281-283, 288-289, 293-294, 304-305
Mobile Device 293-295
Modeling 255, 266, 269, 272-273, 306-307, 309-310, 312, 317, 320
Motion Graphics 80-81, 109
Motivation 253-255, 277, 281-282, 286-287, 299-301, 305
Multi-Display 1-3, 7, 11, 15-17, 22-23, 25-26
Multimedia 52, 80, 85, 88, 99, 104, 109, 154, 185-186, 196, 199, 250, 282, 287-289, 299-300
Music Education 287, 298, 301

N

Narrative 82, 84, 87, 89, 104, 132, 150-160, 164, 176, 273, 276
Nasal Language 221

Network Connection 1-2, 7-8, 11, 25
Nonverbal Behaviour Research 47

O

Ocupar Espaços 131, 135-136

P

Photography 100-101, 142, 154, 171, 187, 190, 192, 198, 202-206, 214, 216-217, 287
Pictograph 80, 109
Pinch Gesture 26
Pitch 18, 61, 110-113, 119-124, 126, 128, 220-221, 223-224, 226-230, 233, 238, 242, 244
Pitch Class 244
Platform 2-3, 6-8, 14, 17, 22-23, 29, 40, 133, 150-151, 153, 161-162, 176, 196, 247, 252, 274, 276, 286, 296
Playful Interaction 129, 131, 134-135, 138, 145, 148
Plurality 141-143, 173
Polyhedra 270-271, 273
Procedural Modeling 307, 320

R

Reconfigurable 1-3, 5, 7, 11, 15, 22, 25-26
Relative Placement 3, 9-10, 16, 26
Representation 1, 3, 54, 80-81, 94, 99, 101, 108-109, 122, 132, 135, 137, 167-168, 170-174, 184, 189, 202, 204, 250-251, 269, 272, 283, 285, 308, 320
Road Network 307, 309, 313, 316, 320

S

Scientific Driving Simulation 306-307, 320
Self-Assessment Manikin (SAM) 38
Semiotics 54, 81, 172, 184
Semitone 114, 244
Sequential Art 83
Serra de Arga 175-176, 184
Sign 54, 56, 81, 172-173
Sketch 64, 77, 82-83, 96, 102, 308, 310-311, 316-317, 320
Social Anxiety Disorder (SAD) 28, 48
Social Semiotics 172, 184
Socio-Spatial Transformation 129-132, 135-136, 139, 141, 145, 148
Sonority 239-241, 244

Sound Waves 61, 118, 121, 128, 244
Spectacle 83-84, 130-134, 136, 141, 145, 147
Spontaneous Divergent Thinking 247, 249, 253, 261, 265
Storyboard 80-81, 88-89, 95-98, 102-103, 108
Storyline 88-90, 96, 101-103
Storytelling 49-51, 53, 59-61, 65-66, 69-71, 77, 82-85, 87-89, 91-100, 102-104
Subjective Phenomenon 186, 202
Symbol 53-55, 80-81, 85, 109
Symmetry 61, 193, 267-271, 273, 279-280
Synthetic Visualization 252-253, 265

T

Terrain Erosion 320
Tessitura 233, 244
Tone Language 220-222, 224-229
Tonotopic 128, 244
Tonotopic Organization 244
Topology 280
Tree Structure 81
Tritone 128, 244

U

Usability 20, 30, 38, 40, 42, 282-284, 289, 291, 296-298, 300-301, 305
User Experience 2-4, 22, 283
User Interface 1, 13

V

Vanguards 167, 184
Virtual Humans 27-28, 30, 40, 43
Virtual Reality (VR) 28, 283
Virtual Reality in Exposure Therapy (VRET) 48
Visual Artifacts 187, 202
Visual Complexity 188, 202, 214
Visual Perception 219, 250, 252
Visualization 2, 30, 40, 52-53, 81-82, 85, 88, 99, 104, 152, 246, 250, 252-253, 255, 258-260, 265-270, 273-274, 306-307

W

Wallpaper 268, 280

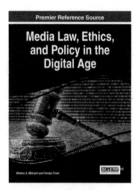

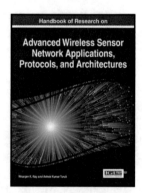

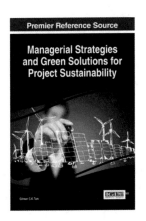

Information Resources Management Association

Advancing the Concepts & Practices of Information Resources Management in Modern Organizations

Become an IRMA Member

Members of the **Information Resources Management Association (IRMA)** understand the importance of community within their field of study. The Information Resources Management Association is an ideal venue through which professionals, students, and academicians can convene and share the latest industry innovations and scholarly research that is changing the field of information science and technology. Become a member today and enjoy the benefits of membership as well as the opportunity to collaborate and network with fellow experts in the field.

IRMA Membership Benefits:

- **One FREE Journal Subscription**

- **30% Off Additional Journal Subscriptions**

- **20% Off Book Purchases**

- Updates on the latest events and research on Information Resources Management through the IRMA-L listserv.

- Updates on new open access and downloadable content added to Research IRM.

- A copy of the Information Technology Management Newsletter twice a year.

- A certificate of membership.

IRMA Membership $195

Scan code or visit **irma-international.org** and begin by selecting your free journal subscription.

Membership is good for one full year.

Printed in the United States
By Bookmasters